Cécile Dargnies

OUT OF FRANCE

Chronicle of an escape

Published in 2009 by YouWriteOn.com

Copyright © Text Cécile Dargnies

First Edition

The author asserts the moral right under the Copyright, Designs and Patents Act 1988 to be identified as the author of this work

All rights reserved. No part of this publication may be reproduced, stored in a retrieval system, or transmitted, in ay form or by any means without the prior written consent of the author, nor be otherwise circulated in any form of binding or cover other than that in which it is published and without a similar condition being imposed on the subsequent purchaser.

Published by YouWriteOn.com

TABLE OF CONTENTS

Prologue :   **Africa, the Book of the Jungle**   p.   5

Part I :   **Going West, America**

America 1   p.   9
Back to France 1   p. 69
America 2   p. 113
Back to France 2   p. 173

Part II :   **Going East, Greece**

Greece 1   p. 195
Back to France 3   p. 213
London   p. 229
Greece 2   p. 263

Epilogue :   ***"Pyrame ti zoï mas, lathos,***
               k'allaxame zoï"   p. 399

PROLOGUE

It all started with Africa and Mowgli. In 1958, I was seven years old. One November night, I flew from Paris, France to Douala, Cameroon with my family. A year and a half later, we were back in Paris. And I hated it. I knew now that the world was bigger than France. But to escape I had first to grow up for a good decade.

At ten years old, my parents gave me for Christmas the *Jungle book* by Rudyard Kipling. It was a big book, in quarto, with beautiful illustrations of Mowgli and his animal friends. In fact, there had been a mistake. Kipling was for boys, not for girls. The book should have been given to my brother. But Mowgli had landed in my shoe. «*Brave heart and courteous tongue will lead you far into the jungle*» said Kâ the snake to the Jungle boy. It became my motto.

Part I : Going West, America

AMERICA 1

The first end of the world - A Château in Bray - Sandwich, Kent - A pragmatic lady – Visa

Washington D.C. - Bill and Kathie's house - Arthur from Berkeley – a Texan party - A Sunday with the Millers – A taste for soap operas – A hoarse and husky voice named Bob Dylan - Arthur from Berkeley - The Vermont farm of John Kenneth Galbraith - Big steak in Maine - Philadelphia, a sooty old city "The art of love" by Erich Fromm - Edgar Allan Poe's dark alleys - A boat party on the Chesapeake bay - Dinner with the grandparents

Ambling along the East coast - Brown University - A Professor's family - The crazy Lubin family - A party at Penny's box in Manhattan - Elisabeth's grand suite in Spanish Harlem - "A nous deux, New York" - Mondrian the magician - Guggenheim, MET, Frick, Cloisters - "Last year in Marienbad"- Taking off

The first end of the world

Everything was drifting away from me. It was like standing on the quay and watching the world, my world, sailing off. Home, school, family and friends were still standing where they always had, but they were escaping me. The first twilight one goes through is frightening. If the sun goes down, why should it rise again ? On that 4th June 1969, everything was going awry. It was my eighteenth birthday. After thirteen years, it was the end of school. It was the end of balls also. At eighteen, after three years of parties, I was supposed to have found my match for life. Those balls after all had an end in themselves, making girls and boys meet and mate. School friends, dancing partners, they were all going their own way. It marked the end of God also. A whole architecture of verticals and horizontals was collapsing on my head. On a grey day when the sky was unbearably low, I had looked out of the window above the patches of gardens in the back of the apartment where we lived. All of a sudden, the grey sky had broken like a sick skin, letting out a dirty liquid. There was no God up there anymore. I was left with the world in front of me.

A week later, I was sitting for my baccalauréat exams. My first degree in the bag, I would be out there on my own. There was no compromise possible. I could not stay at home, prostrated, in the shadow of Papa and Mama. I had to find a job and make a living. Or I had to marry. But could marriage be the definite solution? A boy, hardly older than me, would take me in charge and take over my life, making the money and all decisions. No one had applied yet beyond a dance or two at the balls. And together with awe for the beauty of those balls, I had often felt a strange feeling of loneliness in the middle of so many boys and girls and so much splendor. Like weddings, balls were utterly out of sync with normal day to day life. Like ephemeral fireworks, they hit you with regrets even before dying.

I had to move on. If everything had ended in the land of my birth, I had to move somewhere else. West, I decided. Because west was the ocean, wide enough for my longing and, beyond, America, the land of Gatsby. When I had sat down for my baccalauréat exams, I had written for four hours a long essay. The subject was a defense of literature. I had quoted my three chosen kings: Stendhal, Proust and Scott Fitzgerald. *"As the moon rose higher I became aware of the old island that flowered once for Dutch sailors' eyes –a fresh, green breast of the new world. For a transitory enchanted moment man must have held his breath in the presence of this continent into an aesthetic contemplation he neither understood nor desired, face to face for the last time in history with something commensurate to his capacity for wonder"* wrote Fitzgerald.

West was my path, then.

A Château in Bray

The first tip opening the way to America had come from the most unexpected place. I had gone for a fortnight at the château of a schoolfriend. Her parents had bought it the year before, part for prestige and part to keep the unemployed agronomist father busy. The family lived on the mother's substantial real estate dowry in Paris. My friend, Gabrielle, was seventeen years old and the château would be a good asset to marry her and her younger sister to as good a match as possible. We were in the summer of 1968. After the Paris riots of May, the château and Gabrielle's family felt all the more surreal and farcical. The château was set in a dull countryside, the "pays de Bray", two hours north of Paris.

Those two weeks there were to be my last well-ordered vacation. From the summer of 1969, I would not have *"grandes vacances"* anymore. University recess would be used to work and make money.

The château was a rather elegant eighteenth century *"logis"*. The roof had been repaired, a few bathrooms set up and a Versailles style motif of green lawns planted along the ostentatious alley leading up from the iron gate to the main door. The rooms were many, crummy and huge, with very high ceilings. Besides Gabrielle, her sister and three brothers were there, so were her parents, an aunt with her three daughters and the paternal grandmother. Counting me, we were thirteen around the dining table, but no one was superstitious. I had been invited as a guest, a free one. Otherwise, Gabrielle's mother took every month of August paying guests to add some dough to the family kitty. They were American girls forwarded by an astute American lady who got a handy commission as a go-between. Gabrielle herself had told me that the sum paid by those girls was huge. The most essential requirement for would-be host French families was to have a "château" and to demonstrate upper class biases such as a distinctive French U-class accent, listing in the *"Bottin Mondain"*, the French social register and, even better, that tiny "de" in the family name which meant that the family was of noble descent, as went the popular belief.

Gabrielle's family had all the requisites. The grandmother, Marchioness de la Croix-Barrois, added even more to the aristocratic picture. *"Grand-mère"* was in her mid nineties, terribly deaf but very impressive with her long horse-like face, long aquiline nose and long giraffe neck. Her mossy yellowish hair was tied in a heavy chignon on her nape. She had it washed once a month, Gabrielle had told me. She rarely had it cut. Since her teens, it fell down to her waist when she undid it every evening before going to bed. She talked to herself most of the time, usually while sitting in the still embryonic sitting-room where the paint job was not finished yet, or sitting at the dining-table. Nobody paid much attention to her, although she sat regally at the head of the table, presiding on loud and agitated grandchildren that, due to their majority numbers, no parents could keep quiet. Never having had a grandmother myself, since both had died very young, I was interested and touched by the old lady that to me seemed to be treated like a dog by the two-generation horde yelling on all sides of the long oblong table. Since she was deaf, the children shouted jokes bordering on the insult to the old lady that remained smiling and affable, trying to eat the budget dishes concocted by the maid to feed everyone at the least expense.

There was not much to do at the château besides helping the one and only maid in cleaning dishes and setting the table, and wandering on the rundown estate. The boys pushed each other and whatever girl they could find into the tiny pond full of water rats. We sailed bravely on a makeshift raft the four meters from the shore to the island in the middle of the pond, where barely five of us could stand up together. We shouted at placid cows while the boys tried hard to entice them to a wild corrida in the fields. The whole family was very keen on throwing and breaking things and beating or crushing lots of stunned insects or mammals. At best, we went for walks in the neighboring woods, gathering wild mushrooms in big baskets. There were no *cèpes* nor *girolles*, but loads of black trumpet-like mushrooms called "trumpets of death". Those were served in self-styled quiches, with loads of insipid white sauce. Once in a while, the grandmother ventured to ask what was exactly in her plate. The hilarious children yelled at the top of their voice, "Trumpets of death, Grand-mère! Trumpets of death!" "What did you say?" squealed the old woman, "Trumpets of death, Grand-mère!" I was horrified.

But to the American girls that had come to spend the whole month of August with them, that yelling and insulting family felt like the epitome of French high class. Could the huge sum paid for the privilege have been the reason for such reverence? Or were those girls so innocent that they could not have conceived of such malice on the part of such an exemplary noble family? Incidentally, Gabrielle had told me that Mrs. Rodnick, the American manager of that bright paying guest scheme, was actively trying to put up the same system for French girls, so they could spend time in America with American families. She was having problems though, Gabrielle had said, because French families were not terribly interested in sending their daughters to America. Moreover, nobody in France would have paid the exorbitant fees asked by Mrs. Rodnick. "She is thinking of putting up instead an au-pair system for French girls, but not me, thanks a lot!" She had added, with a sneer.

Sandwich, Kent

A year later in 1969, I was going to Sandwich, Kent as an au-pair girl for the whole summer, determined to make my first real pile of money. Announcements in *Le Figaro* listed families asking for au pairs. A French lady married to a British man in Sandwich, Kent was looking for one. I had got the job. Being an au pair was an heresy among my girl-friends and my parents did not like it much either. Of Sandwich and its beaches, I did not see much. I got up at seven and prepared a complicated English breakfast from kippers to toasts, bacon and porridge for a dozen people. I went on cleaning up and making beds and emptying chamber pots from eight to twelve. Then I set up the lunch table, emptied and cleaned it up after the meal, cleaned the kitchen and the dining-room and prepared coffee. Besides, I helped the young cook prepare the meals. Between three and six thirty, I could breathe before setting up the dinner table and helping prepare dinner, clean up the table, and set up the table again for breakfast. I polished shoes and silvery too. But being an au-pair, I sat at the table with the family and their guests. That allowed them to have a live-in maid working ten hours a day for four pounds a week. In America, I had heard, things were different. An au-pair was not a cleaning lady nor a cook nor a housekeeper. American families hired au-pair girls only to baby-sit when they were going out. Slaving it in England was tough, but I had made money and lived on those earnings for three months. I felt better at knowing that I could. Part of the money I had squandered on pretty Shetland wool jumpers that were the rage in 1969. But I had put aside two thirds of my pounds.

A pragmatic lady

The au-pair stint in Sandwich, Kent had not improved my English very much since everyone spoke French in the house and the English-speaking guests could not have cared less about talking to the French au pair. Back in Paris, I started to work on my English. In America, I would have to rely on English only. Out of my own pocket, I got and read Herald Tribune at least three times a week. I also read all the English novels I could find in libraries. At "Smith & Son", on rue de Rivoli, I could leaf for free through English magazines and books until my legs got numb.

One day, when my parents were out, I had called Mrs. Rodnick. Right on, she had enthused over my wish to go to the US with an abundance of exclamatory adjectives and a strong assertive voice, which I had found marvelously supportive. The clamoring empathy of the American lady gave me wings. Soon, I was breaking the news to my parents about my plans to go to the US. I was not asking permission neither was I asking them for money. The au-pair scheme would pay for the plane ticket and for room and board. My Sandwich savings would pay for extras. My parents were not at all enthusing like Mrs. Rodnick. The US was a faraway country, and I was barely nineteen years old, still a minor, since majority age was then twenty-one. I had shrugged my shoulders at their objections. My determination was absolute.

I would go. In fact, my father had listened to my detailed plans and agreed, telling my mother that I probably needed some fresh air. He even had designed a kind of grant for the trip. So as not to offend my fierce independence and respect the equality principle between his four children, he had decided to give me an amount corresponding to the value of meals for the three months I would be away: two months au-pair, and one month to travel on my own.

Mrs. Rodnick had given me an appointment to meet her in her Paris abode. She came to Paris every spring and stayed in a private apartment on the boulevard Saint Germain. I had walked up Rue Cortambert to the Avenue Henri-Martin to catch bus 63 that would take me across the Seine and onto the left bank. It was one of those dreamy Parisian days, epitomized in poems and prose but very rare indeed. The perfect harmony of light, sky and white horse-chestnut blossoms sticking like candles on top of the rich green canopy mingled with the buzz of just born insects and the trills of young sparrows. Eyes, nose, ears, body and mind could be stunned on those days, and an ordinary walk became bewitching. Waiting for bus 63 under the long arch of horsechestnuts, I felt strange, as if split in two. This was my city, my country, the long-tamed beauty of my native surroundings which I enjoyed and breathed carelessly everyday. That city had stunned, and would for ages stun people from all over the world. Paris opened to me that day as to an American. I was in and already out. I was dying to get away, and filled with wonder at Paris, fallen to my share by virtue of birth. I was falling in love that day, yet plotting my escape. Bus 63 was not very crowded in mid-afternoon. I knew the ride by heart, but I always liked the low balanced skyline along the Seine, the bridges from a distance looking like piled up one on top of each other along the lazy meanders. At the moment you die, they said, everything came back in a flash, yet as dense and detailed as all those years lived through. Just on the edge, of before and after, of past and future, I was feeling for the fist time a fleeting moment both present and eternal.

Mrs. Rodnick, her hands up and her face slit by a smiling mouth, let out a furious sound of American welcome. Her hands went down and pressed mine with words of wonder and contentment. "Céciiile…" she chanted at least three times with the maestria of a diva. Sun flowed into the vast sitting room through the high windows wide open above the plane trees of the boulevard Saint Germain. The buzz and hiss of traffic and pedestrians came up as a jazzy background. I didn't pay much attention to my words, neither to Mrs. Rodnick's. Like on the bus, I was still sailing in a world of my own. I knew that woman was not extraordinary, neither could she have been that enticed with me, but she understood my craving for the world out there and she was handing me the ticket to get there. From the minute I had stepped out of her apartment building, my days had become building blocks. The blurred hours that weighed so much and went nowhere were over. I was up and ready to fly, ride or walk. May and June went by. The day of departure approaching gave me a lot to think and do, but the emergency it fuelled erased any fear, apprehension or worry. I leave therefore I live, I thought.

Mrs. Rodnick had put up the programme. First, I would spend the month of July in Washington D.C. at the home of Bill and Kathie and their adopted baby girl. In August, I would stay in Philadelphia at Ben and Eliza and Sarah. In September, I would travel on my own. Plane ticket, room and board were secured for two months. My father was giving me the promised allowance and his blessing. I was lucky. Since I was still a minor, he could have prevented me from going abroad on my own. But, in spite of some reservations, mostly about the length of my stay, too long according to them, both my parents had respected my decision.

Visa

Before leaving, I had to get my visa. The US Consulate was situated on rue Saint Florentin, off the place de la Concorde and just at the beginning of rue de Rivoli. That corner of the city was my favourite. Since the age of twelve, I had come alone to walk around there, pacing slowly under the arcades, stopping at "Smith &Son" or "Galignani", both English bookshops, and going to the Louvre on deserted Thursday afternoons. Rue de Rivoli was also the way to the Comédie Française. The whole area in fact felt like a theater set, because of the arcades, because of the ornamented façades and the perfect lines enhanced by the green motifs of the Tuileries.

When I entered, the waiting room at the Consulate had already dozens of people filling their visa forms. The form was about twelve pages thick. I started to read the questions the US government wanted me to answer. Was I or had I ever been part of, or a sympathizer of, the Communist party? Had I ever planned to overturn the US government? If yes, could I please give details in the next box? I looked at the other visa candidates. They were all absorbed in their task. I finished filling the form, signed it and gave it to an employee standing behind a desk who told me to sit and wait to be called. The others around me were silent and impassible. Outside, the day was vibrating and the flow of cars was swelling on the place de la Concorde. I shut my eyes. I felt like on a plane. "Miss Dargnies!" called the employee.

I went through the door held open for me by the guard. Madame Consul was standing up behind her desk to greet me. She invited me to sit. The stern lady wore thick tinted tortoise shell glasses and a prim taupe suit. She asked me why I wanted to go to the US and I told her right on about Scott Fitzgerald, my desire to go abroad and get new perspectives. The new perspectives were my first attempt at using pompous and void concepts. The straight gaze of the lady had not flinched and the small spark of smile in her apples was but a reflection of the sunray. Madame Consul took a seal, stamped my passport and handed it to me. She got up again and held out her hand, this time for a vigorous handshake. "Good luck" she said, like Mrs. Rodnick. Nobody in France ever said "good luck". The French said "au revoir". Out on the Place de la Concorde, I felt bursting with all that luck and the boundless space that had opened. I had a visa, a plane ticket and places to stay. I was ready to take off.

My father had driven me to the place des Invalides from which the Air France bus left for Orly airport. I was eager for him to leave me. I wanted to be alone. This was day one of my life. I was going out of France and out of Europe. I could see the shapes of America and Europe, the Atlantic, in the back of my mind. The prosaic gestures and words of any ordinary traveler felt like new rites. The old white skaï suitcase where I had piled all my things was appropriately an old great-aunt relic from her adventurous trips to Tahiti in the early fifties. The perky stewards and stewardesses on the ground and in flight looked and sounded like magic dolls. The perfume smell in the minuscule toilet and the colored patchwork of little foods on the lunch tray felt like Alice's wonderland. I fell asleep above the ocean, tired and blind from focusing on the sky through the window. I was a new born baby carried by the stork.

Washington D.C.

Like protesters, they held a sign, which read "Cécile" in red letters on white cardboard. He was very tall with long jaws and long sideburns and a jutting chin split in the middle. She was much smaller, plump and round with fat knees showing under her mini plaited and red-dotted white dress. Her chubby face was coiffed with short dark fringed hair brushing against her glasses' rim. She held in her arms the baby, a pale and blond infant with a big and bald head and buttonhole eyes like Charlie Brown. Bill, Kathie and Christine were standing right in front of the gate through which passengers emerged into the arrival hall. In glaring sun and African heat, we walked to the red Beetle Volkswagen.

Washington looked white and gleaming, with large and leafy avenues and European looking buildings. The small car had no air-conditioning, which allowed the hot air to blow in with the smells. It smelled wonderful like in the Cameroon of my childhood. Strong putrid and sweet smells, piquant lemony ones, milky dewy ones and, most inebriating of all, honeyed and sharp magnolia scents. We stopped on a sloping street with small front gardens and trees all along. The trees were gigantic with gracious crowns of fluffy foliages. Bill and Kathie's house was not very wide, with the living-room and kitchen on the first floor, the main bedroom and the baby's room on the second and an attic under the roof. That was my domain. A small window looked down both onto the small patch of dry lawn that was their back garden, and the neighboring ones. The slanted roof was low above my head and the temperature under it was like a sauna's. The naked wood beams exhaled a spicy smell. "America" I told my reflection in the tiny mirror pinned on the wall above the sink. I was still incredulous, but I was abroad and away for sure. As I glanced again through the small window, I saw a Cardinal, a flaming red and black bird with a small hoopoe, perched on a tree.

Bill and Kathie's house

Everything around the house was efficient and comfortable as no château in Bray would ever be. From the giant all-purpose double fridge to the electric can opener and the multiple sofas. Every morning Bill and Kathie went out to work while I stayed home with Christine which I had privately baptized "the Peanut" since she looked so much like a creature of Schulz. She played or drowsed in her pen on the Chinese carpet in the living room and I fed her at noon with ready-made baby food. Kathie came back in the afternoon, setting me free. A few evenings every week, I was baby sitting while they went out. Bill was a reputable lawyer on the rise and an alumnus from Harvard Law School. Kathie was doing social work on a part-time basis. While Bill came from the East coast, an Irish-American from Boston, Kathie was from Billings, Montana and she had graduated in sociology from the University of Michigan. She longed for the West and its space, not relishing much the pretentious and go-getter spirit of Washingtonians. We chatted with coffee in the afternoon when she got back. My work, if I could call it work, was being around when she was not. Kathie was thrilled to have me at home. In the US, she had explained, it was impossible to have an au-pair arrangement. Baby-sitters were paid by the hour and, if hired every day, cost a fortune. She had gently offered me to take the Beetle any time I felt like since Bill had another car. When I had said that, at nineteen, I had no driving license, she had been flabbergasted.

On Saturday nights, before going out all together, they invited friend couples at home for drinks and I shared with them tough concoctions like gin and tonic or dry martini, which I had never drunk before. Those detonating cocktails left me dizzy long after they had all gone merrily to a Georgetown restaurant. Bill and Kathie's friends were always jolly, laughing and full of pep. It was impossible to actually decipher their real mood, but that was not the point. I enjoyed that surface benevolence and discovered happily the American feelgood approach.

The rumors of creeping dangers around Washington annoyed me. Kathie had told me to keep not only the front door locked at all times, but the back door also, even if I was just going down the wood staircase into the back garden. In any case, she recommended I not go into the back garden through which potential muggers could easily sneak. But when I ventured out alone on the street the first time, I quickly forgot the fears nurtured by the daily TV reports of robberies and murders I watched on my long baby-sitting hours. This was difficult to reconcile with the magnificence of the city, designed by the French urbanist L'Enfant as I had been told already hundreds of times. I didn't care about the Frenchness of Washington, but I relished its sprawling beauty. Nature was so dominant and gorgeous everywhere around that I was not terribly attracted by the classical tourist staples. More than the Capitol and the White House, I was thrilled by the vegetation and the Potomac river. After making the requisite visits to the Museums, I turned to the list of friends of friends I had duly concocted before leaving.

A Texan party

I called Laura one evening. She had been the neighbor of a school friend of mine who had stayed three years in Washington while her General father was posted as military attaché at the French Embassy. Laura proposed to come by one evening when I was baby-sitting. She was a tall lanky girl, with long dark hair tied in a tail. Her huge blue eyes looked strange rather than pretty. She started to explain her job to me. She turned and wrenched her long hands and kept mentioning records, which I misunderstood as being music records. Laura was in fact working as a MD's secretary, keeping files and records on all the patients. When she left, she invited me to her birthday party that was taking place a week later. I had no party clothes. Besides two jeans and shorts, and ordinary flat sandals I had only a shirt frock, which I had made myself. Kathie drove me to Laura's house, which was in an upscale district where most diplomats and military officials resided. The upscale feel came from the enormity of the houses and the spacious private parks surrounding them.

Laura's place was a white stone building with tall French windows shaded by huge rounded awnings. A crowd of guests chirped and chuckled around the pool. Laura's parents were standing in the alley just in front of the gate to shake hands with every newcomer. Her father was dressed in close-fitting pants, bending his corseted body every time he shook a woman's hand. His smile, like the one of his wife, stayed constant on his lips. Laura's mother was dressed with sophisticated and sober elegance in a Chanel type cream dress. Laura stood a little further by the pool, her hair dripping. She was in her bathing suit, having just finished a series of jumps in the pool. Quite a few boys sliced through the water with powerful butterfly strokes that sent waves in all directions, splashing now and then guests standing too near. Laura had gently taken me by the hand to introduce me around. A Mexican-looking boy had quickly put a colorful cocktail in my hand and I had joined in the chirping.

The sun was low and glowing on faces, turning people and things into gold. A girl from Austin, Texas, was asking me eagerly about France and Paris. She was telling me that Texas was really the heart and saviour of the USA and that Laura's parents both belonged to Texas society, as did most of the people around us that night. As she exhorted me to come and visit her home state, a gaunt young man suddenly came up to me. "Are you engaged?" he asked. I didn't understand what he meant. Engaged to be married? Before I could answer, he had already turned towards the Austin girl. "Are you engaged?" he asked again. The gaunt young man looked strange. His pale and pimply skin was grayish, his minuscule eyes deepset above salient cheekbones. He seemed to be blind as he moved agressively and clumsily at the same time in his worn out dark suit. People were watching him. Abruptly, he took the hand of the Austin girl, and dragged her with him up onto the diving board. They jumped on it once and both splashed all dressed into the pool. The girl's pretty coral pink dress was clinging to her thighs, and she grimaced a smile as someone was quickly wrapping her in a robe.

The gaunt young man was now standing a little further, his arm tightly held by Laura's father who chided him as if he were a child. People around me whispered that he was mentally ill and dangerous. A tall and enormous man, dressed in a pilot outfit appeared in the alley. His Roman emperor's face, with virile features and heavy eyebrows, was crimson with rage. He was the father of the gaunt young man. He first took Laura's mother's hand and kissed it politely, apologizing for the incident. While he had a drink with the hosts, his son stood silent, his head down like a guilty dog. After a last gulp, the formidable air force general grabbed his son by the neck and dragged him away. Some guests were leaving and I followed them in the queue to say goodbye to Laura and her parents. "Do you have a car?" asked Laura. I was hoping to find a cab on the avenue. But in no time, she had found two boys that were going to the same part of town to give me a lift.

A Sunday with the Millers

My next hosts were an old couple, military people too. The husband was a retired officer. They lived in Virginia. They had come in the morning to fetch me with their Cadillac. Although there was all the room in the world on the back seat, Mr. Miller had insisted I sit on the front seat together with him and his wife. Tucked between the voluminous thighs of Mrs. Miller and the car gear, I could sense some tension in the couple. She was growling at something, smiling at me though every time our eyes crossed. Her pallid but chubby face striated with fine wrinkles and her silver compact perm hair didn't let much personal feeling out. She made me think of one of those blank and unappealing standard wood fiber wardrobes. The husband glanced at me now and then with a wink. The powerful air-conditioning made the Cadillac feel like a fridge on wheels. I felt terribly cold, besides being uncomfortable on the slippery and cold white leather seat. A few times, Mrs. Miller let off gas that she was obviously trying to keep at bay by moving her heavy body from one buttock to the other. We arrived at their one-floor house, stepping on cement tiles in front of the garage and immediately onto plain carpet past the entrance door. In the living room, everything was silver grey, creamy white and well-padded, like them. We had a drink. All around, curios and trinkets from their overseas trips lay on multiple shelves. They had been everywhere for at least a few hours. Mr. Miller talked of Paris with twinkling eyes and again lots of winks towards me. Enthused by a gin tonic, he was talking about the Lido nightclub in Paris where he had spent many an evening, including one with Mrs. Miller, he said, slapping her on the shoulder, which she did not seem to like.

We were to have lunch with friends of theirs who had children my age. Their house was big and their lawn generous. Besides the usual travel souvenirs, that house was filled with flamboyant furniture, a rococo interpretation of the Louis XV or XVI style. The supposed crest of the family hung on the wall and the two big Chinese carpets were exactly the same as the one in Katie and Bill's living room in Washington. Beige with blue motifs, I was to see that carpet all over America. The meal was good and strangely formal. I had rarely seen that many different glasses in front of my plate. Plates and cups were multiple and changed all the time. The daughter got up to do the service. John, their friends'son, was going to Georgetown University the coming fall.

While the parents were having coffee with the Millers, John took me with his sister to have coffee at their neighbors. The neighbors were two girls, one going to school with John and the other, Jane, preparing a BA in ethnology at Brown University. I was very impressed by Jane. She was beautiful in a Scandinavian way with very blond hair, very blue eyes and a tall athletic body. But more endearing than her allure was the energy she radiated. She embodied exactly what I expected from an American student, and what I would have dreamt of becoming myself. She was barefoot with impeccably depilated and milky legs, dressed in boyish shorts but with sexy long hair dangling around and a blue shirt tied with a knot rather than buttoned up. Jane was not all seduction, she talked about her research as a very serious intellectual. Now in her freshman year at Brown, she was going on with her ethnology studies, specializing in Asian countries. Japan was her main interest and her boyfriend, studying at Brown too, was Japanese. We all drank coffee in mugs, sprawled on the carpet floor of Jane's room. "If you are still here in September, you should come and visit me at Brown" she said as I was leaving with John and his sister. She scribbled her phone number on a little pad and tore off the note to give it to me.

A taste for soap operas

My mornings at Bill and Katie's were now a comfortable routine. After cereals in milk and watery coffee, I sat in front of the TV set. We had never had a TV at home, and even if we had, there were only three channels to watch in France. There were more than a dozen in America and the programs were quite extraordinary. Besides interviews, reports, news and variety shows, surreal and endless drama shows filled the screen all morning, probably intended for women at home, bored and alone. Katie had smiled when she had caught me watching one of them. It was called "Love is a many-splendored thing". Teenage love, post–menopause love, adulterous love, love between old and young and young and old, any kind of love was taking place every day every morning of the week. The show was interrupted two or three times for advertisements, which always occurred at some decisive moment like the first kiss or the first sight of a loved one with someone else. "Soap operas" had said Katie with a smile, "They are an institution here in America". Soap? "Yes because their main function is to sell soap and soap products. Didn't you notice that all ads are about soaps, shampoos and washing powders?" "Love is a many-splendored thing" took place somewhere by the sea, Florida or California as the palm-trees and hair blowing in the breeze bore witness. It had the lazy and addictive charm of sweets filled with preservatives. One could sit all day long, every day and all one's life watching those beautifully formatted puppets. There was no story but a long cry for love unattainable or love lost.

Besides the soaps, the most intriguing program was a story in progress, that of a real American family living in California. A voice off was telling what each of them was doing or going to do. It was the first reality show and it would go on for more than a year. A middleclass Californian family was being shown at home, in the office, at school, shopping, partying, meeting friends. A lot was shown, but the whole family and each of its members remained totally elusive. It was as if the camera could not catch anything, no feeling, no atmosphere, no substance in the life of those people. It was as if the eye of the camera, the perfection of the screen just killed them softly. The mother was a trendy yet harsh woman. She had long black hair, huge Jackie O' sunglasses, sporty trench coats or safari type jackets. All day long, she drove from one appointment to the other, smiling at all times. She hosted parties and dinners and went out with her executive husband. Her face was a perfect mask and her words lightly self-mocking as if she had to put a brave face at all times, but for whom and what? The father was mostly in his office or in conference rooms. He smiled too, but his smile looked tired and constrained. He joined into the light joking tone of his wife when they met every evening back at home. He drove a striking sports car and talked with a manly bass voice and brief sentences. The son was artistic, sporting long hair and fancy tribal jewels. The show puzzled me but I couldn't help watching it, as if all that vacuity attracted and numbed me. The son confessed his homosexuality. The man announced his divorce. The woman had an affair. The carving up of all those lives into moments was horrifying and riveting at the same time.

A hoarse and husky voice named Bob Dylan

On baby-sitting nights, there was nothing on TV that I felt like watching. I was attracted neither by talk-shows about people and facts I knew nothing about, neither by loud variety shows, and even less by game shows like "Let's make a deal!" where obese and hilarious people ended up with three refrigerators and as many washing machines which must have given them a lot of headache as to where to stash them in their apartment. I contented myself with LP records. Still fresh from her University days, Katie had a big collection of everything in vogue in the sixties. I had got tired of Joni Mitchell and Joan Baez endless complaints, but I was enthralled by Bob Dylan. I had heard his name in Paris when he had come on his first European tour. He looked like an owl, with sleepwalker eyes sunk into an enormous mass of hair that bubbled all around his head. From that frail body and hallucinated head came a throaty, nasal, hollow voice supported by a nerve-racking high-pitched harmonica and a bass guitar. The words came up like dripping blood, like hurricane wind or the sad pace of a man in pain. It gripped body and mind and sent shivers up my spine.

"*Come gather around people wherever you are, if you're tired of the US we are saving*" he cried, with bells ringing the tocsin in the background, calling up everyone to wake up and be ready. The urgency, the exuberance of life and the imminence of death, all of those were into that song "*Times, they're changing*". The fear, the joy, the excitement, the disarray and the mad hopes that were mine and other youths all around the world. Bob Dylan resurrected the utopia of a world where everyone would give his or her hand and no one would be alone anymore. Tears came up to my eyes every time I heard the bell ringing, and then that enthralling, "Come gather around people wherever you are!" The comradely bible of Dylan was friendly and grandiose at the same time and his lines sounded like desultory prophecies. *"The moral of the story, the moral of this song, is one should never be where one does not belong".*

Arthur from Berkeley

I still had one girl to contact on my Washington list. Sophie was French-American, with a French mother and an American father. She had come to fetch me one evening for dinner out and she had brought her brother Arthur. Arthur didn't speak very much, he had very blue eyes behind round glasses that seemed to peek at me like someone stuck behind a boat porthole. His hair was frizzy and overgrown all around his lunar face. His virile neck was pale against his light blue shirt and he half-smiled all the time. He looked like Bob Dylan. But on top of it, he was living and studying in Berkeley. I was all eyes and ears.

Berkeley was, or, rather, had been, the twin campus of Nanterre, my own campus in Paris, nicknamed "the French Berkeley" following the wave of protests of May 1968. But, in 1970, the "French Berkeley" was in bad shape and nobody cared much anymore for the American brotherhood. I did. The desolate and muddy wasteland, next to the biggest French shantytown, where the first campus "à l'américaine" had been built, way out of the city had been like an airlock for me. Out of school, out of that well-ordered pattern of childhood and teen age, thrown from one day to the other into adulthood, I had liked Nanterre for its isolation and its absence of any kind of story or history. It was only a series of cement blocks planted on polluted soils. But out of that grayness and harshness, I had picked friendliness and togetherness.

The students of Nanterre at the department of human sciences and literatures came from starkly different backgrounds, from the west and the east of Paris. There was not even a cafeteria to meet on the campus. There were only coin coffee machines and dirty tile floors to sit on in winter, or stiff couch grass outside in spring. Professors, assistants and students were all equal. Far from the madding city and all its French manias, Nanterre was an oasis of straightforwardness, mutual aid and real communication between individuals. Beyond social backgrounds and political clans, we all slummed it carefree and happy in the brand new yet already rundown Nanterre. Hailed as a groundbreaking formula, the campus was already ignored and avoided by the new students who all wanted to flock to the Sorbonne and other Paris Universities. I could not afford the cafés of the left bank anyway and didn't care much about the heavy centuries hanging over those historical buildings. The shabby airport toilet charm of Nanterre fitted me perfectly. From that no man's land had come out a tentative experiment of students and professors all stuck in the same boat. That was the best way out of the past and out in the world.

Arthur fitted in my dream, perfectly. Berkeley was my target, my far away Spanish castle. He was in computer engineering and mathematics, working on his MS. At my mentioning Nanterre, he had laughed lightly. Being half-French, he knew well the situation in France and apart from René Thom and other famed French mathematicians, he found the French boring and pretentious. But he mocked American girls too as we sat in an Italian restaurant on that Friday night when all Washington employees went out to make whoopee. Women in pairs or trios sat at many tables and Arthur laughed at what he saw as their gross female temptress ways, heavy make-up and loud laughters. "Secretaries" he had said snobbishly, "Washington is just full of sex-starved secretaries". Sophie and Arthur had driven me back home and Arthur had said he would call me.

He was in Washington until mid-August to see his father. His mother was mentally ill, in and out of a psychiatric hospital. Arthur liked his father and pitied him for the terrible life he had because of his sick wife. He couldn't stand

Washington though where he didn't know a soul. Besides working, Sophie was engaged and already pregnant. Arthur was left to himself and his rambling mother. He came walking by a few days later. His house was not very far. He was telling me about Marshall Mc. Luhan. I had to read *The Gutenberg galaxy* by all means. His other mentor author was Theodore Roszak who had just published *The making of a counterculture*. It was the first time I heard the word "counterculture". As for my intention to go to Berkeley, he was all for it. Berkeley was the only place in the world he wanted to be. He couldn't stand Washington, neither the East coast. He had deliberately ignored the Ivy League universities which he found passé, sham and deadly boring. Berkeley was top of the range for vanguard social organization, daring politics and pioneer research in sciences. They had the biggest computer in the world. He couldn't wait to be back there. I had listened to Bob Dylan again after he had left. *"Come gather around people..."* I was on my way. Times were changing.

We had set for a meeting on Dupont Circle for the last Friday I was to be in Washington. After that, Bill and Katie were taking baby Christine and me for a week of holiday to Vermont and to Maine before my leaving for Philadelphia where I would stay the whole month of August. Dupont Circle had a very bad reputation. From its earlier distinguished days, it had fallen abruptly downhill in the sixties, with houses dilapidated and squatted by derelict people, mostly black. Katie, because she was a leftist, had not said it clearly but the tremendous crime rate around Washington was due to the very high percentage of poor and destitute black Americans in the area. When I had told her I was going to Dupont Circle, she had told me to be careful. The place was swarming with gangs, drug dealers and customers, ready for anything to get a buck or a fuck. I had got off the bus at four in the afternoon under a sun and glare worthy of "High noon". Lots of black guys hung around the unattractive garden at the center of the Circle. In unknown whereabouts, it was wise to look matter-of-fact. Any sign of being unfamiliar to the area was bound to attract attention. I glanced at my watch while walking assertively towards the other end of the Circle. I was five minutes ahead of time. Arthur would show up soon. At five past four, I was still waiting. There were benches along the alley, but Paris had taught me long ago that sitting alone in public places, for a woman, was calling for trouble. I went on pacing for a while and stopped.

A black guy, slim and wild-eyed, got up from his bench and came up to me. I didn't move, although I could see him well, moving my eyes incognito behind my sunglasses. "Where are you from?" he asked with a husky voice. I pretended not to hear. "Where are you from?" he repeated, this time with a crying tone. "France" I dropped, pronounced the French way. "Where are you from?" he asked again, getting nearer. "France" I shouted this time, angry more at myself for being frightened than at the guy that seemed to be a loony rather than a baddy. An old woman with a beret sat on the nearest bench shouted: "Leave the girl alone!" " That's none of your business" retorted the guy. I got away fast towards the bus stop. I didn't intend to wait forever. As I fumed and panted, Arthur appeared ahead, hands in his pockets, smiling mockingly. I had no desire to sit on a bench on Dupont Circle. There was an ice-cream parlor on the avenue nearby. Something I had seen only in cartoons. A counter, plenty of taps giving out bright-colored ice creams, more taps and jars giving out all the toppings one could add to a mountain of icecream. The ice cream was served in a heavy glass jar as tall as a flower vase. It was very good but the huge amount made the sweet overwhelming. The parlor was empty. We sat alone on pink bar stools with mirrors in our backs and mirrors in front behind the counter and the magic taps. At six, the sun was getting softer. We went out.

Going across a green park, we arrived in Georgetown. The Flemish-like red brick houses lining the red brick tiled sidewalks felt quaint and homey in the twilight. The air was still warm and thick like jelly but with night falling it was no longer stifling. It was made for the shawl I had not thought of taking with me when I had gone for my rendez-vous with Arthur. The heat of the night made the sky look blue, if a darkened one. We walked up and down with a crowd of people in search of a place to eat. It was a happy crowd. Car traffic went by at snail's pace. I knew Georgetown had become the Neuilly of Washington, but even if trendy and chic, it felt like a tropical Latin Quarter. We ate black beans and sausages in a Mexican place. Near midnight, the whole area was switching gear. Laughs and congratulations flared up all along the avenue, which had turned into a kind of Fellini's Via Veneto. A warm breeze rippled through the frail green trees. We were pacing again on the red brick sidewalk. Tired, we sat on a low wall, watching people go by like a parade on Carnival day.

We walked back to Arthur's house and slipped silently down to the basement. He sneaked upstairs in the kitchen and came back with cokes and biscuits. Sitting on the floor, I was yawning. When I woke up, Arthur was asleep, his head on my lap. Faint noises of water running and feet tiptoeing came from above. Milky light trickled from the narrow windows at street level. Arthur yawned and stretched and jumped up on his feet. Outside, sunlight swept the ground with white gold. Night was over. We walked under giant trees, arched like a nave. A cab appeared on top of the sloping avenue. Before I went, Arthur had written down his address and phone in Berkeley, and those of a friend who lived in Philadelphia. Sleepy and dreamy, I was holding the paper note in my hand like Cinderella's slippers. That was all that remained from the Washington night.

The Vermont farm of John Kenneth Galbraith

Like Chevy Chase on a driving holiday with his family, Katie and Bill had rented a station wagon to accommodate the baby pen and the stock of paper diapers. The Beetle was too small. I had the whole back seat for me. Katie was nervous on the highway where cars were going barely five feet from each other and all at the same speed on the multiple lanes. It felt like a huge parking lot creeping away all together. No one overtook anyone; they just all went forward in one block. Up to New York City, the traffic was very dense. As we were getting on the New Jersey shore, I turned my head and saw the dreamy skyline of NY, like a blow-up from a book. We stopped once in a while on busy cement patches with junk food and lousy toilets. Baby Christine got a change of diapers in the back trunk. In Massachusetts, the air was cooler. We stopped at a motel for the night. The highway was quiet and almost empty now. We entered Vermont the next day at noon. The curvy road went along the valley meandering among the hills. It felt like a sea of green, its canopy shivering under the slow and powerful wind. It felt wild and fresh, the very green breast of the New World I had been fantasizing about. We got on a dirt track. A rundown wooden gate was open.

The summer farm cottage of John Kenneth Galbraith was spreading its low roof in the middle of the forest. It was not far from Canada where he was born. Bill was an ex-college mate and friend of Galbraith's eldest son. French style, his wife showed us our rooms as if we were part of the family. We then all shared refreshments ahead of dinner. The small and portly black maid, as wide as she was high, chuckled and laughed non-stop while she kept cooking, cleaning and preparing the dinner table. As the sun set, in Colorama grand style, the temperature dropped abruptly. We had drinks indoors before the meal in the long low-ceilinged living room. Tall, oak-like, Galbraith smiled ironically at all times, but behind the creased eyelids, the eyes were stern and alert. His long face had regular features with prominent cheekbones and an imperious aquiline nose. He looked like a princely horse, or like Abraham Lincoln, minus the beard. He towered above everyone and his head almost brushed on the beams. He had to bend to go through the diminutive doors from room to room. His wife could have fitted in his pocket, minute and pretty, sporty and alert in her sixties. She spoke French fluently and, out of perfect breeding, seemed to make a point of having a conversation with me. Besides my comparative literature and Berkeley ritornello, I didn't have much to say. But she convincingly expressed interest and told me about her student past at Radcliffe.

Dinner was served the French way with a well-ordered succession of dishes. The black maid sat at the left of the big man but she sprang on her feet every minute to check her pans on the stove, to carry off or bring the next course. Velvety claret was being served with the meal like in France. Besides Galbraith and his wife, there were his eldest son and his wife, the third and youngest son with his girl friend and the maid's niece. Baby Christine had been put to bed in her parents' room. The dishes were all fruity and spicy in the native Louisiana way of the maid. She fitted her role perfectly, with a tinge of self-mockery in the just too much perfection. It was both a performance and a play for her. That night was her birthday and all lights went out abruptly after cheese served at the end of the meal like in France. Mrs. Galbraith appeared suddenly in the dark, her stern face illuminated by the candlelit birthday cake she had gone to fetch discreetly from where it had been hidden. All members of the family piled presents in front of the maid. She tore them open with cries of delight. There were many different gaudy hats in canvas or cotton, which she put on obligingly while parading around the table to much applause. We concluded the birthday with champagne, the real one, and as we all got up from the table, the maid ran back to the kitchen to prepare coffee and start cleaning up the mass of plates and cutlery before putting them in the dishwasher. She was perched on her little wooden platform in front of the sink, joking and humming and gesturing, happy and gently keeping to her servant's station.

As for myself, I retired early, keeping to my au-pair station. My room was cool and I decided to take a hot bath before going to bed. The tub was wide and deep, a huge cast iron tub with its enamel chipped off in places. The hot water poured massively, and apparently unlimitedly, from the old faucet. I lay in marvelous oblivion in the heat and steam, floating in the water. On entering the bathroom, I had noticed that it had two doors as it served two bedrooms. I had prudently locked the one door going to the other room. My bed was small and the mattress worn down to great softness. The sheets were used up also, but at just the right amount to have the smell and feel of childhood countryside summers.

The next day, the sun banged its gold with all its Vermont might on the window. I got up and dressed, hurrying out. Galbraith and the maid were the only ones up in the house. Mrs. Galbraith had gone at dawn to ride her horse in the hills. The maid greeted me with chuckles and kisses, calling me the little Frenchie and making me sit at the wooden table outside with coffee, milk, boiled eggs, crispy corn bread and pancakes with maple syrup. As the day before, she couldn't stop working, gulping some liquid or munching some food on the go as she ran to and fro non-stop. Galbraith had nodded at me, with the slight ironic smile that seemed carved on his gaunt face. His small grey elephant eyes scrutinized me. As everyone arrived in pyjamas and nighties, he announced that he was taking us for a walk in the woods.

The woods were dense enough to suppress any view in the distance. Walking on the path, there were no rolling hills and rolling clouds to watch, just trees, smells and sounds. Any walk I had done in the past had always been a walk to a high spot where a spectacular valley or mountain range always sprang magically as we panted up the last slope. That Vermont walk was like a forest bath. Galbraith quickly outpaced everybody with the maid's young niece, disappearing ahead. I came second all by myself while Bill, Katie and the rest of the family followed leisurely. Katie had got bad blisters, which Mrs. Galbraith took care of with ointment and bandages she had wisely taken with her. As I progressed on the path, I heard a splash in water. Not far ahead, Galbraith was sitting on a rock, smiling and talking to someone. As I was going up, a wide pool appeared behind the rock, the head of the niece floating on top like a wild duck. I put my hand in the water. It was freezing. The girl wallowed in it happily, inviting me to join in. Her body showed through the ripples of water, naked and blurred. I took a sip from the pool and put water on my face. The girl was getting out, her muscled body at its best in the sunray dripping down from the foliage. She was zipping up her jeans shorts just as the others arrived. Galbraith and the girl were already up and going, singing summer camp songs together and playing with his cane. As they all took off their clothes to jump in the cold water, I sheepishly started off.

In the afternoon, there was another swim programmed by Mrs. Galbraith. "You don't need your bathing suit" she had told me, "It's only girls this time." She seemed intrigued by my prudishness. I had taken my swimsuit all the same. The sun was already low and its rosy rays were lighting our heads and the heads of the spruces around. The light waves on the pond were reddish. The sinewy Mrs. Galbraith had jumped first in the water, crawling away elegantly while Katie giggled uncomfortably as the cool water tickled her thighs. Birds cried and squealed, flying low. Night was falling fast as we hurried back home.

Big steak in Maine

After Vermont, Maine was another choice cut of America. A land and a climate with yet another incredible whiff of wild to breathe, Maine had something from Brittany but on a giant scale. Land and seawater were so entangled together in patterns of gleaming pools with thick manes of kelp and rocks and brackish ponds that there was no way to know where the continent ended and where it got cut off. Bill's sister, Maeve, a sporty ruddy blond mother of five had a summerhouse right on the beach. We were to sleep in a tiny wooden bungalow just above the tide line. It was barely bigger than a beach cabin with two small closets as bedrooms. Katie and Bill were in one and I was sharing the smallest with baby Christine. The surf hissed and breathed but in July the wind was very mild.

Maeve's family was very gentle but policed with an iron hand by its *"materfamilias"*. The father was very quiet, prudently letting his wife run the show. For dinner, we had the biggest piece of rumpsteak I had ever seen, ruby red under its grilled surface and juicy like an orange. We had several helpings each of us with plenty of baked potatoes and cream. Between every dish, two of the children got up and efficiently cleaned up plates or cutlery to replace them by new ones. I joined in the kitchen for the final cleanup of the table. As I was putting some glasses in the dishwasher, I saw the daughter throwing the remaining piece of steak in the garbage can. For a split second, I remained mouth open and eyebrows raised. Maeve suddenly caught the expression of bewilderment on my face and swiftly grabbed the piece of steak as it was falling into the garbage. "We can have some spaghetti with it to-morrow" she said blushing while the children seemed to wonder what was the matter.

For their two weeks yearly holidays Maeve's family lived exclusively on the beach. Nobody swam much nor for very long. The gorgeous surf was great to watch and breathe, but as icy as the iceberg it had been shortly before. No gulf stream in Maine as we had in Brittany explained to me Jane's husband. Instead of swimming, people sailed in all directions with all sorts of boats. The funniest was a very big woman filling her whole tiny boat equipped with a minuscule sail no bigger than the smallest jib. Nearby a noisy, candy and grease smelling beach resort served as a place for the evening stroll and ice-cream cone dessert. The crowd was huge, fat and dense, moving like a colony of sea lions on the boardwalk, eating and drinking on the go.

Philadelphia, a sooty old city

A couple of lawyer friends of Bill and Katie were giving me a lift on their way to Chicago. They also had a little baby and a rented station wagon. They fought non-stop, the husband putting down his wife at the same time he was smiling engagingly to me. I was new to couples' politics and I felt embarrassed for the little brunette wife being rebuffed all the time. We were driving in the middle of the night and the highway was as full as during the day. The air was hot and damp and we had all the windows down because the air conditioning system was broken. In spite of the asphalt and thousands of cars, it felt wild in the kind of chiaroscuro of car lights and faraway illuminated towns or diners. "At night, the baby sleeps" had told me the mother with a sigh of relief to explain why they traveled in the dark. I still was amazed that so many Americans chose that solution. Suddenly, it felt as if we were approaching another planet from our dark limbo. A thick fog engulfed us. In the distance, the lights of Philadelphia were blurred and diffracted like a lighthouse lost in a tempest. "City pollution" explained the husband.

In a matter of minutes, we had arrived in a narrow and tiny street lined up with red brick townhouses. Benjamin and Eliza were yawning on the doorstep. As I was ushered in, the couple was already waving goodbye, going on non-stop to Chicago. Benjamin was barefoot in falling shorts, his tummy bulging out and his short torso hairy like a chimp. His round chubby face was ensconced in frizzy hair like Bob Dylan. Eliza in a long tee shirt looked like a little girl, her long black hair down to her hips. The house was a pyramid of tiny and dark rooms with a sundeck on top. It was small and dark since sunlight could not shine through because of the narrowness of the street. Out, the sun was tough and merciless. August in Philadelphia had a feel of Paris. The same grey asphalt exhaled an acrid smell of bitumen, and buildings were black with soot. It was easy to go around its European web of streets and public squares. We were one stonethrow from Rittenhouse square where I took the child, Sarah, every day for a stroll.

She was only two years old, but big and determined enough to be four or five. My luck was that she liked me and seemed to appreciate the attention and entertainment I provided. With her mother and grandmother, she tended to shriek and kick, but whenever I announced to her that we were going for a walk, she went to sit all by herself in the stroller. Mother and grandmother were surprised by my authority and even more by the fact that Sarah seemed to enjoy being directed. I had heard of Dr. Spock because of whom American children had become totally unmanageable, so went the saying in France. But Sarah had taken splendidly to my empiric methods.

"The art of love" by Erich Fromm

Benjamin was a 1960 iconoclast and a very successful business lawyer in Philadelphia. He and Eliza went out for dinner almost every day and I baby-sat every night until late. I didn't watch TV very much at those hours. I read instead. There was a whole library in a den off the sundeck on top of the house and the living room had plenty of books too on shelves and tables. I had opened "The art of love" by Erich Fromm at random. From the first lines, the book had taken hold of me. Fromm was describing and analyzing the complexities of love and human relationships with clarity and ease. I was both engrossed in his words, and lightened by his grace. What could have been a stern treaty or a trivial joke was a profoundly sympathetic voice. The meaning of tricky phrases and new words often escaped me, but I was drawn to them as by incantations. Benjamin and Eliza's house, in the silence of the hot night was the perfect environment to read the book. So was Philadelphia, that old city that seemed to have been shipped direct from the old world into the new. "Our main task is to give birth to ourselves" said Fromm. I had a lot on my plate.

Edgar Allan Poe's dark alleys

Philadelphia felt like a pentimento of the first migrants to America. As if they had wanted to build anew their smelly and intricate European past. The streets of Philadelphia were many and labyrinthine, going in straight lines that somehow got lost like in oriental souks. On my free time, I had begun to tread the dark and dusty sidewalks. There were not many people on the streets. It was too hot to walk for the working people, and the leisure class had gone off to the ocean or the mountains like it did everywhere. I had only a very sketchy map of Philadelphia that showed a chessboard of streets stabbed by a few diagonal ways that had survived from pioneer times when no one felt compelled to go at right angles.

One afternoon, I set off for Edgar Allan Poe's house. I had sunglasses, but no hat. The sky was hazy but the blurred sunrays turned silvery pounded heat and glare even more. Bathing the sooty city, that mercury silver was dazzling, shooting at me from the ground below and the sky above. It felt as if an eclipse of the sun had overtaken Philadelphia. Neither day, neither night, it could have been dusk or dawn. I walked in a daze. I had no clear directions and no sense of orientation either. I was alone and lost in the city of Edgar Allan Poe.

The dark, grey and silver of the scene reminded me of something I had seen once upon a time. An old man in black walked along an unknown street, in a part of town he didn't know, with empty streets stretching ad infinitum. A pedestrian appeared ahead and as he turned his head, his bland face, eyeless and featureless, stared at the horrified old man. The sound of a horse galloping suddenly broke the silence. A black carriage appeared at the corner. A carriage wheel got stuck on the pavement and the horse broke free, running away and disappearing. The old man approached the carriage, a hearse. Slowly, a black coffin was slipping out. As he bent above, the cover of the coffin slid open and a naked hand appeared, held out as if crying for help. The old man took that hand which grabbed his own, voraciously. The old man tried to pull back and free his hand, but he could not. And he woke up, in his bed. That memorable nightmare I had not forgotten. It happened in the first movie I had seen at twelve years old. *"Wild strawberries"* by Ingmar Bergman.

I was walking in the middle of crumbling and banged façades where black birds nested. Bits of rusty wire fencing, weeds and undisciplined bushes mingled with broken pavements and sidewalks, tired cars, there was nobody around. Amid that dereliction, a fresh oasis appeared unexpectedly. It felt like a mirage. The buildings were old but neatly cleaned up and restored. Bruges-like frail red bricks gables pointed anew. The elegant and light townhouses lined a street planted with fragile linden moving gracefully their pristinely green foliage. Vermeer land resurrected in the middle of Poe's world.

A boat party on the Chesapeake Bay

When I had called on the phone, I knew from Mrs. Cross's melodious and volubile elocution that I was going into American bourgeoisie. She had announced brightly that we would be going for a trip on Chesapeake Bay in their motorboat. As I was coming down the train from Philadelphia, she was waiting for me on the quay, wearing white gloves and a wide umbrella straw hat, together with her little girl, Teenie, in jeans shorts. At the wheel of her formidable black Buick, she seemed to me like the embodiment of a perfect American hostess, well mannered and magnificently organized. The house was off the main road, at the end of a shady alley meandering through tall woods. It spread like a manor around a theatrical paved yard with cropped borders. A small pond and a stream completed the scene. I was swiftly whisked to my room in the adjacent guest house. When I entered the living room, Mrs. Cross had taken off her umbrella hat and gloves and had changed her blue and white dress for a slicker silky one in a creamy tone. Teenie was playing outside with her dog, still in her shorts, while her mother was checking preparations for the dinner, all laid out by the maid who had left earlier.

Mr. Cross arrived, with frumpy face and clothes. His large tummy was crushed by his leather waist belt and sweat oozed from his shiny parted black hair. His head and face were small on top of his vast body and he fixed me coldly as I nodded to him. Mrs. Cross came in and hugged him, introducing me. "You are a friend of Tom?" He asked me. I had no clue who was Tom. "No, no" said his wife, "Tom's girl friends will be arriving later." Mr. Cross disappeared for a while and came back to sit in a deep armchair. He had combed his hair and changed his shirt. Mrs. Cross was buzzing around him like a bee, bringing him a glass of scotch on the rocks, exchanging some jolly private jokes and obviously trying to lighten the atmosphere. "Where is Tom?" he growled. "Tom has been fixing the gutter the whole afternoon", she announced emphatically. I still wondered who Tom was until Mrs. Cross informed me that he was their son. "My son is an idiot", growled Mr. Cross. As we were sitting at the table, Mr. Cross insisted on pushing my chair under my bottom, something I disliked very much. Buttocks had to grope for the seat that way, with the risk of missing their target.

Tom appeared just then, a tall and pale boy with a tortured face. He mumbled something as he sat. "What did you say?" asked his father. "I said good evening" said Tom, his head down. "You can say it louder, son. And keep your head up." "Tom fixed the whole gutter" said Mrs. Cross again. "This is good, son" conceded Mr. Cross. Teenie was silent, sitting by her father's side. The chandelier above the table gave a dim light in spite of its many bulbs and the meal routine felt endless like a bad play at the theatre. It was a five-course meal, but dishes seemed to be there as a pretext for a change of china plates and silver cutlery. Tom asked permission to get up as his mother was bringing dessert. He had to go and fetch two girl friends at the train station. "So" said cheerily Mrs. Cross turning to me, "We'll be all cruising on the Chesapeake to-morrow! We should leave early". I took it as a hint to go to bed.

The night was surprisingly cool after the warm summer afternoon and the woody landscape quite dramatic. The guesthouse was in the dark and I groped for a while, looking for a switch. I was beginning to undress when the outside door opened and I heard Tom and his friends coming in. I delayed going to bed and, instead, came out into the small living room. Tom now smiled and joked. He introduced me to his friends, Elisabeth and Joy. Elisabeth was twenty something, living in New York and working in a graphics agency. She was thin, blond, blue-eyed and fair like a Swede, while Joy was brown-haired and brown-eyed with puppy fat. Tom had met them while working for the summer in a carpentry shop near Lake Champlain where the two sisters spent their summer holidays in the family cabin with their widowed father and their other brothers and sisters. Tom had gone to the kitchen in the main house to bring food for his starving friends. All lights were out there while we ate and drank wine. "If there is one thing I am glad of" said Tom suddenly, his face drooping for a moment, "it's that I am not their biological child." "Don't say that" said Elisabeth, "Even if they are awful, that blood thing doesn't mean anything one way or the other." "Still, I am glad not to have any gene in common with him." "Come on! Just one year and you'll be free" said Elisabeth. The two girls were going to sleep together on the couch that converted into a double bed. Both were going for the cruise, but Tom would not. He swiftly gathered food and plates on a big tray and helped open the couch-bed. "See you at breakfast" he said, going to sleep in his den above the garage.

We were piled up on the back seat while Teenie sat on her mother's lap. Mr. Cross seemed in a better mood, patting his wife every now and then while they chatted happily together. The ride was short to the marina where the motor-boat was moored. The boat was a huge affair, towering with its three levels and decks. Mrs. Cross jumped in sportily, dressed in white pants, blue jacket and striped white and red shirt, a red eyeshade tied back on her hair. Elizabeth, Joy and I went to sit in front, watching the prow knifing the water with white foam and sun sparks splashing on both sides. The day was gorgeous and the air exhilarating, we lay there while the Cross couple stayed on the top deck, behind the wheel. Teenie, the little girl, still had not said a word except before we left when she had asked permission to take her dog with her, which had been denied. I went to help her set the lunch table on the back deck. Mrs. Cross came down to direct us as to where to put the many salads and pâtés she had brought. We had a glass of white wine for aperitif. Mr. Cross declared that he was very happy Joy was the friend of Tom, that she had a very good influence on him. Joy remained silent.

I was chatting with Elisabeth who was telling me about New York where she lived, about her father who was a medical doctor and her mother who had died prematurely of cancer. The wood cabin at Lake Champlain where she had met Tom was their family summer camp, the narrowness of the house supplemented by old army tents. For all her nostalgia of family life and her love for her father, Elisabeth had not wanted to live in Chicago near him and her siblings. She felt that fending for herself and living alone in New York City were necessary for her to grow and develop as a person. She had been smitten by "The second sex" by Simone de Beauvoir. The book had galvanized her, convincing her that solitude, breadwinning and tough life experiences were not only for boys, but for girls too if they wanted to become full persons. I confessed that I had only glanced at "The second sex" which I found rather professorial. I was more interested by the new world feminists, Germaine Greer, Kate Millett, and even Betty Friedan, the ancestor.

The boat was stopped in the middle of the bay and we all sat around the table for lunch. Frizzy water was missing on the table and Mr. Cross jumped with all his big body to go and fetch it, making his wife sit down and kissing her hand with whispered love names. The sun was becoming a nuisance and, in spite of sun hat and glasses, we were all turning crimson and ill at ease. The pretty lunch table looked now like a dead picnic site and the day suddenly felt dragging along. The boat was going on its course like a drugged turtle. Mrs. Cross was at the wheel to let her husband relax. Joy had gone to lie down in the cabin, so had Teenie. Mr. Cross was drinking coffee with us. He started to chat in a friendly way with Elisabeth. I went back and forth to the kitchenette to clean up the table while Elisabeth sat upright, her chin in her cupped hand, smiling flirtatiously. I heard suddenly Mr. Cross's voice choking, "What?" I came back to the deck. "You mean you would have provided the gun yourself?" asked Mr. Cross, his face red and his small black eyes jutting out. "Yes", answered Elisabeth, still smiling. "I'll have you reported to the FBI!" screamed Mr. Cross, pounding the table with his fist. He got up and went back to the top deck. Mrs. Cross came down, her face stiff. Elisabeth had taken a cigarette out of a pack and was holding it, looking for a lighter. "Would you have a match?" she asked Mrs. Cross.

"The establishment has no match", said Mrs. Cross on a dry humorous tone. Mr. Cross remained at the helm, his face grimacing, looking straight ahead. Elisabeth was shrugging her shoulders. I took out my lighter and we smoked. "I am not afraid. I was expecting that reaction, actually I provoked him on purpose." She explained to me that a shoot-out had occurred a week before in a California courthouse where members of the Black Panther party were being tried. The guns were registered in the name of Angela Davis, a twenty-six years old philosopher, disciple of Herbert Marcuse, who taught at the University of California. Angela Davis was on the run, on the most wanted list of the FBI.

We were speeding back to the marina. Everyone was fed up with the cruise. Elisabeth wrote me her address and phone number in New York for me to visit a few weeks later. "Elisabeth is inviting Cecile to New York" I heard Mrs. Cross say ominously to her husband. We all drove back to the house, mouth and face shut. Tom came to the guesthouse as we were all packing in haste. "They said I could still see Joy because she is a nice girl", he said. "But they want to report you", he nodded to Elisabeth. The cab he had called had arrived. We got in and left without goodbye. The little silent girl, Teenie, stood up behind the living-room glass door, watching us go.

Dinner with the grandparents

I had barely seen Benjamin and Eliza during my stay in Philadelphia, not even sharing a meal with them. But I was sent for Saturday dinner at Eliza's parents where I was to fetch Sarah. It was my last evening in Philadelphia. The kid ran amok in the grandparent's apartment, thrilled by the space. It was a vast place with high ceiling, in a soot black imperial building off Rittenhouse Square. Eliza couldn't stand her mother and found a pretext every week to miss the Saturday night family dinner. The big apartment was crammed with oriental carpets. The grandmother welcomed me with a warm embrace trying to remember my name. The two brothers of Eliza, having shed ties and jackets after a hard business week, were there with their wives. The grandfather in waistcoat and tie sat at one end of the table and the grandmother at the other. Sarah and two other small children raced around and under the table.

Above the hubbub, the grown-ups talked. "I am so sorry you lost the baby" said suddenly the grandfather as we had started to eat. One of the daughters in law had had a miscarriage, which they all commented on expertly in between mouthfuls. Spicy and colored food dishes had been laid all together on the table, oriental way. We didn't drink wine but beer and beverages. A big cake with a warm cannella smell was served in the sitting room with coffee, German way. One of Eliza's brothers drove Sarah and me back to Locust Street. They would not let me walk the short distance at night. I regretted it. Before leaving Philadelphia, I would have liked to feel the mellow asphalt one last time.

Ambling along the East coast

I was riding the Greyhound, but this time I was not going to work anymore. After two months, I was free to do as I pleased for four weeks. Going back home was far, far away in time and space. I would drift slowly along the coast from Providence to New York City.

Brown university

First port of call was Brown University. On that first week of September, the postcard campus was bubbling with activity and swarmed with students. The green grass and lunchtime made the place look like a holiday club. I walked around, waiting for Jane. She appeared in jeans and belted cotton jacket, impeccable with her long hair braided, showing off her beautiful face. She embraced me with a loud "yeah!" as if I were an old chum and took me to the cafeteria for lunch. Everybody was busy and hilarious and I felt a pang of regret not to be part of it. "You can apply if you feel like it" Jane was telling me gently. I was taken in by the great mood and atmosphere of the beginning of the schoolyear. Of all the months of the year, September was the prettiest and most enticing to be on a campus. Some trees were still blossoming while others already had turned their carnival gaudy fall colors. Jane took me to her room where I was to sleep in her roommate's bed since she was away. In the evening, Jane had to go to the library to prepare an essay. From College Hill, I looked down at the pretty colonial houses and walked on Benefit street, taken by the tide of students going up and down. A fresh breeze blew from the river and near ocean.

Early the next day, I walked with Jane through the dewy grass to the building where she had her class. On the way, we met Saki, her Japanese boyfriend who studied economics. I saw Jane blushing at seeing him. Saki was unusually tall, and dark next to her. They slapped each other shoulders, parting fast as if resisting attraction. Jane said that she was going to Japan the next year with Saki. She was studying Japanese too. "It's been my lucky day", she said dreamily as Saki disappeared.

I still had a few hours to kill until my bus would leave for New Jersey. All the little shops were open along Benefit Street. I picked LP's and teeshirts to be my Tom Thumb's little stones once I would be again in France. The shopkeeper played *"Times are changing"* and *"Freedom"* for me and I took Bob Dylan and Jefferson Airplane under my arm. I put on a batik tee shirt splashed with what looked like ink stains. My hair had grown quite a bit in July and August and I was beginning to get a hunch of how American girls achieved their distinctive allure. With the teeshirt down to my thighs and hair tied with a thick strand of pink wool, I went down, wind blowing in my face, to board the bus.

A Professor's family

Professor Graff, a philosophy professor at Hunter College was a sweet man, if quite traditional. An aunt of mine studying philosophy had met him at a seminar in Canada. The house was in a very quiet district in New Jersey, not far from New York City. He commuted every day to Hunter College. Lawns and trees stood alone in the empty streets. The mother had her hair in a chignon and an apron on her grey skirt, busy working around the house. When we sat for lunch in the kitchen, the three children showed up. The perky daughter was studying at Wellesley College where she was going back the next day. She was upset because a registered letter she had been waiting for had still not arrived. Neither parent paid any attention to the two sons. The youngest was twelve years old, talking and moving all the time, trying hard to be noticed. The eldest son was silent. Very thin, with a diaphanous skin, he seemed absent-minded, deep in his thoughts while looking at his plate or at the sky beyond the window. His father stole a glance at him now and then, looking worried. He asked his son about his holiday with a tinge of admonition, as if he were a priest in the confessional. The son was just back from Provincetown. The mother and the sister looked at him as if pouting. The son calmly told them of the beauty of Cape Cod and the many arty and bohemian types in the area. Father and mother exchanged a glance full of hurt feelings and disgust. Provincetown, the mecca of marginals and, among others, homosexuals and drug addicts, was not their idea of a place to vacation.

After lunch, the eldest son and I talked a bit on the lawn outside. We then went for a walk along the tree-lined avenue. He pointed to me the wide living-room windows through which one could see sofas, carpets and mantelpieces, more or less identical. "That's what the "movement" is about he declared, "Everybody out of the living-room. You know about the movement?" he asked with a slightly professorial tone, which recalled his father's. He had dropped out of school and was wandering around the country, taking odd jobs. He wanted to be a writer. His parents and siblings belonged to another world he had left now. The same evening, he was gone without telling anybody.

At dinner, we were only four left around the table. The parents were commenting on their troubled son. "I am sure he is hiding something" grumbled the Professor. They obviously were afraid of his taking drugs and of his being gay. The younger brother had not despaired of getting some attention. He had mentioned about five times an essay he had been writing the whole weekend. The theme was "family" and the boy was eager to read aloud his piece. His father told him sharply to behave until dessert. Then, he could read us his masterpiece.

As the Professor was lighting a small cigar and the mother and I were drinking light coffee, the boy stood at some distance from us, ready for the show. He started to read his composition. The theme was a family outing. His voice, still that of a child, described a neat and clean little family having a picnic in a park. But the sweet appearance of the scene was deceptive. Parents and children ended their Sunday outing with some very unorthodox puffs of grass, not the clean green one they were sitting on. Totally engrossed in his story, the boy smiled as he finished and looked up from his paper, eager for recognition of his talent for humor. I thought the essay very funny and sophisticated for a boy his age, but both parents looked appalled. "We don't like it", said the father sternly. "This is not funny", added the mother. The boy's face drooped down instantly. "You should go up to your room and rewrite that essay before to-morrow", added the father. Blushing out of shame or wrath, the boy didn't say a word and went upstairs.

The crazy Lubin family

It felt homey back on the Greyhound bus. Being a lonesome hobo was not so bad. Every evening I was staying at unknown places with unknown people who gently offered me a bed and a meal like farmers of the past when a tramp knocked on the door in the cold night. But my real home was the bus, moving with the road. As we reached the New Jersey shore, Manhattan appeared as a splendid liner, wholesome, animal and perfect. Its spine rose above the waters with head and paws and eyes. It was strange and riveting.

From the Queens Greyhound terminal, I took a cab to go to my next Samaritans, the Lubin family. They lived outside New York in a suburb. We couldn't find their street. The cab stopped at a phone booth so I could call. As I was talking to Mrs. Lubin giving me directions to get to her house, I glanced sideways and saw a girl looking at me as if she was following my conversation. I had not shut the glass door. I hung up and she smiled at me. She was going in the same direction, she said. She just had to call her mother to come and pick her up. If I wanted, they could give me a lift to the Lubins. I paid the cab and waited for the girl to make her call. Her name was Penny. She was a tiny brunette with a kind of helmet-shaped hairdo popularized by the singer Sandie Shaw. She worked as a secretary in New-York and she lived in Manhattan. I told her I was traveling and visiting people in the area before flying back to France. Like Jane and Elisabeth, she spontaneously offered to house me for a few days if I wished. Which came very handy since Elisabeth was not due back in her East Harlem place before a week, and I could not stretch too long my stay with the Lubins.

When Mrs. Lubin opened her door, a baby crying in her arms and a small child crying in her legs, her mouth smiled but her face looked on the brink of bursting in tears. Both children stopped their crying to look at me inquiringly and the little girl climbed on my lap while I was sitting on the couch. The house was a wood cabin, very dark because of the narrow highperched garage windows and the dense forestation outside. Couches, TV and kitchen appliances were all there, complete with round table and low lamp to give the required cosy feel, but it felt gloomy. Mrs. Lubin was fleshy and curvy, looking Italian. Her vivacious movements and loud voice made her more so. After passionate kisses to the baby boy, she moved her arms in the air and turned around in the kitchen corner, opening drawers, making a kind of musical din with pots and cake pans. After that Lucille Ball bit, she started to prepare a cake in earnest. Her parents in law were coming for dinner that night. Her husband came back, with wonder on his face as if he had no clue what he would find at home by way of wife. But Mrs. Lubin was smiling and flirtatious that evening. She kissed him as he embraced her. He was slightly smaller than she was. In spite of all her friendliness, he seemed doubtful it would last. We shook hands as his wife introduced me and he went to change in his room. I baby-talked to the children while the mother was going herself to change into better clothes. She reappeared with a silky white blouse widely open on her Sophia Loren bosom. Her husband had changed his office suit for canvas pants and a sweater and he was feeding the baby sat in a high chair.

The bell rang and the grandparents Lubin stepped in with shouts and cries of joy echoed by shouts and cries of welcome. They were both small and round like their son, and both wore glasses. They had brought candy and toys for the children who shrieked and jumped. "*Enchanté*" said Mr. Lubin the father as we shook hands. The meal was delicious and Mrs. Lubin everywhere. Behind the burners and at the table, juggling with plates and dishes and glasses and bottles, she talked and joked nonstop. The children had been put in bed and had stayed there. It was a flawless show. The grandparents left and as the door shut, Mr. Lubin was already seated in front of the coffee table, his face bland and still, ready for the storm. Mrs. Lubin started cleaning the table with me. She hit a glass on the table. It fell and broke on the floor. Mr. Lubin pretended not to have heard anything. He went on sipping the digestive he had shared a while before with his father. Things were going crescendo in the kitchen corner, tableware breaking as well as rage. I sat as inconspicuously as possible on the edge of the couch. Mr. Lubin's eyes crossed mine. After banging shut the dishwasher and hurling chairs under the table, Mrs. Lubin retired, head and bosom high like La Callas. Her husband passed a hand on his head and sighed. "Is it like that in France too?" he asked.

The next morning, rain was pouring and the road was foggy as Mrs. Lubin lugged both children in the station wagon. The baby was harnessed like a poney in the back next to his sister. I sat in front. First, she wanted to drop me at the bus station. I would have much preferred to take a cab and get away from Mrs. Lubin's problems. But she insisted and I did not want to hurt her feelings. She drove with as many gestures as when she spoke. The car seemed to be a kind of music instrument in her hands, an alter ego to which she communicated her strong inner feelings. Mrs. Lubin was an angry woman. I was worried. She was speeding on the shiny black road. I could hear the water splashing under the tyres. Luckily, there was no traffic in mid-morning and the road was straight. She was driving right in the middle of the road. I held my breath and shut my mouth. The wipers hissed malevolently and the rain was so heavy that the windshield went blind between wipings. All at once, the wagon went awry, as if pushed by a powerful wave. The skidding had been so fierce that we had made a complete U-turn in a split second. Mrs. Lubin had yelled. Now she cried, flat down on her wheel. "The baby" she shrieked suddenly, jerking on her seat and turning her head. The little girl was crouched in a corner, appalled but still. The baby whined and Mrs. Lubin grabbed him out of his seat, pressing him against her heart with kisses between tears and declamations of love. A yellow cab was coming on us. He stopped gently and asked if we needed help. Mrs. Lubin recomposed herself and, blowing her nose, said that everything was all right. I had my hand on the door lever, "Let me take that cab so you won't be late at school with your daughter" I suggested. I thanked her for everything and swiftly passed my rucksack from her trunk to the cab's one. Her car was still stuck in the middle of the road as the cab was quickly taking me to Manhattan.

A party at Penny's box in Manhattan

We cruised smoothly on the rugged waves of cars. From behind a car window, New York was terribly rocky. In a matter of minutes, I was suddenly out of the yellow cruiser, left to myself in front of Penny's building. The column of nameplates was long. Names were handwritten, fading or crossed and replaced by new ones. The bits of cardboard were going to shreds in the green molded copper frames. Penny's last name was there but I could not go to her apartment yet. She was still at work. I had to wait. I walked up to Third avenue. Traffic was heavy, but there were not many pedestrians, only a few men, looking lost. I went down a few steps into a basement deli. Breakfast time was over and all customers had left. I had hardly sat down, a carafe filled with water and clicking ice cubes was dropped on my table. The waiter, notepad in hand, asked me what I wanted. I remembered the pancakes of JKG's black maid. Of course they had it, and hash, and eggs and muffins and juice. While I ate, the waiters were taking a break, smoking and chatting together in the back. They all spoke a language I had never heard before. As a waiter was passing me by, I bluntly asked him what that language was. It was Greek. All the waiters were Greek, living in Astoria, the Greek town of New York.

Sitting below the level of the sidewalk, I watched legs and feet and car bodies going by. The rainy weather was of no consequence where I was. Like a warm submarine, the deli was bathed in maple syrup, coffee and frying smells, and Greek syllables. I felt like putting my head on the table and napping for a while, but I resisted. To fight sleep I tried to focus on a map of New York. The grid lines of Manhattan blurred slightly under my sleepy eyes, giving a twisted look to the cleanly drawn streets and avenues. All those pieces of jigsaw were mine to tread and assemble. But how could one go at those terribly straight lines and right angles?

The staircase was dark. The tiny elevator bumped now and then as if hesitating between going up or down again. The same reddish carpet covered the inside of the elevator and the landings. No light on the landing either. The building was blind. Penny stood up on the tiny doorstep. Her apartment was dark too. Windows were covered with curtains. After a day's work, she looked fresh and relaxed, her Sandie Shaw hairdo impeccable. I let my suitcase into the mini-hall but she took it right away to put it inside a wardrobe in the bedroom. Although totally filled by a double bed, it was the biggest room in the apartment. "I am having a small party tonight" said Penny. Since I would have to leave at eight in the morning when Penny left for work, night would be short. "Would you prefer to sleep with me in the double bed or each of us on a mattress in the living-room?" I wondered one second if two mattresses could actually fit on that floor. "A friend will stay overnight. But you have the choice." I opted for the floor. Penny was busy preparing bites and drinks for the party. I could not decently go to lie on that big bed that looked so tempting through the open door. I could have helped her, but there was not enough room for the two of us in the kitchen. I sat on the couch that filled the living-room the same way the bed filled the bedroom, fighting the temptation to put my feet up on the coffee-table and doze. The doorbell rang and I straightened up.

A smart and small little man was bowing to me, offering his hand to shake. He told me his name was Juan and that he was from Spain. He had brought a bottle of Ballantine's scotch whisky for the party. "Nice, isn't it?" he said, flattering the rounded flask with his hand. Penny had shut the kitchen door when the bell had rung, asking me to deal with the guest, who had arrived a good thirty minutes ahead of the tight schedule. At the second ringing, she came out of the kitchen. Juan rushed to her impetuously and hugged her. He was still holding her tight when the next guest appeared, head bent down, in the doorframe. Jamie was a tall blond Viking, in jeans and sweater, his hair falling on his shoulders. Juan let go of Penny and straightened his back to tower as much as possible above things, if not people. Jamie grumbled "Hello Juan and Cécile", pairing us off, and went straight to the bathroom for a shower. The bell rang again, and again. In a few minutes, the apartment had filled to saturation. We must have been at least twenty in the chiaroscuro of the living room. All Penny's friends had just left work an hour before. Either having jazzed up their work clothes with some jewelry or make-up, or having changed to jeans or jog-suit, they all stood up, a drink in hand, chitchatting with exclamations of wonder or praise or pity or whatever, punctuating their words. It sounded like a business cocktail party. In fact it was Penny's birthday party, as I had finally understood from all the presents brought in by each guest. Everybody looked or acted happy, save Juan and me, out of fatigue.

Juan sat forlorn at one end of the little couch while everyone else stayed standing up. A girl was toying with a key in her hand, she looked worried. Two friends were obviously trying to comfort her. She had just moved into a new apartment. Her things had arrived the same afternoon and a new lock had been placed just hours before. She was freaking out. Break-ins and assaults were the norm. "With three locks, I should be OK" she said as if reassuring herself, "I should be OK with three locks" she repeated while her friends said "Sure!" and patted her shoulder. A birthday cake showed up all of a sudden. We sang "Happy Birthday" and in no time everybody had left, or almost. Juan still had Penny's hand in his in the doorway, telling her he would call soon, that they could go to the movies, that he thanked her so much.

Penny at long last managed to put Juan in the elevator, coming back in with an indulgent sigh, "Oh, Juan!" We gathered bottles and glasses, cups and saucers and put them in the dishwasher. The Viking was lying on the big bed under the sheets, his torso out. Penny asked me if I wanted to have a shower and I told her to go first. When I finally came out of the bathroom, Penny was already asleep. I lied on my mattress on the other side of the coffee table and slept like a log until dawn.

When I opened my eyes, Penny was not on her mattress. I quickly shut my eyes as I heard a faint shuffle coming from the bedroom. Minutes later, she was up already, taking her clothes to the bathroom to get dressed. The Viking was yawning and splashing water on his face over the kitchen sink. We all went down and parted instantly on the sidewalk. Penny had given me basic directions to find the subway station while already walking to her bus stop. I watched the yellow cabs swerving by, tempted to hop on one. But I could not afford cabs forever. It was time for me to grapple with New York.

Elizabeth's grand suite in Spanish Harlem

I would have liked to walk to Spanish Harlem, but from midtown it was a long way to go with a suitcase. Quays in the subway were engulfed in darkness, with here and there small halos of light were people huddled together in silence. I took the somber ride as a necessary purgatory. Up from the subway, I emerged on Park Avenue, pretty as a garden-party. My route was straight down from there into "El Barrio". Elisabeth had told me of her Puerto Ricans neighbors, vast families with tens of children, solid and static mammas and wandering interlope fathers. Going from Park to Elisabeth was like leaving a rose garden for a back street. I walked like through the layers of a cake, icing on top and hard biscuit at the bottom. But the bottom part was livelier than the top one.

Guys, a foot against dirty walls, looked like a pack at rest. "Don't worry" had said Elisabeth, "They don't move from their wall corner. They just go about their business between themselves." I walked briskly as I was nearing her building, head high, trying to have the look of a girl who knew her whereabouts. I was even careful not to look too eagerly at the numbers on buildings, so as not to appear too much like a stranger. I caught the right number in a glance and got into the building hall. There was no one in the wide staircase but I could hear women and children's voices and noises through the rickety doors I passed on my way up.

Elisabeth's lair was on top of the building. I could hear Joan Baez's voice singing. I knocked with my knuckles on the door. Elisabeth came to the door, radiant like a Flemish Virgin in a triptych with her gold hair floating around her pure oval of a face, milky and rosy. Floods of sunset light bathed the huge living room. We sat on a woven carpet on the floor. Out of the window, the roofs of Manhattan spread in the sky. I had reached at last the canopy of the city. New York spread in front of me, like the Greek Gods' Elysium, elegant structures evolving in the sky at the top of the world. Elisabeth's domain ran the whole length of the building with a string of linked rooms like in royal apartments at Versailles, but a Versailles abandoned for a century, its paint flaking off and its glassed windows broken here and there and held in place by tape. The wooden floors were totally dilapidated, with broken boards and stains all over. The generous daylight was unhindered by the absence of curtains on the windows. The glare of the sun was weakening though with its slow descent. Sunk behind the forest of buildings, it kept its firebird extravaganza for the finale. Night fell, but its somber blue still kept traces of the vanquished sun. There were neither greenplants, nor anything vegetal whatsoever in Elisabeth's apartment, yet it felt like being in nature's most remote area, up there above the petrified forest of Mannahatta. I was speechless amid such strange and endearing beauty, a beauty I had never seen nor imagined from the many popular photographs of New York. As any real beauty, it was alive and changing, in permanent modification with time and seasons passing, along the hours of the day and of the night, be it cold or warm, wet or scorched. Cement and stone registered the changes like any vegetal or mineral. The fresh breast, after all, the fresh breast of a new world, was still alive, transmuted but still there.

Elisabeth had gone to cook food for dinner in the kitchen. I sat mesmerized by the spectacle of New York at night with its piles of lit windows, and streaks of clouds or fumes turning stars into comets. No moon had showed up yet. We sat with crossed legs next to the coffee table, drinking beer and eating spaghetti with meat sauce. "It's great here because it's so big", said Elisabeth. "And I like El Barrio. It's a community of families." I told her about Penny's place in midtown. "I had a place like that for a month, I couldn't stand it", she said, "It felt like being shut in a coffin".

She went to bed early. I tiptoed for a while, cleaning up the table and bringing everything into the kitchen. I didn't dare wash the plates for fear of making noise. The night was very silent, save for a buzz from the street far below, a mix of voices and engines. The bathroom was far enough away from Elisabeth's room and I decided to have a bath. The tub was wide and deep and the water burning hot. I had no clue if the quantity of hot water was finite or not. It took some time to fill the tub. I had not switched on the bathroom lights for fear of being seen naked. The night sky and the city halo gave enough light to move around. I climbed into the tub and lay in the steaming water, floating free like in a dark pond. Afar, in front of me, the moon was emerging like a very ancient planet resurrecting from the dead, shapeless and lackluster. But as she rose above, she asserted slowly her power on the night.

"A nous deux, New York"

The sun had long been up when I finally was. I had opened the eyes at the first rays, quickly getting undercover to fend off the blunt attack. I had heard crockery clicking and smelled coffee but I had stayed in bed until Elizabeth had gone. This was my first real morning with New York. I wanted to be alone with her. Outside, the cement forest was glittering as if wet from sea surf. The white morning sun defined lines sharply, reverberating itself from façade to façade, multiplying itself. Mirrored suns everywhere reflecting each other ad infinitum, splashing more light all over. A human shape glowed in the distance, a naked fragment that looked as glorious as ancient Greek marble. Contours were imprecise, limbs unclear, just flesh shaped by bones and muscles beaming in the sun. So mesmerizing was New York seen from Elisabeth's place that I could have remained there for hours, for days, watching the change of colors and the passing of time. I shrugged and shook myself.

Now, it was time to get down to earth and to start treading the city for real. I ran down the flight of stairs and went straight to Fifth Avenue. That was the spine of the beast. Down on the avenue, the sidewalk was still in the shade, cool and dark like a path in the woods. The canyon was at its deepest. People flowed straight ahead. Once in the stream, it seemed to carry you further and further, effortlessly. Block after block, it was one single wave rolling on. Faces floated on coming against the current. Heads bobbed ahead in front of me. It was multitude as I never had been in, and that multitude carried you away, body and soul.

Mondrian the magician

At the MOMA, I got off the wave. A Spanish guy, his torso protruding and his head high, was being photographed by a friend in front of "Guernica". I ambled in the rooms, aimlessly. Braque, Degas, Van Gogh. They looked lost like expatriates in the museum, akin to a warehouse with blunt square volumes. Suddenly, a room opened like a giant flower. Flashy forms danced all around. Abstract paintings firing at me from all corners. Ellsworth Kelly, Rothko said the cartouches on the wall. In mid-morning, the rooms were empty. I went around, and around again. A grid with black, yellow, red, blue and white lines looked incongruous, like a child's painstaking little work. I came close to the painting. Bits in five colors were stuck on the canvas. *"Broadway Boogie-Woogie 1944"* said the cartouche, by Piet Mondrian, born 1872 in Holland, dead 1944 in New York. Piet had been 72 years old when he had made his boogie-woogie. I went backwards, to the other end of the room. The grid was still there but the little patches moved, or rather they danced. Broadway? Of course, the painting impersonated the one oblique avenue in the city.

I went out and walked right away up to Broadway. The little man had got the trick. Those paintings had been dubbed abstract, but Manhattan itself was abstract: vertical and horizontal lines, height above and perspective ahead. It was a perfect abstract feast. I whistled as I walked in rhythm with the other pedestrians. Later, when I looked for that Piet Mondrian, I learnt exactly this. The week before his death, Piet was still so entranced with New York that he could not take the excitement out of his system. He had just arrived a few months before. An old silver print showed a very small man, with big glasses, smiling like a schoolboy. After walking through the city like in a dream come true, Piet was coming back to his little apartment, painting and dancing in the tiny studio. He was painting "Broadway boogie-woogie" and he boogie-woogied all along, drunk with happiness and fever too. He had gone out the day before and the wind blew icy cold, rushing into the avenues like the wind on the steppe. He had gotten seriously ill, a bad case of pneumonia. The fever grew, but he couldn't stop painting. He had gone to bed in the early hours. At noon, he was delirious and at night he was dead.

My feet burnt on the way back. I had walked tens and tens of blocks. I was not dancing anymore. I longed for Elizabeth's place to rest my feet. That night we went out for Chinese food. The takeaway was down on the street. More guys hung around on the curb or lounged in their cars going at snail's pace and honking helloes. The lemon yellow Chinese take-away was as tiny as the man and woman working behind the counter. There were two little red tables with chairs for whoever wanted to eat on the spot. We waited a few minutes for the dishes to be put into cartons and climbed back to the gods. Elizabeth was tired and forlorn that evening. Her boyfriend was leaving her. Actually, he had bluntly spilled out the news to her that morning. She cried silently as we sat on the floor again with all the cartons open on the coffee table. "I had washed my hair one day and he smiled to me. We went out for coffee." Stephen still lived with his parents and many brothers and sisters in Harlem. "I got along with them and they did with me. But I think Stephen got fed up with me. He thought I was far too fanatic about the cause of Black Americans." She wiped her tears away. "God, I loved that guy." She got up. "Listen, to–morrow we'll go to the movies if you want. There is a festival of French movies near Tompkins square."

Guggenheim, MET, Frick, Cloisters

The next day, I didn't go as far as I had the day before. I went gorging on all the splendid museum fare piled along Fifth Avenue: the Frick Collection, the Guggenheim, the Metropolitan. Out on the avenue, it was too hot and inside the museums, it was too cold. The Frick smelled and felt like an old attic with dusty furniture and objects crammed in every corner. All had been bought and imported from Europe, it said, and then tentatively reassembled like a DIY kit. The strange thing was that they had imported the French smell of mold and dust too. But they could not give life again to what had been cut out and severed from its original home and land. The Guggenheim was more successful, but the container eclipsed almost entirely its contents. Ignorant of the set-up, instead of taking the elevator up to the last floor, I began the visit from the bottom. The slope was steeper than it seemed and I was going up panting and spinning around the snail-like structure. The funny pyramid had the feel of a mall with art hanging all along like shops' windows. The Metropolitan's large entrance hall was stupendous, like a grand hotel which fires all its big guns in a glorious lobby to catch the attention all at once. The rooms after that sumptuous entrance hall were too small and too crowded. I then went to Wall Street. Employees were still stuck in their offices and the street was quiet. I went to rest for a while in little Trinity church. Its nave was crowded with noisy bums and hoboes. It was noontime and they were waiting for a daily distribution of sandwiches. Bored waiting, they were discussing loudly their problems of the day. I would not get rest there. I went uptown to the Cloisters. There, the assembled pieces of pirating were surprisingly oozing some of their original grace. Although coming from many different places, the colonnades, fountains and sculptures had been combined successfully. The sky and green and the Hudson river gave life to the lost old world remnants.

"Last year in Marienbad"

Elisabeth was serene again when I came back to her apartment. We had a bite and a drink before getting to the subway station for the long ride down to Tompkins square. Elizabeth knew her way in the dark corridors like a trapper in

Canada. In no time we were at the movie theatre, an oldish formerly plushy theatre with red carpet, red velvet deep seats and red curtain. The grapes of bulbs on the walls dimmed slowly while the curtain went up. I knew the name "Resnais" and I had heard of *"Last year in Marienbad"* but I had never seen it. A woman ran and ran along rooms and rooms, pursued by a forgotten lover. The story and the couple went on through Marienbad, hopeless. He ran, she ran, they would run forever. I liked the melody of images and the dry dialogue whispered off screen, but I disliked the lack of resolution. The story had turned hellish. She could not get out of his life and he could not stop running after her. When the grapes of bulbs started to shine again, I felt relieved.

Outside, we stopped under the canopy. Torrential rain poured and drowned the streets of New York. We waited a while, hoping for the rain to stop. When it slackened a little, we took off, pulling our sweaters above our heads. In no time, we were in no man's land. No street lights, no home lights, no shops, no cars, nobody. The wide avenue stretched wet and dark between lines of seemingly bombed out houses. Packs of rags were piled on the sidewalk. A coughing face emerged, someone mumbled. The rags were human beings. Dead or dying, they lay as far as the sidewalk went, forever. The rain poured on them. They would not get up, they would never leave anymore, dying or dead they would stay there. "The Bowery" whispered Elisabeth. We were not afraid, but death was pounding too strong to stand for long. Out of nowhere, a yellow cab came cruising along. We rushed into it and fled.

Taking off

From Elisabeth's place, I watched again the sun conquering his kingdom above New York. Hours later, I was in the sky itself, flying above New York. Below me, the city dissolved. I was away from America. The wheels banged on the tarmac. I was back in France. Back? No, only stopping by.

Soon, I would be off again. Home country, home city, home itself had lost their power. I had left, I was back, but I would leave again.

BACK TO FRANCE 1

Backwards - Nanterre, the French Berkeley – Susan from Boston - America in Paris - Martha from Atlanta – Theodore Roszak – The Vassar plan - The sleazy Professor

Looking for plan B - Goethe Institut - Cambridge Mass.? - Minerve Intérim - Universidad Internacional, Santander - Remembrances of my father - A bad hangover - Linda from Cambridge, Mass. - Tübingen - Rita in München, Ludwigstrasse, Nymphenburg - The Becher family, Shopfeim - Oktober Bierfest

Backwards

Back, that word exhaled all its numb and malignant stupidity. Back, like backwards, like backwater. Back in France, back in Paris, back in life as destiny had it for me. Born here, grown up here, programmed to marry here, procreate here and die here. The line seemed straight and clear, so much so that it was doubtful such a linear life was worth living. If the scenario was all written down already, I didn't want to live it through. But, if I could cross again the Atlantic, everything would be new and unwritten over there. My motivations were neither to escape hunger nor destitution, neither torture nor deprivation of liberties. My urge was to break free from any obligation to replicate the normal good girl destiny. I longed for space, for distance, distance from family, home, roots, all hurdles to the birth of that self I had read, eyes out, in Erich Fromm's *"The art of loving"*.

"Why do you want to go back to America?" Parents and friends asked. "Because I want to study there for a Ph.D." I would say. It had to sound serious enough. "But can't you get a Doctorate in France?" they objected. I did not answer that one. Declare my love for America was unthinkable. It would have sounded preposterous, childish and silly. Like saying "I want to be Marilyn Monroe".

Nanterre, the French Berkeley

My first luck was Nanterre, the first French university campus *"à l'américaine"*. I had not chosen to go to that faraway western outpost of the Paris conurbation. I owed it to the so-called "sectorization system", a new concept of the

French Education Ministry according to which the place one lived determined the place one had to study for a degree. That "sectorization" applied only to State Universities. Any *"baccalauréat"* laureate was free to go to private higher education establishments, provided one could afford it, which was not my case. Living on the west side of Paris, Nanterre University, or Paris X, was my designated campus to study and get degrees. It cost only a few hundreds of French francs to enroll which my father had given me distractedly. My path back to America actually started on these muddy outskirts. With a BA or two, and, even better, an MA under my belt, I could apply to American Universities and maybe even get a scholarship. If accepted, this would entail a Student visa allowing me to stay in the US for the duration of my studies and for a few years of salaried work considered as complementary learning. That was the rosy scenario on paper. But getting rejected was far more likely than being accepted. Getting a scholarship was even less likely and, without one, I would have to solve the financing problem. To begin, I had decided to focus on the first step: get degrees, get top marks, get top recommendations.

Nanterre was a wasteland. On one muddy edge sat the campus buildings. On the other edge sprawled shanties like in Calcutta. The French Berkeley was damp and cold in October, its cement bits looking drab and already aged after four years of existence. To get there was a long and variegated trip. It took more than two hours by subway and trains with sixteen subway stations to Gare Saint Lazare to begin with. From Saint Lazare, it was all cement forests on both sides of the Seine. The greyish and sepia colours made the landscape look like an army map. The train line was not direct to Nanterre. I had to get off at Bécon-les-Bruyères. There, the cement gave way to rusty millstone houses with tile roofs and little garden patches. The quay was always empty after the morning peak and wind-swept most of the time. There was no shelter for waiting passengers. I would tread on the quay, tapping my feet now and then to keep them warm. The fashion was clogs that year, which didn't improve comfort and warmth, even with thick woollen socks. Time stopped at Bécon. The daily wait for the connection to Nanterre froze time as well as my feet. Sky and earth were often lost in drizzle or mist. When there was no sun I would feel out and away like in a space ship, sucked by a vacuum. My brain stopped too. I felt like a paramecium, that smallest of animals I had observed and cut in pieces under a microscope at the high school lab once upon a time. On hot summer days on the contrary, the quay at Bécon was gleaming in the sun like the one on which Gary Cooper stood in *"High noon"*. Fall, winter or summer, it was a test that tried one's patience and determination. Sometimes, I had to resist the urge to quit and hop on one of those trains bound back for Paris, to forget Bécon, to forget Nanterre with its mud and poverty, its cold naked classrooms and its graffiti-covered walls. But I knew I had to stand the test. Nanterre was my only way out, my only hope. Only with degrees would I be able to apply to a University in America.

And then, unexpectedly, Nanterre opened to me as a bizarre treasure trove. Astonishingly, out of that wasteland came warmth and comradeship and a huge territory for the mind. It gathered the friendliest people I had ever met in France. An uncertain environment and the distancing from Paris, away from normal social life, made everyone more open. The inhospitable place, its amphitheatres, its classrooms, even its corridors were quickly locked after lectures and courses. Between classes, we had only coffee machines and the tiled floors to sit on. The library was in another building and in any case, you couldn't chat or bring drinks into the library. We all made do with what we had. I had gone once to the restaurant where so-called meals were served. The few francs they cost were better spent on coffee. I had sampled a pea soup with shining bubbles that looked like soapy water to wash the dishes. Noodles disintegrating and spongy ground meat was the *plat du jour* that day with pre-sweetened yogurt and small tasteless apples. Since that meal, I brought boiled eggs and cheese from home and ate them with the coffee. I smoked too, a lot, like everybody. The smoke and scent of burley and Virginia tobacco gave air to the wretched surroundings and feel to the atmosphere.

That academic year 1970-1971, carried away by my first transatlantic crossing the summer before, I had decided to put on a spurt. I was now preparing two BA's at the same time, one in comparative literature and one in English. I ambitioned to complete both BA in two years so as to tackle right away an MA on my third year at University. Speed kept me focussed and blurred anguish about the morrow. I believed that the more the degrees, the more attractive my academic profile would be. This I would find out was not the case. What mattered in US Universities were the marks rather than the content of courses taken or their quantity.

Comparative literature matched my desire to explore and get out of a strictly national perspective. Its basic principle was to put on an equal footing all literatures and languages of the world. I was discovering the notion of "ethnocentrism" and I was going centripetal with the zeal of one subjected to centuries-old national centrifugation. I was required to read works in the original language with a target of fluency in a minimum of five languages, including my mother tongue. I had French, English and Spanish and was beginning German at the Goethe Institut. I immersed myself into foreign literature as a would-be swimmer ignorant of swim strokes. Once immersed in the book, I would find a way I thought, grabbing the few words I knew to build a kind of semantic springboard from which I could rebound to a higher level of understanding. Language, I was convinced, was more a densely textured material than a collection of pearls. Words were not as important as their relationship to each other and their connecting tissues. The august linguists I had to read had taught me this: Saussure, Martinet, Lyons, Jakobson. My years at school with Molière and Racine, dictations and recitations seemed as remote as a tiny Fidji island from that vast and powerful ocean of knowledge I was now navigating.

My studies in English blended perfectly with comparative literature. My heavy load of eight courses per semester was not only manageable, it allowed cross-fertilization of one subject with another, be it linguistics or literature. The keyword at the Faculty of literatures and human sciences was *"pluridisciplinarité"*, an awkward neologism that meant building bridges, all kinds of bridges, between subject matters, civilizations, languages, people and customs, art genres and styles and, to begin with, between the contents and goals of the various courses on offer. Beyond my studies in literatures and languages, I was now jumping into art and human sciences with courses on the Symbolist painters, on psychoanalytic methods of analysis in art, and on different human societies like the Trobrianders seen through Margaret Mead's studies.

One of my art professors was a stern looking dark-haired and dark-eyed man, dressed with meticulous Italian elegance: the color of his suit and tie matched the handkerchief blossoming on his chest. Under his guidance, we contemplated works by Gustave Moreau and Odilon Redon, trying to decipher hidden motives and repressed feelings. He lectured us calmly and methodically on the inner depths of figures standing in the paintings. I had been most impressed, and half hilarious, when he had analyzed a painting depicting Jesus Christ falling under the weight of his cross while Véronique was brandishing the white cloth with which she had just wiped his face. The cloth bore the stained imprint of the Christ's face. The gaze of Véronique had mesmerized our professor. Those female eyes, he concluded, were looking straight into the groin of Jesus, castrating symbolically the male God. The demonstrations were rigorous and the tone always quiet and slowly persuasive. Once in a while, though, I had caught a slight grin on the professor's face. All students enrolled in his course were preparing a BA in art history. I was the odd sheep coming from the literature department. All those people knew each other since two years. They shared private jokes and a peculiar language using specialist terms with the ease of colloquial ones. Once, they had mentioned a known art critic, known to them anyway, named like one of the students. "Oh yes indeed" the Professor had said, "This is an "agnate" of Jacques." The ethnology professor had defined the term to my class sometimes later.

The ethnology course was equally interesting and non-competitive. The professor was a mature woman, dressed hippie-way with a scarf tied on her nape and covering her head, her frizzy dyed hair coming out on her neck and shoulders. Her face was clearcut and full, with a "Pasionaria" charm coming from her long green eyes. Her torso and head were still beautiful and enhanced by black tight tops *"à la Juliette Gréco"*. She cleverly concealed what was below waist under vast skirts or Turkish pants. In spite of her radical chic appearance, she was very old fashioned in her teaching, speaking slowly and emphatically like traditional professors. That revisionist style had alerted a team of *gauchistes* who liked to burst in and disrupt courses they judged old hat.

Two guys had come one afternoon, sitting on the floor in front of everybody while the lady discoursed with her usual august manner on the merits of love rituals in the Pacific islands. The subject was erotic but her tone serious, bordering on the monotonous. The two guys were quiet. The twenty of us in the class didn't know who they were, only that it was the first time they showed up. As our Professor was drawing diagrams on the blackboard and explaining the complex syntax of male and female relationships, the taboos and signals of love among the islanders, the two boys had uncrossed their long legs, which sprawled now almost touching the Professor's feet as she strode back and forth. The boys' faces were hilarious. One had rolled a cigarette, which he had lit, taking a whiff and passing it on to his friend. The Professor didn't budge, but her eyes glanced at those legs she had to mind every time she went by. She was explaining to us the symbolic significance of a girl showing her inner genitals to a boy, a custom called "to show one's scarlet" by the native Trobrianders. The boys' faces not only shone with hilarity, they were beginning to squeal with repressed laughs. They lay down completely now, their heads resting on one hand, legs apart, scratching their balls with the other hand and making sure the lady professor couldn't miss the view of their groins. She stopped all of a sudden, in the middle of her stride back and forth. Hands on her hips, she faced the boys and the whole class. "I can't go on" she said simply, instead of yelling or cursing. "As long as you are around, I can't go on." She stood up, still and silent, her arms crossed, waiting. We all caught our breath. Finally, the boys folded back their sprawling legs, jumped to their feet and went. The lesson resumed. No outsider showed up anymore.

No course bored me. Even English grammar was attractive. Each class was a different group and all Professors or Assistants were accessible, knowledgeable and admirable. Classes often lasted longer than scheduled, if nobody claimed the classroom. Perched on tables, sitting on chairs or on the floor, sometimes on the grass outside, we were gathered around a woman or a man who had the power of making knowledge shine and explode like fireworks in the night.

Susan from Boston

Susan was the best flag for America. She was bright, young, talented and the perfect American beauty. Blond, blue-eyed, slim and longhaired, with a rosebud complexion and the tight, clear speech delivery of a New Englander, like Jane of Brown U. She considered herself a radical, which an aspiring lover and French colleague at the English department called, with raised eyebrows, her radical chic. To him it was her way of excusing herself for an impeccable WASP pedigree and education. But Susan was no Barbie doll. I liked her. Against the dull background of Nanterre, she was luminous, a breath of fresh American air blowing in my sails which badly needed a boost.

Odds of ever getting back to America seemed against me. Competition to be enrolled at Berkeley was formidable, and even more formidable getting a scholarship. Besides, as a foreigner, I was barred from holding any job in the US. It was very likely I would be grounded forever in France. Susan's permanent good mood helped my spirits soar again. She taught a course titled "US current affairs" which was a kind of hold-all for a wide array of American issues, from Woman's lib to Black power, American-Indian renaissance, protest singers, the Vietnam war, the Hippies, the Yippies. To me, her course was the great symphony of America, orchestrating all ongoing movements, ethnic, gender and political ones. To sit in the amphitheater where she taught, since we were a good hundred students enrolled, was like listening to a siren. Susan was the voice of America and I listened, enthralled. In the American campus tradition, she tutored us as well as she taught us. After the lecture, she rolled slowly a cigarette between her fingers, sticking the paper around the tobacco with her tongue, listening while the student uttered his or her problem. She recommended a book or a song or gave the address of a library or bookshop to the inquiring student and she left, holding the mass of her files and papers in both her arms, shaking her blond hair and galloping away on her slim blue-jeaned legs.

I had not been long to go and talk to Susan after the course. I had mentioned comparative literature, Berkeley and my intention to go there to prepare a Ph.D. "I am almost jealous of you!" she had declared, which had startled me. She was herself finishing her Ph.D in social sciences at the University of Illinois. Her family was from Boston, Mass. At that first encounter, she had given me all the tips to trace America right in the middle of Paris and to get as much information I could to prepare my return. The very fact that she had reacted positively to my American plan had comforted my, sometimes, wavering determination. I needed hope and encouragement. Not only was it difficult, but nobody in France could understand such a longing to go to the US. It just didn't make any sense to anybody, my family or even to my Nanterre Professors, why should one want to go to that land of dubious opportunities and non-civilization. For them all, the US were a creation of colonists, who had crushed mercilessly the local natives and carved domains in areas they deemed free for grabs, from plantations to industries. The US were nothing but a land of lucky robbers, provincial minds and vulgar culture.

Susan was a US citizen, but she didn't seem to mind, ignoring with all her fresh beauty the jokes and snarls she probably heard everyday. I had a project and she respected it, while for my peers, it was mere whim. In fact, around me no girl had a project. All seemed to follow a system, not even a path, as if they were programmed for a life of spinster, bride or mother, or eventually nun. I had first believed it was a bourgeoisie thing, a Catholic fixed idea. No, it was the same in all walks of French life as I could gather from my female classmates at Nanterre and from the women I met on temporary jobs.

America in Paris

I was a lonesome hobo, I was a soldier, I was battling, against the odds and against myself. I was an ant, a minuscule insect, lost in the multitude of crashed or crashing insects, but I had a purpose. Like Jay Gatsby, like Benjamin Franklin, I woke up every morning in my child's bed, the same I had slept in for more than fifteen years, ready for a day's walk towards my goal. Some of those steps were meaningless and useless, but they kept me going, myself and my aim. I was investigating every possible source of Americanism I had found. There was the "Benjamin Franklin Center" on Place de l'Odéon. Besides a nice ride on the left bank, the Center offered free lectures and a documentation center with papers, magazines and books. It was a pretty and comfy place, its large windows framing the neoclassical columns of the *Théâtre de l'Odéon*. The "American Library" on rue du Général Camou, in the seventh arrondissement behind the Eiffel tower, was a bigger affair. For a monthly fee, I could consult their big collection of colleges and universities yearbooks and directories. There, I was looking for Professors names and list of courses, trying awkwardly to decipher the ways and meanders of Berkeley, but too Harvard, Princeton.

Thus, I had found out that a Rene Wellek was head of the comparative literature department at Harvard, himself a specialist of French nineteenth century literature and, in particular, of Stendhal. An American interested in Stendhal, this awoke my interest. I had immediately started to read Wellek books. Shortly before, I had come across a phrase coined by Michel Mohrt, a French novelist and specialist of American literature. In an essay, *"La prairie perdue"*, Mohrt dwelt on the nostalgia for the lost wild prairie of the west, as the recurrent theme and background of American fiction. Commenting on Scott Fitzgerald, he saw Gatsby as a dreamer, for whom ambition was but a way to the dream. "Gatsby", wrote Mohrt, "is a Julien Sorel from Minnesota". That had pricked up my ears. I knew Julien Sorel and Gatsby well. In my private pantheon, there were foremost Stendhal, Proust and Fitzgerald. Julien and Gatsby, that would be the theme of my research. My plan was to compare those two incarnations of success and crash. Across a century, across thousands of miles and an ocean, I would demonstrate Gatsby and Julien were twins.

Martha from Atlanta

On my list of American places in Paris, the "Shakespeare and Co" bookshop, the famed lair of Hemingway and other American writers lost in Paris, had deceived me. It was a bookshop with a pedigree and accompanying pretentiousness run by an American man, bearded and disdainful, who biked around Saint Germain des Prés and seemed to consider most customers as undesirable intruders. I much preferred the American Church. I was not going to church services but to weekly free jazz and spirituals concerts that were held on the church premises. My interest in those concerts was not musical. I was going because American kids gathered there. Sitting on the marble steps of the church, legs crossed, I had met Martha from Atlanta. She was in Paris to finish a degree in French she had started at the University of Georgia. She didn't know any French natives and coming for lunch or dinner at my parents' table pleased her. The rest of the time, she met only American fellow citizens. We went together around Paris. Surprisingly, it was Martha the American who, with her zest and enthusiasm, was making me discover the *"quartier latin"*. I knew the *"Boul' Mich"* and the cafés and the existentialist folklore, but they had no interest for me. Their charm was passé, touristy and too expensive for my pocket. The only reason I went there was to buy books at bargain prices at *Gibert*, the big bookshop on boulevard Saint Michel. I much preferred the other side of the Seine, along the Louvre and beyond on the quai de la Mégisserie where they sold birds and exotic fishes.

Martha was a fan of the small movie theaters around the boulevard Saint Michel. One afternoon, we had gone to see *"La Salamandre"*, by a new Swiss film director, Alain Tanner, which was becoming a cult film. La *"Salamandre"*, that fabulous lizard of medieval fantasy that can survive fire, was the name of the female heroin, a dropout girl named Rosemonde played by Bulle Ogier, as new a name then as Alain Tanner. The story took place along meandering narrow mountain roads in a dull Valais village covered in snow and peopled with cows. In the gloomy Swiss valley, the girl drifted in winter fog and snow, as did the story. Martha and I relished its drift rather than its plot. The *"Salamandre"* trotted along the roads and village streets, lost and happy like a cow on the run. It seemed to us like the epitome of a girl's life in 1971: foggy, shaggy, a new lost generation but this time, couldn't- give-a-damn type girls, and numbering millions. Bulle Ogier was a baby-boomer like us. For years on, *"la Salamandre!"* would remain our rallying cry whenever we met again.

Theodore Roszak

The American Cultural Centre on boulevard Raspail was radical and arty. Besides, music concerts and painting exhibits, writers and thinkers came along to talk to and meet their audiences. Theodore Roszak had been programmed and I was thrilled to see in the flesh the man behind the invention of the counterculture. At seven p.m., we were all seated and waiting for him. After hours, he finally showed up, a long, thin man with a sallow face, narrow and angular like a fox's. His eyes were too small and deep-set to let out any hint of personal feelings. His voice was low and slow as if he were in torpor. His agent, an alert blond man, was doing all the talking and all the smiling. Roszak appeared totally controlled by him, his bored face and his long arms dwindling aimlessly on both sides of his chair making him look like a chimpanzee on show.

I waited patiently for a spark but the cult writer seemed dead like a device devoid of batteries. At the end of the talk, he stood in front of the platform while some people came up to shake hands with him. I went too and looked in his minuscule eyes at arm's length. To no avail, nearer or further, Roszak seemed burnt out. We talked for a minute of power's corruption. The blond agent cut in, taking him away abruptly for yet another show. The encounter had been a flop, which, in itself, was of no consequence. But I felt uneasy. As if that forlorn man was a signal that something was dimming in America. People were hunted down, people were arrested. In five years, between 1966 and 1971, the "movement" had already lived and died. That shadow of a man, sad and tired, embarrassed me tremendously. What if my dream future was already passé?

The Vassar plan

Susan had told me to come by her place, rue Maurice Ripoche in the fourteenth arrondissement. She was in a good mood, in woolen socks and poncho, in a flurry of activity and smoking nonstop or, rather, holding a cigarette nonstop, which she took a whiff from once in a while. The apartment was a *"trois-pièces"* she shared with two fellow researchers. On the naked oak floor, piles of books, papers and cardboard boxes collapsed along the walls. There were no shelves, nor any furniture save one table in the living room and four chairs, all in thick and heavy carved wood, a kind of Art deco style for rural homes. We sat at the table drinking in mugs the coffee she had made, using a small Italian steel *"cafetiera"*, the nearest thing to a real espresso one could make at home. I was telling her about Wellek, announcing without a wink that I would apply to Berkeley and to Harvard since I needed a plan B. Harvard though was not much of a plan B to Susan. Both were equally competitive and near impossible to get in. "In any case, you have to wait until you finish your MA", she opined.

Susan took a deep sexy whiff at her cigarette. "I have another idea", she said, putting her chin on her hand. I was all ears. One of the Professors at the Nanterre English department had connections with Vassar. He had taught there at the beginning of his academic career. Every year since then, Vassar asked him to recommend one of his students for an assistantship in French. The assistantship meant about twelve hours of teaching a week and carried a stipend of four thousands dollars. Room and board were provided on the Vassar premises. Moreover, Vassar curricula were varied and rich and I could take any number of courses I wished, free of tuition. I could make extra-money with jobs on the side like private lessons or translations. "Don't you think it's fantastic?" In fact, no, for me Vassar was off track. It was neat and chic, and it sounded like the girls school I had attended in my teens. Gently, slowly, Susan was trying to reason with me. Vassar was a good way to get a foot in the door. Once in the US, I could go to whatever campus took my fancy, I could meet with faculties and more easily secure admission to a Ph.D. program for the following years. Besides, with a Vassar background, I would have a much stronger application.

I knew the English Department Professor she had mentioned. He was the one who jeered at Susan for what he considered her WASP radical chic. He was also rumored to be chasing females, Susan among others. He was not very attractive however, and rather sleazy. His greasy dark hair overgrew over his shirt collar, his reptile-like dark eyes under heavy eyelids moved a lot as if alert to whatever opportunity. I didn't feel at all like asking that man a favor. I was not one of his students anyway. There was no reason why he would propose my name to Vassar for a French assistantship. But Susan was ready to talk to him, in fact she had already mentioned me as a strong candidate for the job. She was convinced I would be an excellent assistant in French, all the more since I was doing a BA in Comparative literature on top of my English BA, which gave me the lead over other candidates from the English department.

It was the beginning of March and winter was at its saddest stage, wet, cold and devoid of any sunlight. As Susan was waving her hands in the air and shaking her hair, talking with her usual enthusiastic tone, rain splashed on the curtainless windows and a dead forest of black roofs, antennas and chimney pots spread in the distance. Coming out of my reverie, I looked at Susan. She seemed almost pleading with me to accept the Vassar assistantship. I came back on earth. The offer was incredible. In one shot, all my problems were solved. I would have a job, money, possibility to study, a good reference for later endeavors, a perfect scenario to present to my parents and all this in America! The only thing I had to do was to contact the sleazy Professor and talk it over with him.

The doorbell rang and Susan went to the door. A couple of friends were coming by. The girl had Warhol make-up and high-heeled red boots into which her jeans were tucked. The mass of her flashy red hair was tied in an opulent tail jutting out from the top of her head. A pink woolen bolero, with the wool threads cut to look like fake fur, made her little torso bubble on top of her long booted legs. She looked like an exotic bee. Her boyfriend had trendy high boots too, jeans and a flashy blue nylon bomber jacket. His curly blond hair and blue eyes made him look like a model. He was French and didn't speak English. He seemed a little awkward, like a pup next to his girlfriend. Susan had all of a sudden changed persona. She was squealing and shrieking her delight at seeing her friend and I left quickly. From the staircase, I could still hear the flow of superlatives and congratulations the two girls were bombarding each other with.

Vassar. I liked the name. The next day I went to the Library to look for Poughkeepsie on a map of the US. It was not New York City, but New York State. At least I could go to NYC once in a while. I had never taught a class in my life yet. But I was not supposed to give lectures, Susan had said. The assistantship meant mostly grammar drills and conversation. Besides, I was welcome to organize "French" events such as film showings, song singing, cooking, whatever. Basically, I was to be a "French" presence at Vassar. It was the first time I was asked to market my French nationality and culture. I had no clue one could make money just by being French abroad. When I had been an au pair the year before in Washington and Philadelphia, the fact that I was French had counted only because it was cheaper to hire a French girl than an American one as a baby-sitter. Neither my hosts nor the babies had any interest in the French language or culture.

The sleazy Professor

I called the Professor. He proposed to meet at the Gare Saint Lazare a few days later, at seven p.m. He also took the train to and from Nanterre. I knew what he looked like, but he didn't know what I looked like. At seven p.m., the train station was hectic and crowded with commuters colliding in both directions, going in and out of Paris, like two sea tides rushing towards each other. Having fended off the countercurrent, I looked around. The Professor was leaning against a metallic pillar, reading from a book, lost in his world. I spied a minute on him before coming up. We shook hands. He put his book back in the satchel he held between his feet, grabbed its handle and we went out, down the wide steps. We crossed the jammed *Place du Départ* and went into one of the cafés lined up all along the rue Lafayette. He had a beer and I had a coffee. We talked or, rather, he talked. His voice was soft and slow, slightly caressing. His eyes had heavy eyelids, but they were attentive. Time was going by. Both tides of commuters had long receded. Everyone was home now. The café was empty and he was still talking.

Daniel D. had taught at Vassar for two years after he had passed the much coveted *"agrégation d'Anglais"*. He was born in Algeria. In 1960, he had arrived in Paris with his family, a refugee like thousands others who had left everything there. Bright and precocious, he had been admitted at the *Ecole Normale Supérieure* right after secondary school. At twenty-two, he had been the youngest laureate of the *"Agrégation"* in English. "Great" I said. "Yes" he said somberly, "for two weeks". To celebrate his success, he had taken his girlfriend to Corsica, camping, slumming it carefree and happy on beaches and rivers. Back in Paris, his girlfriend was nauseous. On their first holiday together, she had gotten pregnant. A month later, he was married. Smoking nonstop "*Gitanes maïs*", black tobacco French cigarettes rolled in corn paper, "the worst thing in life", he confided, "is to know that you are clever, but only clever enough to know that you are limited. Average. Mediocre." Once upon a time, Daniel D. had been also watching a green light far away in the distance. Daniel D. was, in his own way, a sleazy Gatsby.

Outside, night had fallen and lights had sprouted everywhere. "I am hungry", Professor D. said, "Are you?" I was. We paid our drinks and got up. On the boulevard Haussmann, not very far away, the wide red awning of a new restaurant spread its silly name and logo: *"Hippopotamus"*. It was part of a chain, a new thing in France, imported from America. I had never been to a *"Hippo"*, but I had heard about their gigantic steaks. "That's not bad if you like beef" said Professor D. The restaurant was organized in a series of little compartments like on a train. The lighting was very subdued and reddish to match the red velvet on floors, walls and benches. I could not see very well but there didn't seem to be many patrons around on that weekday. We ordered T-bone steaks with *"frites"* and green salad, the staples of the house and finished off with a huge ice-cream *"coupe"* covered with crushed caramel and nuts. Daniel D. went on talking. He was not a great fan of the US, neither of Americans. He found them loud and superficial. He mentioned Susan and told me that she was attracted to him and willing to have sex but that her typical WASP Puritanism made her hesitate. He himself was still married and had three children. "In fact, I am now separated from my wife" he announced with a shrug.

I was now getting tired and annoyed, unsure about how to ask him about Vassar. After five hours together, he still had not told me a word about the assistantship. The waiter brought the check as a clear indication that they wanted to shut the place. We were the only diners still around. Glancing at my watch, I saw that it was well past midnight. "Do you think I could get an assistantship at Vassar?" I asked softly but determinedly. His eyes seemed to roll and wake up like some amphibious beast's. "Vassar?" he uttered, as if it were a non-recognized onomatopoeia. "Vassar" he repeated, getting slowly back his whereabouts and brushing his face with his hand. "Sure. This can be arranged. I shall write them about you. I don't think there will be any problem." That simple, I thought. Daniel D. sure had *"le bras long"*. If he was that influential, I was bloody lucky. I had my wallet in my hand, but he took out a checkbook, wrote a check and gave it to the waiter. Outside, the boulevard Haussmann was deserted, the air mellow, plane trees and pavement oozing night dew. Daniel D. hailed a taxi and offered to drop me somewhere. "I am going to my bachelor pad at Odeon" he informed me. "I'll get the bus 32" I announced. The bus stop was further down on the boulevard. He proposed to drop me at the Place de l'Etoile, nearer to my destination. The taxi let me off, I waved goodbye as it was already rushing down the Champs Elysées. The lampposts blinked their glare behind the acacia trees blown off by the May breeze. It was the perfect moment to stand on the edge of the Place de l'Etoile. The same moment I had read about somewhere in *Tender is the night.* So Vassar, I thought. That surely would have fitted a Fitzgerald's debutante.

More than a month later, at the end of June, nothing had come from Vassar yet. The engagement was supposed to be confirmed a year ahead of the 72-73 academic year. I had sent transcripts, biography, a motivation letter as instructed by Professor D. On his side, he was writing himself to the Head of the French Department at Vassar to nominate me as his choice for the assistantship. I ran into him in Nanterre corridors and casually asked if he had any news from Vassar, since I had none. He looked at me startled and scratched his forehead. "I'll get in touch with them" he said. I went down everyday in the morning to check the mail in the box in the entrance hall. In July, a long envelope with the Vassar logo arrived. "Dear Miss Garnier" it started. Miss Garnier? "Dear Miss Garnier, we thank you so much for your interest in

Vassar, but..." The address on the envelope was correct, but the name was not. Professor D. had blown it completely, not even taking the pain of checking my name or asking me to spell it for him. The biography and other documents I had sent of course bore my correct name, Dargnies. They must have been wondering who was kidding whom. They had given the assistantship to another candidate. Vassar was gone for good, like the eggs of *Perrette*, the milkmaid of La Fontaine.

Looking for Plan B

I felt low, as low as the ground. In spite of all my running around, I had put on weight. I was now one hundred and forty pounds. Walking in Paris or going to the campus, I was grinding my teeth and looking at my feet. "You've got to play this right" I mumbled to myself as I walked through the corridors of the metro, along the boulevards and down the shabby halls of Nanterre. *"Il va falloir jouer serré"*, the words had become a strange leitmotiv I was telling myself as a mantra. My face was tense. My muscles were tense. I stiffened, body and soul, as if fighting for life. What would happen with me, my life, all those days, all those years ahead? America didn't seem to loom ahead. In fact nothing loomed ahead at all. It was as if time and space had shut and I was shut in. The terrible anguish and sadness of my eighteenth birthday was trying again to take hold of me. I had to resist. Plan A, going back to America, to Vassar, was postponed *sine die*. But I would go on all the mini plans that were to lead to the success of the big one.

Goethe Institut

I had started German at the Goethe Institut where a heteroclit mix of students met at evening courses. My class was run by a small blonde woman who made us repeat structures over and over, shaking her heavy fringe in rhythm and teaching us summer camp German songs. German was difficult for me The build of a German sentence was radically different from French, Spanish, Italian and all the Roman languages I could more or less decipher even when I had not studied them. In german, the verb always had to be at the end of the sentence. All kinds of complements could be inserted between the auxiliary verb and the past participle in the case of compound tenses, but still the past participle had to stick at the end. It felt absurd to have to wait for the end of the sentence to really make out its meaning. The classes were pleasant though and it helped time to go by when I felt so miserably stuck in life.

One of the students was a lady in her fifties, with large blue eyes and generous dyed blond hair. Her wide face and luminous complexion had a lot of make up that shone under the neon. She could have been a captain of a girls' chorus in a forgotten life. She rarely opened her mouth and every half hour she excused herself from the class, I suppose to go to the bathroom. Her beautiful eyes looked a little strange, mellowed and their apples enormous. Some students wondered if she was not disappearing to get a shot of something, alcohol or drugs. I found her intriguing and when she invited me for a drink at her place one Sunday afternoon, I accepted.

Her one room apartment was off the rue de Franqueville, near the *Bois de Boulogne*, on the groundfloor of a building in the opulent Haussman style. The only window opened right on the sidewalk. It was very hot that summer afternoon and the window was wide open with people passing by slowly and sometimes peeking in. The apartment itself, a one-room *"studio"*, was dark and claustrophobic, filled with a bed, a bed table, a dining table, low tables, chairs and stools. I had landed on the bed arranged as a sofa with pillows against the wall, and draped with something like a Spanish shawl. Her dog, a white small hairy thing, sized me up for a while with a stern look and resolutely started to yap and jump at the other end of the sofa. My fellow lady student had invited a girlfriend to that afternoon drink. Her frizzy brown hair was as dry and worn as her small face. She talked with the Parisian drawl of Madame Bérard, who had been the *Concierge* all her life in our small building until she had been taken ill to the hospital, never to return. Our hostess had prepared glasses, tomato juice and a bottle of gin. At five in the afternoon on a Sunday while the asphalt was melting and smelling from the heat just out the window, gin felt heavy to me. I kept to the tomato juice while the two old girls downed cheerfully gin after gin mixed with tomato juice, more cheerfully with each gulp. Their drink was a variation on the "Bloody Mary" they informed me, the authentic one being made with vodka.

While they giggled and talked about things and people I had no clue about, the two women seemed to have forgotten me. Only the dog kept a vigilant eye on me as if I were going to rob something in the room. The conversation had turned to men. They mentioned *"les hommes"* several times, followed by a deep sigh. Obviously, *"les hommes"* had amply harvested the two women, taking away their *"jeunesse"* and their best treasures. I never knew what was or had been the actual life of the lady, only that she was learning German because of her father who was from Alsace and spoke German. They were both dressed and made up to go out after our drink and they invited me to go with them to the restaurant *"de quartier"* they were walking to on rue de la Pompe. I said I had an engagement and I left as they had another round of gin and giggling, oblivious of the dog facing a solitary evening.

Cambridge, Mass.?

No matter what, I was going to the US. I had asked for a tourist visa again. I had bought a one-way ticket to New York, with Loftleidir, the Icelandic airline company, the cheapest. Since Berkeley was out of my reach, I had decided I would do research at Harvard's Widener library for my thesis on Scott Fitzgerald and Stendhal. A tourist visa was valid for three months maximum, but my intention was to stay as long as I could find a way of making money. I could find only odd jobs like any illegal immigrant. Real jobs required proper documents and I knew that a green card was impossible to get, unless one was either a refugee, the spouse of or the direct relative of an American citizen. I was none of those. Susan had supported my plan. Martha had said "why not?" and "if worse comes to worse, you can always fly back." My parents did not agree at all, but I had not asked their opinion. I was turning 21, the majority age. No one could reclaim me anymore.

Susan had introduced me to an eccentric girl whose family was from Cambridge, Massachusetts. The girl had thick round glasses, masses of hair billowing down her back, abrupt gestures and an incredibly fast delivery, which I had difficulty to follow. She was the daughter of some prominent people and happened to know Helen Deutsch, the renowned psychoanalyst. Helen Deutsch was in need of a househelp. I could maybe get a room at her place in exchange for housecleaning. I had written down her address.

"Minerve Intérim"

Before the big leap, I had to make money, as much as I could, to carry me as long as possible. Temporary work agencies were beginning to open in Paris. The most famous was *Manpower* with its Leonardo da Vinci logo. But they looked for real professionals with training and experience. I had taken typing courses at eighteen so as to type a novel I had embarked upon writing but I had never thought I could work as a secretary. The most salient result of my writing attempts was that at least I could type, fairly fast, even if only with two fingers, and typing was a skill that could be moneyed. I learnt that from a girl who worked at *Minerve*

Intérim, the only existing French temporary work agency. One could work whenever one felt like it. When she wanted to stop, she just quit for as long as she wished and resumed working again, at will. That sounded like a splendid idea. Making money without being prisoner of schedules, even less a career.

A rather striking French woman, who was also the manager of her own company, had founded *Minerve Intérim.* She was an invalid, stuck to a wheel chair since her childhood and moving only slightly and with great difficulty on crutches. Her offices were off Avenue Victor Hugo, not far from where I lived. One morning, I decided to go to the place and ask for work. The lady at the reception desk handed me a form to fill and made me type a text. That was the first big hurdle. The test took place on an electric typing machine, an IBM *"boule"* with a running little ball darting from left to right and back with a smack. The typing room was off the reception hall and I hastily tried, and tried again, and threw a handful of paper sheets in the basket before mastering to some extent the wild jumps of the "ball". It was a far cry from my tame and faithful *"Hermès baby",* a mechanical machine without fuss nor whims. When I gave back my typing test, the reception lady asked me to wait as she went in the manager's office. She came out minutes later and held the door open for me to enter.

"Mademoiselle" was the head and soul of the agency. She was as impressive as a *"Mademoiselle Chanel",* running her business knowingly, passionately, expertly and, obviously, enjoying it. From the end of a vast room plunged in near darkness, behind a giant desk, *Mademoiselle* was studying me like a casting director. Blinds were pulled down because of the summer heat. Her body was immobilized but her face was incredibly mobile and, most alert of all, her dark eyes were looking straight into mine. She was silent as she indicated the chair in front of her desk for me to sit. Her gaze was intrigued but not hostile. "Why do you want to work

here?" she asked without preamble. I told her my new tale: America, Harvard (which had now replaced Berkeley), my comparative literature master thesis. "I need to make money", I said and this was the first time I was saying it straight and simple. "So you know English well?" she summed up helpingly. I said yes with unflinching self-assurance, which surprised me rather than her. Mademoiselle liked the US very much. She was the first French person I met who praised America. That was where she had seen temporary work agencies for the first time, quickly understanding that this was a good business opportunity still unheard of in France. "*A l'américaine*", she had boldly embarked on creating her own company, a rare feat for a French woman. Emboldened myself by the daring yet courteous woman, I had declared bluntly that my secretarial skills were non-existent, but that I could manage to type in French and in English. That first day she proposed me a job, a bottom–of-the-typing-ladder one, but a job. I could start the next day at a bank to type bank checks. This involved only figures and country names, nothing more. From the end of that first week, I could already collect an advance payment. I would have social security, which I did not care much about, and could go on getting better jobs, like typing reports in English.

The bank, the *CIC*, was on rue de la Victoire, behind the Galeries Lafayette. Rue de la Victoire ran at a right angle from rue de Provence, the most famous sidewalk bordello in Paris. I had to walk the rue de Provence twice a day, coming from and going to the subway station "Chaussée d'Antin". By day, the girls in small shorts and mini-skirts hung on the curb, like dolls popping on top of the constant flow of workers and shoppers. At night, they were more conspicuous. The sidewalk then was empty like a beach at low tide and customers loitered in front of their hotels' doors. That first job was dumb but very exacting. I typed all day long money orders into bank checks format. The money orders were piled up in front of me in a metallic basket by the *"Chef"*, a tough lady with a big mouth and a red brick wine lover complexion.

Her name was Madame Carton, also the name of a very famous woman comedian, Pauline Carton, who was still performing *"théâtre de boulevard"* at an already respectable age. Our Madame Carton knew her homonym and prided herself to be as facetious and sidesplitting as the famous Pauline. We were a dozen typists lined up in four rows of benches. I sat in the last row, the least distinguished one for the temporary employees. There were no expensive electric machines there, which was a relief for me. The racket was incredible. The typing machines rattled like machine guns, faster as the day went by as we had to finish those bloody piles of checks that seemed never to end. Until the last minutes, Madame Carton went on distributing them. But tied to the same bench, the women were merciful and helpful. They knew what beginnings took, they had begun themselves to work in their teens and I looked lost enough to awake their sympathy. No bigger than a single executive office, the room had a low ceiling with long neon tubes hanging from it. The window opened on an airshaft.

For all its bonhomie, the typing pool had a very strict code and hierarchy. We were not *"secrétaires"*, we were *"dactylos"*, as remote from the secretaries as a bum from a king. But where the *"secrétaires"* were haughty and lonely, we were friendly and together. The *"pool des dactylos"*, a group of typists all working in the same room was supposedly more efficient. Our *"pool des dactylos"* luckily was a pool of chums, albeit with some protocol. All married women were called "Madame", followed by their husband's patronym, a working class custom far more practical than the bourgeois polite "Madame" which would not have allowed us to identify each other. Madame Carton, Madame Biraud, Madame Haussoy and a couple more were the *"doyennes"*, with already a good thirty years of experience under their belts. They sat on the same benches as all of us, behind the same long tables and with the same terrible "bikes" as the typewriters were nicknamed, as democratically unaffected as royalties ambling on feast days among their subjects. On the other hand, the non-married women were called by their first name as befitted their "girl" status. Girls could be chided for lack of productivity, but they were easily forgiven and often helped by the *"doyennes"*. Madame Biraud, a small rabbit-looking lady with a flippant smile, had been my mentor/tutor from the start, because we liked the same radio series. *Bons baisers de partout* was a spoof on the James Bond's movie, *From Russia with love*. All personages' names were puns. The hero was *"Colonel de Guerre Lasse"*, "tired of resisting" assisted by the perky *Mademoiselle Truscotte*, his secretary, a pun on "Triscotte", a famous brand of packaged rusks. The mastermind and star of the series was Pierre Dax, an irreverent, hilarious and tireless writer comedian.

    The working day unrolled ritually, the same way every day of the week. We all arrived at eight in the morning and, before sitting in front of our typewriters we all shook hands with each other. Madame Carton, the *"Chef de pool"* was the only one who didn't type and didn't sit with us. Her office was a minuscule niche in a corner, enclosed with glass on two sides. Her job was to register all the incoming work, distribute it to the typists, check quality of work here and there and send on the typed money orders to the credit transfer people where they would be duly processed. At ten, all machines stopped for the *" la pause"*, heralded by Madame Carton getting out of her niche, arms up and hands waving. We all quickly finished to type the bank check in progress and got up to get a plastic cup of the coffee prepared by one of the typists. Most women brought some snacks, biscuits, sandwiches or boiled eggs. Most of them lived in faraway suburbs and started off on the train at dawn, needing therefore solid food to go on until evening. The pause was time for a chat and for marketing too. Madame Haussoy had a kitchen garden and a chicken coop, and she represented some neighbour farmers. Every Friday, she was taking orders from all the colleagues for vegetables, fruits, eggs, chickens, cream, even jams and marmalades. The next Monday she brought on the train full baskets and crates and the distribution took place at the mid-morning pause.

Madame Carton was the head and the soul of the team. She was tough and demanding, keeping all of us busy non-stop. No empty basket escaped her alert eyes, and as soon as our "in" pile of checks was down, and the "out" one full, she rushed to drop new piles of money orders in our trays, taking away the work done. There was no end to the work. We emptied our tray, she filled it again and again and again. It was like an assembly line, but to be part of the team lightnened the monotony. I liked the village gossip and the sensible routine. We worked hard and tediously but we stopped, talked and conferred like women on market square. Madame Carton recalled the days when she was coming to work on her motorbike until one day Monsieur Carton surreptitiously broke the feed tube to the engine so she could not use it anymore. She referred to her husband as "Carton" and talked about him all the time. Theirs was a decades long love story and he was dead afraid of her having an accident with the bike. But Madame Carton was not someone to quit easily, she had been pedaling for days all the way to work, wondering what was wrong with the motorbike. Monsieur Carton was a pastry cook and the couple was childless because Madame Carton did not want any. At most, my colleagues had one single child or maybe two if the first one was a girl. They had all started to work around sixteen years old and children, I suppose, required free time they could hardly afford. Their one treat was to go to eat at a restaurant every Saturday night to unwind and relax. Madame Haussoy kept a double life of employee and farmer, going to the Sunday market in her suburban town to sell her garden and coop surpluses. The typewriters rattling kept us rolling like army guys running under submachine gunfire until, all of a sudden at five pm sharp, Madame Carton got out of her niche, arms raised, shouting "Stop!" like a general on a noisy battlefield. We instantly stopped, covering the typewriters with their plastic cover, getting up and grabbing bag and jacket. In less than a minute, everybody had disbanded on the street.

I stayed six weeks with Madame Carton's battalion. After that, *Minerve Interim* decided to assign me to a better paid job as an English typist. I typed endless reports at many companies, correcting some terrible turns of phrases and spelling mistakes, which the guys didn't like at all when, rarely, they would see my corrections. Gone was the stimulating camaraderie and fun of Madame Carton's team. I was now alone in a small office with the weird IBM electric typing machine, with only the stupid sound of the little running ball for company. Far too often the executive who had produced the report came to check on my progress, hanging around in my back, which I could not stand. Those jobs were short, two or three days usually. I had a lot of autonomy in that new job but, alone in my cell, I missed the Carton girls. Money was piling up steadily in the bank account I had opened all by myself, and its gentle trickling week after week was reassuring when life looked like a blank in front of me, save the seven letters "America" still floating like a banner in the void.

To strengthen my chances to get accepted one day in a US university, I decided to enroll for summer courses in Spanish and German. I would go first to Santander, Spain at the pompously titled "Universidad Internacional Menendez Pelayo" for the whole month of July, and then to Tübingen, Germany in August. End of September, I would pack and go to Cambridge, Massachussetts, no matter what.

Remembrances of my father
Universidad Internacional, Santander

On Nanterre walls, I had spotted a sign advertising for the "Universidad Internacional Menendez Pelayo", a summer language program for foreigners taking place on the premises of the University of Santander, a low-key non-touristy town in the Basque region, north of Spain. The program lasted four weeks, offering seven hours of courses every day and plenty of movies, music and theater evenings organized on the spot. Tuition, an individual room and full board cost a modest sum I could afford with my typing gains. On 30 June 1972 at eight in the evening, I was on the quay at Gare d'Austerlitz, the train station of my childhood holidays in the southwest and the station of trains bound for Spain via Irun at the border. I was traveling by night in a second class *"couchette"*.

My father had driven me to the station and lingered on the quay with me, brooding but merry, recalling his one time voyage to Spain in 1943, his only luggage a Basque beret in his pocket that he would put on his head once in Biarritz, to look like a local Basque. That had been his fateful and only escape from France. He was refusing to go for compulsory work in Germany, the *STO*, a system put up by France's occupiers and supported by Pétain's collaboration government. From Biarritz, he had made it safely to Saint Jean Pied-de-Port at the foot of the Pyrénées. From there, at night, together with a handful of other French men, led by Basque shepherds, he had started the long climb and walk. His way went through the narrow gorge of *Roncesvalles*, the *Roncevaux* of the *"Chanson de Roland"*, that had been fatal to the medieval French hero. At dawn, the fugitives had arrived in a farm in Spain. Having hardly gulped down a coffee and a piece of dried ham, the Spanish *Guardia civil* had broken in to arrest all of them. They had been instructed to declare that they were Canadians and not to carry any kind of identification on them that would have established that they were French, hence enemies of Franco's Spain. Spain's policy towards Canadian nationals was not overtly hostile. Therefore, the Spanish police could not jail them forever, and at least could not execute them summarily. My father and his companions had been thrown into jail in Pampeluna for six months. He had then been sent to Miranda, the worst Spanish concentration camp with only parched land and stones he had to break and carry to build a road to nowhere. My father didn't talk much about his yearlong Spanish ordeal, which had left him scrofulous, covered with lice and pustules, and very weak since he was afflicted with TB since his teens.

But all he remembered was the elation of freedom in Madrid where the Red Cross had cleaned his wounds and given him clean clothes. The Spanish authorities had given in to pressures from the Allied Forces to "free" the "Canadian" prisoners. Suddenly, they were free to go wherever they wished. After a day in Madrid, my father had gone to Malaga to board a cargo boat and rally the French army in exile in Casablanca, Morocco. There, he had joined the 2nd *division blindée*, the famous "2nd DB" tank corps under General Leclerc.

As I leaned out of the window from the wagon, my father paced the quay, moved and happy. Thirty years before, the same train had been his way to hell, and his way to victory. From Morocco, he had disembarked in Marseilles in August 1944, advancing on his tank all the way to Bavaria to push the enemy once and for all out of France. I could feel his urge to hop on the train and recall the past. The railway man had yelled *"En voiture! Fermez les portières!"* blowing his whistle, and I had leaned my head out of the window while my father waved, waved, until his still silhouette had disintegrated in the dark of Gare d'Austerlitz.

Santander was a town by the sea but not a sea resort. There was a beach, ice-creams stands, sun, sand and plenty of boys and men ready to deliver the age-old *"piropo"* to any girl passing by, *"piropear"* being a must for any Spanish male. It meant delivering staccato a litany of compliments on a girl's eyes, mouth, feet, whatever, but all in the limits of a gentle flirting. I don't think those men expected any kind of answer from the girl. The campus where we boarded and took the classes was on a hill above the town. In July, the heat was tremendous. Classes started at eight in the morning after an enormous breakfast, complete with *"jamon crudo"*, peppery sausages, bread slices as thick as steaks, mounts of butter and homemade marmalades and tons of very dark and strong coffee. Jose, my assigned teacher, was a young guy in his twenties. He was slim and elegant, with a light frame and a small mustache, but so controlled and well proportioned that he made me think of a kind of male doll. His hair was thick and perfectly contained by some shiny gook. His voice and words were slow and measured. Even the way he held his left hand in his pocket and his slow pacing on the wooden platform felt studied, as if he were not a teacher but the impersonation of one. He had taken an interest in me, which was annoying, and I had to fend off his invitations for drinks or dinners as politely as I could. I just could not figure out how to be face to face with such a man for the length of a meal.

A bad hangover

Students at the *Universidad Menendez Pelayo* came from Europe mostly, but there were a few American girls. There were different age generations too. Some were well into their thirties, married men and women taking time off as singles and obviously sex was the main goal. The French students were the youngest, most of them around twenty. All meals took place in the big diningroom and it seemed that we were eating non-stop. After breakfast, lunch was served at one o'clock with three courses every day, plus cheese, fruit and pastry. Wine, red or white, flowed freely, served in huge ceramic pitchers obligingly refilled by a maid as soon as they were empty. We ate *"comme des cochons"*, by big mouthfuls, getting second servings of dishes that were both plenty and succulent. Between cocidos, *paellas*, grilled fish, almond cakes and creams, it was hard to stop. I weighed now sixty-eight kilograms and I burst in my three or four pieces of clothing. That didn't seem to bother Santander males, nor my teacher. Everyday I heard that my *"ojos"* were as mesmerizing as those of the *"Madre de Dios"*, my *"cuerpo"* was *"hermosisissimo"*, my *"cabelos"* were *"lindos"* and all in all, I was the most *"guapa"* in town. This was a nice compliment, but I couldn't care less. I was totally at sea. Santander could have been anywhere on earth, to me it was just one more stop on my way out into the world for good.

Evenings were balmy and scented and most students managed to get into a twosome configuration. I joined one or another group after dinner until they would disband in couples. The rules were strict however. Boys had to keep to their buildings and girls to theirs. But the gardens were large and shadowed from the moon by many trees and bushes. One evening, I had stuck later than usual with two Swiss boys and a German girl. Peter, one of the Swiss, was a very tall, dark haired boy from Saint Gallen. Half lying on the grass, they had drunk a few beers, already quite tipsy from all the dinner wine. I could see that the girl was head over heels for dark Peter, already sitting on his lap. Peter had brought a bottle of wine and had been drinking from it first before the girl had grabbed it from him, putting avidly the bottleneck in her mouth. She had then handed it to me. I took a few sips. It was cheap Spanish red wine, rough and too dry. Dying to get kissed, the girl had to contend with the bottle of wine that Peter much preferred to her lips. The other boy stuck to beer.

Feeling very sleepy all of a sudden, I left them. Walking to my room, I was feeling funny, my head swimming. I had sat down on my bed. The window of the little bedroom was open and I could hear my "friends" joking and giggling. I leaned out of the window and started to sing, and sing, and sing, all the songs I could remember from school trips, from family trips, even from church. They seemed to seep uncontrollably out of my throat. I couldn't stop. Next thing I could remember, the whole room reeled and reeled. It was like being a ball, rolling in a sphere. I went to the adjoining small bathroom and threw up on the floor. I put my head under the faucet and let the cold water run to cool down the horrible sensation of a bursting brain. I cried for help. I rolled on the floor. I pulled the sheets and covers from the bed. It kept reeling and reeling until I drowned in sleep. Sunlight and heat woke me up. I was tangled into the sheets on the floor. Vomit made cakes and puddles all over. It was eleven past. A sharp pain axed my crane. The cleaning lady opened the door as I was up at last, screaming in horror while I mumbled excuses. I went out to the shower room to drench my hangover and my shame. Twenty minutes later, the room had taken back a more human appearance, but I had not completely. The nausea was too much. I went back to bed while the cleaning lady kindly brought fizzy water and some biscuits.

I had attributed the nightlong malaise to too much food, the July drought and the bad wine. Years later, I recounted the story to a friend. No way, she said, food or wine can make you feel like that, not even a few sips. That bottle was the culprit for sure. The wine had been doctored with some powerful drug. In fact I was lucky I had not jumped out of the window under the influence of god knows what substance. The golden rule, she had made me swear, was never, never to drink from an already opened bottle.

Linda from Cambridge, Massachusetts

One day at lunch, as I was looking for a place to sit, carrying a tray filled with the usual mountains of food, I saw a table empty save a girl sitting by herself at one end. Linda Mc. Williams was from Cambridge, Mass. She shared a house there with other students. When I told her that I was going to Cambridge in the fall, she right away suggested that I stay in that house until I would find a more permanent solution. The offer of Linda was a lifesaver. After my courses in Spain and Germany, and after paying for my plane ticket to Boston, I would have very little money left. In fact, I would have exactly three hundred French francs, barely five hundred dollars.

Out of the blue, I suddenly had someone waiting for me in America and a place to stay. Linda was positive that in a few weeks I could find easily an au pair arrangement to have a room in exchange for housework and babysitting. A friend and a home to start from were worth all the Vassars in the world! Linda's forebears had come from Scotland. Her parents lived in Watertown in the greater Boston area. Her small blue eyes always twinkled with irony and her pale skin had reddened a lot in the Spanish sun. She was most of the time by herself, focussing on her courses and writing daily to her boyfriend, John, a Harvard graduate preparing his Ph.D in Chinese literature. After the course, she was going straight back to Cambridge via London. She had already been in Paris and some of France with a couple of girl friends the month before. Santander was her last stop on her way back to the US.

Tübingen

My six weeks in Tübingen, a mediaeval gemütlich town on the Neckar river, would be integrally paid for by the OFAJ, the *"Office Franco-Allemand de la Jeunesse"*, an organization dedicated to bringing together French and German youths in the spirit of post war reconciliation. The scholarship included the roundtrip train ticket, room and full board. At first sight, Tübingen was lovely and leisurely, filled with students hanging along the green river. But my mind was elsewhere. Apprehension was creeping, six weeks before flying solo to America. Besides, August was a painfully hot month in the continental German climate. The pretty Neckar river only brought dampness and mosquitoes. Day and night, the atmosphere was stifling. I was sneezing non-stop, my nose red and running, with a bad case of hay fever. It seemed that my body was swelling more every day. My head ached non-stop and I could not sleep at night, attacked by clouds of mosquitoes. Nearly all students who followed the German course were schoolteachers, thrilled to have found a free six-weeks vacation since they had a three-months summer leave to kill every year. We were a dozen students in my class. I was getting so fat and swollen that everyday I wondered if I would get into my jeans, the seams of which were beginning to give.

In the class, a guy from Southern France kept making jokes and puns non-stop which our German teacher, a woman, suffered patiently and silently, waiting for him to stop babbling and for us to stop giggling irrepressibly. The guy's jokes were rather primitive, but like childhood jokes about poop, they were most effective in making us roar into laughter for almost the full course. His favorite one, which he kept repeating, was about the Munich *"Pinacothek"* which some of the book lessons talked about. The unfortunate Pinacothek had become the *"pine-à-Cotek"*, i.e. the schlong of Cotek. The pun was going on and on. Who was Cotek? And how long was that famous "pine"? And dear Cotek... The teacher sat, her face burrowed in her thick hair, pretending not to understand the salacious jokes and waiting politely for the guy to stop talking and for us to stop laughing.

Rita in München, Ludwigstrasse, Nymphenburg

Because of the 15th of August, a public holiday all over Europe, the school was closing Thursday and Friday, giving us a four-day holiday. To distract myself from Tübingen, I had contacted Martha's sister, Rita. She was living in Munich where she was studying to become a translator. She had invited me to spend a few days with her on the campus. I could sleep in her *"Mensa"* room since her roommate would be away. Besides, a German family whose elder daughter was a friend of my sister had invited me to Shopfeim, a small town right in the middle of the Black Forest where they lived.

It was a fairly complicated trip to get to Munich from Tübingen by train. I had no driving license and no money to rent a car. I decided to hitchhike. Early morning on Friday, I posted myself on the high road. A small truck quickly pulled aside. The man was transporting a load of chocolate bars. He gently asked me how old I was. His round face and funny crewcut didn't alarm me much. He left me on the outskirts of Augsburg where he was delivering the chocolate, giving me two big bars of milk chocolate and asking hesitatingly if he could come and see me at the school in Tübingen. Gone the chocolate truck, I was on the road again, my thumb up. A couple stopped to give me a lift. The shorthaired woman wore sunglasses and didn't say a word. The man in shorts and sleeveless cotton underwear wore thick glasses that made his eyes look watery. They both sipped non-stop from a bottle of wine and handed me the bottle, which I refused politely. The Santander experience had taught me enough. They left me on the outskirts of München where I got on a bus.

Rita had told me to take the brand new subway to get to the University campus. With my handful of German words, I found my way and arrived at the campus. It was still surprisingly alive in the middle of the summer. Students stayed around to prepare second chance exams in the fall, others came for special summer sessions. Rita was as tall and thin as a willow tree, the opposite of her sister Martha, plump and round. She had a steady German boyfriend whom she was going to marry. The first evening we went out for a glass of wine on Ludwigstrasse. The evening was balmy with a sweet breeze and none of the dampness and heavy heat of Tübingen. My sneeze had stopped, the white wine was cool like spring water and summer night in Munich felt enthralling like oriental ones. Sidewalks and terraces overflowed with students and the wine flowed. Glasses clicked, hands clapped, they chanted and shouted, got up and down, the ones sitting hailed the ones passing by. I had never seen such a tide of students in Paris, neither such joyful and carefree tipsiness. It felt like wine going from one to the other, a kind of merry communion. That image and feel would remain in my system, so much that I had many dreams afterwards of Ludwigstrasse bathed in light, wine and people, all sharing happily each other, the luminous night and the sweet white young wine. The next day, I went around Munich, cool and deserted. I also went to that much-derided *Pinacothek*.

For the evening, Rita had scheduled a chamber concert at the castle of Nymphenburg. We took the train and arrived early enough to marvel at the Château and the park. Its exuberant stuccoes in all kind of pastel colours snaking up and down walls and ceilings, its high windows shaped as if by draughts, Nymphenburg with all its precious décor felt wild and like nature itself gone mad. It didn't feel like a grand home to stay in but rather like a weird place to haunt. Even as prosaic a thing as heating had been turned into surreal monsters of tortured earthenware creeping in corners as high as prehistoric beasts. The concert though was civilization itself at its highest degree, Mozart and Haydn concertos. The music caressed ears and mind but Nymphenburg remained unfazed. Sunlight still lingered in the woods when we left after nine. The train was filling with yet another batch of wine drinkers. Munich was readying for another summer night.

Schopfeim, the Becher family

From Munich, I took the train to Freiburg-in-Brisgau. I looked forward to a compartment all by myself. But a huge weirdo of a guy irrupted, looking wild and uttering a language I could not decipher. I quickly went to another wagon with a handful of quiet passengers. Uli, my sister's girlfriend, had worked out a nice plan for me to reach Schopfeim in the heart of the forest. Once in Freiburg, some friends of hers who studied there at the University would meet me at the train station. I would spend the day with them visiting the city. In the evening, they would drive me with their VW Beetle through the Black Forest down to Schopfeim. Freiburg was smaller and homier than Munich. Streets with medieval façades recalled Normandy's streets with half-timbered houses, some still cobbled. It was surprising to find so much *"douceur de vivre"* in Germany, as much in dwellings as in people themselves. Two boys waved at me as I stepped down from the train. Peter, dark-haired, hairy and tall, and Jurgen, shorter, blondish, bespectacled and sweet-faced. After a drive through town and stops at the Cathedral and town hall and photo shots, we went to Annette and Ute's house, Uli's friends too.

It was a modern little house, complete with little front border and back garden like in England. We went to lie on the grass under a cherry tree in the back. Both girls were barefoot in shorts. We ate kilos of cherries. Annette, a small framed and curvy girl with hair neatly combed and fringed, had prepared a salad with salami cuts, potatoes and a creamy sauce. We drank beer from the bottle. Sweet-faced Jurgen seemed totally mesmerized by Ute. She was taller than Annette and much thinner, with an edgy profile, wide foal-like brown eyes, a beautiful aquiline nose and a long swan neck. Jurgen's eyes just could not let go of Ute for a second, yet he seemed to keep his distance as if not to frighten her away. Annette meanwhile had taken all the plates and cutlery back in the kitchen with the help of Peter. She had changed her shorts for an impeccable white frock and, a summer cotton bag on her shoulder, she was off to some appointment. Ute decided to accompany us on our trip to Schopfeim.

Along the way, the landscape was marvellous. Dark green and rocky, the mountains and the forest spread their wings all over. Patches of cultures made yellow and light green motifs here and there. The evening cool was falling on the land, what my mother called *"le serein"*, the serene hour. Indeed, the four of us in the Beetle were silent and serene as we went through the valleys. Ute started singing with a soft and fragile voice and Peter and Jurgen took her song in their stride with sonorous male tones. I listened and breathed in the smells of the first evening dew. We arrived in little

Schopfeim, nestled in the heart of the forest like a town in a tale. The whole Becher family was out in front of the house to greet us: Uli, her two sisters and two brothers, her father and mother. We all had dinner together, with soup, stew, beer and, afterwards in the sitting room, *"kaffee mit kuche"*. Peter, Jurgen and Ute left quickly to drive back to Freiburg. Jurgen looked quietly jubilant as he was opening the Beetle front door to Ute who shivered in her shorts. He had taken a plaid in the trunk and was motherly arranging it on her lap so she would feel warmer. Honking and waving, they disappeared in the forest while Uli was showing me my room for the night. I got quickly under a down comforter, which felt like sleeping in a bird's nest.

Next day we were going for a picnic in the Black Forest. Uli's mother was staying home busy with her house duties. A portly, imposing woman, Frau Becher had an old-fashioned chignon and a brooch on a piece of silk around her neck. She wore a hat most of the time, a kind of combination of sun-hat and church hat, wide-brimmed canvas with rows of straight stitching. She seemed to work non-stop, pausing only to devour a bit of cake or a slice of bread, standing up, biting fast and concluding with a glass of water before resuming housework. Uli's father was a somber man with an endearing but sad face. He had spent a year on the Russian front in 1941, sent back with near-fatal wounds. He limped and walked with a cane, his face tense with permanent pain. He was a clergyman but I did not see his church and parish. He talked very little and mostly seemed to observe. He drove Uli, her sister and me to a lovely spot in the forest. We were in the middle of the fields. The second crop of hay was imminent and the sweet smell of ripe grass was exquisite. We walked on the grassy slope for a while and sat comfortably in a spot sheltered from the wind. Uli's father walked very effectively in spite of his stiff leg. I was going back to Tübingen the day after but I had not decided how. He pointed out to me that a bus was connecting Schopfeim directly to Tübingen. It took a certain amount of time, but the scenery all along was very pleasant and I would not have to hitchhike again which, I could sense, he thought rather dangerous. From the bus, without tiring of it, I took in for hours green valleys and villages crowned by gracious bulbous bell-towers. Just as Uli's family, the german land exuded a peculiar charm, very endearing but nostalgic, as if a draughtsman had been at work, painstaking and gifted, but unable to shake off a lingering melancholy.

Bierfest

Back in Tübingen, Patrick, a French boy at the language school, took me to the annual end-of-summer *"Bierfest"*. Patrick had met another French boy, Jean-Claude, who was living permanently in Tübingen with his German girlfriend. The couple had first invited us to a barbecue party held by German friends of theirs. The charcoal smoke spread its acrid smell and black smoke all over the garden, lingering in the hot air. The hosts were a loose group of Germans in their thirties, two girls and one guy. They drank wine by the pint in stemmed glasses as big as salad bowls. There were two girls, with heavy make-up, heavy fringes and huge red mouths, looking like Andy Warhol's Factory girls. They were dressed in a kind of hippie Burne-Jones style with high-heeled sandals, purple red nail polish on toes, deep décolleté dresses flowing from below their big breasts and slit on each side for a glimpse of their fleshy legs. Their names were Gudrun and Walltraut and, after being with them for a while, they reminded me a lot of Gudrun and Ursula in *Women in love* by D.H. Lawrence. The guy was strange and disquieting. His name was Manfred. Huge and tall, with a blond beard and a kind of ecstatic face, he was telling me about the art of fencing. He had been fighting duels, he said, but only the face could be targeted, "Only the face! Only the face!" he repeated like a mantra, his eyes rolling as if he were seized by a fit, his own face hovering above mine. I suspected that Manfred's frenzy over duelling had to do with some repressed sexual desire. He had shown me proudly a long scar on his cheek slashed by a sword. Gudrun and Walltraut looked like sexpots all right but Manfred was obviously not their sex toy. They seemed rather to consider him as their housedog. After eating half-carbonized sausages and drinking far more than we had eaten, Jean-Claude and Matina, his girlfriend, finally decided to leave and to bring Patrick and me back to the school. Matina looked like a gymnast. Every now and then, she performed a trick with her boyfriend. Her crotch tightly pressed against his, Jean-Claude pushed her high up in the air with a pelvis swing. The slim Matina flew up in the air and Jean-Claude threw up his arms to catch her swooping down.

We had decided to all go together to the annual Tübingen Bierfest. It was the first time I was going to one. Under a gigantic tent, swarms of men and women yelled, sang, drank and banged tankards bigger than chamber pots. With gross but common sense, considering the mass of beer ingested and the beer influence on bladder activity, toilets were posted left and right of the entrance to the tent. Each respectively bore in letters big enough to be deciphered by the drunkest of the drunk, "MÄNNER" and "FRAUEN". Tottering guys made it to the toilets and back, only to sit again on their bench and order more beer. Middle-aged waitresses, with curled hair, boobies and cleft well in evidence in their Bavarian dresses, roamed the alleys, bringing full tankards, taking away the empty ones, taking money, giving back change, their faces stern and focussed as if collecting for the church. After a moment of shock, I plunged into the *fest*. The beer was good, but one tankard was enough for me. Faces around seemed as enormous as the bellies, which many revellers seemed prone to show, pulling off their shirts. It was crass and gross, but in a childish way. Driving us back to the school, Jean-Claude told us that that bierfest was a total addiction for most people in Tübingen and it lasted for two weeks. The year before, he had gone with a friend only to come out at dawn, seriously tight. A bad morning hangover had made him pledge to keep away from the fest, to no avail. The next evening, and the next, for fifteen days in a row, drawn like by a magnet, he had gone back to the big tent with his friend, drinking all night, every morning swearing nevermore and every evening coming back.

Tübingen had become like hell to me. I was exhausted for lack of sleep. The constant sneezing left me gasping for air, and a diet of *"würste mit kartoffeln"* every day made me swell like a montfgolfier. The mosquitoes descending into bedrooms every night, roaring and jarring like combat airplanes, bit badly and extensively. I had had enough. The course was scheduled for six weeks. After four weeks, I decided to go. I was not learning much anyway. That would give me two weeks more to pack and prepare for the big leap to America. I took a bus to Stuttgart and, from there, the train to Paris. The trip was dull and endless, but I was on the road again. The clanking and hissing of the train heralded good bye and a new life ahead. A hard rain was falling in Paris as I arrived. I took the storm as an omen of change. *"A hard rain is gonna fall..."*

AMERICA 2

Going, gone - Suspense at the Customs - A clapboard on Prentiss street - Helen Deutsch – A father-only home – Harry Levine - Widener, a formidable forest - Alumni from Berkeley - Odd jobs – A Russian lady - Would-be Kennedys

A real Sargent lady – Algonquin gas company - Mount Monadnock – A providential sect - Halloween - A party at the JKG - NYC, the grand way - At the Metropolitan Opera - The alpine charm of Montreal -

Coast to coast - Berkeley – Shadow of Arthur - A lucky charm against the evil eye – San Francisco – Carmel in the clouds – "Che sera, sera" - Disneyland – Phoenix in the dark - New Orleans under the rain - Martha at Duke University - The Brattle theatre – A long way back

Going, gone

I had three hundred French francs in my pocket, sixty kilos of luggage and, this time, no return ticket. Everything I possessed was packed in two veteran suitcases and a black forest rucksack. My Hermès typewriter, my Nordmende radio from Munich and all my notes and files on Stendhal and Fitzgerald were the heavy pieces in the lot. The address of Linda was the lightest of my luggage but my only real buoy over there. America this time was an ocean I would have to swim in by myself.

From the *Air France* bus on that fall morning, Paris was glaucous and endless. But beyond the dour and dull landscape, I already saw the wide map of America, as if it had been put in front of my eyes. My blurred reflection on the rain-spotted glass seemed to talk to me as a serene angel. "Don't worry, it's all right!" There was no room for regret or fear, or too much room. So much space ahead, so much hope, had swallowed them. My Loftleidir flight had been delayed for twenty hours, but there was no coming back home. I had slept in a bed with another girl bound for New-York, erred in Orly airport another morning, landed in the middle of the night in Iceland and finally arrived at Kennedy Airport, tottering like a sleepless toddler.

Suspense at the Customs

The Customs room was gigantic with very low ceiling and blinding neon lights. Bulky and stern officers herded us into queues uttering brief commands with a sharp voice. "US citizens? This way!", "Non-US, this way!" It was tough to stand up and wait in line when body and mind wanted to lie down and rest. All US citizens had long disappeared. I was still far from the Customs officer, my Customs officer, behind a long queue of "aliens" as we were all called now. The officer had frizzy black hair, a small face with small glasses over his dot eyes and, below, a vast expanse of flesh reined in by a black belt. He worked steadily, efficiently, a perpetual frown on his face, asking questions without looking at his interlocutor while he leafed through passports before stamping them with a big knock of his powerful fist.

He took my passport, firing his questions. "Where are you from, Ma'am?" "Where are you goin", Ma'am?" "Where are you stayin', Ma'am?" As I answered, he was leafing through his bulky list of unwanted persons. I had passed the exam. He had grabbed the seal. His big hand was descending upon my passport. Suddenly, he stopped, seal and hand hanging in mid-air. "Do you have a return ticket?" he asked. "No." "I can't let you in, Ma'am." He looked at me for the first time. I was speechless, trying to gather whatever brainpower was still awake in me. I had declared that I was going to stay for a few weeks at my friend's Linda in Cambridge. Thank God, I had only my rucksack on my back. I would pick my two suitcases afterwards on the carrousel. The Customs officer had no clue about my sixty kilos of luggage. "I can't let you in, Ma'am". He had put down the seal. "What proof can you give me that you will leave the US?" The blank in my head would not lift, like a too heavy fog. "I am a student in Paris", I said suddenly. He made a pout. That did not help. But my brain was awake now. "I have to be back in October to resume my MA courses. Here..." I showed my student card. In his big paw, it looked like a subway ticket. He glanced at it and gave it back to me with a shrug. He grabbed the seal again and stamped my passport. I took off, breathless and dizzy.

From the cab, I looked at the Charles River opening wide on the horizon. It was now late afternoon, I had been travelling for forty hours. The sun was low and the water glinting. We crossed an arched bridge and went on drifting under leafy trees. The driver was not separated by a glass partition from the passenger back seat like in New York. After the Customs officer, he was my first interlocutor. "Where are you from?" I asked, intrigued by his accent. "I am from Greece", the bulky guy answered. "Know Greece?" "No." "Going to study here?" "Yes" I said determinedly. "They are OK here" He said. He meant the students. "Not like over there, in Ohio". "You mean Kent State?" I ventured. "Yah, Kent State. They should have shot them all!" I remembered. The National Guard had fired on and killed twelve students a few weeks before. "That will teach them!" fumed the Greek-American driver. I shuddered. Thankfully, the turrets and ivy-covered red brick façades of Harvard were coming up, spread beyond a princely gate like a Tudor château. The sun had just set.

An old clapboard on Prentiss street

Linda lived in an old clapboard house with a porch. She shared the rent with Jim and Cindy. They were looking for a fourth lodger. Until then, I would occupy the free room. Apart from space, the house had not much attraction. At the end of Prentiss street, off Mass. Avenue, it was dark and rundown. Bits of flooring were broken on the porch, which served mainly to store the vegetables and fruits they went to buy direct from a farmer in the countryside. This was for environmental, political and financial reasons. Like all her friends, Linda believed in organic food and environmental protection as well as beating the system by circumventing the standard distribution channels. Buying direct from a farmer was cheaper, ensured him a better profit and deprived supermarkets from some of their outrageous ones.

Jim, another tenant of the house, was a real radical. With thick curly black hair and a long curly beard, he looked a lot like Abbie Hoffman, the Yippie author of "Hell". He sported blue overalls at all times. While Linda and Cindy, both employed part-time and studying, were out most of the time, Jim had a lot of free time during the day. He had refused to become an engineer at the end of his graduate studies, taking a job as a manual worker at a steel plant near Boston. He worked the night shift. The pay was good and the job flexible. He could take days off and resume work anytime. Besides, he could get to know firsthand the life of the blue collars.

My first days on Prentiss street, I was sleepless and hungry at all times. The huge refrigerator filled with food was a permanent temptation. On one such craving, I had eaten a whole bar of cheddar to the not so happy surprise of Linda. There were no bakeries in Cambridge like in France where, for a few cents, I could have easily and nicely filled my stomach. Whenever Jim was around the kitchen, I devoured the peanut butter and blackcurrant jelly toasts he made with gulps of brown coffee. He had told me about Suzanne, a girl that had been living with them for a while before going back to Florida to her mother's. "By the way" had added Jim, "a guy for whom Suzanne was baby-sitting is looking for a replacement". I was all ears. But babysitting for a guy sounded funny. Jim meant in fact that the guy was a single father whose wife had left. A freelance advertising photographer, he wanted a woman around the house for his two children, a boy and a girl, whom he was raising himself. He wanted her to be there on evenings when he was going out, and when he was away for shoots around the country. That was Jim's brief about the job. Linda had added a few personal details. Mike was in his forties, eccentric and bohemian, always dressed shabbily but probably very rich. He was no nuisance as he was very busy with his photography and his own social life. The good point was that there was no cleaning to do. The bad point were the two teenage children to manage when the father would be away. Aware of Dr. Spock's methods and the American way of raising children, I was a little nervous. But I had no choice, I had to leave Prentiss street. The new co-lodger was coming soon.

Helen Deutsch

Before contacting the photographer, I met Mrs. Helen Deutsch whose address I had got through Susan at Nanterre. Mrs. Deutsch was also looking for an au-pair arrangement but to help with household chores instead of keeping an eye on some awful brats. That could have advantages. I knew that Mrs. Deutsch was a world-famous psychologist although I had not read any of her works. Her house sat on a quiet street like most Cambridge streets were. With shuffling little steps, a small stooped woman with boyish cut grey hair had come to the door. She was dressed like a church mouse. Her small black eyes were as piercing as the little rodent's. In spite of that frailty, the little woman was impressive. At a second look, those piercing eyes were mesmerizing but sharp as a knife's edge. Her whole home exuded an atmosphere of strangeness and coldness, of death in fact. Maybe she was terribly ill, I thought.

She made me sit in the living room in two shabby-looking leather chairs, like dilapidated design pieces that looked out of place. Those chairs rang a bell in my memory. "They look like Le Corbusier chairs" I said. The piercing eyes got more piercing with their apples dilating the way cats do. "They are" said Mrs. Deutsch with surprise, "They actually are originals that were given to us." That sudden outburst of knowledge on my part seemed to destabilize her. I was not exactly what she expected from a prospective au pair girl. On my side, I was not terribly thrilled at having to clean Mrs. Deutsch's house. All the furniture and art pieces were tough to clean for sure. The 1940's and 1950's had delivered a lot of degradable objects, judging from their discoloured greys, off whites and beiges. As the minutes went by, the mistress of the place started to feel strangely menacing. I was not sure I could put up with her for long. I parted with a polite goodbye and the promise to Mrs. Deutsch to consider her offer. Mike the photographer was now my only trump card. At least, he lived a stone throw from Linda, which was reassuring.

A father-only home

I dialled Mike's number the morning after. A polite voice answered the phone. The intonation sounded British, bass and melodious. He asked where I was staying and offered right away to come to Prentiss street to talk things over. Minutes later, an old beige Volvo swerved in front of Linda's house. A tall guy in leather boots and an old parka half-buttoned up the wrong way got out feet first. His thick brown hair was cut like myself at age five, even around the head, covering the ears. Under a heavy fringe, two big brown eyes winked at the façade of the Prentiss street house. His face was crossed in the middle by a big and thick brown moustache. He went up the steps onto the porch and knocked on the door. We sat in the living room, facing each other on the two run-down couches. Arms spread and legs wide open, he asked me where I came from. I poured my brief story. I was from Paris, here in Cambridge to do research for my thesis. His eyes were very alert. He seemed to be scrutinizing and thinking at the same time. "I have a daughter", he explained, "It's not good for her to have only her father and brother, that's why I want a woman around the house." I was thinking as much as he was, trying to sketch what life could be in that household. I had never met a single parent before. He got up abruptly. "We can go to my house right now if you want, so you get an idea of my place." Flabbergasted by the sudden proposal, I got up obediently and went upstairs to take my reefer's jacket. "Maybe you still have your suitcase all packed, since you've just arrived here," he said, following me upstairs. "We can take it with us" Before I could say anything, he was in my room, grabbing one of my suitcases. He was already down and out, putting it in the Volvo trunk.

He drove with his tall back bent on the wheel like a racing driver. We crossed Mass. Avenue into a maze of pretty leafy streets. The houses, made of red bricks or wood, looked like cottages or mock manors and children played in front of them.

As we went up Avon Hill street where he lived, I spotted a rather small house compared to its neighbours on the street. It had off-white stuccoed walls and a domed red tile roof that made it look like a mushroom. Out in front a large round awning, which looked like rescued from an old hotel, was set above the large small-glassed living-room wall window. We stopped and veered in front of the garage below the stucco house. We got out. An imposing line of green plastic garbage cans stood right outside the front door. The small entrance hall was filled with a baby grand Steinway. "I am learning to play piano. My German girl-friend is a musician" he informed me. Dust shone in the sunrays, Moroccan carpets were losing their wool and books were lined up on all walls from floor to ceiling, even in the staircase. We went up to the third floor, a big loft with a very high-elevated ceiling, filled with a *bric-a-brac* of wood planks and tools. At the end of the loft, a door opened on a bedroom. I went up to the window. From the room, I could see far above the roofs and down the whole street. It felt like being on top of everything in a small tower. The room was as large as a small flat. After weeks of camping, it felt good to have a place of my own. Up there, the kids were not bound to come and harass me.

We went down again and sat in the living room on a worn out blue-velvet couch. Mike sat at one end and I at the other. "Do you like music?" he asked gently as if I were a guest. "I have many records" and he bent towards the wooden floor where hundreds of LP's were stacked below the books. "If you help me with the cleaning and cooking, fine. But you don't have to do it", he said lightly. Besides the garbage cans outside, I had noticed some more on every floor. I asked him why. "So the kids can throw out their junk right away, and all

I have to do is gather the cans once a week to put them on the sidewalk." He shrugged. "So, what do you say?" I glanced around again. "OK" I said. He got up. "Let's go get the rest of your things then." I told him we could move my other bags the day after. It was time to get back some control over the situation. Linda and the house on Prentiss street had given me my jumpstart in America, I wanted to say goodbye properly.

I went to Avon Hill street the next morning. Mike was off as he would be every day, first to drop the children at their respective schools and then onto either one of the agencies he worked for to discuss some new shoot or straight to his studio on Copley square. Until the afternoon, I had the whole house to myself. I sat in my room that first day. Since Santander and Tübingen and a fortnight in Paris, I had been travelling all the time. Being in temporary lodgings for so long had been exhausting. To be now in a real home, not really part of the family but benefiting from its cosy atmosphere was in fact ideal. I had a home without home obligations. We were only living under the same roof. Out of the window, the New England October sky was illuminating the whole land beyond as well as the room inside. I was a stranger but it felt nice. People were new to me, I was new to them, and so was Cambridge. I had licence to invent myself, and my life, like an offshoot cut off and ready to flourish in a new soil. My head was buzzing with all the mottoes of America, just like any immigrant waking up the first morning on the land chanted by Walt Whitman. From that attic room on top of the house, I towered above a good part of Cambridge, with the sky and sun as if within reach. That room would be my boat for months. I was at sea for sure, but God, I loved it!

My excitement was such that I hardly ate anything the whole day. I crashed in the afternoon and woke up to see the last purple trails in the sky. I heard voices. Father and kids had come back home, night had fallen and the wide star-studded sky was as wonderful as the sunlit one. There were no lights on the street. Every lit window hanged like a coloured and animated vignette. A face, or a silhouette, or several silhouettes, were bending, talking, moving about in every house. I lowered the sash window, leaning out to breathe in the acrid and sweet smell of wood smoke.

I went down, stopping on the second floor to go to the bathroom. I could hear voices coming from the kitchen, the shrieking voice of the girl and the patient voice of the father. As I pushed open the revolving door, the two kids sitting at the dining table looked up at me coldly. "This is Cécile," the father told the children. I smiled politely. The boy smiled back while the girl went on watching TV with her squinting eyes. The father was standing in front of the burners, frying pork shops with a lot of smoke. The fan was making a terrible noise. He took the pan with the smoking meat to the table and splashed a chop in each of the plates, including mine. There was white packaged bread soft as a feather pillow, butter and jam on the table. They all ate their meat with their fingers. Once done, the girl got up, pulling down her skirt that had gone up on her plump waist, and shuffled in her socks to the big double fridge. "Where are the frozen yoghurts?" she whined. I had never heard of frozen yogurts. "We are out of them", said her father. "Damn" she said, rummaging into the deep-freezer. She came back to the dining table eating with a spoon directly from a carton of ice cream and resumed TV watching, oblivious of us all. Mike smiled at me and shrugged his shoulders. The son was gently and quietly eating an apple. He got up and excused himself while I was eating some fruit too. "You like pork chops?" I asked. "Not especially" answered Mike, "It's just easier." Besides pork chops, they mostly ate omelets or chicken nuggets from *Kentucky fried chicken* on Mass Avenue. The favourite desserts of the house were peanut butter and jelly sandwiches and frozen yogurts. The father cleared away the table and proceeded to rinse plates and cutlery before shoving them into the dishwasher. I sat watching that mother of a man. A bewildered cat's face appeared behind the window above the sink. She was quadricolor with staring eyes. Mike opened the door and the cat darted in, disappearing fast in the house. "That's Paddy. Since she was neutered, she has become very wild" he explained.

After dinner, I had taken the habit of listening to music for hours with earphones, spread on the big blue velvet couch. I lied down submerged by torrents of sounds and emotions. Long after everybody was asleep in the house, I finally mustered enough courage to sit up, get up and go up the stairs to my remote abode. No wife in the house was there to remonstrate with me. Just like Mike's children, I was relishing complete freedom. When not listening to one of the thousands of cassettes, I looked at the books piled up everywhere, a mishmash of history, literature, philosophy, photography, and also chess, golf and scuba diving which must have been the hobbies of the father. When I emerged from those music sessions on the blue velvet couch, the silence in the house and on the street was absolute as if we were in the countryside. I went up to my room on tiptoe and looked through the window at the scant lights outside, above doorsteps and on top floors. I got into the narrow bed against the window watching the night sky, smiling at my luck.

Harry Levin

Every morning I was now setting off for Harvard Square, going either straight on Mass. Avenue, or through the maze of streets lined with little match-box houses, all the same and never the same, painted in pastel hues. They all had a patch of garden and some had very big ones. The walk was just long enough a transition between the house and Widener library where I was now spending most of the day.

I had gone first thing to the Comparative literature Department at Harvard to remit a letter of recommendation from my Nanterre Professor to René Wellek, the Head of the department. Wellek was on sabbatical in Europe. His secretary had passed on the letter to Harry Levin, Head of the English Department and acting Head for the Comparative Literature Department during Wellek's absence. I was asked to come and meet him a few days later. Levin was a blue-eyed silver-haired punctilious gentleman who seemed hesitant as he shook my hand, as if embarrassed that he could not decipher what my calibre, academic and social, could be. I asked him permission to read at Widener Library and exposed to him the gist of my comparative study of Julien Sorel and Gatsby around the theme of success, *"Les ressorts de la réussite"*. I don't know how impressed he was by my subject, but he granted me researcher status instantly. That was better than I had hoped for. The special researcher card not only opened to me the doors of Widener at all times, from dawn to midnight, but the stacks also. I would be allowed to amble and sit at leisure in the shadow of thousands of books lined up like well-planted alleys in forests. Levin had bowed to me as I was taking leave, urging me very urbanely to come by anytime I needed.

Every morning, long after Mike and the children had gone off, I went down to the kitchen. Cardinals and squirrels hopped around the messy back garden while I gulped coffee and cereals down before setting for a brisk walk down to Harvard. When I had been at Brown University two years before, I had felt a pang of nostalgia for an American campus life I would never have. But here I was, treading the lawns of Harvard as a dignified researcher. I did not feel like a stowaway, I was involved and legitimate. I didn't know a soul on the campus and I didn't try socializing. That was not the point of my being at Harvard anyway. The point was to have a foot in the US and to finish my MA dissertation as soon as possible. Then, I would apply to Berkeley. Mr. Levine would have been horrified to hear that Harvard was just a stopgap on my way to California. I had hinted at Berkeley when talking to him and I had seen his eyes looking absent.

Widener Library, a formidable forest

At ten, when all the regular students had already long been shut in class, I climbed up the wide steps of Widener. I read for five hours, taking references and quotations, jotting notes and sketching chapters. In the afternoon, I loafed around the Square, roaming the second-hand bookshops. My favorite books were the "hurt" Modern Library volumes. The stigma "hurt" was printed coarsely on the first page, and everytime I bought one, I felt like rescuing a wounded. They were beginning to pile up on my big desk made of wooden boards I had found in Mike's junk in the next room.

On the way back home, I had the wind in my back on Mass. Avenue. The sunlight was dwindling. From crisp during the day, the air turned to freezing. I held the collar of my black reefer jacket close to my neck and I walked faster. When I turned left into Agassiz Street, it was already dark and lights began to sprout in the houses. Every time I walked back, I enjoyed the absence of street lamps turning the area into a tale-like landscape. Barely seeing my feet and my way, I moved in the dark watching but unwatched. In front of the house on Avon Hill Street, raccoons tumbled down from the garbage cans they were looting, in a din of steel lids falling on the ground. I just had time to see funny grey and white faces made up like carnival masks and long black and white striped furry tails. Mike hated the raccoons, which were said to carry rabies. But I liked them, as much as the gorgeous red cardinals flitting around. There had been a jungle before Harvard square.

Alumni from Berkeley

The month of October was drawing to a close and the marvellous colors of the Indian summer were fading out. Linda and her boyfriend had taken me with them for weekend walks around Cambridge. We had spent an afternoon picking

MacIntosh apples in a private orchard where for a few bucks you could pick and eat fruits at leisure. The sun was still very warm in the middle of the day and Linda had turned crimson in her shorts while we shook apple trees and jumped to reach the highest branches. We had eaten as many apples as we could and had taken back four huge brown paper bags full of them.

Answering my inquiries and stated plans of joining the comparative literature department, Berkeley had sent me a list of alumni I was to meet to get tips and advice on my Ph.D. prospects. They could also recommend me to the department. The first I had gone to see was a woman teaching and completing her Ph.D. at Harvard. I had come on a Sunday afternoon. She, her husband and child were in their pyjamas gulping down brunch amid cries and TV shrieks. I felt like a dog in a game of skittles. We exchanged a few words and promised to meet again, but I swear I could hear them sighing once I got in the corridor. The second alumnus lived two streets away. I had left a message and he had called back inviting me to a drink he was giving for his students from Tufts "which would be a good opportunity to meet with fellow students". This time I had put on my one and only dress, a "maxi" mauve jersey one with short puffed sleeves. The alumnus drink was starting at five. I walked there and arrived at a quarter of six. About a dozen students were standing stiff in freshly pressed shirts and ties, all with the same expression of mute benevolence on their faces. They held glasses and looked as if they were talking to each other although barely any sound came out of their mouths. As I was taking off my jacket, they were forming a circle around their teacher, holding their drink higher, ready to toast.

I joined hastily as the teacher wished them all the best for the college year. They gulped down their drink and instantly disappeared. Within five minutes I was alone with the teacher. Even his wife had disappeared in the kitchen. In less than an hour, the party had lived and died. As I was telling him of my settling in Cambridge, Wellek, Levin, Widener and whatever could make me sound like a winner, the teacher kept his benevolent half smile, looking at the floor. We both stood in the middle of the carpetless living room where all chairs had been pushed aside for the now vanished guests. The smile opened wider and I heard the same wishes of good luck he had said before. Good luck sounded like goodbye and I left, feeling gypped. The walk to and fro had lasted longer that my attendance at the "party".

After all, I wondered, was Berkeley really Berkeley? The free speech movement was born there, but to judge from those two alumni, campus life was a very different story. In 1972, in fact, all the free-talkers were in jail, on the run, or exiled abroad. I decided to go and see one more alumnus on my list. That time, it sounded more positive. For one thing, the woman was a graduate in comparative literature, while the two others had majored in American lit, and she had suggested lunch at her place.

Competition to get to Berkeley was fierce, she told me straight out, and even more so at the comparative lit. department which took only twelve post-graduate students. There would be no hope for a scholarship on the first year of my post-graduate program. I would have to wait at least for the second year. The first goal was in any case to get enrolled. For that she strongly recommended to get an interview with the Head of the department before decisions were made on applications. In parallel, she said, it was a good idea to apply for an assistantship in French, which I could get easily since very few French natives were coming to Berkeley. The stipend for an assistantship was about four thousand dollars, which would cover tuition and part of my living expenses. Besides, I could give private lessons or do translations and whatever odd job would be available. In no time, the woman had outlined for me the steps and tasks necessary to transform my fleeting dream into a real plan. I was not to see her again, since she was going to Europe a month later but she promised she would write to the Head of the comparative literature department in Berkeley to say she had met me and was confident I had the necessary credentials to do post-graduate studies there. She had wiped out my qualms. By December, I would have completed my research. By end of March, I would have written my MA dissertation. In April, I would set sails for Berkeley, going coast to coast for the first time.

Odd jobs

For the time being, I had to keep on reading and writing, and making money. In exchange for sitting some evenings and weekends with the children, sometimes a few days in a row when Mike was on a long shoot, I had room and board but I was not paid. Harry Levin's secretariat had directed me to the Harvard employment office where they kept a file on job offers. Officially I was looking for freelance jobs, an acceptable name for moonlighting, since being on a tourist visa I was not allowed to get paid jobs. My visa was expiring at the end of December and I would have to convince the Immigration office to renew it. But December was still a long time away. Seeing my respectable "Harvard researcher" card, the girl at the Harvard Employment Office had handed me the card file. There were plenty of demands for French lessons and translations. By virtue of being a French abroad, it seemed that I had just to bend down to pick up money. I wrote down a few names and phone numbers and the girl took down mine to give to people looking for a French national.

A Russian lady

My first potential employer was in a faraway suburb. So far that it had taken me three hours on different buses to get there. Even before meeting her, I had already renounced the job. Six hours on the bus for two hours of teaching made no sense. The jolly fat Russian lady with a generous bosom was a prominent writer and Professor of Russian literature at Harvard and Boston University. She had a rosy face with high cheekbones and a permanent smile, ready to cry or laugh just like I had imagined Russian ladies after reading Tolstoï. She drenched me with words of welcome, served me tea and cakes and kept whining for an hour about how beautiful the French language was and how critical it was for her beloved and only son, a ten years old little blond boy, to learn it. She said all this in torrents of French with rolling r's dribbling down.

Her plan was for me to stay with them as a live-in teacher. In exchange for the room, I would teach the little boy one hour per day and I would baby sit in the evening. As I left, she followed me outside, still begging me with her high-pitched voice to reconsider. I had repaid myself the trip in a reckless way. While she was making the tea in her kitchen, I had remained alone in the sitting room where I had grabbed the phone to call Arthur in Berkeley. Hastily, I had said hello, telling him that I was in Cambridge and goodbye. Two minutes later, the lady was back, carrying the tea tray with ample hip moves and a smile worthy of a diva. The opulent logorrhoea started again.

Would-be Kennedys

My next potential pupils were living in a faraway suburb as well. Leaving the bus, I had walked along the road up to a house perched on a cliff above the highway. It looked like a miniature palace with an enormous number of rooms, but no bigger than closets and with very low ceilings. Even the living-room was no more than a box. It was a Catholic family with five children. The mother, blonde and pretty in the style of Grace Kelly, seemed terribly efficient and eager to be the perfect mother and wife. This had a lot to do with her husband's career. He was a budding politician, candidate to the coming local council elections. I arrived just as they were all getting out of the family wagon. All the children were blue-eyed and dressed like little Kennedys for a seasonal clothes catalogue. They greeted me sternly but impeccably while the mother was hectically trying to take all the grocery bags from the trunk. She shouted instructions to the kids like a chief scout. "Wipe your feet, leave the boots under the shed, go wash your hands! Lucy, put the kettle on!" I helped carry a few bags, which the mini-hall and corridor could hardly contain. The mother told me to sit in the living room where two small couches faced each other like in a train compartment. She came back from the kitchen with the two eldest children, continuing the conversation that had begun before. "I told you not to talk to them! Just stay out of their way until after the election!" A fight had erupted between her sons and the children of their father's contender for the election. A photograph of the father stood in a frame on the lamp table. His face grinned, with chubby cheeks and sure eyes.

    The mother recomposed her pretty face and smile as she introduced me to the girl and the boy that would be taking lessons with me. We would do it in that trainlike little living room. The house was a long way from Cambridge, but the determination and dedication of that woman touched me. I sympathized with her craving to do everything right. The French lessons fitted into her complex plan for success. I took the job. In October and most of November, I could still manage to walk along the road from the bus stop and back, even though it was pitch dark when I left and there was not much room to walk alongside the long uninterrupted file of cars blinding me with their lights. The road was not intended for walkers. When snow began to pile up, I resisted for a few weeks, but it had become too perilous to get to the bus stop and, once there, I still had to wait alone in the cold, beating my feet on the ground. Around Christmas, I quit. The father had been elected.

A Sargent lady

The last on my list was not far from Harvard Square, on Sparks street. Her house was an enormous sombre stone mansion probably built in the 1880's. Behind an old unattractive wall, it was invisible from the street. The large gate opened on a vast courtyard planted with gigantic maples and beeches that further hid the house. The lady was tiny and unconspicuous in the old gentle tradition. She made me think of the old lady who mentors Babar the elephant. Her hair was undyed, a natural grey, which was rare in America. Her clothes were as low-key as her allure: a worn out tweed suit, heavy brown leather lace-up shoes and thick brownish stockings. Her smile was soft and genuine and her eyes interested. She seemed really keen to learn. She led me through the hall to the vast sitting room filled with belle époque settees and wing chairs. No lights were on and we sat next to the high French window at a round table in a corner. The darkness and feel of abandonment of that huge room recalled the crumbling and forlorn house in *"Great expectations"* by Dickens. She offered me a cup of tea that she went herself to make in the kitchen. We decided that I would come twice a week for one hour and a half. As we crossed her huge sitting room together, I glanced at the paintings hanging on the wall: century old portraits and landscapes. I remarked that a portrait reminded me of a John Singer Sargent. She looked surprised. "It is a John Singer Sargent" she murmured, "and I am a Sargent myself".

We had started to work right away. Her French was already beyond basic and I had looked for books to read and comment together. She had insisted to come and fetch me twice a week at ten a.m. with her own car, although I didn't feel terribly safe when she was at the wheel of her big Chrysler. Her driving was erratic and, even with an automatic gear, she seemed to have difficulties finding the right one. Having to go in reverse one day on Avon Hill street, she had zigzagged from one side to the other down the street, thankfully deserted at that time. The house was always empty in the mornings when I came, but I had met two of her sons on their way in or out, every time in a hurry. They were dressed in sport shoes and training clothes under formal grey coats, as if they were going to jog at lunchtime. She had nine children, and only the three youngest, all boys, still lived at home. I had met her husband by chance too. He had popped in from his nearby office. He ran a family-owned manufacturing business whose plants were outside of Boston. He looked very old, with one round glass eye forever staring in surprise. His formal clothes were in disarray, the jacket ill-buttoned, the tie too loose, a dirty handkerchief hanging out of his grey flannel trouser pocket. In fact, sons and father alike, they all looked as if they had mental ailments, running around aimlessly. The father was very deaf and hardly paid attention to his wife. I could see the concern and permanent worry in the childish blue eyes of my pupil, as if she were always afraid everything would go awry. Our quiet French lessons enchanted her, as a much needed oasis of calm and normality. One day as she was driving me back, her husband had appeared in the middle of very heavy traffic, looking lost and disoriented. "What is he doing here?" she whispered, terribly worried yet unable to stop and talk to him as we were carried away by the car flow.

One of her eldest daughters was suffering from a deadly cancer. She lived in Pennsylvania but kept traveling to every therapist or doctor she could trace that promised a new cure for her illness. She was away from home very often, and my pupil worried about her little boy, her grandson, alone with a baby-sitter most of the time. I had brought Marcel Pagnol's story of his childhood: *"A la gloire de mon père"*, as a textbook. The hills outside Marseilles and all the games of catching and hunting Marcel and his brother played in the Provence countryside mesmerized her and she wanted to find an English translation of the book for her grandson. When I came out of that misfit place out on the streets of Cambridge, I was surprised to find myself in America.

For Thanksgiving, she had invited me for lunch. Besides her husband, there were her three sons and the girl friend of the eldest one. The table was set up with the common French feast paraphernalia. The Champagne was as real as the crystal and silvery. But all the dishes were the traditional mixture of English and "Indian" dishes to commemorate the dinner of the Pilgrim fathers with the autochtons. Squash dishes, pumpkin tarts with cinnamon, a gigantic turkey with oyster filling, sweet orange potatoes. Those flavours were new to me as was that weird celebration to thank God for having given America to the Americans.

The three sons looked at me as a curiosity. The youngest was a teen-ager, very tall with a huge wisp of hair falling across his face like his old father. He looked like the young son of the noble family who holds a château party in *"La dolce vita"* by Fellini. The old maid, usually hiding in the pantry, was helping to bring and serve the dishes. The girlfriend of the eldest son, a pair of jeans tightly fitting her big buttocks, looked like a Martian at the table. She drank beer and not wine, she smoked while eating and she kissed her boyfriend between mouthfuls. Her face and style mimicked Gloria Steinem. A pear-shaped body, long thick hair parted in the middle, small round glasses, bra-less boobs rolling under her teeshirt, bell-bottom jeans. She laughed loudly and giggled when her boyfriend tickled her under the table. She had suggested we meet for a beer some time. Months later, I ran into her on Harvard Square and she dragged me into a café to tell me all the troubles she was going through. Her boyfriend had broken his knee playing football and had been hospitalized at Mass General. The nurse in charge had befriended him so much as to give him nice massages. When he had been discharged, he had moved in with her in her small apartment. The girl felt totally betrayed and, worse, she had no place to stay anymore. She was now camping at a girlfriend's place waiting for better days.

Algonquin gas company

My dissertation was advancing fast now, leaving me more free time. Besides the French lessons, I decided to try my hand at translation. The Algonquin Gas Company on Soldiers' Field road in Boston was looking for a translator and an interpreter. This was another complicated trip to get there. I had no "office" clothes at all anymore. I had exchanged my tartan Scottish skirt and a wool frock for a damaged US Army green jacket with a bullet hole in the heart and a pair of old jeans ripped at the end at a second hand shop on Kendall square. To go and meet the Director of the Algonquin gas company, I had tucked the patched up jeans into a pair of black plastic boots because of the snow. But I had chosen my black reefer's jacket over the US army one not to freak him out too much.

The young and energetic chief executive didn't seem worried about my looks. His sole concern was to solve a serious communication problem the company had with Algeria. First, we had settled pay and conditions. My fee was fixed on an hourly basis. I stated my demands to be paid in cash or checks since I could not have a bank account. They frowned for a second, but quickly said they would find a way to account for the expense in their books. I would be required for as many hours as necessary to assist in the correspondence and communication via telex with Sonatrach, the Algerian public company they wanted to buy natural gas from. Negotiations had already started months before, but they were stalled because of their inability to communicate with each other. Besides Arabic and Berber, the Algerians spoke and wrote only French. Americans used only English. No deal could be made and the Algerians were ready to drop the talks. I was there to resume them and to arrange a meeting with the Sonatrach executives in Boston.

First, I sat at the telex machine with the Director's secretary to send messages and retrieve them. I wrote in

French and translated into English the telex from Algeria. Transmission was often interrupted, but on the other side, the male Algerian secretary was getting excited, answering profusely and always with flirting compliments. After a few weeks, a date was confirmed for a meeting in Boston at Algonquin. A delegation of five Algerian executives arrived at the end of January 1973. The meeting lasted three days. For hours on end, I stayed sitting in the middle of the row of armchairs, Sonatrach on my right and Algonquin on my left. Repeatedly, the American side and the Algerian side would try to talk directly to each other, and, every time, they would have to turn to me. I was the medium and the message, and totally exhilarated.

The Algonquin executives were trying hard to appear relaxed and smiling, treating the Algerians as if they were buddies in a spirit of friendliness. The Algerians, however, remained tight-lipped and haughty, knowing they had the upperhand in the negotiations. They barely answered questions and yawned while the Americans talked at length and laughed spiritedly. At long last, after three days, Algonquin got an invitation to come to Algiers to discuss "possible" elements for a "possible" contract. I was not very proud of such a shaky result, but the Algonquin boss was exuberant. They had talked, they had sat together and they had shaken hands with the Algerians. For the CEO, this was already a done deal. The day they flew to Algiers, my job was over.

Mount Monadnock

One Friday morning, as I was sipping my coffee in the kitchen, I looked out in the back garden. October was ending but nothing was falling yet. The air shined as crystal against the sky, it was more than sunlight on a pretty autumn morning, it was preternatural. I couldn't get my eyes off that sky. From the French Alps, I knew that this superb weather would not go on for long. It was my last chance to hike before next spring. But where could I go and with whom? Linda would be busy with her China specialist boyfriend as she was every weekend. Besides the books at Widener, I did not know a soul. I had to go alone. In my "Student America" guidebook, I had come upon Mount Monadnock, a geological phenomenon in the middle of New Hampshire. The rocky mount, said the guidebook, rose above the plain with views extending for miles around, a survivor from prehistorical times before rivers had carved the vast plain at its foot. I looked on the map and called the Greyhound bus service. There was a bus to Troy, the nearest town, at eleven.

As we got out of Boston, I could see for the first time the real Indian summer. On miles and miles, the forest spread, like waves of red and yellow and all their orange shades. I arrived in Troy around two in the afternoon. The town seemed asleep and village-like. I could see Mount Monadnock in the distance, rising above the flat land like the cathedral of Chartres. Its perfect pyramidal shape gave it power and force. I couldn't keep my eyes off it as I walked on the narrow road. It did not look that far. I could even discern the silvery rocky peak and the forested slopes shining in the afternoon sun. The road was a country road with no traffic at all. It was meandering like the peasant path it had been to begin with, going around fields and terrain undulations. As the road was going down towards a river, I saw an old lady in a cotton smock with very blue eyes and her very white hair in a bun. She smiled at me and I stopped to say hello. She offered some coffee. She was living alone in a small brick house. When I left, she waved at me as long as she could see me. Mount Monadnock was still ahead and looking at my watch, I saw that it was already four o'clock. It seemed that the mountain was receding as fast as I went forward, or at any rate it was not getting closer. I heard a car approaching. It was a farmer's pick-up truck with two guys. I raised my thumb.

They were two foresters carrying timber. I climbed on the front seat with them. They didn't talk much, but offered to go out of their way to drop me at the beginning of the path to Mount Monadnock. "It's late to go up now", said the one who drove the pick-up, "It's going to be dark." I waved goodbye and started going up the path at once. Groups of people were going down, red-cheeked and laughing. They had the long and easy stride of the happy hiker at the end of his hike. Soon enough, the path was empty. The forest gave way to rocks and, all of a sudden, I was out in space, well above the entire area. The landscape was growing as I went up, opening and blooming like a magic flower. The earth extended for miles on end with multiple details coming to life in the slanting sunrays. Lines, dark spots, shiny pools, different textures of trees, deciduous, evergreen, all the greens and yellows and reds and greys and pinks. The spectacle was starting. The sky was changing colors, some well trained clouds were just beginning their act, swelling, stretching and changing hue every minute as the sun was setting. I was stopping now and then, recording with my little Kodak camera the shifts of the landscape: from gold to pink to red to scarlet to purple to violet and, finally, to black. At last, I scrambled among the treacherous giant rocks piled up on top, the ones that shone from Troy. Standing up at the summit, I breathed hard and looked. I felt like a bird atop a giant tree, full of songs and ready to fly. I took a last shot with my camera. The sun had set. The dark violet land was slowly turning black. I was all alone on top of Mount Monadnock as cold and night descended ineluctably.

Going up the path against the current, while all hikers were going down, I had felt happy and brave. Now, I had to go down. The last hiker I had crossed had been a man alone. He had stopped to turn his head as I was going on up. In the last agony of light, I could still make out the rocky terrain I was on. I zipped up my anorak and put a scarf on my head. As I was reaching the beginning of the spruce forest, it was pitch dark. I couldn't see a thing. I could only feel the ground with my feet and hands. Cautiously, I was propelling myself very slowly on my behind. I could hear though. Minuscule sounds felt as conspicuous as a glaring light. Night birds howled and things cracked around. Suddenly, I slid downwards. My feet were hanging in the air and my hands were badly bruised. I remained still, panic mounting in my chest and throat. It was too dangerous to go on. The best thing to do was to nestle in a bush and wait for daylight. But the cold was growing. Without a sleeping bag, I would freeze. Besides, guys or animals could be wandering around, maybe already on my trail? I remembered the odd look of the last hiker. He could have stopped somewhere along the way, waiting for his prey. I was frightened and shivering with cold. Tears came up to my eyes. But if I couldn't see anything, neither could anyone else, I reasoned. I had to move on, if only to stop the cold creeping up my body. I crawled on cautiously, putting a foot forward, another, moving arms and hands and bum slowly in step. I was not thinking of anything, but the path going down in front of me and the next step, and the next after the next.

In the night limbo, the moon appeared, white like a lily on dark water. Tears came to my eyes, but of relief this time. I had never known that the moon could light one's way as much as the sun. The track was now clear in front of me and I could walk erect. I stepped from the last rock onto the wide and easy dirt path. There were lights ahead. I was out of the dark, out of the forest. Happiness was flowing in my veins like a powerful drink. Rather than walking, I was bouncing with joy. The chalet at the bottom of the path was lit. I came to the door. Some hikers were spreading their sleeping bags on the wooden planks aligned on two levels. I asked a Ranger if I could sleep there. He asked what gear I had, and when I said none, he shook his head. The temperature was going to go below zero during the night. I needed a down-filled bag. But where was I to sleep? I had no car, no way to reach Troy other than walking along the road. He said there was a kind of hostel run by some Christian association down the road, on the right side. They would not charge much.

A providential sect

I left behind the chalet and the merry group of hikers and stepped on the asphalted road. It was totally solitary and pitch dark again, the moon now hid by a cloud. There were no houses anywhere. Once in a while, a truck with blinding lights would dash by, honking like a boat coming home. After the forest and the strange cries of fauna, the road felt more frightening. I could see vehicles arriving from the left side on which I was treading, but they could not see much of me which was a mixed blessing. If they did not see me, they could hit me and, if they did see me, they could easily pick me up, want it or not. I kept walking. A tiny light appeared dimly in the distance. It was on the right side of the road, as the Ranger had said that hostel was. Approaching, I could see that it was a single bulb on a painted wooden façade. The building looked like a huge barn, with just one door and one window on its front. I swiftly crossed the road and walked towards it. I knocked on the door. No answer. I knocked and shouted, "Is there anybody in, please?" The door opened. A thin and small man, with blondish hair very neatly combed and a shiny reddish face, as if soaped too often, opened the door and looked at me impassively. He was no taller than me, holding his neck and head backwards like a bird. "I am looking for a place to sleep, a Ranger at Mount Monadnock told me you had accommodation for hikers." He retreated slightly for me to go in and shut the door.

I was standing in a big kitchen. Two boys were busy peeling potatoes. "This is Chris and Peter, my name is George, where are you from?" said the little man, his hands in the pockets of his cotton bomber jacket. France did not seem to ring any bell for him. "Do you know the Bible?" he asked suddenly. I nodded. It seemed enough to get a bed for the night. The little man asked Chris to show me the dormitory. Chris stopped stirring a stew on the burner, wiped his hands on a towel and went with me.

The dormitory was across the corridor from the kitchen. He switched on the neon lights. There was a huge room with a few windows and five or six rows of beds like in a pre-war boarding school. It was not freezing but it was not warm either. I was shown the showers, washstands and toilets on the side. Chris said goodnight and left. I still had no clue where I had landed, but the bed was real and I lay down on it. I gathered what remained of my strength to get up and go to the bathroom and then take off my clothes. The sheets were cold, but not damp at least. I grabbed two more covers from the neighboring beds and let the voice of reason in my mind talk to itself. Yes, I was in an unknown place with unknown people, apparently all male. If I were sound asleep, I conjectured, bad things could happen. I fell asleep instantly.

Bright sunrays were shooting through the mean little windows when I opened my eyes. The place looked now like the cow stable it must have been. From outside, I heard cheering voices and the sound of car doors banging. I took a shower and got dressed. It was ten o' clock, I had slept a good ten hours. I went into the kitchen, a woman was there, dressed in a long wide skirt, a scarf tied on her nape like a peasant from Anatolia. Her hair and eyes were very dark. "Breakfast?", she asked me. I had coffee, and toast with jam and butter. "My husband is busy, he says to say good bye to you. It is ten dollars for the night" she told me. I gave her a bill and left. Outside, cars were arriving non-stop with middleaged couples: big women and men, all cheerful as if going to Carnival. Chris was welcoming them. Seeing me, he came forward. "Are you having a meeting?" I asked. "Yes, it's a three-day seminar for couples." Chris was holding leaflets. "Have one" he said, handing it to me. I put it in my bag. "Thank you very much for your hospitality" I said. "You are welcome", said Chris, "I hope you have time to read the Bible regularly." "Sure" I said diplomatically.

I got my knapsack on my back and went out. From the road, I could see the barn and adjacent buildings, painted deep red and looking quaint against the green grass. It looked homey in daylight. The little man was the centre of attention, surrounded by all the merry couples. The frights and trials of the dark night and forest had evaporated with the sun. Another gorgeous North American day was starting. I could walk to Troy easily and catch a bus back to Boston, but I felt like trying my luck again. I stopped on the right side and raised my thumb. A few cars passed by, the men driving ignoring me while their plump wives watched me with worried eyes. After a flurry of half-empty cars, which turned me down, I resumed walking on the road when I heard a loud roar and a honking behind me. A huge blue azure sports car stopped abruptly, its tyres screeching on the road. A young guy with pilot sunglasses bent on the front seat to open the door. "Want a ride?" I got in. "Name is John" he said. John was going to Boston and offered to drive me all the way there. He had a big head with bony jaws and a mass of lacquered hair that looked permed. He was studying law at Boston University. "What car is this?" I asked. "It's a Thunderbird", John explained. And it went as fast as lightning.

He dropped me at a subway station on the crimson line. Riding back home, for the first time I felt a bond. I belonged here now. My fright at Mount Monadnock had made me long for the comfort of that Avon Hill street home. I got off at Harvard Square and called Mike's house from a coin telephone. His voice sounded slightly worried. He had wondered if I would come back. He insisted on coming to fetch me with the old Volvo on the Square. I waited on the corner of Harvard Common and Mass. Avenue. As I emptied my knapsack, the leaflet Chris had given me in the morning fell on the carpet. *"Fear Jehovah!"* it proclaimed.

Halloween – A party at the Galbraith's

Halloween had come down on Cambridge like a comic strip. I remembered Schultze's "Peanuts" frolicking in carnival clothes and gorging on candies on the last page of the Herald Tribune. This time it was real. The carved pumpkins were out on every doorstep. Their flickering light made the walk back home like a trip in Fantasyland. Mike and the kids had prepared kilos of candies for the costumed children that came knocking on the door singing and threatening tricks if they didn't get treats.

Halloween was also the time for the Galbraith's big year-end party to which I had been invited. Since visiting at their Vermont farm in the summer of 1970 with the Mc. Daniels, I had kept in touch with Mrs. Galbraith who had answered my thank you note expressing her best wishes for my American plans and her readiness to see me again if I made it to Cambridge. I had called her and she had suggested my coming by one morning at her house, a solid and vast redbrick home, just off the Harvard campus. The black housekeeper had opened the door and greeted me very civilly as if she were the hostess of the place. She remembered me from the more than two years before or so she politely pretended. She took me upstairs to Mrs. Galbraith's bedroom. She was sitting on her bed sorting out papers. The papers spread all over the bed, were lists of prospective guests for their annual winter party. She was putting up the final list of elected and told me, with a flicker of irony in her eyes, that I was included.

Like at a debutante ball, the Galbraith party gathered crowds of tuxedoes and evening gowns, real champagne and great New England food served as a *"souper"* by hoards of waiters on a permanent run. In the middle of the entrance hall stood John Kenneth Galbraith with his second son, both as tall as temple pillars and bending courteously towards their more normal-sized guests. We had to queue while the host chatted briefly with everyone, smiling, kidding and sometimes punching people's ribs or shoulders in the comradely way of high academia. When it was my turn, I was the only guest coming unaccompanied. John Kenneth Galbraith looked at me, his elephant eyes stretched like his lips by a powerful smile. You could meet those very alert eyes only by surprise, when he was looking at you sideways. "You really recognize me?" I asked flippantly. "Of course" he answered, with a good faith frown, putting his arm on my shoulder and already looking beyond. Another guest was coming forward and John Kenneth Galbraith's wide smile was already engulfing him. That next guest was in fact a Democrat House Representative followed by a handful of photographers. John Kenneth Galbraith's son had been named campaign manager for Senator Mc.Govern who was going to run against Richard Nixon. Politics was in the air. Swiftly, Galbraith whisked the Representative in his study for private talks and a photo session. At the door to the grand salon, Mrs. Galbraith welcomed guests on a less formal foot.

Past the hosts, I was left freewheeling. Two or three young men in elegant tuxedos came up to me to chat. One of them asked me if I was a model, which was surprising taking into account my almost one hundred forty pounds. A small man, the only one in casual clothes, was looking at me with wide, intense eyes. "It's Erich Segal", said the dashing young man I was talking to. *Love story*, his novel, was a much talked about bestseller.

There was no dancing at the party. It was not a party for fun but, rather, a very formal affair for the many colleagues and acquaintances of the Galbraiths. The resulting ambience was very social and jolly, but with rigid self-control. Hopefuls could get next to their stars and maybe climb a step further to a fateful handshake. Stars, meanwhile, were on the alert to fend off charm offensives. I had spotted early on the blue eyes and fittingly jocular face of Harry Levin. As he was moving on to his next interlocutor, I approached. He bowed, shook my hand and kept smiling while I mumbled my gratitude to him for the great time I was having at Widener. No word oozed through that steely smile as he gently moved on, as if sucked by an invisible current to the other end of the room. The general smile had stuck itself on my face and I went on smiling while I drank and ate at the buffet, while I passed by people or met their eyes. Either they were a fantasy or I was an invisible ghost, either way it felt unpleasant. Before exhausting my stock of smiles, I walked towards Mrs. Galbraith to say goodbye. She asked me if I had a car to go home. I didn't. Snow had been falling steadily since morning and the whole of Cambridge was heavily coated by now. "Wait", said Mrs. Galbraith, "Abigail and her boy-friend can drive you home, they are leaving, it's on their way." She called a girl who was giggling and making mock waltz steps in the arms of John Kenneth Galbraith.

Abigail had a grand white ball-dress, strapless, with matching long gloves. Her hair was gathered as a high chignon with curls cascading down her nape. She sat at the back of the two-door car, insisting on my seating in front next to her boyfriend, since I would get out first. She was full of questions about how I had met the Galbraith, and what was I doing exactly in Cambridge. I told her about the visit to their Vermont farm and she got very excited. "What happens there?" she asked with glinting eyes, "Tell us. Is that true what they say?" I had no clue about what they said. We were going up Avon Hill Street. She was looking at the houses. "You rent an apartment?" she asked. I told her I was an au pair for a single father who was raising his two children. "Single?" she said, chuckling, "And what does he do that single father?" "He is a photographer." "And what do you do with the single father?" "That's none of your business", said the boyfriend, putting his hand on her mouth. He swiftly parked the car, let me out and went off, not even letting Abigail get out to sit in front.

NYC, the grand way

That Christmas was my first away from family and a flurry of nostalgia was falling like snow on me. Mike's children had trimmed a spruce tree in the living-room and we had all exchanged gifts on Christmas morning before they would go on to their grandparents for brunch and more presents. I had been given an orange-yellow-blue six-footer wool scarf to wrap around my neck and a XXL burgundy Harvard sweater that could go through the dryer and remain big enough long enough. I had paid a fortune to have a pot of azaleas delivered to my parents in Paris with a Christmas card. In the empty house, I was brooding, half melancholy and half plotting next steps. I had now completed my research and written my dissertation. I had to type the final draft, make the last corrections and send it over to Nanterre to get my MA degree by mid 1973. In April, I would be in Berkeley for interviews with the comparative literature department. The present was swelling like a bubble, dense with hopes and some anguish. But I felt larger, like my plans and like the continent I was going to cross from coast to coast.

I had sent a letter to Mary R. in New York City. Mary was a very old lady who had been a guest at my great-grandmother's during her "finishing school" year in France in the thirties. My letter had remained unanswered until the beginning of January and I had forgotten about it when, quite unexpectedly, I had received a longhand note where she explained that she had been cruising the Aegean on a ketch, coming back to New York only to be absorbed into all her Christmas obligations. She hoped I was still around and she expected my visit any time in January or February. I wrote back and she called me. Her voice was stentorian but very warm and humorous. And I longed for New York. Elisabeth had vanished and I had no way to know where she was. This time though it sounded like the grand way. Mary had inquired if I liked the opera and the theatre. I had told her that I had been only once to the Opéra Comique to see Strauss's "Nutcracker". As for theatre, I mentioned a play with Alan Bates running on Broadway I had heard about.

For a change, instead of travelling with the Greyhound bus, I decided to take up an offer for a car ride. There were plenty of them stuck on a billboard at Widener library. The two girls I was joining had given me an appointment on Kendall Square, a forlorn and freezing place with bums hanging around. On January 20, temperature was way below zero and a screeching icy wind was blowing. I had put on my maxi-coat and I held close its wide hood, hoping the girl would not be late. I had crammed my mauve dress and whatever essentials in a small leather suitcase I had found in the attic of Mike's house. It was supposed to look better than my rucksack. A creaking Dodge stopped by and I got in the back. There was another girl passenger seated in front. The seats were ripped off and shaky, the doors didn't shut well, letting freezing air in, neither did the glass windows. Worst of all, the heating system was broken, breathing or speaking, we made as much fog inside as out. At least the car could run and the girl at the wheel seemed to know how to drive. My feet and legs, hands and buttocks were going numb. I had only my stringiness to blame. For a few dollars more, I could have been comfortably sitting on a Greyhound bus.

The girls were going to Queens and we had agreed they would drop me at a subway station. As we drove along New Jersey, I looked at Manhattan. Two tall white bars like giant sugar cubes stood now at the bottom end, disrupting the boat-like shape. Manhattan now looked like a dredger. It's the WTC said the girl driver, the tallest skyscraper in the world. WTC? "World Trade Center" she translated for me. A whitish platinum sun lingered on buildings' façades as we crossed into NYC. On a busy street, the Dodge stopped. The subway was right in front of us. I gave the girl my ten bucks for the gas and got out. Down the subway, the employee barked the name of the line I had to take and the stop I should get off to change line. Hundreds of people were pressing behind me, I could not ask for details. It was my first time on the NY subway and it gave me the creeps. Dark, tortuous corridors, narrow like pipes, lack of light and lack of air, it was like creeping in an abandoned mine. There were both fast trains and omnibus trains, but I did not know the difference. To get away fast from the gloomy quay, I got on the first train. It was Sunday and there were plenty of red-cheeked families and couples muffled up in coats and hats, coming back from a walk or a family lunch. The train emerged from the tunnel for a while and I looked at the city landscape, terribly ugly but strangely arty.

Little by little, the families and couples were dropping off the car. There remained only myself, a sporty couple looking like students and a weird human being. It was a male looking like a horse with a long muzzle-like nose, his shiny black hair tied in a long tail. His face looked like a copper mask with cakes of rouge on the cheekbones. His eyes, like two long slits with lashes heavy with mascara, cast a flippant and weighty glance at me. He was standing up, his back against the wagon door, his very long and thin legs morphing into black leather boots. He looked like a horse. I had remained standing up to be able to get off wherever it would seem right. The sporty couple got up, ready to get off at the next stop. The train stopped. I would be alone with the horse and that frightened me. I hesitated one second and then got off, with the intention of boarding the car ahead of us. But it was completely empty. In a panic, I rushed to catch up with the couple already well ahead of me. As we got outside, it was dark. I had no clue where I was. The couple were kissing each other goodbye. As they parted, I hailed the girl who looked at me, surprised. I told her I didn't know the city at all and asked for directions to Fifth Avenue. She said I should have stayed on the same train for two more stops, gotten off, changed lines, and gone on for another five stops. She seemed perplexed at my silliness. "Or maybe take a cab!" she urged me, "and good luck!" I raised my arm to hail a cab. Instantly one drew along the curb.

It was now a piece of cake. I could look as safely as from a movie theatre seat at the six-lane traffic, the bazaar of shops along the streets and avenues and the variegated crowds moving in all directions and at all paces. The driver slalomed like a pro, tacking within an inch to turn into streets. And here I was, as if dropped by Batman, standing on a neat Fifth avenue curb as wide as an esplanade. The doorman came out to hold the door for me and take my suitcase. We got into the wood-panelled elevator. He drew the iron curtain and asked me for my name. He dialled Mary's number on an old bakelite phone to make sure I was expected. The doorman was a very old man, keeping his eyes downcast and trying to contain an irrepressible yawn.

The door of the elevator opened right into the entrance hall of Mary's apartment. There she was, very tall and slender in a crimson red wool pantsuit, her endless neck very straight, her face smiling with a childish surprised expression. I took her hand. She took mine into both hers. "Your hands are freezing, my dear!" she exclaimed as an old peasant-looking maid took my coat and suitcase. "Nora will show you your room. When you are ready we can have drinks before dinner." Nora had the gait and volume of maids in Ingmar Bergman's movies. She wore a long skirt with a blouse buttoned up and an apron. Her hair was neatly combed backwards and tied in a small bun. She didn't seem to speak English. She was from Norway.

My room felt like a slipper, warm and totally insulated from the outside by three sets of curtains. Little ones on the pane, thicker net curtains and all-lined draped curtains pulled shut for the night. I went to one of the windows and pushed open the three layers to look outside. The buildings, on the other side of 52nd street, didn't let out much light nor reveal much behind their windows, also well hidden also behind thick curtains. The ride in the broken Dodge and on the dark subway felt like nonsense bits of a half-forgotten nightmare. To expel all the bad vibes, I took off my clothes and turned the faucets in the bathtub. My skin was turning scarlet in the steaming hot water. I felt sleepy too. I dropped on the queen size bed and bounced off like a ball. I dressed in my best pair of jeans, and blew my hair dry, ready to socialize. Velazquez paintings hung on the walls of the living-room and a little forest of Giacomettis was set among green plants in a small conservatory tucked into a huge bow-window overlooking Central Park. We had dinner, and herbal tea afterwards in the living room. I promised to be up by eight the next day so as to share breakfast with her.

Before going to bed, I pushed all the curtains again and I opened the window to feel the night of New York. The air was so cold that it felt like a sharp knife. It smelled like sea air. Down below, very far from the twelfth floor I was standing on, cars were hissing on the icy avenues. I would have liked to be the girl in the arms of King-Kong, to hop around town. I remembered Elizabeth's eerie apartment in Spanish Harlem, and Penny's dark rooms. Shivering with cold, I shut the window and got quickly into bed. The springs and the linen, the covers and the quilt made it feel like a nest of feathers resting on a cloud. With my little Kodak camera, I took a shot of my two feet up on the bedstead.

As I hurried to the dining room the next morning, Mary, still in her bathrobe, was already drinking her tea. The morning maid was younger than the one of the evening before. She was a niece of the other. As I left, Mary waved at me from a staircase going up to her study. From Mary's place, I was in the heart of town, minutes from the Metropolitan Museum, the MOMA, the Frick and the Guggenheim. I walked the few meters to Fifth Avenue and joined with the flow again.

At the Metropolitan Opera

Mary had reserved seats for "Othello" at the Metropolitan Opera. I had never been to the opera in my life. Renata Tebaldi was to interpret Desdemona. Mary had arranged dinner at home before with two lady friends, a writer who had written a novel called "The rise of the lark", and Beatrice, a short and grey-haired lady rather masculine in her ways but dressed in a flamboyant gold brocade long dress with ruffles and wide skirt. With her cold and piercing eyes, Beatrice reminded me of my Latin teacher. She seemed to know everything and neither Mary nor the writer dared argue with her. Beatrice could sneer also. I don't remember in which context, I happened to mention "turkish blue". The lady pointed at me her two damning dark round little eyes. "You mean "turquoise" she said dryly, reprimanding me. "Turquoise has nothing to do with Turkey", she said peremptorily. "I didn't know that either" Mary said lightly to save me.

To be in tune with my jersey dress, Mary had put on a long cotton patchwork skirt bought at a charity bazaar, with a black cashmere polo neck jumper. Next to her, her two friends looked overdressed. A black car with a driver engaged for the whole evening dropped us at the foot of the steps and we made our way through the elegant crowd. Inside, going up the vast staircase, Mary was waving and nodding nonstop. Our seats were in the seventh and fourth rows. We were not sitting the four of us together, but two and two. Mary sat with me for the first part, while Beatrice and her friend sat together behind us. Lights went off, the curtain rose and cymbals banged. A storm was gathering. A ship was coming into port. Standing up on the prow, Othello was saluting his people assembled on the quay, all chanting and celebrating his return. The wind was blowing hard, the sea was crashing against the pier and the boat. So this was opera, what a music teacher had tried long before to make me understand at school. A maelstrom of sounds, voices and sights and above it all, the miracle of chant made soul. Back home, Mary had taken me to her study where she hung her Miros. In front of it, a wide terrace opened, overhanging above Fifth Avenue on one side and 52nd street on the other. She wanted me to see the nice view, even if it was pouring rain.

On my last day, Mary decided to go with me wherever I wanted to. Wet umbrellas dripping, we took a crowded bus to the MET Museum. Her name, and the names of her relatives and husband were engraved in stone all over the hall walls in giant letters. All the same, she dutifully bought tickets to go in. As we puttered around the Museum shop, she asked me to choose something as a souvenir. I chose a silver brooch, a facsimile of a Celtic horse buckle. We went back on the bus again, this time so crowded that we had to grab the same leather handle standing up. Mary dominated the crowd by a good head, her face impassive but her eyes twinkling with irony. We made another stop at the Guggenheim and she grimaced a lot at the contemporary paintings on the walls. She preferred her Miros and Giacomettis. Before I left, she gave me the address of one of her nieces who lived in Berkeley where her husband taught philosophy. She would call her to tell her of my coming in April.

The alpine charm of Montreal

Before starting the long road coast to coast, I decided to go to Montreal, as a warm-up. I had called a Madame Racette, who rented rooms in the centre of Montreal. Her jolly old rural French sounded cozy. The bus was leaving from Boston late in the afternoon and the whole trip was by night. Around 10 p.m., we stopped at the border with Canada. A Customs officer came onboard asking if anybody had a non-American passport. I was the only one. I went down to get my passport stamped. The chief officer was a tall, blond, blue-eyed, Brit looking officer. He asked me what I was going to Canada for. I said I was going to visit Montreal for five days. The answer didn't seem to satisfy him and he kept asking what was the real reason of my trip. "You have a boy-friend in Montreal?" He finally suggested. I smiled and he took the smile for a yes. "That's it!" he exclaimed jubilantly, and he stamped the passport. As I hurried back on the bus, the whole team of Canadian officers waved at me.

From the bus depot, I walked to the house of Madame Racette. The snow was thick and high in the streets. Montreal felt like a town in the Alps. The white sidewalks creaked under my shoes. Houses and buildings were low and curved, giving streets an ancient meandering feel. Madame Racette was on foot, waiting for me. It was well past midnight. A small brunette with a Jackie style perm, her backcombed hair curling up around her neck, she was wearing a Chanel-like suit with a skirt tight on her thighs and a jacket open on a big bosom. Her B&B was her own home. She showed me my small single room and the common bath on the second floor. For breakfast the next day, she made me sit at a small table under the staircase, off the narrow entrance hall. As I ate, she talked with her son, lulling me with French-Canadian. Through the fanlight above the entrance door, the sky glistened like a blue sea. I coiled my six-footer scarf three times around my neck, buttoned up my jacket and, hand in my pockets, I went out.

The air was freezing but dry. It was tonic mountain air. Mount Royal dominated the city, high above the sloping streets. The white snow covered every inch of asphalt and roofs, and the Mount too. It felt like Chamonix. Amid red squirrels and birds running up and down spruces or racing on the snow, I walked up the mountain. As I was reaching the top, a guard in red jacket and Baden Powell hat, rose like an apparition from the other side, framed by blue sky and white snow. He was ambling along on his black horse. As I looked up, he took off his hat, smiled regally at me and swiftly took off, galloping. French Canadian was sweet to my ears, but people could not understand my French. They kept answering me in English. I went into a restaurant to have a hot soup.

At noon, the place was crowded with employees from the downtown offices. In a matter of minutes, they had all gone back to work, save a couple in front of me, against the wall. They were sitting close on the same bench, a large mirror glass above their heads. The man had his lips and dark moustache against the woman's ear, whispering while she licked slowly her spoon full of ice cream, every now and then scooping more when she had cleaned it. On top of her head, she sported a fur hat. She had long, fluffy blond hair. I couldn't see her face, which she kept bent towards the ice cream. Her jersey sleeves were pulled up on her arms. I couldn't make out the words they exchanged but I could sense the slow grinding of the man's whisper, his relentless courtship. The long pale face hiding behind the big moustache was getting nearer to the woman's face, and his torso was turning slowly. His fishy eyes were glued on her, but he glanced around now and then, like a rabbit on the alert. Getting nearer to the woman, inch by inch, his lips finally reached hers and they kissed passionately. The spoon fell on the table and her hands reached for his waist while he caressed her breasts. Suddenly, as if a clock had struck, they broke apart. The man waved to the waitress who brought the bill. He grabbed his attaché-case under the table, she rearranged her hair in the mirror and they both put on their coats. Since the movie was over, I left too. Montreal at dusk looked like a small town, with the whole repertoire of reds and violets of mountain sunsets. The city lights were as scarce as in Cambridge. I went back to Madame Racette, while melted snow was turning to ice. She served me dinner on the little table under the stairs. After that dreamy whiff of France, I was going west, the far one. My head was already in California.

Coast to coast

"Coast to coast", that was the magic mantra. When the bus left Boston, I was as excited as the pioneers, as thrilled as Kerouac. The wind blowing free through the giant plains seemed to echo the magic word, "West!" I had not read Walt

Whitman for nothing. His wide sweeping verses were just the right music for the huge flat land where the mountains had receded, like at low tide, far away into Colorado. Through the tinted glass, I was looking at the hail and snow falling on the endless highway merging with another, separating, merging again. To look at there were only car lanes, drab buildings and giant billboards, no human nor tree in sight. We were approaching Pittsburgh and smokestacks had the whole stage for showing off their fumes. There we would change driver and have a chance to go to the bathroom and eat a snack. I had put away Walt Whitman celebrations of America. We were now in the US, the country of hoboes and lost souls, toiling workers and people from everywhere.

Passengers were new in every city. There had been a flabby blond girl with swollen face and blue eyes that was called Marlene and dreamed to leave Ohio to go to the Hollywood of her pet TV programs. There had been a thin, dark-skinned Puerto Rican that looked at me all the time and kept me awake for hours at night from fear of his getting a little too near. A middle-aged lady in jeans and white sneakers, all frizzy hair like the Simpson sisters, smoking at every opportunity, and drinking coffee, which she pronounced "kaffee", at every diner we stopped. The diners were all the same with soft, greasy and salty food in gargantuan portions. In their cheap flashiness of metal, plastic and bulbs, they still had the mysterious appeal of lighthouses in the dark night. At all hours of night and day, bosomy waitresses in clean cotton whined orders to the kitchen and welcomed customers with "Welcome Ma'am!" or "Sir!" What do you have?" Plenty of trucks were always stopped at the diners. Their size and structure surprised me. Their height was unbelievable. With their multiple shiny metal pieces on the hood and the roof, they looked like Roll Royce caterpillars. Loneliness on the road felt formidable at times. And as formidable was the vastness of the plain in front of us, and the sky above us, belittling our size as individuals and our pains as well. At night, I looked at the stars unrivalled by any lights in the semi-desertic landscape. I had delved for months in the soul of Jay Gatz, a boy from Minnesota who had dreamt of the cities of the East to become "Gatsby". I had in mind that "Julien Sorel from Minnesota" invented by Francis Scott Fitgerald as the Midwest unfurled, huge and tedious.

After Ohio, the land was boundless and bare. During the day, I spotted a moose, a bird of prey, a rampant mammal. But the land was poor and colourless and the sky dull. We had entered the purgatory of the long voyage. My body ached from sitting so long, my limbs wanted to spread, my spine to lie flat. But I had to keep knees bent and back straight. When I gave in to sleep, at least I could rest my head on the cold glass window. The heat in the bus was so much that I could use my jacket as a pillow. The "kaffee" lady was still on the bus, going to Oakland. She was sitting right behind the driver. Her bass smoker's voice purred non-stop like the engine. She coughed sometimes and begged for "kaffee" anytime we approached lights on the road. I was now too tired. I didn't get off anymore. There was a toilet on the bus anyway. And we were off again, the faithful purr resumed and we were lulled again for another chunk of road. With the straight line of the road in front of us, stops every three hours at diners that seemed to have been planted just where needed, our existence was cut in chunks, with food, drink and bathroom the sole three acts of our sleeping lives. We were like babies in a cradle.

The sky was beginning to change imperceptibly, the smell of the air too. The road was still flat and straight but ghostly sombre masses appeared ahead. We were approaching Colorado. It was cold and snowy, with blue sky and shining rocks. The plain suddenly was behind us. A perky young woman who had fussed with her fat husband and baby non-stop since she had got on in Saint Louis was already up in the aisle to gather their coats and bags from the rack. We were arriving in Denver. It was my first stop after two days and two nights on the bus. I was spending the night at a cousin of

Kathie, my ex-host in Washington D.C. Carrie had married a French man she had met while spending a sabbatical in Paris. They were both teaching and living at the University of Colorado. She had told me that she would come to fetch me at the Greyhound depot. I just had to call. After the confinement of the bus, the light and the mountain air were a blessing. The campus was perched on a high plateau, all green and clean buildings. Their house was part of a housing complex built for the faculty. Twenty-four hours to breathe, walk and take a shower. The next day, I was on the road again.

Down to the Pacific was the last leg of the trip,. The bus felt as happy as I was, descending the Rockies under a sun that seemed invincible. I put on my sunglasses. At the foot of the mountains, the valley opened, lush and green and golden, true to Hollywood's best Technicolor rendering of the frontier saga. We stopped in Sacramento. I had a couple of hours to stretch before riding to Oakland. The tropical park in front of the State Capitol exhaled the scents and feel of paradise regained, after all those miles squashed like a tin sardine. The air was warm, tall palm trees floated their palms in the breeze, birds flew in schools and bees zigzagged erratically. Oranges had fallen on the grounds and I bent to pick one and feel it in my hand. If I had been through purgatory, this was heaven. Nothing bare, nothing cold, nothing grey and dull. Far from the wintry east, I had made it to the West, a land as big and elusive as its name. I kept the orange as a token.

After a few hours, we were in Oakland on the ocean. The sun was going down, infusing the air with gold. It was dusk but daylight was bright as fire and, because the sun was low, its rays reflected on faces and cars, even on the asphalt, beautifying everything it touched. On the huge parking lot, buses veered in all directions. But there was no bus to Berkeley before seven in the evening. I took a cab to Mary's niece.

Berkeley

The house of Mary's niece, Lucy, was a wooden chalet perched above the ocean on a steep piece of land. Yet, it was in the town's limits with Telegraph Avenue only a short walk away. Lucy was barefoot, in overall jeans with a pretty minute face half covered by huge glasses. All rooms in the house were empty save mattresses on the floor in the bedrooms, a rundown couch in the living room and batik cotton prints on the walls. Lucy had shown me the woody garret on top of the house where I would stay. Her voice was slow and patient while her two little daughters were shrieking and jumping around. The oldest, Gaby, nine years old, was studying me carefully but shyly while the baby one, Beryl, was horsing around and smiling. We had a slice of Lucy's cake and organic apple juice on a sun deck looking over the Bay side.

The round hills cascaded like a green herd down to the ocean. I was surprised by the gentle landscape after so much bigness and roughness crossing the continent. Berkeley felt like the Riviera with a tinge of the green mountains of Savoie. When the sun disappeared, we went into the big kitchen where a stew was simmering. Vegetables and fruits were spread all over the counters and the floor. The little girls darted away all of a sudden, yelling and clapping. Daddy was back. He had a boyish face with a small blue wool bonnet on his head. He was going to leave the next day for a lone hike in the hills. He sat on the floor of the kitchen and grabbed his guitar while Gaby crouched in his lap. Lucy had sat on the kitchen floor too with her knitting. Baby Beryl frolicked around. "I've built the house myself" he told me. "Henry is a carpenter besides being a philosopher" explained Lucy. The next morning, Gaby was crying hysterically as her father pushed her away to get into his car. "Daddy will be back" repeated Lucy softly, "He will be back in a few days". Tears turned to sobs as the little girl buried her face in her mother's lap. Soon they were off, Lucy walking Gaby to school and

Beryl coming along with a big basket for the errands they would make at an open market on the way back.

Shortly after, I was off too, striding along Telegraph Avenue towards the incongruous *"grand siècle"* iron gate. The gate was wide open and a flow of students went in and out. I merged in and wandered around the park. It was a real park with beautiful trees, flowers, benches and lawns where students spread like on a beach, kissing and rolling in the grass. Beyond, the San Francisco bay opened wide. The blue waters looked tame and enticing, like a summer resort where summer never stopped. I had taken off my sweater and, like everybody, I lay on my back on the grass. I pictured briefly the "French Berkeley" in my mind. I was now more than twelve thousands kilometres from it. Paris and France were in the Far East now. If I went on, navigating the Pacific Ocean, to Japan, to China, going on through the Indian ocean, and through the plains to the land of Gengis Khan and Alexander, one day I could see Europe and France again appearing on the west in the setting sun. Here in Berkeley, I was the farthest I had ever been from anywhere. If I settled here, my life would be entirely new. As a small cutting from a plant, I would grow new roots and develop new branches and flowers. I would be a new plant in my own right. It felt strange. I got up and went around Berkeley's grounds. Looking at the ancient gate from Telegraph Avenue, walking towards the campus had pleased me immensely. Inside though, the feeling was different but I couldn't make out clearly what it was.

Shadow of Arthur

The next day, Arthur was coming to fetch me. His massive frizzy hair was the same, so were his mocking blue eyes and his moon-like face, but he was much thinner. We got into his old car and went up the hill through a dense forest of eucalyptus and down to a long beach. Arthur was silent as we walked along the ocean. I took off my sandals and walked on the wet sand. A wave caught up with me, I was drenched. The water was icy cold and the currents certainly deadly. Arthur was friendly, but he seemed estranged. On a bored tone, he mentioned his research, his new girl friend. His eyes, I could see at close range, were not really smiling. It was like a reflex, his eyelids contracting as if blinking in the sun. His gaze was haggard. We went on to a park in town where we laid in the grass. "Have you ever taken mescaline?" he asked me out of the blue as I had shut my eyes, basking in the afternoon sun. "Mescal is an old Indian drug, they took it to explore themselves and the cosmos. You should try it."

The Chinese restaurant he took me to was crammed with Chinese families celebrating the marriage of a daughter. They were all dressed up with black ties and lacy dresses. We sat near the door while they made merry with high-pitched voices. The Chinese diversion was welcome. I didn't have much to say to Arthur. Whatever spark there had been when we had walked all night in Georgetown two years before was gone. He drove me back to Lucy's and when I kissed his cheek, I was surprised how cold it was. "Well" Arthur said as I was getting out, "If you are to do your Ph.D. at UC, I'll see you again". His car rattled away. I felt sad all of a sudden. I looked up at the starry sky. Times were changing, and people too. But without the lure of Arthur from Berkeley, would I have ever come that far west? I wondered.

A lucky charm against the evil eye – San Francisco

The next day I went to San Francisco. The shape and plan of the city by the sea was simple and intricate at the same time, like a sprawling village built daringly on an undulating peninsula with vertiginous slopes. I headed for Ferlinghetti's bookshop, "City lights", and bought *"Howl"* by Allen Ginsberg, another idol of Arthur. Following my whim, I found myself in Chinatown. I bought a box of tea, a red and green cylinder that, as I was told later, was the type of box students used to keep their stocks of marijuana. The district was dark like a cellar and damp like a rural town by a river. Near the adorned Chinese wooden gate on Grant Avenue, I entered a restaurant. A line of dead ducks hung on a string in the shop-window lit by a line of naked bulbs. The restaurant itself was in chiaroscuro behind the pallid dead flesh. Behind a counter, a few women and men stirred into big pots and cut on boards, their eyes turned inwards, like automatons. A greasy and sour smell pervaded the whole place with the steam from the pots floating around in little clouds. Suddenly, I felt nauseous. My head was swimming. I wanted to throw up. I had not ordered yet. I got up and fled.

I went down to the harbour. The block-wide warehouses were abandoned. It smelled fish and salt. Birds hissed and cried in the sky. An old wooden boat was moored for show, its old masts mingling with the tall buildings on land. The sun beat hard on the bay. I looked for shade in a small bazaar that was beginning to root itself in one of the abandoned warehouses. I got a sandwich and went to sit on a stone near the water. A street vendor had put his stuff on a shaky stand nearby. He was not American and didn't speak English. But he made it up with a lot of gestures. I picked a blue glass marble on his stand, bigger than any marble I had seen. It was a composite of king blue, sky blue and white. I liked it in my palm. The vendor held out his hand, offering me a leather boot lace and mimicking with his other hand the gesture of tying the lace around my neck. I did as told. The big marble was a glass eye, a lucky charm to keep away the evil eye. But this I didn't know yet.

Carmel in the clouds

The next day was cloudy and damp. It was a long ride to Carmel and, when I arrived, it was drizzling as densely as in Brittany. The place looked deserted and all the prettiness of the houses shut until the summer could not do much to make the town alive. The waves broke powerfully against the rocks. I walked along the white beach festooned by the deep green of cypresses. Along the river, which flowed into the ocean, a white horse grazed, shaking his thick mane and running in the high grass on sudden impulses. The sky was still cloudy but with wide patches of glinting silver where the cloud cover was thinner, lighting the beach like a lamp. A gleaming white little tower emerged from the green grass. I figured it was the Spanish mission, a surprisingly minute construction.

The wind was cold and I was glad to sit on the south side of the chapel for a while, sheltered from the wind. Carmel made more sense now: the pastures, the river, the bell tower and the powerful slap of waves breaking on rock and sand. The changing grey sky gave a dark tragic lustre in tune with the deadly Spanish invaders that had brought their crusade to these Pacific shores. When I left Carmel in the afternoon, the streets were as deserted as in the morning. All the wealth accumulated in the sumptuous villas had not been able to do more than mummify the place. On the ride back, the day was ending in a slow fade-out. In Oakland, night had fallen. The bus to Berkeley left right away, but Lucy's house was a fair walk from the depot, and it was already dark. I took a cab. The driver was black with a face like eaten into by acid. Its colour was uneven and myriads of lumps dotted his cheeks and forehead, even his eyelids. The apples of his eyes were enormous, with a shining blue line around it. His upper lids fell down like awnings and his lower ones fell down also, uncovering blood red tissue. The white of his eyes was yellow. He wore a hat and looked at me like the wolf at little red riding hood. "Where are you from?" he asked, looking at me in the mirror. "From France" I said dryly. "I used to have three women, you know", he informed me for no reason. I asked him to let me off at a corner, hoping to find my way. I paid and got off, going down a oneway street on the left. The streets of Berkeley were dark and sloped. Seconds later, he could not see me anymore. I heard his engine roaring away.

"Che sera, sera"

Next day was the day. Walking on Telegraph Avenue felt like a rehearsal of months and years to come. I would stroll there every day. I spotted the mansion-like faculty building, with vine climbing on its walls. My appointment was at twelve. It was only five to. I went up white steps and was directed to the upper floor by an employee in the hall. The staircase was wide and stately, a world away from the Berkeley hairy free speakers. I was told by a secretary to wait and sit on a chair while she went to announce me to the Professor. He was engaged in a phone conversation. I could hear the sound of his voice, uttering brief onomatopoeias as if trying to get politely off the phone. When I heard a generous exclamation of thanks and good-bye, I straightened my back and worked a faint smile on my face. The Professor came out, his eyes looking at me as if not seeing me. He talked to his secretary. Tall, blond, portly, with a pink Rubens complexion, curled hair and pointed beard, he had the incongruous allure of a 15th century courtier.

The secretary pointed to me with her chin, recalling him his appointment. "Yes, yes, of course" he said hurriedly. As a welcoming smile, his very small blue eyes engulfed in fat turned from round balls to slits for a split second. He bowed slightly, holding out his right arm to show me the way into his office. The blue Riviera sky and a magnolia with birds chirping appeared in the frame of the large window, wide open. I sat, legs crossed, in front of his desk. I spelled out my little ritornello once more. Stendhal and Fitzgerald, my BA's, my MA, Nanterre and Harvard, Wellek and Levine, pouring all the cream I had in stock to convince him. He listened with a faint smile and opened slowly the file where the secretary had put my letters and application. My head had been cut already months ago I sensed it immediately. But like a beheaded duck walking, I kept talking, delineating the courses I was planning to take, the pursuit of my French-American comparative studies. The Professor kept smiling non-stop. Official answers would be given to applicants the following month of June only. But he was telling me ahead of time, terribly politely, that there would not be enough room for me. The Comparative Lit graduate programme could only accommodate twelve students per year. Priority was given to the Berkeley undergraduates and to minority students. But who knows? Maybe the next academic year, or the next after the next, maybe an opportunity would arise. He sighed and looked out of the window absent-mindedly. Promises are free of charge. Blood was going up to my head, my mouth was dry, my tongue stuck. My feet got up.

I was out again in the radiant sun. Berkeley was gone. It was past already, a stop on the way. But where was my way going? My scenario was rejected. I walked out of the campus. On Telegraph avenue, flights were advertised on boards outside on the sidewalk. At random, I entered a shop and came out a wink later with a Loftleidir ticket New York-Paris. I moved along with the carefree crowd on Telegraph avenue. A self-styled gaucho sold me two carved leather belts on the sidewalk. *"The moral of the story, the moral of this song is one should never be where one does not belong"* Bob Dylan's rattling voice and harmonica came up to my ears. *The Ballad of Frankie Lee.* A trip is a trip is a trip, no more, no less, I thought. The next day, I left on the Greyhound again. This time I was going meandering for the sake of it, but I was going back to France again ultimately. I would not go back through the harsh and desolate plains of the Midwest. I would never go back to California.

Disneyland

The slanting California sun illuminated everything and everyone at ground level, but darkness fell fast as if someone switched off the light on the set all at once. The city bus was going along Harbor Boulevard, all lined with the blinking neon signs of hotels and motels. Families yawned after a long day at Disneyland, flushed and giggling, and eating candies. I stood up in the aisle to get a chance to evaluate the hotels we stopped at while people got off the bus. They all looked terribly posh, but I had to make up my mind. I was now the only one aboard with the driver who went on yelling hotel names, slowing down and looking in the mirror to see if I was ready to get off. A creepy wood shack with the letters *"Sunshine Motel"* glaring sheepishly was the last outpost before the boulevard got lost. I jumped in the dark while the wayward lighthouse of a bus sailed away.

    I crossed the boulevard and went under the stingy garland of naked bulbs. A no-colour, no-face guy was standing up behind the counter, his empty eyes turned towards me. "Can I have a room?" "It's thirty dollars payable now" he uttered while grabbing a key on the board. With their wall windows, rooms looked like big TV screens. When the light was on, people appeared like shadows. A guy, a couple, it was disturbingly easy to understand who was inside. I decided not to take any chance. I did not switch on any lamps, groping my way around in the glare of an outside light. I took a shower in the dark and slipped between the sheets, watching the big glass window. Since I had no car parked in front, hopefully the villains would assume there was no one inside. Night would go by, willy-nilly. In the morning, all cars had left and light made everything pretty. This was a perfect day for Disneyland. Hundreds were already queuing up in front of the booths.

    The asphalt esplanade spread like an airport. We had to trample like sheep before taking off in silly-land. After a few hours, I had enough. Another bus was taking me away. California and the West were behind me now, forever. I had put around my neck the blue glass bead from San Francisco.

Phoenix in the dark

The south route I had chosen to go back east was slow. It lingered through the desert. On my way coming, the plains of the Midwest sometimes had seemed dead, grey and flat, but, here and there, animals sprang or birds took off. But in the sandy rocky flats of the Mojave, nothing seemed to live, save rampant reptiles. All passengers were dozing along with the purring bus when suddenly a big bang startled everyone. "Fire" yelled a woman. We all turned our heads. A black lady in the back had got up, running up to the driver, screaming. We stopped. The driver was a very tall guy with a long neck and a very small head perched on top. He straightened his Greyhound cap on his head and took the matter in his expert hands. He went down last after having called his Greyhound General. The ship was in bad shape. Smoke still came out thick from the exhaust. The black lady had walked a good distance from the bus, as fast as her high heels and long mink coat could allow her. The driver was standing up tall, his arms wide open as if to protect us from evil. We had to wait on the narrow berm while the super trucks went by honking like organs. The spring air was very warm already but the lady felt cold in her mink and the driver patted the mink to pacify her. The driver tried hard also to put up a good show, but he was tired. I could tell from the sweat on his forehead and his drawn face. "Everything will be all right" he was saying every minute, with a slight smile and his hands lifted like for a blessing. Another Greyhound appeared in the distance and we all started to wave frantically like summer camp children. In no time we were off. Our valiant driver stood up erect next to his bus that he could not abandon, saluting us again and again with both his hands up.

Phoenix had a bizarre name and nothing attracted me there, other than the comfort of people I had on my list of good Samaritans. Downtown was hot, dusty and glaring with stocky mustachioed men in sombreros and signs in Spanish everywhere. I got out of the cab in front of a low house that looked completely shut. But I had called an hour before, there had to be someone in. The bell I pressed made no sound outside and no one seemed to move. It was maybe still siesta time. A tall and strong woman with a heavy helmet of hair opened the door. "Come on in!" she said with a stentorian voice. Her husband came up from behind, frail in comparison, with soft eyes that followed every whim or hint of his wife. After the blinding sun, the house was plunged in darkness, like a cellar, but all carpeted. It was cold too. The air-conditioning was on at all times. I was shown my room and we shared a drink. Husband and wife were dressed the same with red velvet cotton jumpers and polyester pants, ready to go to a barbecue party. I was left with the fridge to visit at leisure and the TV to watch. The area was but a long line of houses along the road. At least, I could have a shower. I was still a long way from New Orleans.

New Orleans under the rain

All through Arizona, New Mexico and Texas, the throng of round and dark Mexican-Americans was big at every stop. The land was parched and brownish, uneventful and dull, but for the grace of the moving sun drawing lines and contours, like sparse bits of a giant puzzle. I would have to sit for a day and a night and still another day, but I could not care less. In fact, I relished the bus. It knew where it had to go and I was in its hands like a child. I did not have to think nor decide. We were going somewhere, no matter what, living by bits, naps and snacks, wherever the bus decided. The bus was never empty, not even a quarter empty. People came up and down at every stop. An old lady with a delicate face and funny little hat had smiled when I had told her I was French. Her voice lingered and went up and down as a melody. Her father was French she said, he had died long ago.

From Texas on, hard rains started falling non-stop. The land was not dry or rocky anymore. For miles on end, rich green grass spread in all directions. As we got to the gulf of Mexico, the land was flooded. Only the narrow road, shiny black, emerged. We splashed through pools coming up the wheels and the rain did not stop. Here and there, immense trees sprouted above the grey-green waters, turbaned in masses of that strange witch hair-like vegetation, Spanish moss. We passed the strangely named Corpus Christi and Bâton Rouge. The rain had stopped in New Orleans, steam oozed from the warm asphalt. A city bus dropped me on a tranquil avenue shadowed by tall African trees.

The Hotel Columns sat proudly above a green lawn, its Greek neo-classical front flanked with the promised columns, its white paint flaking here and there. I went up a curvy flight of stone steps into a vast hall. The house had not been altered at all, only abandoned as a home and emptied of its furniture. Rooms were absurdly tall and large with high French windows. They let out a sour smell of mold and past. In the morning, the grass was dripping with heavy dew and the tree leaves wet and shining. There were lots of mosquitoes and I had been bitten during the night. Birds flew around the giant trees with shrieks and trills. The hotel had only a dozen rooms for rent and very few customers in April. Breakfast took place in the original dining room on a salvaged mahogany table. A couple with a small child was sitting at one end discussing and jotting notes as I came in. They had just arrived in the US. A Copt from Egypt, the man was fluent in French. His wife was a sturdy Irish woman. She had gone off in a hurry to search for a home to rent. He had stayed with the baby. "I would love to find a house just like this one, full of family and history", he said, looking up appreciatively at the high ornamented ceiling.

Disneyland had showed me a mock face of New Orleans in reduction, complete with black men sporting boater hats and playing the trumpets and black ladies in crinolines loafing on a gaudy replica of the French quarter. In the real one, there were very few people around and the houses were pretty and fragile like pieces of gauze and lace. The town seemed beyond the grave, quiet in its after-life. Books were spread on stands outside a shop under an arcade and I started to go through them. They felt reassuring on that trip, as if armfuls of books were a reassuring continuity. I was going back to France for the second time. After that, I had no real plan anymore.

I had bought a dozen more hurt books, Edgar Allan Poe, Nathaniel Hawthorne, Thoreau. I now had to drag them back on the bus, all the way to Boston and to Paris. I had chatted with the shop owner that seemed to have all the time in the world. He had offered to package the books so I could mail them direct to Paris. It felt strange to mail those books to Paris, ahead of me. The shopowner carried the box for me to the Post office a block further. I sent the books by surface mail. It would take a month at least for them to travel. I would be in France long before them, I realized.

Martha at Duke University

Just when my castles in America were collapsing, Martha remained proof that they had existed. She had been in France when I was building them and, thanks to her, I had been an American in Paris, speaking English on the street. Over more than a year, we had become sisters in exile. Martha was now at Duke for a special program on French teaching methods. The coming fall, she was due to take her first post in Georgia. Her sister Rita was finishing her BA in German at Duke too before going back to Munich to marry her German boyfriend.

Duke was an impressive vegetation of spires and gargoyles, of gothic towers and princely tropical gardens, like Harvard turned Angkor-Vat. The campus was a colony out of the world, surrounded by green lawns and woods for miles on end. Martha was driving nonchalantly a big Dodge. We were far away from Paris and *"La Salamandre"* and she laughed while we recalled the girl in the movie, chewing gum and bumming around. Why not apply at Duke? Martha suggested gently as we were walking through the giant lawns. No, I was now leaving. For all the dreary lack of future ahead of me, I had surrendered to that powerful current taking me back home. Did anyone ever ask salmons why they swam back?

The Brattle theatre

The Brattle Theatre, the Cambridge cinematheque, had become my haven, against the sadness of leaving and the endless vacuity of last days. For two weeks, I sat in the dark from noon to night. When I got out, it was dark too and I was grateful for another day gone by in movies. At the first show at noon, the theatre was empty. I chose a seat in the middle of the second or third row, to be right in front of the middle of the screen, head low and feet up on the seat in front of me, ready to plunge into the first soul that bared itself on the screen. The knight of the seventh seal, the blue angel, the mutineers of the Bounty, any Truffaut, any Godard, any Lubitsch, any Wilder, they all took away my pain.

A long way back

The flight back took two days. The plane from Boston had circled for an hour above Kennedy airport, waiting for a slot. I had missed my connection to Paris. With eighty kilos of luggage, I had pushed one by one my two huge suitcases, a few meters at a time to keep my eyes on the first while I moved the second. Alarmed by that mountain of luggage, my Stetson hat and my shell-torn US army jacket, Loftleidir had put me on an Air France flight free of charge, but bound for Copenhagen where I had to change flight again. I remained stranded in the Danish airport for a whole day, forbidden to go through Customs since I was a transit passenger. I arrived at Orly Airport in the evening, nauseous and exhausted. No one waited for me at the airport. I didn't wait for anything or anyone either.

BACK TO FRANCE 2

Home, sweet no more, home - Reporter at l'Express - Researching cockroaches - Picnic with the MLF feminists - Lunch and disgrace at the Fouquet's - A night with SOS Médecins - Back in limbo again - Researching at the Bibliothèque Nationale – Becoming an English teacher

Home, sweet no more, home

I was back to my childhood. Same bed, same room, same street, same parents. But I was not the same girl. I had room and board at their home, but they didn't expect my stay to go on forever, neither did I. At twenty-two, I was the only child still at home. My sisters and brother had left already.

Every day, the postman was bringing loads of books. They arrived from New Orleans and from Cambridge in tatters. The cartons had been ripped to shreds and the books arrived in big sacks that the postman, grumbling, dumped like potatoes on the entrance floor. My parents grumbled too. Because I was going around barefoot, because I was wearing patched-up jeans, because I was sporting a buffoon US army jacket, because I was listening to music on earphones, because I took too much room. My father rolled up his eyes, my mother recriminated and I watched them, thinking they looked like James Dean's parents. But I had no intent to be a rebel. My only cause was to be on my own as fast as possible. It made no sense for me to play the child and for them to play parents. After twenty years raising four children, they had a right to peace and privacy. And I would not stay home as an aging little girl.

The money amassed with lessons and translations in Cambridge was not over yet. I bought a record player on which I could pile up three LP's, playing one after the other for two hours of music uninterrupted. I bought a pair of earphones and I started listening to music day and night like way back in Cambridge. Before I left, Mike had let me choose all my favourite records and had given them to me. Bruckner, Brahms, Haydn, Schubert and Verdi's Othello with the libretto. I had brought back Nina Simone also, and Jefferson Airplane and Bob Dylan. I lay on my bed, eyes shut, sometimes opening my eyes and seeing the irate face of my mother who had been trying to talk to me for god knows how long. The walls of the apartment, the façades on the other side of the street and the back gardens felt like the appalling horizon of a jailed man. Nothing would ever change. Paris could never be an escape. Any walk was a repetition of the past. Even Nanterre had lost its murky attraction. I now knew the detours and the limits of the little campus. If anything, the campus only aroused regret for my having failed to get to its onetime twin, Berkeley. In 1973, students were not stars anymore. Watergate and the oil crisis filled the papers and fuelled anxieties. Anna Karina in Godard's *"Pierrot le Fou"*, walked on a Saint Tropez beach, repeating as a mantra *"Qu'est-ce que je vais faire? J'ai rien à faire".*

Reporter at L'Express

What was I to do indeed? I had to do something. My savings were melting like butter in the sun. I liked to write, but I was not the only one. If I wanted to make money writing, the most obvious career was journalism. I had pressed my mother to call a journalist, Jean-François Revel, a youth friend of hers. The guy was powerful, writing features and editorials for *L'Express*, a French news magazine, the first of its kind in France. I had declaimed to him my love of America, of American literature and American affairs. All this with good reason: Revel was a specialist on America, having published a best-seller, *Ni Marx, ni Jésus*, analyzing the US youth movement and its radical differences with the '68 French one. He was part of my new plan. If he could get me an internship at *L'Express*, I could maybe get another internship at Time or Newsweek and launch a career in the US. Luckily, he had liked my enthusiasm. *L'Express* did hire interns for the summer. He had talked to Rémy Grumbach, editor-in-chief who had looked at my short biography, returning it with his scribbled comment: "How can one reject someone that likes so much Scott Fitzgerald?" Luck could strike for any reason, but Fitzgerald was an unexpected one. I was granted a three months internship starting on June 1st at *L'Express*'s headquarters on rue de Berri, off the Champs Elysées, another turf for hookers and lovers of small bars.

I now sat behind a table in a corner of the chief copy editor's office, a stern and silent guy scribbling and talking on the phone all day and also on Thursday nights when the weekly edition was put to bed. Once a day only, around noon, he got up when his girlfriend came in. That was to go and lie down at the "California", a posh hotel next door. He took his plump mistress in his arms, kissed her passionately, both hands on her hips, and they both went out, locked in each other's arms. I looked sideways, so did his two assistants sitting behind their table at opposite corners. One was a shorthaired blond woman with a big mouth, in charge of typing, deleting or inserting non-stop bits of text in the magazine. The other was a perky little man who seemed to jeer at me behind his silent lips. He thought that I was a protégé of the chief editor, hence a despicable creature who had pulled strings. My work to begin with was to proofread and to look for suitable quotations to put on the front cover. After a month, I was moved to a specialized team in charge of *"culture et société"*, an alluring title for mild heteroclite subjects.

In August, Paris was empty like a schoolyard after classes and summer was hot on the asphalt. I was alone at home as on the street. Every morning, I woke up early when it was still cool and got on a deserted bus. I stepped off on the Place de l'Etoile, going down the Champs Elysées Avenue, sunny and vast like a Britton beach. The grand sun splashed the vast perspective, but the rue de Berri simmered in the dark all day, too narrow to catch daylight, quiet like a street in a provincial town.

Researching coackroaches

I was now a reporter, sent on assignments. The subjects were discussed weekly at a meeting of the five-strong team for *"culture et société"*. Jean Claude, the recently promoted head, smoked giant cigars, filling the little meeting room with smoke. Each journalist, three men and two women, had his or her subjects territory, well circumscribed. I was given the fillers.

During the summer, rat and cockroach exterminations were at their peak in Paris. My best remembrance of cockroaches was Elizabeth's Spanish Harlem apartment where they congregated at night like pilgrims at Mecca around food crumbs dropped on the floor. Jean Claude had decided that it was a fun and informative subject, perfect for the holiday mood. No one had budged, so I had been assigned for reporting on cockroaches. After calling half a dozen cockroach-exterminating companies, one had finally agreed to take me on a round for an entire day. I had gone to their offices in Boulogne. It was a family business. The old father had explained to me the basics of the job, the chemicals used. He had become lyrical about the armies of "blattus" and rats they had to combat without respite from condo to condo, from block to block, like in guerrilla warfare. Rats like cockroaches were terribly prolific and terribly resilient and relentless vigilance was necessary. The fiercest one was the "blattus germanicus", an enormous black terminator cockroach complete with super helmet and antennas. Founder of his business, the old guy was a pro and a preacher, relishing his yearlong crusades. His only son, a gaunt and giggling young guy, was destined by birth to inherit the business, and with as much enthusiasm as many a crown prince. He had decided to take it as a pastime. Unlike his father, he was not going to put his hands in the dirt. He would be a clean and up-to-date manager. As a reporter from *L'Express*, I was welcome since

I could give some much-needed glamour to a rather tedious job.

    We both got aboard a little van with a technician in blue overalls that would officiate with the heavy pump. We started the round of apartments, breaking carelessly into people's privacy. They looked at us, slightly annoyed and impressed, as if we were a kind of commando they had to let in. The exterminations were done at the request of condominium managers. The tenants didn't like it. The technician put in place his tubes and wires and sprayed floors and cupboards, crawling behind pipes, in dark closets and corners. Some doors remained closed, the tenants had gone off on holiday and the concierge had no key. That meant a safe retreat for enemies that could build up again their armies.

    All day, thankfully nobody had paid any attention to me. I followed in the steps of the boss and the technician. Early afternoon, I had enough material to write my article. We had one last job to do on Boulevard Richard Lenoir. The client was an old lady. She was fastening her robe when she opened her door, her hair in a net and her feet in slippers. She adjusted her glasses on her long aquiline nose and examined our faces as we entered. The enormous apartment was antiquated and in need of new paint, with rooms and rooms in an endless row. The lady followed close on our heels. "Who is this?" she asked the young boss all of a sudden, pointing her chin at me. "Madame is researching on cockroaches" he said, " She is doing a reportage." "A what?" exclaimed the old lady, her voice choking. "A reportage" said the boss, instinctively going backwards as the lady seemed ready to bite. I was behind him. "What? This lady is a journalist? What does this mean? I don't want a journalist in my house! Out!" She was still screaming as we ran down the stairs.

Picnic with the MLF feminists

After May, which had become the month for protests of all kinds, June was quieter and devoted to seminars and conferences all over France. The *Mouvement de libération des femmes*, the *MLF,* had been launched in the wake of May 1968 when the girlfriends of radicals had suddenly realized they were ruthlessly ignored and exploited by their guys. Gay female pride and abortion had become their two big battles. Before busy holidays, they were holding a three days meeting in the countryside, not far from the city. That was my next assignment for *L'Express*.

I was interested in the French feminists. So far, it had been an American experience for me. I had read Kate Millett's *Sexual politics*, Germaine Greer's *The female eunuch* and I had listened to Susan at Nanterre explaining to us the progress of Women's Lib across America. The June day was almost too much, too beautiful and too hot, as I looked at Paris in the haze from a slow and empty suburban train in mid-morning. Two girls in shorts with long hair had come to pick me up at the station with a rundown Peugeot 201. The *MLF* had rented for the summer a dilapidated house in the middle of pastures where herds of bovines were quietly grazing. Women ambled around naked or half naked. With the heat and remaining dew, the grass smelled wonderful with a faint hint of dung.

The participants were varied. The core group was a known one, organizing events and stunts since 1968. Their leader, A., was a very masculine woman, older than the rest, in her forties. Stocky and short, she was dressed in a pantsuit and her frizzy hair was cut straight above the neck with sideburns. Her laced shoes had thick heels. As she went around, she moved her body and swayed her shoulders like a guy. The girls were preparing a huge picnic on long trestle tables. It was high noon and the sun scorched badly. Naked bodies were turning red. The rumor had gone around that a journalist from *L'Express* had come to the gathering. Involuntarily, I was to be the first item on the agenda of the meeting. I had confessed unashamedly. After which, the leader had concluded that some publicity was not so bad for *MLF*, provided they had a look at the article before going to press. Democratically, they had taken a vote with raised hands. I had been accepted with a slight majority.

The weather dictated a rather slack agenda. After barely an hour of meeting, a break was taken to eat and drink and frolic. No list of issues to discuss, no preparation of a protest or program, no motion or conclusions. The agenda was more Club Med' than activist cell. But actually, each participant, as far as I could see, had her own agenda. Anna, a model pretty girl, admirably tanned with tight and round breasts as perfect as Gabrielle d'Estrée's, was walking in her wide hippy skirt, her hair stylishly tied in a Greek scarf with sequins. She held a basket on her hip like a medieval washerwoman, filled with leaflets on abortion. But her leaflets were not for free, she was selling them with as much gusto as little girls selling cookies. A much older lady in her late fifties had been my most vocal advocate when the group had considered throwing me out. With her proper suit and permed hair, she looked discreetly conventional. She felt in sync with feminism because of the two men in her life: her husband and her lover. The husband was impotent but she liked him, the lover did not mind a measure of independence, the unorthodox arrangement was known by all parties and agreed. She spent afternoons with her lover, and always slept at home with her husband.

After lunch, we were all gathered under a splendid oak tree while a herd of young bulls, trying to find some shade as well, had flocked against the fence separating us, watching us with wide eyes. A. was sitting legs crossed like a boy-scout in the center, soliloquizing like a preacher. A pioneering feminist in France, she was also an aspiring psychoanalyst and a publisher, founder of a publishing house run by women and publishing only women writers. She spoke with a southern accent and a soft enticing voice. A. was reflecting about the freedom for women to be whom they wanted. Her own sister, she said, was a hairdresser. She always had wanted to be a hairdresser and that was fine. There was no reason for everybody to be an intellectual.

As everyone was lying on the grass, listening absent-mindedly to A.'s lulling logorrhea, a trio of women in black arrived, arm in arm. The woman in the middle was terribly thin and unstable on her feet. The two others held her tight. A few weeks before, I learnt, that woman had been paralyzed, unable to walk or even to stand up. Psychoanalysis had miraculously cured her. She suddenly had got up and walked like the paralytic in the Bible, appearing with her *MLF* friends in a trendy restaurant.

The arrival of the three women in black had signaled dusk and a perceptible change in the game. The air was cooling and a light breeze rustled through the oak. The young bulls had gone away. The naturists had put on clothes and many women were putting on make up and brushing their hair. Dinner was to be served indoors followed by music and dance. The last train to Paris was long gone, but the double-love lady had offered to give me a ride back to Paris. In the warm night, the atmosphere was turning partyish. Women were dancing rock'n roll. Looking on, A. was sitting backwards on a chair, like a man, arms resting on the back. A slow song started and she got up. She bowed very manly in front of a pretty woman in a chiffon dress who had told me earlier that she had two children. A. was dancing slowly, her eyes half shut. She held strongly the young woman's hip with her left arm while her right hand was rummaging on her breasts. The woman blushed and looked around the room with embarrassment. She was the loved one that evening. In a matter of minutes, A. had become a conquering male, with the cunning and determination to possess her prey. I looked on, fascinated by the metamorphosis, like the one of Baron de Charlus courting the concierge, as described by Marcel Proust in *La recherche du temps perdu.*

The lady who had offered me a lift agreed it was time to leave. To get back to Paris, we had to cross the *Bois de Boulogne* and she was a little nervous at the wheel. The *Bois* was also renowned for its wild parties after dark. In the tiny Fiat 500, we kept silent. Not far from the "Cascade", a belle époque café in front of a waterfall in rockwork where people went for elegant drinks, we had to stop. A number of cars had stopped in the middle of the road. Amazed, we witnessed the strangest of ballets taking place in a kind of ring formed by the carhoods. After the heat of the day, fog was drowning the *Bois*. Tall beings draped in pastel scarves, faces painted like Pierrots and Columbines, stood up in the haze illuminated by car lights. They moved like swans and seemed to hold a meeting too, but as secret as the one held by the Doge of Venice. We watched for a while, mouth open. We could not go through. The Fiat swiftly went in reverse and made a quick U-turn towards the Porte Maillot. The lady dropped me on the Place de l'Etoile.

Lunch and disgrace at Le Fouquet's

The month of August was my third and last one at *L'Express* as an intern. After, I could stay freelance but I knew I had no chance against hundreds of experienced journalists. *L'Express* had a buffet dinner every Thursday evening, the day of the *"bouclage"*, when the final weekly issue was put to bed. Everybody talked to everybody in an apparently friendly atmosphere, filled with cigar smoke and a lot of scotch. The *"grand reporters"*, stars of the magazine, always came to that evening. We were neck and neck, but that did not mean a thing. If I did not see much future for me at

L'Express, I was toying with the idea of trying my luck with the rival magazine, *"Le Nouvel Observateur"*, a rising star, more radical and irreverent.

During those three months, I had barely seen Jean-François Revel, the very respected editorialist who had handed me the internship on a plate. The Watergate scandal had just burst out. He had been sent to Washington right away. But before the end of my internship, he had made a point of inviting me for lunch. We were going to *Le Fouquet's*, an extravagantly priced and famous restaurant, which I had seen only from the Champs Elysées sidewalk. The temperature had risen considerably that day, it was *"la canicule"* and people panted like dogs on the burning asphalt. Offices had no fans nor air conditioning and quite a few journalists had settled at the *"piscine Deligny"* anchored on the Seine. The managing editor was day and night at the Hotel California with his girl friend, popping in only when necessary. Revel had courteously come to fetch me in my minuscule office all glassed in, which I had hijacked from a high flying contributor of the magazine who never came in, the very sister of the editor-in-chief, Brigitte Gros. Revel was just back from Washington having landed early in the morning. After being kept in the back pages, the Watergate Opera was now opening on front pages and magazine covers everywhere.

As we walked under the red canopy, the old Maitre d' came up, bowing and whispering something in Revel's ear. The latter suddenly screamed "What?" he said, grimacing and fuming as if ready to bite and fight. "My secretary called for a table outside. I don't want to sit on a bench indoors with the gangsters." He wanted a table on the small terrace outside. *Le Fouquet's* indeed was a famed rendez-vous of top crooks and informers. The Maitre d' bowed again like a Japanese, waiting patiently for the furious tempest to calm down. We went to sit on a crimson velvet bench next to each other. It was warm inside, but pleasant in the rosy light filtered by the red awnings, certainly much better than frying outside, barely protected by scraggy and dusty box trees. Sitting in the sun, there were many Japanese and American tourists. When the chilled champagne arrived on the table, Revel began to mellow. As usual, he had set to bestow on me some of his extensive knowledge. Sipping *"Veuve Clicquot"*, I listened distractedly. He was explaining to me the meaning, and consequences, of an "impeachment" procedure, an awkward English word anglicised from the French original word *"empêchement"*. I read about President Nixon regularly but I was not particularly interested in the personage. I had foud funny his beatific face at the burial of Charles de Gaulle, as he confessed to TV reporters his elation at "History" hovering above him while the casket went by.

The meal had started with an entire *"foie gras"* washed down with a sweet white wine I had never had before, *Sauternes*. In spite of the heat, I felt very hungry and Revel, sleepless and still on US time, even more so. The main course was a melting although very rare *Chateaubriand* with a *Chateauneuf du Pape*. I had never drunk so many different wines in one single meal and never on such a hot day. There was no water on the table. Revel managed to devour the food while talking non-stop as if making up for the jet lag with mouthfuls of food. We finally wrapped the meal with cheeses, of which he ate a good pound, with yet another grand cru, a *Margaux* this time. He asked for the menu to choose a dessert. I still managed to eat the sherbet and almond cookie put in front of me. The buzzing *Fouquet's* had now quietened down. It was three past. Revel suddenly seemed tired. He stretched his arm towards me and turned flirtatious. "And now, tell me what you want to do in life" he said engagingly.

All those wines had made me slightly floating but also uninhibited. Head on, I declared that I did not find *L'Express* that appealing in the end. I considered *Le Nouvel Observateur*, the rival of *L'Express,* to be a much more interesting news magazine. Revel looked at me aghast, his face frozen, his round eyes petrified. He frowned as if incredulous *"Le Nouvel Observateur? Mais ça ne vaut rien!"*. I realized I had blown it. Trying to make it up, I proceeded laboriously to explain why I preferred *Le Nouvel Observateur* to *L'Express*. "The best thing to do is to go and work where you wish!" he said, throwing his napkin on the table. We drank our coffees. He paid the bill. We went out and parted on the Champs Elysées. He still looked like a dog ready to bite. A few years later, however, the same Jean-François Revel had become the top editorialist at *Le Nouvel Observateur*.

A night with SOS Médecins

On the 15th of August, Paris was at its lowest ebb, half its inhabitants away. This included medical personnel that left hospitals and clinics strongly under-staffed. In that situation, medical emergencies could turn into nightmares and *L'Express* wanted a first-hand account. I was to follow the whole night a doctor from *SOS Médecin*, a private medical emergency service people resorted to when public services could not cope. At nine in the evening, I boarded a Renault 5 with a young doctor. He had a phone in the car. We had to wait for the *SOS* desk to contact him. Our first assignment was in a south suburb. The patient was a coughing mechanic whose wife worriedly tried to contain the over-excitement of four kids, spying on us from behind a half open door. While the wife wringed her hands dramatically, the guy in his underwear obediently coughed. As the doctor wrote down the certificate of sick leave and a prescription for syrup, the woman seemed to hesitate between joy and tears. As soon as we were on the landing, we could hear the children screaming and running. The doctor smiled as we drove off. "Did you see all the suitcases stashed under the dining-table?" The family was ready to leave for its summer holiday. The father needed the sick leave to drive them all and have some extra holiday for himself. The only snag was the price to pay. SOS Médecin was not cheap and badly reimbursed.

The next call was not a joke. A woman had ingested a massive dose of barbiturates and had lost consciousness at the Hotel Commodore on Boulevard des Italiens. Her husband and son were waiting for the doctor in the reception of the rather showy hotel frequented by foreign tourists, due to its proximity to department stores and theatres. The woman, a peroxyded and permed blonde, was laying in a pink chiffon dress on a gold adorned king size bed, snoring sonorously, her heavy whale-like body rising up and going down staccato. The husband and son spoke broken English. They were from Praga. Just as they were ready to leave for a show in Pigalle, they had found her on the floor with an open tube of pills near her. The father, a stout man with a cold face, looked annoyed, but not terribly shaken. It was not the first suicide attempt of his wife. The teenage son, with his long disheveled hair, looked terrified. The doctor sounded the chest of the woman and poked in her mouth, lifting her eyelids. He called an ambulance and two bearers in white came up, placing swiftly the loose body on a stretcher. The lobby was quite busy as many of the hotel guests were going out in evening attire. Nobody seemed to pay attention to the stretcher. The ambulance started, its siren screaming while husband and son followed in a big Mercedes.

Around three am, we had stopped for a drink and a snack in a café on the boulevard. The doctor was in a good mood, that 15th August night seemed to unfold just like any other. Even the suicide attempt did not worry him too much. The woman would have her stomach pumped and she would be fine. Just as we relaxed with a *"croque-monsieur"* and a coffee, his beeper started to squeal in his pocket. He got up and went to the car to answer the phone and came back hurriedly. A newborn baby was in trouble. A panicked nursing aide had asked him to rush.

The small clinic was on a quiet street of Passy in the 16th arrondissement. The aide, a young girl, rushed the doctor to the labour room. The baby was lying blue and inert. The doctor took some blood, called the ambulance and in a few minutes had the baby transferred to a hospital. The parents were in a small adjacent room, waiting for news. The mother was already dressed, her eyes dilated, sitting on a chair while her husband held her shoulders. She wanted to get up and go wherever her baby had been taken. The young doctor was comforting them while they both looked at him as their only anchor in the abysmal nightmare they suddenly had fallen into. When they had arrived a few hours earlier at the clinic, there was no doctor. The delivery had been delayed until someone could come. Finally a doctor had come, and had left immediately after the baby was born. In a matter of minutes, the infant had turned bluish, a sure sign of a deadly cyanosis. Would their child be handicapped and maimed for life? Would he survive? The doctor comforted them. The situation was preoccupying, but babies were strong and he was in good hands now. As we were off in the car, I asked him if really the child would survive. Survive, yes, he was positive but there would be serious sequels and, yes, the child would be maimed for life. I was appalled and ashamed. The tragic birth was exactly the material *L'Express* was looking for. Journalism was definitely not for me.

Back in limbo again

Summer ended. For the first time, I had not taken any holiday. After my three months at *L'Express*, I was now idle in Paris. My feet felt heavy and my days, frayed. I had completed my two BA's and my MA at Nanterre. I had registered my project for a doctoral thesis on Katherine Mansfield, an uprooted life that interested me. I had toyed with the idea of going to New Zealand. The University of Wellington offered generous scholarships that few Europeans applied for. My chances were good to get one. New Zealand felt like the end of the world, in fact the exact antipode of France. I chickened out. I planned to go to London to the

British Museum Library, which had a good collection of Katherine Mansfield's manuscripts and most of the needed bibliography. But my priority was not to get a fourth degree. As prestigious as a doctorate in English literature could be, it would not be an asset to find a job, no more than my BA's and MA. At least, that doctorate could be an alibi. Having nothing to do in life did not sound good. But rather than studying, priority was to make money. Not much, being poor and frugal was no problem, but being totally penniless was. Even to take the subway, I needed money. It was as crucial as being able to walk for a child. To make a living one had to make money. If no money, no life.

The temporary typing stuff had been a good solution, but it alarmed me. I didn't want to be a typist forever. I had sold clothes at the *Bon Marché* one summer before, neither did I want to be a salesgirl forever. Those jobs were not only badly paid without any hope of much progress along the years, but they were absurdly, maddeningly repetitive. What could a girl with three degrees, three languages and a normally constituted mind hope for? Apparently, there was no other choice than to be a secretary or a salesgirl. I was not a lawyer, I was not an engineer, I was not an accountant. I was only literate and wanting to write, which didn't lead anywhere. A school friend had started a career in a publishing house owned by her uncle, another wrote book reviews for *Le Monde*. I was not blind, without friends or relatives in the right place to help, I would not get where I wanted. France was gradually becoming the place where I was born and raised, not the place I would grow. The doors opened, but there was nothing behind those doors, just other doors and finally, vacuum.

There was a tenuous, but tenacious, feeling that permeated the air I breathed, the Paris I roamed in, a feeling of impossibility. In my country, nothing felt possible for an individual. One had to rely entirely on family and social ties for work, for money, even for love. Husbands landed on your doorstep, brought by mothers or won at those balls, which were a marketplace of sorts. Helplessness drove me up the wall, but the worst was the absence of visible wall. I was battling in the dark against my own powerlessness.

Researching at the Biblothèque Nationale

Unexpectedly, a celibate aunt of mine, herself living a precarious life, handed me a job. She was a librarian and book researcher. The *Reader's Digest* had asked her to gather descriptions of landscapes in European literature. She had no time for it and she had secured the job for me. I had five months to scour the *Bibliothèque Nationale*. The offices of the *Reader's Digest* were on the Boulevard Raspail, plush and comforting. The woman editor who had interviewed me seemed prosperous and secure. I would have loved to ask her how she had got there. Her young assistant was smiling and friendly too, to begin with anyway. But when both women scented another bitch looking for a position, they switched off instantly. I was asked to deposit the texts and all useful references with the receptionist in the entrance hall. There was no need for me to go upstairs in the office.

Against the vacuum, the foggy obstacles that dampened any enthusiasm and left me like a blind man in the cold, the *Bibliothèque Nationale* was a haven. The rue des Archives was narrow and sunless. The traffic was heavy and the sidewalks too narrow to walk safely, but a stone throw further, the Palais Royal and the avenue de l'Opéra provided vast and airy space. I had nowhere to go, but for a while the *BN* was my stop. Going there with a bus, walking part of the trip, coming back in the evening, I had a line to follow, a path to tread, a direction and something to do. The employees, dressed like schoolmasters of the past with grey blouses buttoned down to their knees, had quickly identified me as a troublemaker. I usually asked for five to six books at a time, refilling a demand before I had given back the previous batch.

Widener Library had given me bad habits. My method was fast and efficient, I went quickly to the chapter or part liable to yield the type of text I needed to find. As a result, I could easily finish ten books in one morning. That was not tolerated at the *BN*. To kill time, I went to the bathroom, which was the only place to chat with the other readers. In the basement, the bathroom was vast and prettily art deco, which made it suitable to linger.

When it rained cats and dogs, I went to the café across the street, crammed with the specific fauna of the *Bibliothèque*. Middle-aged professors and a few young students, shabby and pale, were eating on foot a sandwich or a *croque-monsieur* at the counter, but mostly drinking, red or white *"ballons"*, round glasses of red or white wine. Their cheekbones turned scarlet and they chatted with the garcon before going back, dutifully, to the austere *BN*. In February, I was through with my work. I had assembled about thirty texts from hundreds of books. As prescribed, I had covered every European country, save Russia. I had tried Cholokhov and Paoustovski, but their evocation of nature and landscape were too fragmented to fit the format necessary to edit the collection of texts. *"Merveilles naturelles de l'Europe"* was to be published as an in-quarto book with photographs accompanying the various extracts. From Carinthia to Carelia, the French Alps, the Julian Alps, the Pyrenees, Andalucia, Galicia, Portugal, the gulf of Napoli, I had had a good time jumping on and off the many lands of Europe. Six months later, *"Merveilles naturelles de l'Europe"* was in bookshops with the woman editor credited with all the work.

Becoming an English teacher

Belatedly, Berkeley had sent a letter to offer me an assistantship in French with a handsome stipend of three thousands and five hundred dollars for the year 1974-1975. Why not? I wrote back accepting the job. They wrote again.

They were sorry, but I could not get the assistantship without having secured first admission at one of Berkeley's departments. I went typing again, but now I was paid as a bilingual secretary, hired for a week or two to type endless reports in English. Some companies seemed to have tons of secretaries but only to answer phones and sit pretty. They purred and squealed, they cried, they pretended to be mad, courted and teased like kittens by their bosses. Their working life seemed easy and lazy, but devastatingly boring.

I was beginning to consider teaching. With still dynamic demographics, there was demand for teachers in Paris. The perk of a teaching job was a long summer holiday and plenty of free time between classes. The maximum schedule was twenty hours per week. The pay was enough to fly solo, rent a room and earn my bread. I had applied for a post as an English teacher in a Catholic nuns' school in Sannois, a faraway suburb of Paris. The Mother Superior had accepted me after I had decared on purpose that I had been schooled in a convent school myself. Job and income, however modest, secure for the next fall, I decided that it was now time for a well-deserved a holiday.

Part II : Going East, Greece

GREECE 1

Colossus of Maroussi - Athens at first sight - High on the Acropolis - In the Athens bazaar - Sparta, a sibylline officer - Peace of the past: Epidaure, Olympia, Delphi - Crete – Aghia Galini - Alexandros of Phaistos - Along the Lybian sea - War - Freedom

Colossus of Maroussi

Standing up in the crowd at the *Gibert* bookstore, off Boulevard Saint Michel, I had picked up and started to read *Colossus of Maroussi* by Henry Miller. It was a rather dog-eared pocket edition I had grabbed at random in a mass of second-hand books for sale on the top floor. Not that I was especially attracted to Miller's works. I had been bored by both *Tropic of Capricorn* and *Quiet days in Clichy*. But *Colossus of Maroussi* was totally different. It started with a walk in the French countryside.

Miller was recounting his trip to Greece in the summer of 1939, just weeks before World War II. Curiously for me, the story started in Dordogne, right where I had spent my childhood summers, digging fossils and building huts. More surprisingly, Miller made the Neanderthal men and women who had first inhabited the region sound as if they were distant cousins of his. He had been blown away by the artistry and the intelligence of our near-monkeys ancestors. Both the artistry in the caves he had visited at Les Eyzies and the striking intelligence of that proto-man for choosing the Perigord land to settle on. The Dordogne for Miller was just a stopover on his way to Marseilles where he was taking a boat to Greece. He had not expected any revelation from the Dordogne, but there it was. The man of Neanderthal was the perfect introduction to the Greeks, ancient and new, he was going to visit.

People buzzed around me at the *Gibert* bookstore but I hardly noticed them, too hooked by my reading. Miller was now on a freighter eating cans of sardines and whatever he could find to eat free on the boat. The crossing to Piraeus had taken weeks, which Miller didn't mind at all. He liked preludes. The pocket book was in tatters and I had carefully put back in place its loose pages. It cost ten centimes, which was no insult to old Henry. I had gone on reading on the subway and I had arrived at the end of the book some hours later. I did not want it to end. I started reading it all over again.

I had read once upon a time the tales of Greek mythology. I still remembered the trysts of Zeus and the ire of Hera, the tragic story of Persephone, the strange birth of Athena coming out of her father's brain. But about Greece, I did not know a thing besides the eternal Parthenon and the movie *"Never on Sunday"* by Jules Dassin, starring Melina Mercouri. I knew too that behind the islands and luminous sky, there was a more sinister side to Greece. For all Melina Mercouri's lobbying, governments and media kept very silent. The dictatorship went on killing and torturing. The Greek Colonels, to say the truth, did not preoccupy me either.

Miller had been there long before the Colonels, in 1939, and long before Greece had become a catchword for holiday. *Colossus of Maroussi* had given me a reason to want to go there. If even the prolific Miller was at a loss for words to describe his wonder and love for the Greeks and Greece, there had to be something amazing there. He did not even talk about women the seedy way he usually did. Greek women made him stand still. He was in awe of their beauty and power. Rather than writing about sites and views, Miller evoked at length all the Greeks he met, the crooks and the shopkeepers, the boat captains and the card players, and the majestic Georges Katsimbalis, the friend of Miller, nicknamed the Colossus of Maroussi, whence the title of Miller's book. With all manners of strokes on his canvas, Miller conveyed the sense that Greece, in spite of its five thousand years history and language, was like a New World of the East with people from the Balkans, from the Levant, from the Near East and the Middle East, an unexpected melting pot where the original natives had not been exterminated. Miller was American but he had felt Greece to be his authentic home, the real cradle of Man that he had craved to find when slaving it in New York.

Athens at first sight

By that evening, I had decided. I would go to Greece to find out by myself if Miller was right. Since that summer of 1939, thirty-five years had gone by, but I was ready to take the risk. Not alone though. I did not know Greek at all and I did not know anybody I wanted to travel with. A travel agency had just started in Paris offering cheap tours and cheap flights. The tours were "self managed", which meant that there was no determined itinerary, participants could design the whole trip in the limits of a set amount. The group leader was not a professional tour guide but just someone who had already traveled a few times in the country. On the first of July, I went to Orly for the first time since coming back from the US. There were only girls in the group, twenty of them, save a couple on their honeymoon. It felt like one more school outing. But we were not supposed to stay together all the time. The self-management concept meant also going on one's own.

Like all of us, the group leader was in her early twenties and likewise eager to have a nice holiday. Out of the Athens airport, the sun was beating down hard while the rare locals looked struck with sleeping sickness. The motto of *Nouvelles Frontières*, the tour operator, was "get to know the locals", hence no special Pullman to carry us around. We got on a regular city bus, all windows down blowing hot thick air. It was a short ride along the shore before bifurcating into avenues lined with unfinished cement buildings and rundown brick houses. The asphalt was patched and punctured with holes as if war had been raging not long before and the rickety bus navigated as carefully as possible, not always able to avoid serious jerks. Although it was siesta time, the bus was full and we were all standing wherever we could, stumbling whenever the driver stopped abruptly or the bus hit a pothole. The Greeks on the bus were dressed in black or brown, their impassive faces watching us behaving silly.

As we were coming into Amalias avenue, I saw the Parthenon, a faraway planet floating up in the sky above a thick magma of yellowish cement. Syntagma square was the terminus. The driver opened the luggage compartment and I grabbed my Shopfeim rucksack, pretty blackish after the trip. The sun was setting on Athens like in California, a golden dust veiling softly the sky, the buildings and, across the avenue, the tall trees clustering behind the gates of the Zappeion. The Parthenon, now tinged with copper, sailed forth above in the distance, forgetful or forgotten by the city. It looked strange and inescapable. We had now switched to a trolley which leapt brutally now and then, making a rain of sparks when the trolley pole scratched the electric line. The crowd on the street was dense. Women wore scarves, tied all around the head, and black clothes. Men looked somber and dark. Morose mourning seemed to reign over Athens.

We got off at Omonia square. While Syntagma square was a succession of levels interspersed by large flights of steps, Omonia square was like a well sunk amid drab buildings. All sunlight had now gone and the intense activity under the weak streetlamps looked like from another age. People moved around the Square, stopping at minuscule makeshift shops lit by small lanterns. Faces lit from above or below sprouted like masks while darkened people progressed at a slow pace in diagonal or curved lines, but never in straight ones. Athens, at first whiff, smelled and felt like something different. Not Europe for sure, not Africa either, probably in the Orient. But what did Orient mean? This was no Russia, no India, no Middle East, no China. It was not either a dormant city of the past. However there was that Parthenon, flying high above Athens. The past had been put once and for all above and out of the real city, leaving it to live its pulsing existence.

Our hotel was a 1930 Art Déco building on Pireos avenue, the main axis going all the way to the port of Piraeus. The room was hot from a long day of sun, in spite of shutters playing the role of blinds. Outside, grayish cement façades patched awkwardly over the years looked like stained cloths hanging on a line. Cats were out hunting and men shouted between shrieks of car tyres on the hot asphalt. Most of the group had gone to Plaka. I had opted for quiet before setting off the next morning. Breathing Greece through a hot and dusty room seemed appropriate as an introduction.

High on the Acropolis

While all the girls slept like logs, I woke up stunned by sunrays thick as gold bars darting through the slits of the shutters. The day was free for us to do as we pleased. At seven in the morning, the broken sidewalks and buildings looked stylish in the fresh sunlight. The air smelled coffee. Men were everywhere, dark-haired, dark-eyed and tanned. They stood up on sidewalks or sat at cafés, smiling, talking, shouting, merry and carefree. They looked at me, saying purring words with eyes half-shut as if trying to hypnotize a wild animal. Athinas street traced a straight oblique towards the Acropolis. Wide but with small sidewalks, it was bathed in rising sun. I could not lose my route, I just had to look up, the Parthenon stood there like a lighthouse. Men puttered in their basement shops whose goods overflowed on the sidewalk. As I got nearer, the Acropolis looked more and more mountainous with green pines on its slopes. Lightly set on top, a white ship seemed to sway in the breeze. My eyes riveted on the ancient temple, I went on, as if floating in a dream.

I started going up towards the Propylaea. I ascended the large and steep marble steps. Out of a mess of broken marble, the Parthenon rose. I walked awkwardly on the debris and climbed into the temple. Circled by the giant columns that looked so frail from afar, I was alone. A chunk of azure made up for the vanished roof and the white marble glared like a lamp. A white butterfly veined with black arabesques flew nonchalantly around. I sat at the bottom of a column, my back against the fluted streaks of the shaft. Down below, Athens was sprawling its white buildings in all directions, filling the entire basin and climbing on the hills. I shut my eyes and basked in the sun. There was still nobody around. Time had stopped.

The Athens' bazaar

A flock of visitors woke me up. It was time to go downtown. I went down through the ancient agora. Greek, full of unknown sounds, of clamoring vowels and rocky consonants clashing and singing, was resonating loud. The narrow Pandrossou alley darkened by reeds and canvas to shut off sunlight was like a long cupboard full of junk and marvels. A man pointed his finger at my neck. I was wearing the blue glass bead I had bought in San Francisco, a year and half before. In fact since then, I had been wearing it nonstop. The man was moving his hand and stretching his neck as if asking something. "Where did you buy it?" He asked. "San Francisco" "San Francisco?" he asked incredulous. The same blue bead was everywhere along the bazaar, in all sizes. "This is against the bad eye, see", he said showing the dark blue of the apple, circled by white and a lighter blue. Without knowing, I had sported a lucky charm all those months since leaving America. Athens and San Francisco, I reflected. Same light, generous sun, rounded hills and the sea beyond, indeed the two cities could be twin.

The next day, we went to Cape Sounion. This time the promontory was not above a city but right above the sea. Resting against a column, I could now hear the lapping water, oblivious of the tragic death of Patrocles, drowning himself because his son Theseus had forgotten to put up a white sail on his ship, as he arrived back from Crete where he had killed the Minotaur. We then all went to swim at the foot of the temple. It was my first swim in the Mediterranean. Through the transparent waters, I could see pebbles splashed with all shades of grey, white and red. Tiny little silver fishes with a black band across their agile body and a black little snout kept pecking swiftly at my toes. The sun was setting and we still lingered in the warm water.

Sparta, a sibylline officer

The next day we were off to Pelopponese on a small bus rented with driver. We slowly cooked under the tin roof, but we could slide open the windows. The countryside was parched but not desertic. Fields and trees had changed colour like at fall, with deep yellows and browns. The cicadas seemed to bang cymbals for their king, the sun. We were heading for Mystras, a medieval city long abandoned. The road was long and dangerous. There was nobody in Mystras. Houses from the Byzantine era were still standing. Churches also, from whose frescoes deep and wide black eyes looked at you from all corners, in wonder or shock.

In the evening we were to sleep in Sparta, a lean and sad city of drab buildings, wide empty avenues, and gusts of wind whipping up clouds of dust. The modern city looked like a western movie setting. Instead of cowboys, it was filled with soldiers. It was one of the biggest garrison town in Greece, a male dominated place like in ancient times. We were housed in yet another Art Deco hotel with rooms even bigger than in Athens. As we walked around town, we quickly attracted the attention of men pacing around or yawning at the seemingly male-only cafés. Women were nowhere to be seen, save the very old, wrapped like mummies in their black scarves and shawls. Two men in civil clothes approached as we were buying sweets from a tiny *"periptero"*, a stand built like a minuscule chalet and painted a bright yellow. Their French was fluent. They were both officers in the army. They offered us a drink at a café. Their faces were polite but cold, they did not behave at all like men approaching girls. Learning that we would still be in Sparta the following evening, they invited us for dinner. We said a half-yes. Sparta and those army men exuded a silent sadness that dampened our carefree spirit.

At nine, as agreed, my two roomates and I were on the central square, waiting for the two officers. Sparta's main square was huge like Moscow's Red Square, megalomaniac and unnecessary. The older officer showed up alone, looking tired and bored. He apologized for his friend that had been called on special duty. He called a taxi and we got in, slightly annoyed. We sat in the back while the officer sat in front with the driver. We were out in the country, in pitch dark. It would be a long ride on foot in case we wanted to escape. Three to one, we tacitly decided, gave us an advantage. Abruptly, the taxi turned into a small dirt road and stopped above a taverna. The wide empty terrace was illuminated by a collection of bulbs hanging all around. The taverna owner stood impassive as we were going down, bowing like an oldtime servant in front of the officer. With a few sharp orders, the officer sent the man back to his kitchen. In no time the table was covered with dishes, which we started to eat hungrily. Our host however was not eating anything. He just looked at us eating, with a languid and sad face. I politely started conversation. He was married, a wife and kid in Athens. I mentioned the Colonels. He looked away and, instead of answering, asked me where I was from in France. A little behind, the taverna owner sat astride a chair, his arms resting on the back, yawning non-stop. Cicadas, owls, all kinds of mammals and insects filled the night with their eerie cries. As we stopped eating, the officer called the taverna owner who went in again and came back with pastries dripping honey. "Café?" he asked. We nodded and he came back with Greek coffee. I pitied the guy, who tottered like a somnambulist. The officer finally paid him and we got in the taxi, which had come back and was waiting for us. The central square was still busy with kakhi green in all the cafés. We shook hands and thanked him for the dinner. As I retrieved my hand, he said dreamily: "Something is going to happen". He seemed absorbed and worried. "Soon" he added, on a more definite tone this time. I took it for a delayed answer to my careless question about the Colonels. As I was opening my mouth to ask more, he turned his back and swiftly walked away.

Peace of the past: Epidaure, Olympia, Delphi

Epidaure, Olympia, Delphi may have been the most common staples of a trip to Greece but their enthralling beauty felt as vivid and powerful to me as to the millions of travellers over the centuries. The three together composed a perfect triad. Epidaure was all hills, round and sweet like a woman's bosom, Olympia was green and flowered like the garden of Eden and Delphi was mountainous and wild, still oozing mysteries and oracles like in the times of the Pythia. Digging into that Greek past brought unexpected recollections of early childhood and magic expectations for the future. I was seriously falling in love.

Coming down from the ancient site, I wandered in the modern town of Delphi at noontime. I stopped under a plane tree for some shade and rest. A long haired blond guy was already sitting there. Water trickled from a small fountain and he was filling his gourd. I washed my face and hands and put water on my neck and nape before drinking from the spurt. We chatted American way. "Where are you from? How long have you been in Greece?" and other routine questions. He was German, travelling alone around Greece. He had just been in Crete and he said he was going to go back soon. He did not detail the reasons for his wonder and awe. He just said that Crete was beautiful, in a mind-boggling way to judge from how he shook his head and raised his eyebrows. Having cooled enough in the shade, I got up. "If you go to Crete" the guy said, "go to Aghia Galini. It means serenity. It's just perfect." Aghia Galini, I repeated and nodded.

Crete

The moon was full, splashing the upper deck. The ferry ground slowly its way in the sea. Lying on a bench, I watched the constellations oscillating with the boat. It was a night to be sleepless. We moored in Iraklion, at the foot of high walls, rosy in the morning sun. The fortifications made a grand effect. An effect fast diluted once on land. After the Levantine whiffs of Athens, Iraklion oozed Arabia. The sun was fierce and the men looked fierce in their heavy boots and breeches. The women looked like walking catafalques. Everything was stronger, more intense, from the blue eyes of people to the color of the sky, the merciless sun and the faces wrinkled like tortured rocks. The heat, the dryness and the dust had a taste of the Sahara. I had dropped the group. Until our flight back to Paris, I would wander alone.

The bus depot was almost unbearable in the heat and noise. I had managed to decipher the Greek letters of Aghia Galini. It was a fishing port right in the middle of the south coast, facing Lybia. I went to queue up behind venerable old men in wide breeches and women loaded with sacks and baskets who avoided my eyes. The driver had glanced at me in the mirror as he sat in front of the huge wheel, almost flat in front of him. I had got a seat in front, just on his right. The wide windshield let in the whole landscape outside, like in a helicopter. A blue braid ran all around it with a blue glass eye and an icon of the Virgin hanging in the middle. As soon as the driver turned the contact key, strident violin music erupted in the bus, carrying on its waves a powerful male voice, crying a recitative. The violence of the song seemed only to drag passengers further into their thoughts. The driver himself had his eyes half shut, turning sleepily the huge wheel with both arms as we were winding steeply upwards into the White Mountains, the *Lefka Ori*.

The journey coast to coast would take two hours from the Cretan sea to the Lybian one. Like the Touaregs, the Cretans were covered with wool and cotton from head to foot, even the face. Drowsy and silent, summer was their hibernation. Wearing only a teeshirt, my arms and neck naked, I felt suffocating. The faint air coming through the windows on one side was burning hot. The blinds did not help, slamming up at each jostle. When we reached a pass through the mountains at Aghia Varvara, a cool breeze arose. Along the main street, there was nobody but a few cats. A few passengers got off, loaded like donkeys. When the driver jumped back on his seat, he was awake. His eyes were now wide open and there was urgency in his drive. The road was winding down. The endless Messara opened below us like the garden of Eden. Green of the olive trees, gold of the harvested fields, white of the houses clustered like fish schools here and there. Beyond the plain, framed by Mount Ida on one side, the sea of Lybia glared, silver like melting metal. It seemed terribly appropriate for Mount Ida to be the birthplace of Zeus, taken away from his cannibal father Chronos by his mother Rhéa and fed by the goat Amalthea. Sky and land balanced each other in the most perfect proportions I had ever seen.

Aghia Galini

The passengers were dropped little by little along the road, disappearing fast into dirt roads. After each stop, the bus would start again, revving like a truck. We stopped in a town that seemed to be one single big main street expanding into a big open square, treeless and dull. Mires, I could read on the sign. We stayed longer. The driver got out to lug a mailbag into the local bus station. The corral-like dusty square gathered a lot of men and boys. When we left again, the bus was near empty.

Aghia Galini was the last stop. As soon as I was dropped on the esplanade along the water, the bus made a U-turn and left in a hurry. There were no boats moored in the port, and nobody around. I walked up the steps to the village street, hemmed in by steep cliffs on both sides. A few empty tavernas and cafés lined the street. "Room, room?" said an old woman whom I followed up a staircase. She showed me a room with two beds and a naked bulb hanging in the middle of the ceiling. The shower on the landing was a metal pipe jutting out of the wall, dripping cold water. The landlady insisted on my stepping into her little salon, bringing me a spoonful of fruits in syrup and a glass of water. I sat on a macramé pillow on a wood chair, looking at silver prints of newlyweds of yesteryear above the oak sideboard. I went back upstairs to my room for a nap. I had not slept on a bed for twenty-four hours. The rickety door could have been opened any time and all my belongings easily snatched. I barely noticed. Greece so far was like a village community. "You can leave your wallet in the middle of a square and find it again two days later" the German boy had told me in Delphi.

The morning was milky and rosy with colour climbing up slowly on walls and cliffs as the sun rose. Beyond the quay, a stony beach spread with the cliff curving like a grotto above. As I arrived, three old women stared at me, startled like does. They had just got out of the water and they were drying up their swollen legs. In no time, they had put back on their black dresses and scarves and left furtively. I had surprised them in their private dawn bath. Further away, the cliff cracked open into a valley dotted with pink laurel and green bushes. Lying in the sea on my back, I looked at the mountains still capped with snow.

Alexandros of Phaistos

Miller had warned me about Phaistos, but the absolute contentment it brought was unexpected. I sat for hours in the shade of pines and the rattle of cicadas. Past and present colliding, time was suspended, fragile and tenuous. People had gone, their houses were but remnants of walls, their life broken like the jars, pots and basins scattered around. Still, Phaistos was not a tomb but a home. Proof was the Messara plain, shining and undulating under the sun.

Surprisingly that day, Alexandros, the old guardian of Phaistos, now retired, had come back to walk across his beloved domain. He was exactly as Miller described him, small made and thin, with piercing eyes behind his glasses and a polite smile. He was very honoured to be recognized on the faith of Miller's testimony. To be true to his legend, he offered me very civilly to have coffee at the small cafeteria recently installed.

Along the Lybian sea

Tymbakion on the coast was a very modern farming center, the first in Greece to introduce all year round cultivation of tomatoes, cucumbers and peppers under plastic tents, taking advantage of the African climate on that side of Crete. The new plantations yielded big profits, taking over the traditional fields. But NATO was taking over southern Crete, a prime spot in the heart of the eastern Mediterranean. NATO bases had started on the north side in Souda, already a base during World War II. But the south was far more important strategically. From there, Lybia and the Near East could be reached in no time. Walking along the coast, I had fallen upon an enormous road, wide enough to be a highway. The road was straight, heading to the sea. Parallel to it, another road. As I wondered what kind of highway was being built going straight into the sea, a man had come yelling at me. "No, no" he shouted "No walk here, forbidden!" NATO was building a secret airport right on the Lybian Sea.

Bringing me a generous dome-shaped salad with a thick slice of *feta*, the Tymbakion taverna owner, a bulbous unshaved man, had said: "This is not Matala here!" Matala was the big attraction in the area, hence higher prices and smaller portions. Henry Miller had gone to Matala, starting the fad. His first followers had been big hippie families from the West coast. They had come with their children, the women nursing their young long after babyhood, like in primitive tribes. Cretans had liked them. Free love pleased local young men, and the old women liked those young hippie mothers nursing their babies. The hippies had first set camp in the caves carved in the cliffs above the sea.

The Cretan, lighting fires, had originally used those caves to lure ships en route to the Near East onto the treacherous reefs. There they hid their looting also. During World War II, the *"andartes"*, the Greek resistance fighters and some of their Australian and New Zealander comrades had in turn used the caves to hide from the German occupiers. Some tourists now camped there and local men used them for their trysts with foreign girls. Until the inhabitants would grow weary of what they saw as desecration and fence in completely the caves, they were still open with their tables and beds carved in the white stone. The stone and the sand were equally white, turning the Matala waters into a mesmerizing opalescent turquoise. But the beach was treacherous. Just a few meters from the tranquil beach, the seabed plunged down at vertiginous depths. The continental shelf ended there. Beyond were the dry lands, the deserts that brought a red dust when the South wind, the "Livikon", blew.

War - Freedom

The next morning, everything was quiet in Aghia Galini, as if all tourists had left or overslept. I went down to the café on the quay. The daughter of the café owner looked absorbed. She sat next to the radio, which blared military chants. She brought me coffee and went to sit next to the radio again. The chants stopped and an excited voice started to talk. The girl looked up and stared at me. "War" she said. I looked at her flabbergasted. "War with the Turks in Kypro." I had no clue what was Kypro. I asked for a yogurt and she said I couldn't have a yogurt, neither milk nor butter. They couldn't be sold anymore. The daily bus going to Iraklion arrived in the middle of the esplanade. Tourists came out from the street with their sacks, hurrying to get aboard. I got up to ask them what was going on. "It's Cyprus, the Greek Colonels have overthrown Makarios. The Turks have sent troops to protect the Turkish minority. You'd better go, they are rationing food already." I ran to fetch my rucksack and got on the bus.

I suddenly remembered the officer in Sparta. "Something is going to happen", he had said. That was it. On the central square in Mires, tens of military trucks were loading all the men of the area. Some were wearing green military clothes, others their usual ones. For luggage, they each held a blue plastic bag, like the ones used in the shops. As we were driving towards Iraklion, the trucks were lined in an endless convoy. Standing up, the men were chanting. The bus driver smiled and honked triumphantly as he overtook the convoy. "Konstantinopoli, that what they chant. We'll go to Konstantinopoli." I looked at him, puzzled. "Konstantinopoli is the Capital of Greece. Some day we'll go back." I was baffled. In all the villages, for once, all women were out on the streets. Mothers, wives and daughters were crying and waving to the men as they jumped in the trucks and disappeared in the dust.

In Iraklion, the bus struggled to go through the streets. They were submerged by thousands of Cretans, with more chants and cries. The crowd was turning into a mob. The other tourists on the bus were all heading straight for the airport. I had no idea where the rest of my group were. I had to meet them on the ferry two days later. I decided to stay on the bus, which went further along the north coast, up to Aghios Nikolaos. That port town was surprisingly quiet, save for a few trucks still filling up slowly with young men that could not stop kissing their girl friends. Some girls had jumped aboard the truck for a last passionate kiss. Built on a promontory looking to the sea in all directions, Aghios Nikolaos looked like a miniature San Francisco. There were still tourists around and no food was rationed here. But the place felt abandoned as if the party was over. I took a room in a "pension" and went to bed early. It was the heart of summer, but it felt like autumn. People's faces were shut and even the sun felt unfriendly. I felt stuck and unable to shake a boredom that seemed to have engulfed the whole town.

The next evening, everybody was talking on the street. Something had happened. People talked loud and smiled to each other. I could not get the words, but from their happy faces I knew it was good news. *"Eleftheria!"* they shouted, "Freedom!", that was my first Greek word. The war was not over in Cyprus, but because of the Greek army defeat, the Colonels had been ousted from power. The army had abandoned the Junta, rallying the people. On July 22, 1974, Kostas Karamanlis, exiled in Paris, was arriving in Athens. After *"Eleftheria"*, the Greek now shouted *"Demokratia"*. Demobilized men were coming back. All villages were rejoicing and feasting. On the 30th of July, on the eve of my departure to Paris, Greece was a free country and seeing everyone talk and smile, I suddenly realized how silent the Greeks had been since my arrival four weeks before. Free speech was taking over.

BACK TO FRANCE 3

*Learning Greek - Langues'O - Modern Greece History
Teaching English - Down and out in a Paris garret - To
London, on Katherine Mansfield's trail*

Learning Greek

Paris was hot and deserted as usual in August. Until September when I would start teaching English in high school, I had nothing to do. Bizarrely, I missed the Greek language. Voices and words felt so flat in Paris. I did not know Greek at all. In fact, it had nothing to do with any language I had heard before. No sound recalled even remotely the sounds of French, English, Spanish or German. It was as foreign to me as Maori or Arab. There was no way I could make out any meaning from Greek speech or writing. I knew only three words: "Elefteria", "Democratia" and "Leepon". "Leepon" came rhythmically into speech, like "so" in German and English. I had easily isolated the word from the rest since "Leepon" was always followed by a slight pause as if the speaker was pondering or sighing. The Greek alphabet was another formidable obstacle. There was an A, an E, an I, a B and a P that I could recognize. But the Greek P and B were pronounced like an R and a V. With a few vowels and three words, I could not go very far. I had to find a way to walk in that jungle.

I needed a Greek dictionary and a grammar. I went to *"Smith & Son"* on Rue de Rivoli. They had no dictionary, only phrase books for parrots. They told me to go to *"Brentano's"* on Avenue de l'Opéra. Everywhere, Paris was empty and all the space suddenly freed felt strange. In the shade of the blinds in front of the bookshop, I found a Greek-French and French-Greek dictionary in two small blue volumes, but no grammar. For that, I had to go on the left bank, Rue Monsieur Le Prince, at *Klincksieck's*, a *"Libraire-Editeur orientaliste"*. I crossed the Seine and found the bookshop no bigger than an Athens' bazaar booth. In the shambles of shelves and book piled on floors and tables, one could find anything. *Klincksieck* itself had published a grammar of Modern Greek. I could now get down to work.

First, I had to learn the alphabet. In fact, I had to start all over again to learn how to read and write, as I had done twenty years before to learn my mother tongue. I had been taught to read and write French, my mother tongue, with the Maria Montessori method. We were given plastic letters that we could touch. Then, we were made to shape our lips accordingly as we were uttering each letter, to relate sound and graphic form. I still remembered it vividly. I just had to do the same with Greek. I took a small paintbrush and red watercolor. On a sheet of white drawing paper, I sketched carefully every Greek letter, one by one, the capitals and the smalls. I pinned above my bed the two sheets of paper. Every morning, every evening, I read the letters aloud. The grammar was in French with examples in Greek. I decrypted the syllables one by one, then the words. By the end of the week, I was beginning to be able to navigate very, very slowly in that new language. Where I had first felt Greek like a sea with undifferentiated elements, I was beginning to distinguish bits, from which I could step further. Greek was not anymore a complete fog, it was beginning to feel more like a huge map which I was trying hard to decipher. *"Leepon"* was a clear seamark now, written *"Loipon"*, the "o" and the "i" being one of the five ways to write the sound "e". Although I was groping like a blindman, paddling like a puppy at sea, at least I was going forward.

Langues'O

But that was not enough. I needed a teacher. The *"Ecole des Langues Orientales"* on Rue de Lille, or *"Langues'O"* as it was abbreviated, was one of the oldest higher schools in France. They taught all the languages of the countries beyond Germany up to China. Polish, Romanian,

Greek, Turkish, Russian, Arabic, Thaï, Japanese, Chinese, the abundance was cheering. The Orient was an inexhaustible bounty, in stark contrast with the Americas where only three languages existed. Courses for a BA started in October at the *Université Paris-Dauphine*, near the *Bois de Boulogne*.

At *Langues'O.* all the professors were Greek, save for the Head of the Greek section, Professor Tarabout, a raucous and tall man with wavy white hair. Chryssa Prokopaki, a writer, biographer and leftist intellectual, was in charge of the beginners. Her wide and solid face resembled that of Nana Mouskouri. Like her, she had heavy glasses with a dark tortoise shell frame, and long brown hair falling on her shoulders. She would first write a sentence in Greek on the blackboard, then she would analyze every word and syllable, every free and bound morpheme. Then, with her nasal voice, she repeated over and over the sentence, accentuating the morphemes. We read in turn, one by one and then all together. It was kids' school all over. Chryssa sat on top of a table, her feet on a chair, in the middle of the class. At the end of the course, she was disheveled and covered with a film of chalk dust, but still in a good mood. We stumbled at every syllable, it seemed that we would never make it, but she gently laughed and shrugged her shoulders, fatalistic. We had to get into the Greek language or, rather, the Greek language had to get into us.

At Christmas time, Chryssa was going to Athens. She had promised to bring back Greek schoolbooks that we could use to progress. They were the first grade books used by Greek children at four or five, compilations of very short poems, like Japanese haikus. They talked of flowers, of birds and butterflies. Some poems were from a collection by Odysseas Elytis, "Ta ro tou erota". I had memorized instantly that funny title. Chryssa Prokopaki was reading aloud to us the poems with her velvety and husky voice. The intensity of her pleasure in reading poetry was intoxicating and we repeated again the verses until we got the pronunciation and rhythm right. Chryssa knew a million poetry verses. She could recite at will sonnets, poems, and even prose by Cavafy, Palamas, Elytis, Séféris, and many others, but above all by Yannis Ritsos, her idol and the subject of a monumental biography she had just finished writing. After reciting or reading for us, she would put a cassette in the tape recorder and we would listen to the poems set to music by Theodorakis. We all sang along with her, thrilled to feel the Greek words tamed in our mouths. There was a song from a poem by Elytis about cicadas shouting under the burning sun: *"Zi, kai zi, kai zi, o Vassilias, o ilios zi"*, "he lives, he lives, the sun, the Sun King" The *zi* was also the Greek onomatopeia for the cry of the cicada, called *tzitziki* in Greek.

Modern Greece History

Christos Papazoglou was a short plump man with an egg-shaped head where hair was beginning to rarefy, a very pale complexion and slanting eyes embedded in thick eyelids. He was in charge of grammar, history and civilization. His name terminating with the *"oglou"* indicated that his family had come from a part of Turkey which the Greeks still denominated Asia Minor. The suffix *"oglou"* meant "son of" in Turkish. We had nicknamed him PPZ. Uncommon among Greeks, Christos was perfectly at ease with the Turkish heritage of Modern Greece, be it the language, the cooking, the music and songs lyrics, and many other aspects he would reveal to us in his illuminating course on the *"Turkocratia"*, the four centuries domination of Greece by the Ottoman Empire. In spite of his physique, he was very attractive. He was funny, lively and full of humor. He frequently alluded to his love life. Explaining to us the use of diminutives with words, he had told us that often they were used as a sign of tenderness. Thus a man would ask his love if she wanted "a little coffee", or "a little bath", and he would certainly call the kitchen table, "the little kitchen table" since he had certainly made love upon that table.

His history course on Greece from 1452 to 1821, covering the 400 years long domination by the Turks, took us deep into the complicated origins of the country. From being an Ottoman province until its war of independence or "revolution", the Greek people had been an incredibly rich mosaic of populations of different ethnic origins. Greek, Slavic or Levantine, the population of Greece was mostly composed of peasants dominated by a handful of landowners. That wealthy elite had taken advantage of the absence of property law under the Ottomans, for whom, as Moslems, land belonged exclusively to God. Men could only hold the land in usufruct. Those Greek landowners, the *"tsiflikades"* (from *"tsiflik"* meaning estate in Turkish), had therefore been able to constitute huge properties without any need for ownership titles. There was no landmap in the Ottoman Empire, as is still the case today in Modern Greece. In such circumstances, it was easy to appropriate for oneself any piece of land, provided you had some social clout and ascendancy on analphabet peasants who worked the land. The *"tsiflikades"* had had a good time under the Ottomans. The war of independence against the Ottomans was not bound to bring those wealthy landowners much benefit. The same applied to the upper orthodox clergy, masters also of enormous areas of self-appropriated land, which they still own. The Revolution against the Ottomans was therefore the enterprise of a minority of Greek nationalists, local Robin Hoods, thinkers, scholars and poets, together with the harried peasants.

Christos, like all inspired teachers, frequently made his own digressions about Greece. He talked to us at length about the *"Rebetika"*, the songs of the Athens underground filled with Turkish words and concepts, accompanied by Turkish musical instruments: santouris, baglamas, bouzoukis. He told us about the many ethnic minorities in Greece, the Venitian, the Sarakatsanes, the Judeo-Spanish of Salonica, the Slavs, the Albanians, and their respective religions: Judaïsm,

Islam, Christian Orthodoxy, Christian Catholicism. Modern Greece came out as a conflicting but fascinating pot. Today's Greek life was as Turkish as before, he maintained, with the same daily words, the same dishes, the same coffee, the same music and the same dancing steps of *zeïbekiko* and *tsifteteli*.

The moral of his course was that, in contemporary Greece, a Greek was a Greek and yet wasn't a Greek, but still was a Greek. Everebody shared the common Greek language, although the oral daily language had a Greek syntax and Turkish words. The learned and the upper class spoke and wrote the "clean" language, a trimmed down version of ancient Greek, cleansed of all the borrowed foreign words, Turkish words mostly, but also Italian, French and Slavic. This contrasted state of things shaped the peculiar psyche of the Greek people. They were not that sure to be Greek and therefore eager to proclaim it, aggressively sometimes. Like the non-Arab Moslems faithful to the Arabic heritage, they were made to be faithful to a heritage that was not really theirs.

Bloodline was over important. People had to prove their "grecity". Notwithstanding the place of birth, if one of your parents or grandparents was Greek, you were Greek automatically. To be Greek was an indelible characteristic, that you kept forever, you and your descendants even if you didn't ask for it. There was a specific word to name that enduring nationality: *"Ithageneia"*, distinct from the usual concept of *"Ethnikotyta"*. Christos Papazoglou, however, was an iconoclast, and his analysis of Modern Greece and Modern Greeks was far from being the analysis of the predominant intelligentsia which was still faithful to the myth of the uninterrupted continuation of Greece all along the millenniums. And for the common people, the *"demos"*, it was the Byzantine Empire for which they had the most endearing nostalgia, rather than Pericles's century and the celebrated classical times of ancient Greece. Constantinople was their Jerusalem. No Greek ever uttered the name of

Istambul. The teachings of Christos sketched a country divided into many elements, and itself a small element of a much bigger world extending from one bank of the Mediterranean to the other and beyond, up to the Black sea, the steppes of Gengis Khan, the Red Sea, even the Indian Ocean.

There was no limit going east, as there was going west. In America, once reached the Pacific Ocean, the world ended. In France, everything stopped on the Atlantic shore. But from Greece, you could go on forever. The Mediterranean was but an inland sea. To the Orient, the space was boundless yet all lands and people seemed bound together in spirit and things as simple as tea and coffee, olive oil and large communal meals.

Teaching English

On September 23, I went to the *Ecole Notre Dame* in Sannois to take up my post teaching English. Teaching was more difficult than learning, and far more exhausting. Learning Greek, I was amassing knowledge day by day, feeling richer as time went by. Teaching English I was giving knowledge and not receiving much. At least, that's how it felt. The girls I was teaching, aged ten to nineteen years old, were not difficult. But they were not terribly interested into learning a foreign language and, as a result, they were chatting too much. They were happy, simple girls, who loved their parents, rode little motorcycles or bicycles, had boyfriends and lived in spruced little villas surrounded by neat little gardens in Sannois. Their lives seemed all mapped out. They would marry the boyfriend and take up their parents' trade. Most parents were shop owners. They were totally unpretentious, which was refreshing, but they seemed devoid of any personal plan or dream for their own lives. They were contented to be where they were, what they were and how they were. I felt like an odd sheep.

Everything was not smooth however at the *Ecole Notre Dame*, nor everybody equal. Some pupils were much poorer, their parents unemployed or badly paid manual workers. Claire was an awkward, untidy girl, with a reddened complexion that never spoke up. She sat at the bottom of the class and she looked at me intently with her animal blue eyes. Her performance was very bad. At the end of the year, the doctor had found out that she was at least six months pregnant. Neither the nuns of Notre Dame, neither the teachers nor the other girls' parents, were shocked. They just laughed, a fifteen- year old girl impregnated by a boy was funny. After all, the girl had been doing some good practical work after school, they all joked. Her parents had decided that the best thing was to marry her right away with the father, barely older. They would keep the child.

Nadège was twelve years old, very tall and thin but very childish looking. She was dressed like a dance skater with pink and white dresses or skirts adorned with bits of fur or pompoms, a white blond ponytail dangling on top of her head. At first I had thought she was putting on simpering airs. She looked at me fixedly with adoring clear blue eyes from her seat in the first row. Her face was very pale with blue veins showing through her delicate forehead. In spite of her dedication, her results were not good. She seemed mesmerized by my words but nothing got assimilated. Her notebook was the neatest. She carefully underlined or wrote in red ink the examples I gave to illustrate a point of grammar. Her patient efforts had moved me. I knew from my own childhood that a teacher's goodwill could work wonders on a child with learning difficulties. To be given consideration could suddenly instil enough self-confidence for a pupil suddenly to be able to master a subject. I started to pay more attention to her. And it paid, immediately. Nadège was progressing fast. She could make up English sentences, she could read and understand better everyday. The other girls in the class sneered and called her a bootlicker. They genuinely thought that if Nadège had good marks, it was because she was my pet pupil. But I could feel that they jeered at her for other reasons.

At the end of the year, an open-door day was organized to meet the parents. Nadège's parents came to see me. They were an elderly couple. The mother was a pleat-maker for the garment industry, working at home, the father retired. They had adopted Nadège in their late forties. They had tears in their eyes. Since I had appeared, their little girl had started to love going to school, and reward of reward, she had been accepted to pass into the upper grade the year after. I had weighed as much as I could as a junior teacher to ensure that. Nadège was already repeating her school year, if she could not pass in the upper grade, she would have to leave regular schooling for a technical school, a sure way to stay in limbo all her life. I had won. The school council had decided to give her a chance to confirm her progress. For me anyway, Nadège alone had been enough of a reward for a long boring year in that school.

The long hours on the train to get to the school were even worse than the trip to Nanterre University the years before. From Paris, I had to take three different trains to get to Sannois. There was no shelter for the commuters on the quays swept by wind, rain or snow. Adding to my living conditions, the long commute was too much. If I stayed in the same spot, I felt nothing would ever change. I didn't want to go on like this. "No god, no love, no home, alone in a gaol" I had written. I had called my mini-poem, "my side of paradise". On the streets, on the subway, on the train, at the school, in my family, I saw only repetition, dull and omnipotent repetition. I had to escape, this time for good.

Down and out in a Paris garret

I had rented two ex-maids'rooms, cells rather, made into a shabby and cold mini flat under the roof of an otherwise chic 19th century white stone condominium on rue Vineuse, not far from the Trocadéro. This was my first independent home.

Coming in, I first pushed a heavy black wrought iron gate opening on an elegant entrance hall. I crossed the hall, and pushed a door opening on a back courtyard. In a corner of that yard, I pushed another door, this time narrow and shaky, opening onto a steep staircase. There were relegated society's underlings. Students, cleaning ladies and destitute old people had replaced the servants of the past. While the façade building had a wrought iron gate, a lift and a staircase with wide and low steps covered by a thick carpet, the back staircase was steep and narrow. Its sunk wood steps were naked and twice as high as the other stairs, as if the architect had wanted to make sure that the guys in the back would have to raise their knees high enough to feel the pain in their muscles and the short breath in their lungs. There was no heating in that staircase, neither in the long, narrow corridor onto which opened the doors of the rooms, like stalls in a stable.

It was freezing, dark and damp. There were eight floors to climb. Once up there, I felt stranded as much because of that dreadful staircase as because of a surreptitious anguish which seemed to ooze from the walls. My mini-flat was a luxury though, compared to the other lodgings on the eighth floor. I had two rooms, two windows, cold and hot water and a gas heater. The Spanish cleaning lady next to me had a space no bigger than a broom cupboard with a small glass and steel rusty skylight, no water and no heating. We met going to and from the water closet at the end of the corridor which all lodgers shared on the floor. She was carrying zinc buckets of water, which she filled at a whining faucet just outside the toilet. It could freeze of course. She then boiled some water from a bottle in a pan over her small camping gas heater, and poured it on the faucet.

At first, I had tried to take it lightly and positively. After all, I was not the first bloke living in a garret. I marveled for a few weeks at my home, my first real home. There was a big double bed, a real bedroom with a window opening on the sky, at least a slice of it, since the view took in mostly the opposite roof across the courtyard. And I had my first kitchen, although with no clue how to cook food. I had no bathroom. I washed in the sink. The toilet was on the landing and I had a chamber pot for the night. The faint heat from the gas stove quickly escaped through the badly insulated walls and glass windows. Sitting at my desk made out of a long wood plank, I felt cold creeping up from my feet and sinking down from my head. Back from the school, I had courses to prepare and piles of tests or exams to grade. Besides, I was feeling nauseous, I had headaches. If no heat, there was a persistent smell of gas pervading the rooms. The stove leaked. One Sunday morning, I had tried to get up from my bed, feeling awful. I was dizzy, my head was swimming and I was terrified. No matter the hurt to my pride, I packed the same day and went back to my parents, into my girl's room.

My life felt like a joke, like the destiny of poor celibate women in 19th century novels, from Balzac to Edith Wharton. Although from genteel extraction, the poor girl would ineluctably drown into poverty and loneliness. Her fault was to be without a dowry and therefore non-eligible. She was condemned to humble and slaving jobs and solitude. After a life of hard work, the only exit was a solitary death. Could that be my fate? I wondered. I had no *"fortune"* whatsoever. All those boys I had met and danced with at balls and dinner parties, I pondered, were only looking for "a big sack", a wealthy heiress. *"Noémi So-and-so? Oh, mais c'est un gros sac!"* It sounded funny like a cartoon by Daumier, but it was not. After a few years, long gowns and ball parties had gone. Coming back at dawn through a silent and dewy Paris, heeled shoes in hand and sore feet treading the gently scraping asphalt, I could still believe then that my youth was privileged. But behind the glitter of dances, there had been a discreet market place where boys and girls could spot each other. Money was a forbidden word but the wealthy families were known and their daughters sought after. In any case, the boys I danced with had no attraction to me. Even more than the girls, they seemed to be already cast into their life role. I was turning into a misfit. And I hated it.

I was now twenty-three going on twenty-four. My schoolmates were all getting engaged and married, dropping whatever degree they had pretended to prepare, if any. I now had only marriage ceremonies and parties to attend. But, in the profusion of white tulle, lace, veils and flowers, the beautiful liturgy and chants, the triumphant organ music, I saw and felt a farce, feeling perilously out of it all. I could not see nor sense real love in those perfectly staged performances. It was not funny. It was frightening. Either they were mad or I was. It was exhausting to stay on the edge, a foot in that fantasy world, the other foot groping for the real one. Either I would give in or I would be a renegade but, either way, my social peers would manage to define my existence. According to their rules, I could only be in or out. I only wanted to be far, far and away. No matter what, I had decided to quit teaching by the end of the school year. I would not renew my contract with the school. One episode of "down and out in Paris" was enough. But, what next? Money had to come from somewhere.

That sun firing like a ball above the plains of Peloponnese and the Messara had merged with the wheat fields of my childhood summers, taking residence in a corner of my brain. At will, I could make it alive, eyes shut and memory open. Henry Miller had passed me the message. Greece was the sister of Aquitaine and Dordogne. In the mid of worries and fears for the morrow, I had found my haven.

"Langues'0", where I went a few times a week, was a versatile planet where one went out of passion or for enterntainment, rather than out of breadwinning logic. Not many in the Modern Greek classes thought seriously of making a career out of it. Save a few that would try their luck at the competition for the *"Cadre d'Orient"*, a poetic name for the diplomatic corps posted in Eastern countries, from Athens to Peking.

To London, on Katherine Mansfield's trail

America had been my first fling. But I had failed to take off for good. Coming back home had made me more determined than ever to just get up and go. The only clear goal I could see now was to go abroad, to escape being in or out of the system I was born in. The challenge was to make a living abroad. My health was bad. An inspired gynecologist had prescribed me Tranxène and Valium. The first had made me lose twenty pounds in two weeks, immediately regained the next month. Valium had made me insomniac and addicted. I had managed to withdraw from Valium, albeit with pain. I now weighed one hundred and forty pounds. I felt helpless. I could not muster enough courage anymore to get up and go.

In September, I decided to go to London. Just as Scott Fitzgerald had been my alibi to go to the US, it was this time Katherine Mansfield giving me a hand. I had not abandoned my doctoral thesis. Now and then, I read, took notes and worked on it. *"Katherine Mansfield ou la volonté d'être, biographie intérieure"* was its romantic title. KM as she signed her letters had lived in London most of her writing life. The British Museum Library had not only memoirs and writings of all her British contemporaries, but also a collection of her letters and manuscripts. I was planning to stay three months in London before coming back to finish and present my thesis. I had bought a steel trunk, strong enough to endure train and boat trips and big enough to carry books and clothes. The trunk was incredibly heavy, but I would ship it apart as heavy luggage. It would wait for me at Victoria station.

At the Gare du Nord, my perplexed mother had waved at me as I stood behind the glass window, the train shuffling its way along the quay, gathering speed slowly. For all its rickety sounds and smoke, the train had far more allure than the plane. Its lengthy cruise across the Somme up to Calais afforded plenty of time for breathing and thinking ahead. Half a day later, I was pacing a boat deck, watching the coasts of France melt in the Channel waves and autumn sun. The wind in the face, the heavy swell and the boat plowing its foamy furrow deleted any melancholy.

LONDON

Crosby Hall by the Thames - British Museum Library - The Bassae frieze - Maria's lover - Sundays at Battersea park - Nasreen from Baghdad - The Faduah club - A Sunday trip - A baptism certificate - Forbidden love - Abla the ceramist - Wedding day - A Greek bookshop on Tottenham Court road - Looking for a job - In the birds' wake

Crosby Hall by the Thames

Crossing the Channel, sea and sky were equally grey and rocky, clouds and waves rushing from the west. But the wind blowing on the deck felt like a friendly push. Moving on the map gave the comforting illusion of advancing in life. With the past behind, I had only the unknown future ahead. I felt like a snake sloughing, with no idea what would come out of it.

Stepping off the train at Victoria station, a jolly white-haired porter hailed me from the quay with a big smile "Need help, Love?" He took the suitcase and the rucksack and followed me to the Customs depot to fetch the steel trunk. The weight and solidity of the trunk was unpractical, but it was the only home I had left. Wheeling everything to the taxi line, the porter yelled "Crosby Hall" to the first taxi in line who, getting out, held open the back door for me to climb in, arranging the whole load in front. I sat princely on the deep and wide seat. The crowd of pedestrians and the shop-windows lining the sidewalk made an exotic patchwork. I had popped in London years before, but I had never lived in it.

I knew enough of the city and the language to feel acquainted, but being a foreigner gave to London just the right amount of strangeness, and the right space for fancy. I had been delving a lot into Katherine Mansfield's life and writings in the last months. As a doctoral thesis, I intended to write a psychological biography of her, trying to decipher patterns and motives in her brief life. The title I had given to my project was: *La volonté d'être*, the will to be. Katherine Mansfield had steadily refused from her teens to be what she was born to become, a placid New Zealand wife and mother, living happily ever after in Wellington. Her years in London were the ones I was interested in for my research. There, she had been on her own, often on the brink of misery, but determined to go her own way, whimsical and free. There was an enchanting impromptu quality to her moves and deeds, however grim or painful daily life might be. She seemed to have lived like a bird, carefree and trustful, day-by-day. The intriguing thing about Katherine Mansfield was the way she had been considered as an alien by all the trendy Londoners she had met, in particular the "Bloomsbury" group who dubbed her "the little Colonial" with a stiff upper lip.

Katherine Mansfield at sixteen, stuck in Wellington, had written to a girlfriend : *'I'm so keen upon all women having a definite future – aren't you? The idea of sitting and waiting for a husband is absolutely revolting and it really is the attitude of a great many girls. It rather made me smile to read of your wishing you could create your fate—Oh! How many times I have felt just the same! I just long for power over circumstances.'*

Coincidentally, Crosby Hall was around the corner from where she had lived. She had rented rooms on Beaufort street, just above Cheyne Walk where the old mansion of Crosby Hall, a fifteenth century house totally reconstructed in 1910, spread in what remained of the original park on the banks of the Thames. The large red brick façade with its adorned gables and stained glass windows at the end of a lawn left me in awe. Crosby Hall was a foyer for post-graduate women from all over the world. Rooms were rented at bargain prices for any length of time, with daily breakfast and dinner served in a sumptuous dining hall. My room was vast, with bed, night table, bureau and a desk in dark oak, all donated to the British federation of Women Graduates by lady-donors whose names were conscientiously affixed on a plaque on each piece of furniture. There was a closet with a small washstand and a toilet, but the showers were outside on the landing to be shared with the other boarders on the floor.

Behind the large bow window, I overlooked the lawn, Cheyne walk, the Thames and, beyond Albert Bridge and Battersea bridge, the tall plane trees of Battersea Park. At rising tide, the river became wild, swelling with high waves like in a tempest. Along Cheyne walk, the heavy truck and car traffic went parallel with the giant black barges steaming on the water and, above, planes shrieked and roared as they took off or went down to land at Heathrow. The constant move on land, water and up in the sky kept the whole landscape throbbing at all times, day and night. As if a cartoonist had decided to animate the old wonderful Turner view. Turner had actually lived his last years in the house just next to Crosby Hall, thrilled by the land sloping gently down to the river and the wide horizon opening west on flamboyant sunsets.

At seven that evening, I went down for dinner. There was bustle and chatter all over Crosby Hall. Girls from all floors poured from the stairs and from the oak elevator into the hall on the ground floor. We treaded slowly through the narrow passage to the dining room. It felt like entering a church. Dark carved wood paneled the walls and the high ceiling. Giant multicolored coats of arms all around the room glared in the sparse light given by candelabras hanging from the ceiling. The tables were long and bare, of the same dark wood as the rest. Mats, plates and cutlery were already set and everybody sat at random wherever there was room. Two big bosomed and bottomed maids were going from a counter opening on the kitchen to the tables, carrying big trays with bowls of soup. Voices were resonating in the dining hall forcing everyone to talk louder to be heard. Latecomers kept arriving as the main course was being served. The maids held their tray with one arm and scooped with the other in the various dishes of vegetables, sauce and meat according to each diner's wishes. A tall girl, dark-skinned, her hair pulled backwards in a tail had come to sit in a hurry in front of me. After gulping down her soup so that the maid could take it, she took a piece of bread in the basket sitting on the table and looked up, smiling lightly. "New?" She asked me. I nodded.

She held out her hand, "Anna, I am from Greece." She was working on a master in English literature. "We are only four Greeks here" she said, "Practically all girls come from the Middle East."

A dessert followed the main course of meat and vegetables. That day it was a rosy blancmange. The food was hearty, portions as big as anyone wanted with second helping at will. The atmosphere recalled a convent school with only females around and long communal tables like in a refectory. Most of the girls had been eating pretty fast. Anna seemed in a hurry also, but she suggested we have coffee together. One could help oneself every evening in the sitting room from silver coffee pots put on a round table. The settees and armchairs were more comfy and the atmosphere more friendly that in the big dining hall. Some girls were dressed with western clothes, pants or skirts, but others wore baggy dresses, covering knees and legs. They all seemed to know each other, chatting, laughing. They had all arrived already at the end of August to enrol into their respective schools.

Anna introduced me to Voula and Myrto. Voula was small with a childish round face and very short hair, dressed in a girlie frock. She was studying Byzantine musicology. Myrto looked much older, in her mid-thirties. She was doing an internship as a hospital nurse. When I told them that I had been to Greece a year before and that I was studying Greek in Paris, they smiled politely. Like Voula, Anna talked about her father often. They both seemed to be in love with them. While Anna's father was alive, Voula' s father had long been dead, but she still cried at the iniquity of his death. She even seemed to resent the survival of her mother. Anna and Voula were both from provincial towns, Volos and Corinth. Myrto was from Athens, where she lived with her mother. I listened eagerly to their chatting in Greek. As I was leaving with them, a girl in jeans came in, going straight to the only coffee pot remaining. "That's Maria" said Anna as they exchanged a

"Yassou, ti kanis". "Hem! French!" said Maria shaking my hand meekly on her way out.

By night, my room was filled with the thunder and shrieks of trucks and planes, more prominent than during the day. But the lights underlining the banks and the bridges, shivering in the dark Thames waters made up for the din. On clear nights, I beheld the moon and stars overhead. Before I went to bed, I could always hear an old man meowing, just below my window. Mr. Chives was the sole male employee of Crosby Hall and the love of his life was a big black and white tomcat, a female I supposed from her name of "Millie". He was always bad-tempered, sulking or grumbling. He obviously hated the tribe of females he had fallen into. He could be mean, rarely answering good nights and helloes from the residents. He spent every night at Crosby Hall, with a sofa in the back to lie on when he was tired. He had a rough, red face with cold blue eyes that never twitched behind his glasses. He arrived at dinnertime and left twelve hours later at seven in the morning. Around midnight, his grey coat and hat on, he went out in the garden looking for Millie out on her night hunt. He went meowing and whispering sweet nothings in the night to the invisible cat. He bent to the ground to pour the milk in a bowl. Millie would arrive at long last, late enough to have kept him worried, her tail high up in the air and her muzzle vibrating. He managed to caress her while she pumped all the milk, chanting and buzzing his love. But once she had finished, she quickly fled, unless he was quick enough to grab her and take her in his arms.

All the residents, except me, seemed to have tough schedules starting early morning and lasting until night. They ran to London University, Imperial College or various hospitals by bus or tube, both chronically full and non-predictable. Breakfast was the main meal of the day together with dinner in the evening. No lunch was served. In the morning, everybody ate fast but a lot: boiled and fried eggs, fried tomatoes, bacon, sausages, porridge, cereals, toasts, butter and jams. I had no schedule but the one I chose. In any case, it was better to take buses later in the morning when peak hour had passed. I came down at half past eight, when most girls had left. That's how I had met Suzie, a black American, as she was complaining aloud about the bacon. "They have no idea what real bacon is" she said aloud to whoever cared to listen. "In the US we know. It has to be crisp, real crisp, not that greasy, flabby stuff". She was contemplating her plate with a grimace of disgust. She had got up to give it back in the kitchen. Voula was sitting not far from me and she had rolled up her eyes at the fastidiousness of Suzie who was talking with wide gestures and loud voice to an impassive maid behind the counter. Coming back, she turned to me, asking where I was from. "France" she started simpering, "La France, oh my!" "Do you eat bacon over there?" she asked, bursting into a big laugh. "You like England?" "I don't" she answered for herself. "What are you doing here? What a French could be doing here?" But she got up all of a sudden, looking at her watch with a shriek. She had an appointment. Voula sighed. "It's always like that." Suzie did not have anything definite to do in life. She had fallen in love months before with a man from Ghana she had met while strolling on Piccadilly Circus. After raving about going to live in Africa with him, Suzie had come back to Crosby Hall, as bored and fussy as ever.

The London Times was on a coffee table in the sitting room every day. In the empty and idle room, I lingered every morning, reading the newspaper and enjoying the pleasure of being lonely in a place normally filled with lots of girls. I could hear the voice of the Warden, Mrs. Hargrave, a stiff but politely cheerful lady with long white hair framing her long face and long nose, as she pottered in her office with the secretary. Besides them, the charwomen were the only other people around. When I went up to my room to get my jacket, Joy, in charge of the second floor, was busy dusting off and wiping. She had an angular face with alert little grey eyes and a Cockney accent that enchanted me. While her small hands kept busy, she went on talking to herself or to me if I looked interested. Vowels lingered in her mouth wide open, while her speech went up and down and circling like a roundabout. She marveled at a small leather manicure set I had brought with me, or she switched to politics, complaining about the cost of food, or rents. I left her soliloquizing.

British Museum Library

First, I had tried to take a bus to go to the British Museum, but it was helpless. Bus after bus came, at half hour intervals, ever more full, people hanging in clusters on the open platform. They went forward at snail pace, joggling like obese elephants. Frustrated, I walked to Sloane Square and took the Tube to Russell square. I liked the walk, turning into Beaufort Street and into King's road where the sidewalks were narrow but not too busy during the week. Along with the dairy shops and greengrocers were many small shops, all probably born in the sixties, their windows filled with fancy boots and clothes. On Sloane Square, there was a *Smith &Son*, a *Boots* and a *Peter Jones*. But after paying my one hundred and twenty pounds a month to Crosby Hall, I didn't have much to spend. On my way back, I bought tiny tomatoes and cucumbers, a luxury in winter, coming from some faraway sunny country. Behind the shop window, they were neatly presented in impeccable rows on fluffy white paper and the shopkeeper took them one by one delicately as if they could break. The tomatoes and cucumbers were my lunch, with a sprinkle of olive oil. Myrto had given me a bottle of the olive oil, which she brought back every Christmas from the Peloponnese village of her mother.

The British Museum was monumental, a world in itself. To get to the library, I had to cross the large entrance hall and go out in an open courtyard around which the whole Museum was built. In the middle of the courtyard stood the Library, an elegant rotund building with a glass dome. Like

Widener Library and the *Bibliothèque Nationale*, it was not open to the public, but only to students and scholars. The courtyard was cold, damp and often swept by heavy rain and wind. But, crossing the elements to get to the Library made it even more heaven. Tucked under the high glass dome which blurred the bad weather outside, letting only daylight come through, it felt like a magic cavern, or like being in Captain Nemo's submarine. The curved ceiling was painted with delicate motifs in light blue, pink, yellow and white that made up splendidly for the lack of sunshine. The employees talked and moved softly and there was never a stir in the opalescent bubble. I read for hours, sometimes looking up at the pastel ceiling and daydreaming. The Bloomsbury people gave me ample work. Leonard and Virginia Woolf, Roger Fry, Maynard Keynes, Vanessa and Quentin Bell, the flamboyant Ottoline Morrell. I followed them into their trips, their trysts, and their quarrels.

Leonard and Virginia Woolf had been to Greece in the twenties. Their route had taken them to the known Delphi, Epidaurus and Olympia, but they had also ventured through central Peloponnese, the ancient Arcadia, to a place called Bassae. Leonard in his memoirs recounted the frightening road, a track rather, littered with stones falling from the vertiginous heights of the mountains above. The Greek taxi-driver had valiantly gone up the endless canyon to the small plateau where a grey stone temple was standing up, almost intact, in the middle of nowhere. The temple at Bassae had been built by Ictinos, the same architect who had built the Parthenon in Athens.

The Bassae frieze

After many hours sitting down, I would usually get cramped. I would get up, cross the courtyard and wander in the Museum proper. As vast as a forest, it was the perfect place to stretch and get some exercise, going past thousands of masterpieces and through thousands of years of time. There was nobody in the rooms, save a few museum attendants asleep on their feet. My preferred domain was the Oriental collection. In a long room that looked like a hospital ward, I went past a whole population of mummies, all lying parallel in their painted caskets. Further on, I went past giant Assyrian riders and fighters with horses as big as them, and mysterious bulls with wings and human heads. Finally, I arrived in the Elgin rooms. There lay, laboriously reconstructed, the front sculptures of the Parthenon, a giant relief depicting the Gods of Olympia, sitting or lying in a mounting crescendo of size, culminating in the middle and decreasing after. But in the Museum room, big and well lit for sure, the Gods looked lost, like jailed exiles. Their precious marble bodies bore the marks of wounds inflicted on them when they had been savagely carved from the Parthenon and thrown onto a ship to England by Lord Elgin. Those rooms were the only ones that attracted scores of visitors any day of the week. I had always liked the triumphant *"Victoire de Samothrace"*, her wings spread at the top of a majestic staircase at the *Louvre* in Paris, and also the *"Vénus de Milo"* because, in spite of missing arms and noses, they both looked alive. But here, Zeus, Hera and their children looked like pitiful war veterans with their shattered faces and body remnants.

Going a little further, eager for a less crowded area, I had come upon a real marvel in almost pristine condition. It was not obvious to find the narrow and dark staircase that led to a small mezzanine room plunged in chiaroscuro. It was called the "Bassae" room. The name rang a bell. The Woolfs! Bassae was the name of that mysterious temple in an Arcadian valley Leonard and Virginia had gone to see. I was face to face with a complete and intact frieze, a series of grey stone slabs depicting in relief the fight of Heracles against the Amazons, and the fight of the Centaurs against the Lapiths. The miniature personages, running, riding, dying, drawing swords and daggers, killing or imploring, sprang to life as I went around the room, unrolling their story. A cartouche in a corner signaled that the whole frieze had also been brought back by Lord Elgin, carved on the spot from the temple of Bassae, the last, almost intact, Doric temple in Greece. Mesmerized by the expressions on faces, the gracious movement of the bodies, I went around the room twice. While the Parthenon remnants were all damaged, the Bassae frieze didn't have one defect; not one foot, nose or head was missing. The story was intact, as were its actors from 420 B.C. My preferred slab represented Olympia, Queen of the Amazons succumbing to Heracles's strong fist holding her wrist. Olympia was kneeling down, but her face smiled as if she was succumbing to love rather than force, and Heracles's fierce hold was a lover's gesture. For days on end, every time I needed a break from my reading, I went back to that dark room. Again and again, Amazons and Greek soldiers would spring up to life, no bigger than puppets but larger than life and death.

The British Museum Library had a special section where original manuscripts of letters and literary works were kept as treasures. Access to them was highly regulated for limited time and occurrences. I had got permission to consult the "Katherine Mansfield" files. The room for the consultation of those manuscripts was no bigger than a classroom, with a very low ceiling due to the fact that it was under the roof. I had to wait a long time until an employee brought me a series of boxes. I had opened one, shocked to see the handwriting on the paper. I had read already a huge amount of Katherine Mansfield's letters to John Middleton Murry, published in a big volume. I knew a lot about her, besides her writing career, but nothing had prepared me to the shock of the real life jumping from those handwritten ink characters creeping like a vine on the paper sheet. All of a sudden, on the desk in front of me, Katherine became alive, not just a figure of English literature. It felt both sacred and sacrilege to touch those letters and notebooks, the most intimate writing she had intended for her close friends or for herself, certainly not for a stranger to investigate mercilessly.

Coming out of the Museum and Library, I walked for a while, catching the Tube further on down the line. It was always dark when I emerged on Sloane Square, in front of the windows of Peter Jones casting light and color with their chic dummies. The sidewalks of King's road were crowded in the evening, with people shopping hastily on their way home after a day's work. Back at Crosby Hall, the bustle of the residents and the warm smells of food from the dining hall were the right thing after a day floating at the Library.

Maria's lover

Anna, Voula and Myrto were too elusive to be friends. Anna was going to leave soon to go back to Greece. Myrto was going to move to another residence where she could have a small apartment with her own kitchen. Voula seemed walled into mourning her father. Maria was more communicative. I had walked with her once in a while on King's road, going back to Crosby Hall. She was studying economics at London University. Her parents and two brothers lived in Athens. She had asked me one day to accompany her to the office of a Greek businessman that gave her money on behalf of her father in Athens. She disliked going alone and having to chitchat with the guy. The main reason for this dislike was her fear of betraying a well-kept secret. Maria had a lover, a Lebanese student she had met at a New Year's party the year before. Every weekend, Maria was taking the train to Manchester where her boyfriend was studying. Her parents knew nothing about it. At Easter, she had gone to Athens with him, wearing a frizzy wig and Jackie O' sunglasses. Feeling like robbers, they had got into her parents' apartment. But just as they were going out onto the street, her parents and brothers were coming in. Maria had gone past them, head down, while they looked at her wondering who was that woman wearing sunglasses in the dark hall.

One morning, we went together to the Greek businessman to pick up her money. It was a bombed out area. The narrow no-exit street smelled. Black water stagnated in the gutter. From the outside, the brick building looked like an abandoned factory. Inside, typing machines rattled on all floors. Plump and heavily made up secretaries came in and out of offices where fat men smoked and yelled, glancing at us as we were going upstairs to the office of the boss. It was a shipping company. The personal secretary of the boss, an elderly matron, had welcomed Maria with motherly kisses. The boss was yelling in Greek on the phone, but as Maria stepped in, his voice switched to candy. He stayed on his seat, asking Maria and I to sit on the chairs in front of his desk. They exchanged cheerful words with abundant smiles and exclamations from Maria, and a kind of insistent sweetness from the man who looked like Fernandel, with deep lines on each side of his mouth, like an old dog, and dark circles around his big dark eyes. He was from Cyprus and he had known Maria's father in Africa when the latter was running an import business. Maria interrupted their conversation in Greek to ask me if I wanted a drink, at the same time making a quick grimace to prompt me to say no. She looked at her watch and said we had to be at school in a while, but next time, maybe. The man opened a drawer in front of him and took out a bundle of banknotes. He proceeded to count the notes one by one, licking his finger and then, tapping them into a neat little pile, he handed them over to Maria who quickly put them in her handbag. She got up and they started again their Greek civilities, putting their hand on their heart, patting each other and at last, waving goodbye.

"My poor father" said Maria as we walked back to the Tube station. "Every time I call him, he asks me: "Money?" and I feel terrible." Her father had come back from Africa, having amassed a lot of money from his import-export business. He had settled again in Athens and started a construction business. Maria had seen him for the first time when she was already seven years old. She knew her time in

London was counted, and so too was her love affair with her Lebanese boyfriend. Her parents would never accept a non-Greek for a son in law, neither would they agree with her living away from Greece. And since they financed her, she had to abide by their choices.

Sundays at Battersea Park

Sundays were dull at Crosby Hall. I usually went to walk along the Thames, up to Westminster Bridge. Not far, there was a small pretty church, the Chelsea Old Church, with trees and lawns around it. I sat on a bench and enjoyed the Turner view for a while. The church was Unitarian. I had gone in on Sunday afternoons while they were singing lively hymns. The vicar was an affable man, white-haired and good-looking. I had seen him distributing food to bums that came to sit on the steps. Seen from the riverbank, London offered a meandering perspective punctuated by bridges, each decorated differently like a flock of ships. There was no skyline, not even tall buildings, save the Westminster Parliament and London Bridge, towering above like in a Flemish landscape. The size of the river surprised me every time I walked along the Thames. The powerful waters rushed and clashed according to the tides and, from one bank to the other the distance was too big to see clearly. On foggy days, the river, the opposite bank and the whole of London disappeared. Not yet tamed entirely, the Thames looked like a Mississippi lost in England. Crossing the bridges was tricky when the wind blew hard and, with autumn gathering steam, the wind was getting fierce, the type of wind that could "dehorn bovines" as my family said.

On Cheyne walk, just a few steps from Crosby Hall, I crossed Albert Bridge, which was almost parallel with Battersea Bridge. Going that way, the Thames grew larger, as it approached the sea that was not yet visible beyond the flat landscape extending as far as the eye could see. On the opposite bank, Battersea Park rustled and whistled with birds crowding the plane trees, in growing numbers since I had arrived in September. The leaves were falling in packs at every gust of wind while the birds seemed to intensify their shrieks, as if a tough negotiation was going on. Did birds take decisions? I wondered. They did, I realized. They had to come and go, both to find food and find a mate. Once in a while, the cackling birds left their trees and flew around in formation like well-trained pilots. They landed back on their branches and resumed their tergiversations. They were going to leave, I knew, but they didn't seem ready yet. Every Sunday by any weather, mothers pushed prams in the alleys, boys played ball games and dogs ran around. There was no dinner on Sunday at the Hall and I was left to my tomatoes with olive oil and salt. Discreetly, I made rice in the teakettle. The small lid made it tough to get the rice out and to wash the kettle. The rice was sticky and filled with water but it made up for the bread I couldn't find in London.

Nasreen from Baghdad

It was on one of those boring Sundays that I met Nasreen. She had just arrived from Baghdad. I had seen her in the group of Iraqi girls that stuck together at dinner. But while all the others had dark hair, dark eyes, strong features, arched noses, which I associated wrongly or not with an Arab girl, Nasreen was ash blonde, with very blue eyes and a light rosé complexion like a porcelain doll. She looked young enough to be eighteen or less. She was pacing around the garden one Sunday as I was coming back from a walk in the park. We had smiled to each other and started to talk. She had come for a three months internship in a psychiatric hospital. She already practiced psychiatry at the main Baghdad hospital and she had come to London to get acquainted with new treatments. She was an Iraqi citizen, but from the Kurd minority. She was not Moslem, she was Chaldean Catholic, the oldest Christian rite. She talked and behaved with a mix of grace and childishness, her face laughing one minute and frowning the next. She made me think of Tolstoï's *Natacha Rostov*, her gracious features and fair complexion could have been Russian.

Soon, Nasreen had told me of her secret plot. She was a Catholic but she was in love with a Moslem. Ahmed was a psychiatrist at the same Baghdad hospital where she trained. Their relationship had been carried on in total secret and the only place where they could meet without awakening suspicions was the bazaar. In the dense crowd, they could be together and anonymous. Nasreen would put a thick veil on her head on those occasions, ready to drape the scarf on her face at the slightest hint of recognition from someone. Her face was blushing as she talked about Ahmed. Going shopping at the bazaar was the most natural thing to do and Nasreen's parents had had no hint of the love story. On one of those trips to the bazaar, she had seen beautiful daggers and she had bought one for Ahmed, ordering a special sheath of leather and silk embroidered with pearls in complicated motifs. She had told me about it at length, moving her hands and fingers to express the beauty of the dagger in its sheath. I had understood that the dagger and the sheath were like the symbol of their fusion as lovers, although Nasreen seemed strangely unawares of the symbolism herself, as if her psychiatric expertise was vanishing behind her passionate love for Ahmed. She showed an absolute innocence that puzzled me. It puzzled her too. She and Ahmed had kissed and hugged, but they had never slept together.

Their plot was working fine. Nasreen had first arrived on the pretext of a three-months internship. Ahmed was due to arrive in mid-October. They would get married in London after fifteen days of residence in England, as required by British law. After the marriage, they would go up to Birmingham where Ahmed had already secured a position at the local hospital. They planned to stay in England a few years, until the scandal would have calmed down at home, but there was a possibility that they would never go back to Iraq if both families persisted in refusing to accept their marriage. Ahmed's family expected him to marry a Moslem girl and Nasreen's family expected her to marry a Catholic man. All the more since the Catholics of Iraq were a minority community of barely one million people, a sort of endangered species that felt jeopardized by mixed marriages with Moslems, the dominant religion. Nasreen was a true believer however and, although she wanted to marry Ahmed and only Ahmed, she had no intention of renouncing her Catholic faith. As a consequence, she had to have three marriage ceremonies. The first ceremony would be the civil wedding at the Chelsea registrar's office. The second would be the Moslem wedding at a London Mosque. The third marriage would be the Catholic wedding. While Ahmed was getting ready to come, Nasreen was busy arranging her marriages. There would be no reception and no guests, but she wanted a white bridal gown and, most of all, the Catholic wedding. As she was telling me about her preparations, I felt a pang of anguish for her. What if Ahmed didn't show up? Nasreen was not worried about that. She only worried about their sexual relationship. She was perfectly conscious of the gap between her sexual inexperience and her medical knowledge of sexuality. "I have seen men's genitals during all my career as a psychiatrist. I know what is copulation, how it works, what it does. I am not afraid" she confided in me candidly, "But what if it doesn't work?"

The Faduah club

Nasreen herself had brought me one evening to have coffee with the group of Iraqi girls. Weary of the British insipid brew, they sat after dinner in the sitting room mostly to eat the biscuits that accompanied the coffee, but for the real thing they retired to their apartments. Since I didn't know a soul in London, it was pleasant to meet them every day for coffee. They had become my chums. It had not escaped their attention that Nasreen and I had a close relationship and probably shared secrets. The exuberance of Nasreen was a sure sign of deep happiness that those girls knew had to do with love, hence with a man.

Faduah was the leader of the group, a heavy girl who had something of a Buddha, with a protruding bust and tummy and a heavy face whose fat was sitting at the base of her neck like a collar. Her hair was long and rolled in a bun on her nape. Her brown eyes were always alert and her tongue always ready to mock. She had a rough expression and a rough voice, but I found her funny. She had a lot of irony which she exerted nonstop. Sophia, a very stiff Japanese woman who was staying at Crosby Hall, made her roll her eyes and smile any time she was mentioned. "Sophia is crazy" she would say, "All Japanese are crazy" and she giggled irrepressibly. She also made jokes about Mr. Chives the night watch, whom she called our eunuch. Faduah was a gynaecologist like two other Iraqi girls. Besides paediatrics, gynaecology was the only acceptable medical field for a Moslem woman. They could not be in contact with men, only with females and children. Nasreen had been able to become a psychiatrist because she was a Christian, hence freer.

Coffee at Faduah's was a sophisticated event. We sat on the floor on a giant carpet she had brought from Iraq. A little gas burner was put in the middle and lit with a lighter. The girls sat in a circle with their legs crossed or on their heels. They all wore long frocks or skirts, which were in fact in tune with the hippie style of the time. Only a girl from Bahrein and myself wore blue jeans. Faduah went to fetch water in her bathroom and came back, the copper pot in her hand. She knelt down in front of the little gas burner, increasing the flame before putting the copper pot on top. I was familiar with the "briki" and the oriental way to make coffee, which was the same in Greece. But the Greeks didn't sit on the floor like we did, which made Faduah's room feel like a tent out in the desert. One pot filled two cups and

Faduah made more coffee until everyone had a cup. Coffee was a distinct Baghdadi invention as they had pointed out to me with a didactic tone. From there it had spread all over the world. The coffee was strong and sweet with an added heavenly flavour that I could not define, a mix of mint and anis maybe with a hint of lemon. It was cardamom, a spice they powdered lightly on the coffee. As we drank the coffee, we raised our cups and toasted each other with customary wishes of good health and thanks to Faduah who sat on the only chair. Some of us, I included, smoked, which Faduah tolerated.

Faduah was in her third year in London and she would go back to Baghdad at the end of the academic year. She and the others looked forlorn when caught unawares. Only one woman in the group was married. She hated being in London but her husband, a bright and famous scientist, had pressured her into coming to advance her career as a gynaecologist. She was a Kurd like Nasreen, but a Moslem with as dark a complexion and eyes as Nasreen's were fair and clear. She complained of having to examine vulvas of doubtful cleanliness.

The Bahreini girl was different. She giggled non-stop, she made faces, and she joked about virginity all the time. "My most precious thing" she said laughing. She wore heavy make-up, long floating hair, tight jeans pants and jacket and white sneakers. She was tall and skinny like a model, but her heavy make-up that made cakes on her acne-ravaged face made her look rather like a transvestite. Her father was an old sheik who had twelve wives, the latest one younger than she was. When she sat with us, she laughed all the time and made jokes about sex nonstop. Her usual line was that a girl had only one treasure, meaning virginity. She said often with more big laughs that she had already given away her most precious treasure. She had even said it in front of a man who had come up once to the room of one girl.

A man in a girl's room was a complete revolution, although they all seemed to take it lightly. One Saudi girl, barely twenty years old, who studied physics at Imperial College, had brought him to Crosby Hall. He was a Kuweiti and they had met before. They had fallen for each other at first sight. The girls' parents had already arranged her marriage with a fellow Saudi and she knew that she stood no chance to marry the man she loved. But she was still free and living in London, far from the promised groom. The boy had come, they had gone out together and she had brought him up to her room, quiet but determined. To keep a certain amount of convention, her roommate was there too and she had invited us all for coffee that afternoon. Her room was much smaller than Faduah's and we had all sat on the two facing single beds, covered with silky pink nylon that draped the windows too. The room smelled perfume like a tart's boudoir. The Kuweiti man looked like a Westerner, sporting a bomber jacket and no moustache nor beard. For good measure, he had brought himself a Palestinian friend who sat silent on one chair while the Saudi girl sat on the sole other chair, having served coffee to all. The Bahreini girl teased the Kuwëiti Romeo with her usual laugh, titillating him with words and touching him here and there. The Saudi girl didn't seem to care at all, while the guy blushed. "He is the one that took my most precious thing" she shrieked as if choking with her own laughter.

Nasreen had told me that the Bahreini girl was indeed in bad shape, having frequent fits of depression. Walking on the street, she looked lost and forlorn. When she had invited me for coffee in her room one day, I had accepted. As we sipped the coffee, she had taken off her her big glasses. Her long dark eyes reminded me of a camel's diifident ones. The floor was littered with women magazines. Our conversation switched to Nasreen and Ahmed, now their love story no longer a secret, and I told her how happy I was that at long last they could be married together. It must be so tough to be obliged to marry a husband chosen by the family, I added.

She kept silent and, pulling back her long hair with both her hands, she complained of migraine. I asked if she needed an aspirin or something. She shook her head and got up, her glasses back on. I left. Minutes later, she had stormed into Faduah' s room, in tears and enraged. She had yelled about "that French girl and her dirty mind." Nasreen was there. She had tried to calm her down. It was a quiproquo, but from then on the Bahreini girl would change sidewalk if she saw me in the distance.

A Sunday trip

Sophia the Japanese had arranged to go and see Myrto in her new place. Myrto had left to stay in a Catholic convent where she would have a tiny one-room flat with a kitchenette. Sophia, usually very reserved, had decided to rally whoever Myrto knew for the trip. She seemed terribly excited. Even Faduah, rolling up her yes, had accepted to join "that crazy Sophia". Ten of us, with Sophia who had traced the whole itinerary, started out one Sunday at noon. We had to take the Tube and two buses to get there. Impeccably dressed with a smart little coat and matching hat, Sophia turned her head regularly to check on her flock. Faduah was dragging her feet and fuming as we were walking to the tube, down the tube, up from the tube, waiting for an improbable bus in the freezing cold of November, and for another one again. The trip all the way to Chalk farm was endless. The suburb was greenish and gloomy in the weakening daylight. The vaguely gothic convent's yellow brick buildings stood on top of a grassy mound. The day was almost over and dusk was settling in. It had taken us more than two hours to get there. The place seemed deserted. We rang the bell and waited. A mousey nun in grey skirt and grey veil opened the door and shuffled us through the long corridors that linked the sparse buildings.

Myrto was waiting for us in her flat with a table all prepared for tea. We had brought her flowers and sweets. She seemed happy and moved that we had come all that way to see her. The nun started pouring the tea in cups. Myrto introduced her as Sister Joan, her best friend. The nun didn't open her mouth and sat with us the whole time. Myrto seemed to be trying hard to be jolly, but there was something wrong in the picture. Under the plastered smile, she looked lost and haggard. "I am not alone, you see, since I have so many friends" she said repeatedly. We had a cup of tea and a slice of cake before starting the long way back. We had barely stayed two hours there. When we left, the nun was still there, beginning to clean up the table. Night had fallen as we walked to the bus stop. None of us said anything as we waited in the cold. But we all thought that for a kitchenette, Myrto seemed to be paying a dear price. We never heard of her again. She never returned our visit.

A baptism certificate

Nasreen was worried. It had nothing to do with Ahmed. It had to do with a Catholic vicar. Nasreen had gone to meet him to arrange for the Catholic wedding that she wanted at all costs. The Vicar had been very considerate, without any objection to the groom being Moslem. But, at the end of their meeting, he had asked Nasreen for her certificate of baptism. Nasreen had remained speechless. A certificate? But she was baptized of course. Still, the Catholic Church required a certificate to make sure people getting a Catholic marriage were authentic. It was the rule. Nasreen had said she would try her best, but it would take time. She had to write to the Catholic Church in Baghdad. In fact she was not even sure they would find any trace of her baptism. She had been born in the mountains at the beginning of the fifties at a time when the Kurds were fleeing persecution. It was no time to register baptisms then. Her family was on the run. She had come back to the Vicar telling him the facts and the impossibility to produce a valid certificate. The Vicar had expressed his regrets, but had confirmed that the Catholic ceremony could not take place without that proof of baptism. Nasreen was overcome with despair. The Moslem and civil marriages were not enough. She had to have a Catholic one.

I was flabbergasted. Born myself a Catholic, I was ashamed and enraged. What right had a Vicar to screen people like a policeman? Nasreen could well be the last girl in the world so intent on marrying in the Catholic faith. Her story was genuine and the suspicion of the priest was outrageous. I offered to find a Catholic priest that could produce a forged certificate. Nasreen refused stubbornly. To answer stupidity by dishonesty was not and never would be her thing. She would find a solution. A week later, she was relieved. She had found a compromise. The affable Vicar at Chelsea Old Church had accepted right away to marry Nasreen and Ahmed. This was not a Catholic Church, but Unitarians were Christian. That was enough for her.

Ahmed arrived in London but did not show up at Crosby Hall. He and Nasreen were still as careful as in Baghdad not to be seen together. Even if they were both adults, their families could still get in the way and make things difficult. On the part of the other Iraqi girls, there was understanding for Nasreen but no sympathy. Not that they were envious of her happiness, they just thought it was unworkable. In their eyes, a Moslem and a Catholic could not be happily married. They had many examples of such marriages that had gone to the dogs after a couple of years. Besides, for some of them, Nasreen's love story seemed to stir up painful memories. "She won't be the first girl that cannot marry the man she loves" had said bitterly Faduah's roommate, and Faduah had nodded. Many had known an unfortunate and unfulfilled love, broken by their parents in all good faith and for their own good. They had resigned themselves to the only choice they had: either marry the man of their family's choice or remain single. It was my turn to be shocked. Nasreen at least was willing to take risks, boldly and in full knowledge of them. If no one did as she did, their lives would go on being casually destroyed forever.

Forbidden love

There was a solution however to the dilemma, a centuries-old one. Love could be kept secret and one could live a double life. Which was exactly what Nasreen refused to do. I had been arrested one day by the silhouette of a woman walking on Beaufort Street. She walked ahead, as if oblivious of the man who followed her with gestures of remonstrance. They disappeared into a private residence called Beaufort mansions. Later, as I was finishing dinner in the already empty dining room, I had seen the same woman enter the dining hall. Above her black turtleneck, her face was pale and impassive. Her long neck and slim figure that seemed elongated gave her a disembodied appearance, like a creature of El Greco. She was strikingly beautiful and I could not help watching her. It had to do with that strange expression on her face. Her features were absolutely still, her eyes carefully clothed into thick eyeliner and mascara, her spine rigidly straight. She looked like a walking mask, a mummified being. Yes, she looked like a living dead. She was nibbling at the food a maid had brought her, breaking a piece of bread.

I had learnt from a Kurd woman, who was an intern at the same hospital that the girl was from Iran. She was officially a resident at Crosby Hall, but she spent most of her time around the corner in an apartment in Beaufort mansions. Her lover had followed her to London, with his wife and children. He had rented an apartment for his family and another for his mistress. The Kurd woman was sorry for her. The girl had in fact come to London to put an end to their affair, but he had immediately arrived on her trail. Her lover would not let go of her. They had both fallen in love in their teens, but neither family wanted to hear of such a marriage. He had married the girl his mother had chosen for him. The couple now had two children and one on the way. But without qualms, he lugged wife and children and followed the girl he loved wherever she went. I would see them, like a close-knit family, shopping along King's road. The girl with her tragic face, pale and resigned, always ahead of the group. She seemed lost in her inner world, while her lover followed close on her heels. The wife, wearing a veil and a long caftan, dragged her feet at a distance, a child in her arms and another holding her hand.

Abla the ceramist

The arrival of Abla had brought a welcome diversion to the tensions in the group. A renowned ceramist in Baghdad, she was coming for Christmas shopping in London and to meet curators and collectors. A short woman in her fifties, she had a wrinkled little face sparkling with joy. She spoke very softly and slowly, giving a feel of tranquil self-assurance. She was unmarried, yet apparently fulfilled. No marriage would have given her the secluded space she needed for her art. Reading the future in coffee grounds was another talent of hers.

As usual, we were all sitting for coffee at Faduah's after dinner. Abla had begun to turn a cup upside down. Reading coffee grounds was common in Iraq, but Abla was famed for it. She placed the upside down cup on a saucer and waited quietly for the coffee grounds to fall down on the saucer. She checked twice to see if the cup was stuck enough on the saucer, which would indicate the grounds had slipped down. Looking absorbed, she lifted the cup and started to look inside. The younger girls liked it more than the older ones. I could see on Faduah's face that she found coffe grounds reading utterly silly. The future did not interest her anyway. The voice of Abla, high-pitched but sweet like a little girl's, was rising slowly. Arabic words came out like pure music to me. Rough consonants contrasted softer syllables, like dunes or cliffs followed by sweet descent in the soft sand. If only for that music, reading the coffee grounds was worth it. When my turn came, Abla switched to English, which I regretted. The words didn't matter, the sound of Arabic would have told me as well what fate had in store for me. Because I was impatient, it felt like ages while she scrutinized my cup. She seemed to be pondering her oracle that was also a judgment. Abla held the cup as if she weighed your soul, like the God Anubis. She beheld almost tenderly those rivulets of coffee grounds going down the white china cup, she looked for hieroglyphs that only she was able to decipher. Having looked again and again, she pressed her thumb on the bottom of the cup where grounds were still thick to get another interesting pattern of coffee.

I could sense curiosity in the other girls's eyes. After all, I had not said much about myself, except the obvious. I was reading and writing a thesis on Katherine Mansfield and I would be back in Paris in a couple of months. At long last, Abla looked up and smiled, as if back on earth. "There are two persons in that cup" she started slowly. "One is against a tree. The other is walking away." She turned again the cup. "The first one is still. The second is moving. See…" She moved nearer to me and pointed with her small finger at the faint lines sketching a tree, one silhouette against it, another silhouette with two legs, one leg forward. They were no more than a few millimeters, sketched in brown on the white china. "Someone wants to stay, and someone wants to move" she declared. That's all she had to say, no more and no less. Abla had delivered her oracle, I could do what I wanted with it. She looked at me with her alert eyes. Many things were brewing in that cup, and it was time to take decisions, she knew it perfectly well.

The evening before she left, she came to see me. She wanted to say goodbye and tell me she had been glad to meet me. She wished me the best for the years to come and said that whatever happened, it would be good. She told me of

Nasreen too and said it was good that we were friends since Nasreen needed to talk. Abla was the first in the group to speak about her with sympathy. She handed me a necklace she had made out of enameled ceramic squares, lozenges and pearls. This was her farewell present. Nasreen was going to accompany her to Heathrow the next day and I decided to join.

Abla had bought tens of presents and books. She had two enormous suitcases, many bags and shopping bags. We arrived at noon and went to the counter of Saudi Airways. The flight to Baghdad was delayed. At least we could register her luggage. In the queue were lots of fellow Baghdadis and Abla knew everybody. Most of the Iraqi passengers were men. Tall, dark, mustachioed, dressed in impeccably tailored suits, they came to London "to have fun" as Abla said lightly. I remembered the strange caravans I had seen sometimes around Knightsbridge. A man in white keffieh and long dress walked ahead of a flock of women dressed in black, their heads and faces completely hidden behind a thick black veil and a weird beak which covered nose, cheeks, mouth and chin. Their eyes were the only human element visible, otherwise they looked like weird insects. One emir and his harem had come to shop at Harrods. Iraqi men had no harems anymore, but they had their freedom. Nasreen had joined in the chatting with Abla. We all went for a drink, waiting for the flight to be announced. It took hours and Abla finally left late in the afternoon. A day in an airport was not very entertaining, but I knew it was important. The bustle and noise of Heathrow awakened me. That day, I remained on the ground, waving at Abla going away. Nasreen was going to leave in a few weeks. Most of the girls would be going home for the Christmas holidays. How long was I going to stay in London?

Wedding day

The date of Nasreen's marriage had been fixed for the first Saturday in November. As I was drinking coffee in the sitting room, Mr. Chives suddenly came in, looking furious. He pointed his finger at me. Someone was on the phone for me. I followed him and got into the booth by the reception desk. Nasreen was on the phone. She sounded terribly excited. "Listen, my father has come to London. I cannot stay in Crosby Hall. I cannot tell you where I am, but I'll call again. I am all right." As I came back, Faduah looked at me frowning. "Trouble?" Before I could answer, she went on, "Nasreen's father has come to London to fetch her", she said, "I know". Two days later, Nasreen called again. Her father had gone back to Baghdad. She had refused to meet him, but they had talked to each other. He didn't approve of her marriage, but he would not stop it and he wished her happiness. They had made peace. That was all she wanted.

Nasreen didn't come back to Crosby Hall and the girls made jokes about her remaining intact before marriage. I went to Peter Jones looking for a present. I settled on an earthenware tea service with blue flower motifs. The day of the wedding, the weather was abominable. It was cold, pouring rain and so windy that the short walk from Crosby hall to Chelsea High Church was like walking on a boat deck in a tempest. In their best Sunday clothes, Faduah and all the Iraqi girls looked like a procession of mourners. Long dark chiffon dresses showing below their coats, high heeled shoes and dark veils draped around head and neck. They looked sad. We walked against the fierce wind that sent us stumbling. The affable priest was standing in the choir, nodding gently to us as we got in. Chelsea Old Church was in halflight like at dawn. We went to sit in the third row of pews. In front, two chairs stood empty in the middle, with two pillows on the first step to the altar. The church was cold. Outside the pandemonium went on with rain slapping the stained glass, wind howling like a mad dog. There was light behind the organ.

Suddenly, the door opened and Nasreen appeared in a cloud of white. It was like sun after a storm. The organ burst out with a solemn march. Arm in arm with Ahmed, she walked up the aisle, radiant and rosy, her fresh face inundated with joy. She looked to us as she went up. The priest smiled benevolently from the top of the steps and the service started. During prayers, Nasreen knelt down on the pillow while Ahmed, unsure, looked at her. He knelt down but sat on his heels as in a mosque. He was a small man, with dark hair and a moustache. Nasreen's blushing face overflowed with joy as if her love after three years in hiding was springing out, inexhaustible. They pronounced their vows and exchanged their wedding bands. The organ burst out again and they went down the aisle. I had my wedding present all packed with me. We kissed on the doorstep. I shook Ahmed's hand and gave Nasreen the silly package. The church door opened. A taxi was waiting. They ran in the rain, she sat while Ahmed folded the white satin trailing behind. He got in and the taxi drove off. Nasreen turned back and waved behind the windshield, her face blurred by the raindrops.

We went down the church steps. Faduah was sulking, looking disenchanted. A week later, Nasreen called me. She was settled in a semi-detached house in Birmingham. Ahmed was working while she lazied around until she also got a job at the hospital. She had talked with her mother in law and all was well. Both families had accepted their marriage and promised to come and visit. She even planned to go to Baghdad the next summer for a holiday. She said she had one of my cups in her hand, drinking tea and she hoped I would be coming soon to visit. They had two spare rooms.

A Greek bookshop on Tottenham Court road

I was through with my research. I didn't have much to do anymore. One day as he was walking in London, D.H. Lawrence recounted in his memoirs that he had seen Katherine Mansfield and John Middleton Murry on top of a double-decker, pulling out their tongue and making faces at each other. If not pulling out my tongue, riding one of those red elephants sounded like a good idea. At noon, they were near empty. I could sit on the top deck on the front seat. It was like being in a helicopter. I could watch passers-by, shop windows and the whole range of houses from above. The slower the traffic, the more enjoyable it was. On Tottenham Court road, the bus almost came to a halt. The road was as crowded and messy as in century-old accounts I had read. Still tortuous, like the village alley it had been. The shops were crummy and undistinguished, save for giant signs above their windows. "XENOS" said one shop above its door, in light blue letters, "greek bookshop" it said below in smaller characters. I rushed down the bus and out.

In a place no bigger than a closet, books were falling off the bending shelves covering the walls. A man with wavy white hair and blue eyes was considering me. Xenos was his patronym. He stood up in his coat and muffler in front of a gas heater. I told him I was looking for a French-Greek dictionary and he pointed with his chin a shelf where they were. The one I had bought at *Brentano's* was no good. Xenos had exactly what I needed, two in-folio volumes of perspicacious translation both ways, and with sample phrases. As I was paying, a young man entered the shop and started speaking Greek with Xenos. He turned to me laughing. "You are learning Greek?" he asked. I nodded. "Why learn Greek? This is a stupid language and a stupid people". "That's none of your business" seemed to say the old Xenos admonishing him in Greek I could not understand.

Looking for a job

I read the London Times from beginning to end every morning before trying to decide what next. I had moved into a new room since mid-October. The big room with the bow window facing the Thames had already been reserved for October when they had given it to me. I had taken a smaller and cheaper room, overlooking a wall beyond which was Beaufort mansions. It was colder and dull. I missed the lively Thames view. The bed was narrower and shorter. It was another maid's room.

Every day, the Times had a double page of announcements of all kinds, jobs and travel in particular. A whole section was devoted to au-pair positions, which I looked at without much enthusiasm. I had spotted a Greek-English family looking for an au pair. The trip to get there was a half-day journey along endless little streets with little houses and little front gardens. Even a wasteland would have felt like a breath of fresh air in that frightening web, slowly closing in on the innocent passer-by like a spider on a fly. Their house reminded me of a suburban house I used to go to teach French in Cambridge, Mass. It was another miniature palace with an enormous number of rooms, but no bigger than closets and with very low ceilings. A man opened the door. We sat in the box-like living room, choked under multiple curtains and carpets. He was tall and portly, blond and blue-eyed. He was Greek, a writer and journalist as he told me right away, hence working from home.

I listened patiently as he said that he would be delighted to have a French au pair. Besides baby-sitting, I could give French lessons to his children. They had a room for me. He had it all set that I would stay with them. I left saying I would think it over, but I was fed up. It was like a Thackeray or Wharton story all over again. I had had enough of being a *"bonne"*. Fuming to myself, I took the bus and the tube and got off at Tottenham. Going to Xenos would allay my rage. That day, a list of flights was posted in the window. Xenos also sold airline tickets to Greece. When I came out, I felt better. Tons of energy was rushing in my feet. I had bought a one-way ticket to Athens.

In the birds' wake

The birds could understand my departure. They were all ready to go now, clustered by the hundreds atop the plane trees of Battersea park. In a matter of days, they would be all flying to the Mediterranean and to Africa beyond. I still had coffee now and then at Faduah's, but since Nasreen had left, the ritual felt contrived. Faduah was beginning to get very curious, wondering what I was up to. I played silly, weary of the likely ominous pout she would have if I told her I was going to Athens. I had told only Maria and Nasreen. Both wished me good luck and hopefully some day *"au revoir"*. Maria had even offered to house me for a while, since she would be in Athens herself for Christmas.

I still had some money in Paris, but I had to get to it. The last thing I wanted was to go to Paris again. It was not easy. France applied a rigorous exchange control, with a strict limit on the amount one could take out of the country. I had called my elder sister. She was ready to come and visit while I was in London. Could she make me a favor? Bring me cash money. I would write her a check for it. She would only have to shut her mouth if the Customs officer asked her if she had an amount of French francs in excess of what was allowed. She didn't mind.

She had come. We had walked to museums, parks and shops and we had feasted on a splendid Bengali meal in a small restaurant behind Regent Street. As instructed, she had brought me two thousand French francs. I had not told her a word about Athens. Like Nasreen, I feared my parents, if not their wrath, their remonstrance. This time I was going abroad with no plan, no alibi but to go away. Faduah was glancing at me like a secret service agent. She could smell something. But I was not going to tell her. To allay her suspicion, I went during the day, when no one was around, to fill my steel trunk and suitcase down in the luggage closet. Then I went to Mrs. Hargrave, the Warden, to pay my bill.

    The charter flight was leaving from Luton airport at six the following morning. I had had dinner in the gothic dining room, and coffee in the sitting room. A Christmas tree was up in the hall and the Warden would offer a drink to all residents the next day. Maria had already left for the holiday. I had no qualms about leaving London. I had no reason to stay. But there was something new in this trip. For the first time, I was going from one foreign country to another, from England to Greece. I was becoming a nomad. Before, I had always come back home before going abroad again. The night smelled of wet grass and sea when I went out. Mr. Chives was up, his hat on, to help me wheel my trunk on the hand-truck. As I left, he was bending next to a bush, looking for Millie the cat. The taxi driver was a student at the end of his night shift before going to school. "Greece" he said enthused, "That sounds wonderful for the winter!" The girl at the airport counter was not as happy, seeing my luggage. She looked at my steel trunk with a sneer. "What is this?" "A trunk" I said flatly. She shrugged and put a tag on it and off it went on the belt with the suitcase. It was still dark when the plane took off.

GREECE 2

Athens in winter - YWCA - A classy night watchman - Christmas at Maria's - Cleaning ladies - Outdoors for a home - Kingdom of Abyssinias: Vassilis and Tito - Winter sun - Sister souls – Pamela - Training at the French Institute - Discovering Lycabettus - The Arab castle - The Byzantine lady - A Greek Frondistirio - Dithering - Iro from Naoussa - Easter in the deserted city - Off to Lamia - A room "chez l'habitant"- Danae, a budding femme fatale - Expulsion order - Lost and redeemed – Tsangarada

Back to Athens - The streets of Kolonaki - Looking for a flat - Home - An eccentric landlady - Summer in the city - Les amours de Marylena - Careless Ariane - Marie-Christine – A Greek success story - The French Institute nomenklatura – Hitchhiking in Evia - Trizinia, the land of Phaedra -

The Royal school of Anavryta – Gentrifying my home – Private lessons – The comfort of a legal status – At the Kaningos police station – The lake of Stimfalia – Mets, a bohemian haven in Athens - Gladys from Scotland – Exarchia the anarchistic – Fernand, Swiss, ex-1968 firebrand - The tavern of the Communists –

Bassae – Naxos – Katerina, a woman with a past – The Kastro ladies - The Archbishop's house – Stranded in Amorgos - Naxos, the grand way - A cabal against la "Française"- Fire redemption - The old violinist of Apeiranthos – Patmos – An Irishman from Brussels – A wild dancer - A Patmian Gatsby – The battle of Patmos –

Times changing again

Athens in winter - YWCA

The sea was silver grey, the plane almost brushing the waves before hitting the tarmac. Sun and sky were pale and convalescent. Two years before, I had met Athens in summer. Athens in winter was another land. Colors, feel, touch, even perspectives and lines were different. So were the Athenians, cramped in coats and boots. From the yellow cab, I looked at the Parthenon, pallid and wan against the whitish sky, like a boat in dry dock for the bad season.

The YWCA was next to Syntagma Square, on Amerikis street. The large hall, paved in white marble with impressive red marble columns, surrounded a sunk-in atrium. At the far end, a woman sat at the reception desk, the only luminous spot in the near darkness. She looked for my name in the reservation book through her half-glasses. She handed me a form to fill and watched me with her very black eyes while I scribbled. My room was on the second floor. Screeching on the marble floor, I dragged my steel trunk across the hall to the blessed elevator that, notwithstanding coughs and jerks, took me up. Rooms could not be locked, but I had a key for my personal wardrobe or half-wardrobe rather. My room had three beds, one table, three chairs and a glass globe on the ceiling. No night tables, no lamps. The window had a greyish nylon curtain and shutters smelling dust like in Paris. There was no view to the right and left, only the wings of the YWCA building itself. In front stood an empty derelict office building where male shadows wandered at night obviously peeping at the female curves visible through our windows. I took out only my clothes and toiletries, put everything in the wardrobe and went down again with the trunk and suitcase still full of books and notes I had no use for anymore. I put them in the luggage closet by the reception. The residence was deserted. Like at Crosby Hall, all the boarders had gone home for Christmas. I went out.

    The wind was soft and tepid and the thick coats of the Athenians didn't make any sense. I had only a pullover on and I felt too warm. At five in the afternoon, the sun had already disappeared but its whitish glare survived. The city was dead. Since it was Saturday, all shops had closed at noon and nobody went to work on the weekend. Around Syntagma Square, traffic was barely dripping. Life seemed to breathe only in front of the Parliament, higher on top of the square. There, between two white booths, Greek guards in evzone costumes went marching like automats. They met in the middle, they opened their mouths wide, they gesticulated with their big guns, put them back against their shoulder, turned around and went back into their respective booth, standing still and silent for another hour. They wore white wool miniskirts gathered like tutus around their waist, sporting impressive legs wrapped up in white wool gaiters. On top of their head, a red tarbush with a dangling tassel and on their feet, leather babouches with a black pompom on top. None of the rare passers-by paid any attention to the movement of the guards, save the crowd of pigeons that gathered on the esplanade and went up in the air when the guards began to move. Syntagma Square was unpleasant, shut in by buildings and wide treeless streets on all sides. The square was tilted down which suppressed any view, even towards the Acropolis that stood not far. The massive *Hotel Grande Bretagne* looked like an administrative building rather than the deluxe hotel it was supposed to be. Faded and dusty palm trees and scraggy plane trees looked like survivors in the garden at the center. What on earth had I come to do in Athens? Just survive?

    Night had fallen all at once like a curtain coming down. Dark was comforting, Athens became anonymous, just a city at night, easier to blend with. Panepistimiou Avenue opened a wide path going downwards which felt more promising with the wind blowing in my face. A trolley arrived rattling and making sparks and, after a steep curve, dashed down the avenue towards Omonia Square in a formidable din. The sidewalks on Panepistimiou were as wide as the roadway, treeless but here and there planted with tiny yellow huts like minuscule wooden chalets. They were scintillating with lines of bulbs hanging above and around. Their succession down the banks of the avenue made them look like floating pagodas along a meandering river. They caught the eye irresistibly, like fireflies or torches in the night. The *"peripteros"* were my first joy that gloomy December night, a light in the dark.

When I approached one of them, I saw a man's head and shoulders. The guy seemed to carry his home on his back like a turtle. All around him, above and below, small shelves held boxes that were filled with all sorts of goods. Sweets, pens, Kleenex, chocolates, aspirins and condoms, soft drinks and chips, nuts, books, newspapers and magazines. Some of the stuff was on display outside under the roof that made like a mini-porch around it. The guy not only had an opening in front of him, but also one on each side from which he could keep an eye on the merchandise and, also, on the two or three telephones sitting outside on each of the window sills. He could shut or open at will those portholes with a sliding glass and, whenever necessary, he could put out a forbidding hand. I glanced at the newspapers' titles while the guy cast a grim eye on me. I kept my hands in my pockets and moved on without buying any.

A classy night watchman

The YWCA hall was as dark as ever when I got back, save the reception in its bubble of light. There was an old man now on duty. He was the local Mr. Chives but obviously another class of watchman. As I walked in, he was reading a book. Standing up behind the counter, which served as a pulpit, chin resting in his hand, he looked very scholarly in the halo of light. As I came by and glanced at him, he looked above his glasses a split second and went back to his reading, ignoring my nod. I walked up the stairs.

My room was empty. Nobody else had taken a bed. The small globe on the ceiling gave a crude light that didn't light anything. It was only eight, too early to go to bed. I felt hungry. My last meal on the plane was now far away. I went down again. The watchman was not behind his counter anymore. He stood on the doorstep, legs apart and smoking a cigarette while looking down Amerikis street. Down from his reception desk, he stood very upright but he was actually very short. I waited. He slowly turned his head and half shut his eyes as he spotted me at the reception desk. He came back in leisurely and went inside his booth, much taller than me now. He nodded politely, his neck stiff and his face as condescending as a British butler. "Yes, Miss?" he asked in English but with an American accent. I noticed that he wore a faded red pea jacket. "I am looking for a place to eat", I said. "A place to eat" he repeated emphatically. "The restaurant should be open, shouldn't it?" "Which restaurant?" I asked. "The one downstairs." I had no clue. His face contracted slightly. I was getting on his nerves, but he forced a smile on his lips while his eyes definitely took me for an idiot. "On the right, in the corner, just go down the stairs." And, what if the restaurant was shut? I obviously had exhausted the ten seconds allowed. He had put back on his glasses and resumed his reading.

A faint light oozed up into the staircase as I went down. The "restaurant" was immense, covering the whole basement. It was bathed in a white neon light melting from tubes hanging two by two on the very low ceiling. It smelled food, old and new, and it was as deserted as the rest of the YWCA. Dishes were dutifully displayed on glassed-in shelves. A woman in slippers shuffled out from the kitchen area while I was pondering over the rather dull-colored food. I asked in Greek what there was in the marmites in the back.

"Only spinach and rice" she said. She put a portion in a plate. I asked for soup and she plunged another ladle in a pot to fill a bowl. She added two slices of bread. She looked as moody as the watchman, but not condescending. I paid and took the tray. The food was lukewarm but good. The woman had disappeared and I was alone again in the neon pool. There was a mirror on the side and I considered my white face in the glass. I looked like the woman in the kitchen. We all looked the same under the neon. It reminded me of Katherine Mansfield. She had been sitting in a pub one dreary Sunday afternoon in London, with John Middleton Murry. All curtains were shut since officially no pub could be open on the day of the Lord. Katherine and John had looked at their reflection in a mirror on the opposite wall, appalled and amazed. They saw themselves lost but together. Their sight in the mirror had sealed their secret pact against loneliness. A few weeks later, they were married. Coming back upstairs, I took a long burning hot shower, the only luxury of the YWCA. I got into bed, too lazy to shut the shutters.

New Year's eve at Maria's

Maria called me some days after Christmas. She had been to the native village of her parents but she was back. It was New Year's Eve, 1977 was coming in. She would be going shopping downtown and she offered to come by and fetch me. We went down Panepistimiou Avenue and around Omonia. Maria had to buy presents for two little girls, her father's godchildren. We went into *"Minion"*, the only Athens department store. The low ceilings and heavy lighting made the place overheated. Moving with the thick crowd, we got to the toy section. Maria grabbed two dolls and we went out. Her father's office was nearby on a small cul-de-sac, called a *"stoa"*. The building and the area were as dingy as the one where she went to get her money in London. Her father was a tall guy, with abundant hair combed back Onassis-like, big glasses and a well-kept flat belly. He was a building contractor. His eyes were piercing and cunning. He seemed to want to size me up like a potential customer. Maria handed him the two packaged dolls and the receipt from Minion. He looked at it and yelled. "What? I can't believe it! How could you spend so much for dolls?" Maria blushed and looked ready to cry. "What do you want me to do? They are all expensive!" The father calmed down, still mumbling to himself the offensive sum. In a matter of seconds, his wrath made way to a gallant smile as he addressed me. "Would you come to our home tonight for New Year's eve dinner?" He asked me very urbanely. I would, but before, Maria wanted me to go with her to meet Kitty, her cousin, the only person in the know of her Lebanese boyfriend.

Kitty, like Maria, had a double life, one with her family and one with her boyfriend. We went to meet her in a dark basement flat, what was called a *"garsoniera"*. It was the Greek version of the Paris *"garçonnière"*. They were small, usually in a busy area where comings and goings were less noticeable. They were equipped only with a big bed, a bathroom and not much else since they were intended for sexual trysts. Kitty and Yannis were sitting on the rumpled bed when we arrived. Maria and I sat on the carpet while Kitty brought coffee from the kitchenette. They all started talking about Maria's Lebanese boyfriend whom they had met a year before when Maria had made her incognito trip to Athens. The telephone rang and Yannis started to argue with his father who needed him immediately at the family shop, a clothing business. Fuming and still groggy from his long night, he went off in his car to help his father. Maria, Kitty and I walked to Floca, a chain pastry shop, to eat an ice cream.

Maria's family home was a big apartment in Kypseli, a central Athens district on a small hill shaped like the beehive of its name. Massive furniture crowded its huge sitting room and dining room, in a kind of oriental rendition of Louis the 14th with lots of gold and silky shiny materials.

Her mother, an enormous woman perched on high heels, seemed terribly stressed. Elaborate cooking was still going on with the help of a maid while the family frolicked around. The father had a drink with me, while Maria was playing with her young brother nicknamed Bobo, a comic strip personage. While the mother toiled in the kitchen, the elder son talked to me nonstop until his father ordered him abruptly back to his room. The mother came out of the kitchen, an apron around her waist and came up to me, her face worried. "You must understand" she said as if begging me, "My son has problems." The two grandmothers were there too, having come from their respective villages in the Peloponnese where both Maria's parents were born. The two very old ladies dressed in black sat quietly on chairs, a glass of ouzo in their hands. One was almost blind and unable to get up by herself. The other had a childish face, but was in much better shape and looked around with her alert blue eyes.

We all sat around the huge table dressed with the finest crockery and silvery of the house. All dishes were spread on the table and we all picked from them. The main dish was the traditional sucking piglet baked in the oven with potatoes. We ate to our heart's content and drank a lot of wine. Meanwhile, Greek bouzouki music played in the background. Sighing, Maria's father took off his glasses and rubbed his eyes before getting up. He put on another cassette and, raising both arms, snapping his fingers, he started to sway his hips. *"Opa!"* he yelled as he spinned around, raising his leg. He yelled again to his wife who got up and took his hand. She went spinning too, all flushed and breathless. When she came back to the table, I was summoned to dance myself. The mother looked at me with half suspicious, half nostalgic eyes. I spun round the best I could, my hand held up in the father's hard fist. The others clapped their hands. Maria was next. The grandmothers and the brothers were excused. We sat back at the table for the sweets and the coffee. The blind grandmother had gone to bed. The hardier grandmother was beginning to clean up the table. Maria's parents looked flushed and sleepy. The boys still nibbled at a tart. Maria went out with me up to the street corner. A yellow taxi came cruising along, just like in New York.

Cleaning ladies

On the following Sunday night, the YWCA was bustling like a bird's cage. All the girls had come back from their parents' homes. But I still had my room to myself. On the two other beds, the sheets were intact, the top one neatly folded and piled with a bath towel.

On Monday morning, an incredible racket woke me up. I looked at my watch. It was seven am. Heralding the end of winter holidays, the cleaning ladies had swooped down on the YWCA. Brooms and mops banged against floors and walls, along with the shrieks and clamors of the women. I retreated under my sheets and covers, but soon one of those fierce amazons pushed open my door and invaded my territory. Any room was open to anyone. There was a price to pay for the privilege of the cheapest and safest bed in Athens. The locked wardrobe was my only private domain, but I couldn't lock myself up in it. Forced to get up, I went to the bathroom to take one more shower while an amazon ran amok in my room.

When I came back, she was still there, soliloquizing. A pal came up to help her. She had a pad in her hand with numbers and crosses. The rooms were listed according to their number and if a cross was indicated, it meant that they had to change the sheets and towel. But it was tricky to figure it out. There were three or four beds in each room, which one exactly was supposed to be changed? The ones in use were not obligatorily eligible. They may have had another two or three days to go before the change. The clean ones may not have been actually clean. Or they may have been officially occupied, but physically not. Every morning, they pondered and deliberated and tried to figure it out until, fed up, they would change whatever sheets and towel they fancied. The lists were written in a very elegant cursive, but I understood quickly that the cleaning ladies couldn't read any more than they could write.

With their light blue blouses, they looked and sounded like a barking dog pack, but with time I got to know them better. They were free women and quite aware of the struggles of the international proletariat. Single mothers or widows, they all lived in far away industrial suburbs, in Elefsina or Kokkinia. Their boss, the housekeeper, was an old cranky lady who walked with legs plied in two, due to arthritis. They jeered at her behind her back. *Kyria Theodora* reigned proud and solitary from her small office on my floor. Her nose was big and hooked, and curving down towards her mouth. Her eyes were alert and wide like a deer's, dark and thoughtful like the Egyptian Fayoum's faces. Her hair was piled up together in a Maria Callas chignon. She was very short, with a voluminous head and a compact trunk on top of two very thin and very curved legs that could have belonged to a spider.

When the cleaning ladies' racket was going beyond acceptable decibels, *Kyria Theodora* would appear in the corridor and, at the top of her shrieking voice, ask what on earth was going on. She walked like a duck, oscillating from one foot to the other, her big head erect and her face severe. Massed in front of her, their hands crossed on their brooms, the cleaning ladies exposed their griefs or dilemmas and Theodora addressed their complaints regally with her slow bass voice. Then, she turned back on her high heels, almost keeling over, and disappeared into her office. The cleaning ladies usually went on talking, holding impromptu conferences in the corridor, careful to keep their voices down. They uttered frustrations and gossiped about *Kyria Theodora*. The fact that the housekeeper was from Alexandria, Egypt made things worse for her. They considered her a fraud who pretended to be a refined lady just because she was a "Greek from Egypt", and above all from Alexandria, the ancient capital of taste and elegance for the pre-war Levant. At best for them, *Kyria Theodora* was an immigrant. They, born in Athens, resented the prestige of a foreign-born Greek.

Theodora took a mischievous delight in speaking French whenever possible to show the women where she belonged and where they did not. She had been delighted to find out I was French, and from Paris on top of it. I was honoured with a long tirade on France, that land of civilization and marvellous shops and clothes. Greece was but an abyss of uncivil, uncouth, stupid and malevolent peasants. She still bemoaned the forced departure of her family from Egypt in the fifties, after the fall of King Farouk. Greece was but a third world country to her. The paradox was that, for all their sneers and jeers, the cleaning ladies seemed to emulate the proudly decadent Theodora. They spent a fortune to send their children to private language schools to learn French, convinced that their children had to have that chic veneer as a passport up the social ladder.

Outdoors for a home

Day after day, the same shouts and bangs always woke me up in the morning, usually from a deep sleep. I could not get used to it. But, like all the other girls at the YWCA, I had to get up and go somewhere. After all, if I had no privacy, there was a whole territory waiting for me to be explored just at my doorstep. Athens outdoors was cosier than my drab room. Every morning I went wherever my feet or my eyes took me. Sometimes, even a smell guided me. Down Amerikis, I glanced at a minuscule mall off the sidewalk. Inside, there was a barber, a dairy shop with two small round tables and chairs where I could eat a yoghurt or drink a coffee. The owners of the Lilliputian shops hung out in front or pottered inside, always on their feet, always smoking and talking non-stop. Only at the end of the day did they sit on a chair to smoke a last cigarette before locking their shops. Those malls, the *"stoas"*, were everywhere and all winter I wondered what purpose they had. Wondered until the scorching sun of June showed up, making those dark passages a heaven of cool.

Amerikis street ran into the wide river of Panepistimiou Avenue, which carried along torrents of cars until dark. There, I had two options. Either I crossed the avenue to go down towards Plaka and Monastiraki, or I turned right and went down to Omonia square. Waiting for the red light or pondering over my route, I looked at the gold displayed in the windows of Lalaounis, the Greek jeweller, at the corner of Amerikis and Panepistimiou. The metal was thick and shiny, twisted, embossed, engraved, shaped into lions' heads or pomegranates, chokers or ankle-bracelets. Before crossing the avenue, I mused upon which ones I might buy if I could. Cars were roaring all the time, taking any opportunity to progress, regardless of red lights and pedestrians. When I crossed the avenue, the imminent danger always made me think of the walls of the Red sea as the tribe of Moses hurried to reach their promised land.

The avenue triggered fantasies in others as well. One day, an eerie personage, his long mane floating down his back, all dressed in white with a long shepherd's crook in his right hand was taking the lead every time the light turned red, as if he were the Moses of the people of Athens. Flows of ribbons in all colours hanged from his crook and from his shoulders. The mission of that prophet was to help his people cross that infernal avenue. At every red light, he held his crook high in the air and led his people safely to the other side. This happened for hours on end, day after day. The guy had started his mission after his mother had died, run over by a car. This, the watchman at the YWCA had told me on one of his good mood evenings.

Along the way, I met other *habitués*. The crippled were a steady crowd. Spread on the pavement, or standing against the wall, they gave a generous view of what made them special. It was not despair, but a pragmatic sense of breadwinning. Their handicap was their asset, however grim. Stumps of arms, legs or feet, tracheotomies, blind eyes, wounds, everything was exposed during working hours. But there where pauses, to eat and drink or just chat for a while. All of a sudden, the whining stopped, the begging hand folded back, the stumps disappeared under the clothes and the damned of the world resurrected, until the next performance. Many hung around the tiny Byzantine church in Plaka, next to the pretentious Cathedral. The little church was below street level, surrounded by large steps on which they could sit. Open at all hours, shining with gold and candle flames, the church felt warm like a mother's lap.

At the other end of the large esplanade in front of the Cathedral, opened the narrow souk of Pandrossou. There, I thought of Nasreen pacing the bazaar of Baghdad. A few bored and shivering shop owners brandished goods and whispered promises in English, but without much enthusiasm. Athens winter was mild but cold if one had to stay out all day. Besides, business was dead until spring. At Monastiraki, instead of a monastery, there was a mosque with a turtle-like dome and minarets shooting up in the sky, crumbling but still graceful. The sky was king on those green lowlands of Athens at the foot of the Acropolis where small houses built by Asia Minor refugees clustered. The second leg of Pandrossou was the real bazaar. In the shops, tourist souvenirs gave way to solid clothes and hardware, wood, plastic and metal. At the end, the alley emerged into a ring, Abyssinia square. It was a true circus.

Kingdom of Abyssinias Square: Tito and Vassilis

Merchants came from everywhere to Abyssinias square. There were dark gypsies from the north and blue-eyed people from the Dodecanese. A giant rooster walked around, proud and beautiful. His name was *Tito*, he was the mascot of the place. The free souls who populated Abyssinias square let him do as he liked. He perched and crowed and defecated wherever he wanted, but he had no chicks to command. *Tito* was superbly alone.

An old man named Vassilis introduced me to *Tito* who looked at me pensively, with an eye closed and his head bent. He caressed *Tito* and gave him maize in his hand to pick. Like everybody on the square, Vassilis had a shack built out of blackened metal scrap. His was crammed with piles of old gramophones and some furniture. He was dressed as a gentleman, his suit pressed, his white hair neatly combed and parted. His calm blue eyes were quite arresting. Their blue was sheer turquoise. As I looked at his goods, Vassilis, with a strange high-pitched voice, invited me to sit and drink a coffee with him. We sat on empty cans. He snapped his finger and a waiter came from a café to take the order. *Tito* perched on the highest gramophone, opening his wings and puffing out his throat.

Above the shacks of Abyssinias Square, the sky positively twinkled, its blue shine diffracted in the crisp cold air. It smelled of wood fire. Floating high, the Parthenon looked beatific, like a being from the next world. I spent time looking at stuff in Vassilis's shack. He played some of his best gramophones for me. He had huge stocks of needles and vinyl records. Every time I came back, I went to say hello. He lived in Gizi, a district up in the hills along Alexandras and Athinas avenues where terrible fights had taken place during the Civil war of 1945-1949. Every morning at dawn he came walking all the way to Abyssinias. Vassilis was born in

Lesvos and had arrived in Athens as a boy. A widower, he lived alone with his mentally retarded daughter.

Winter sun

From Abyssinias Square, there was a passage towards Ermou Street on one side, and towards Adrianou street on the other. I chose Ermou street for the way back up. Midway up to Syntagma Square, I bought a pitta with souvlaki and onions folded in, which I ate standing on the narrow sidewalk, almost touched by the passing traffic, which was always very dense. From Abyssinias back to Amerikis, it was a steep ascent. The old town was the lowest spot in Athens. Only the sea at Piraeus was lower. Ermou street concentrated textile and clothes retailers, hence the brisk business and heavy traffic. Another route via Adrianou took me longer but time was well compounded by the gentler slope going up and a much better smell, of grilled coffee and fresh leather. Car traffic was banned on Adrianou, which ran along the ancient Agora. Just facing the entrance to the site, a rundown café gathered all the idle men of the area around coffee and *tavli*. Inside smoke burnt the eyes, I sat outside against the south wall warmed until noon by the sun.

The January sun disappeared soon after noon, but until then it splashed all over. It was difficult to resist the drowsiness that spread from head to foot. Any wintry day was balmy against that wall. Opening one eye now and then, I saw a scene out of a dream. The Parthenon perched on reddish rock, seen from the back above the ancient market place now filled with green and birds. Until summer, the few chairs outside the Adrianou café would be empty. My only company was a woman tobacconist with a bilious complexion that sat all day, shut into her cupboard of a shop that had been carved out of the street wall of the main café room. It had a door opening inside which she opened now and then for air or to chat with the waiter. One day, as she was frantically grabbing cigarette packs, holding them out and taking the money in return, she was mumbling to herself. She was having a serious fight with the café owner, her husband I guessed. In between clients, she opened the door of her cupboard and gave him a piece of her mind, quickly shutting again the door as a customer waited on the street side in front of her mini-shop. Between shouts, she shook her head and made faces, trying to calm down by stretching her facial muscles. It was still winter but warmer than usual and stifling in the southeast wind. I had a headache myself and, sympathizing with the woman's bad mood, I made a point of showing her my compassion as I bought a pack of *Karelia* cigarettes. "Heavy weather, isn't it?" I told her with a smile. She looked daggers at me. "You are the heavy one, *Kyria mou*!" she smashed back at me. I remained agape.

Sister souls

Contrary to Crosby Hall, almost all residents at the YWCA were Greek nationals and, every weekend, most of them went back home. They were all students at the University of Athens or at professional schools. Foreign girls were an exception and they did not stay long. They were just passing by on their way around the world, or on their way back home. They came mostly from North America, Australia or New Zealand, often in pairs. Their rucksacks were as gigantic as their bodies. For some, Athens was to be the most eastern place they would reach. Others went on to Istanbul. But no one ventured further east than Turkey. Like me, the foreign girls were all drifters. On weekends, the whole YWCA belonged to us drifters.

One peculiarly cold and damp weekend, there were six of us stranded at the YWCA. Our main recreation all day long had been to take burning hot showers as often and as long as our skin could take it, to kill both time and cold in one shot. The heating clearly was not working on weekends and rooms already not very hospitable were outwardly unpleasant. We could not even take refuge reading or writing in bed. Covers and sheets were too short and pillows totally flat. We had gathered in the room of two Quebec girls who were leaving the day after. No one made coffee the Greek or Iraqi way among us. We made tea and hot chocolate on the small gas stove in the kitchenette, which was on the same floor, and we gorged on "Papadopoulos" chocolate cookies.

Besides the two Quebec girls, there was another Canadian, Pamela from Sherbrooke, Ann from Connecticut and a respectable old lady from New York in plaited grey skirt and grey chignon. She declared proudly that she was seventy-two years old and free as the air since she had put all her possessions in storage and rented her apartment. She was a retired teacher from New York and she had been traveling for over a year now, from YWCA to YWCA. The two Quebec girls after twelve months of wandering longed to be home. They missed their boy friends, the snow, and speaking French. Their boy friends had also been on trips abroad, but having tried their luck with foreign girls, they had confessed in letters they sent *"poste restante"*, that they longed for their *"Québécoises"*. Ann the American looked in very bad shape. Her pale face was covered with red acne and, because of the cold, she had stayed in bed most of the day with all her clothes on. She was waiting for friends to arrive. They were to go together to Istanbul.

The old American lady had joined us for a moment, telling us once more that she didn't regret one second at having left all her possessions behind to roam the world. Her stern expression and drooping mouth seemed to deny her declaration. As for a new life, I wondered if the old lady was not trying to escape death. We made more tea. At the beginning of February, we were having the first real spell of winter. Considering the poor heating system, it was fortunate that winters were so mild. The six of us made the room barely wrm enough thanks to our breathing and body heat, like cows in a stable. One of the Montreal girls suddenly sighed. *"Ah, comme j'aimerais que mon chum soit là pour me chauffer les pieds!"* Pamela sighed also. *"God, it has been such a long time since a man has warmed my feet in his!"* she exclaimed. We all looked around us at the dingy and cold room. *"Not much of a home!"* I said. *"Home, what is home?"* Pamela mused. For a moment, we all stayed silent, munching slowly the word "home". *"Montreâl"* said the two Quebec girls. Ann, shivering under her covers, longed for a fireplace, to sit next to warm embers. *"It's not a house, it's a home"* I grumbled like Bob Dylan, *"I've got neither"*.

That evening, while I was getting numb again under the hot shower to warm in turn my cold bed, that home thing still gnawed at me. I was stuck in the middle of nowhere. That haggard old American lady had alarmed me. She would go on wandering from one YWCA to another, free maybe, but dead already. I wanted a place of my own, and a job, a real life.

Pamela

Pamela had come from Salonica where she had stayed a year. Like the two other *Québécoises*, she spoke singing French with an assortment of American slang and, here and there, oldish French. Greece was a late pilgrimage for her, too late in fact. Her family had belonged to the Judeo-Spanish community of Salonica until they had been deported to Auschwitz in 1943. Some of her relatives had left in time, and they had survived. She was the offspring of the lucky. Her parents had told her of the city of her grandparents. Nobody and nothing remained of the family past in Salonica. Of the hundreds of thousands Judeo-Spanish inhabitants of the city, only a few hundreds had come back alive from Germany. Their whole district had been destroyed by the occupiers as well as by the liberators of Greece in 1945. Pamela had no regret for that past she had not lived. All the same, she felt at home in Greece. Here it felt normal to be an exile or a nomad.

Of all the foreigners that stayed at the YWCA, Pamela was the only one who dressed, in the real sense of the word. The rest of us only put clothes on. She was always elegant, with always a touch of red. A scarf, a belt, a shirt, a ribbon, there was always something red on her. She sported a bob with a fringe. Her features were delicate like in Katherine Mansfield's early portraits, eyelids slightly domed with long slanting brown eyes and harmonious oval face. Her room too looked better than ours. She had a lamp with an orange shade, a red cover on the bed, a cloth and a plate full of fruits on the table. Those tiny dabs changed everything. She had turned the drab anonymous room into a home. She invited me for tea very civilly. We sat on the beds, legs crossed like yogis and we chatted while she sewed or embroidered.

Training at the French Institute

Willy-nilly, winter receded day after day. So did my savings. I had to find a job. The headquarters of the French Institute were on Sina, a street that ran parallel to Amerikis. Its heavy armored doors and its thick cement walls made it look like an army camp. A thick cement arcade painted a Teutonic grey green spelled in pseudo Greek characters *"Institut Français"*. The building surrounded a vast and naked yard. The corridors felt cool and tremendously civilized as I wandered in search of the Director's office. The Director, a tall Alsatian from Strasbourg, got up and took my hand as I came in. I went straight to the point. I had come to Greece two months before and I wished to stay. I needed to work and wanted to know if there was any opening for me at the French Institute. I gave him my biography listing my French and English degrees and added that I was preparing a degree in Modern Greek in Paris. He looked at it distractedly and considered me for a while. "I can offer you some training in French teaching if you wish, and then, we'll keep you in mind if we have a vacancy." He got up, shaking hands again cheerfully. "You are not married, are you?" he asked suddenly. No, I was not.

Training was taking place at one of the French Institute's annexes, on Massalias Street, the next street after Sina. I was to follow a class for a full week. I sat in the last row. The teacher was a Greek woman in her late forties. The pupils were beginners and the teaching method rather primitive. Under the iron hand of the raucous woman, the kids practiced aloud over and over. The teacher wrote a word or a sentence on the blackboard and the whole class yelled it to the top of their lungs. When they didn't yell loud enough, she pulled their ears.

The manual used in the classroom was designed around the comings and doings of a French family, *"la famille Lépé"* which was a way to acquaint quickly the children with the treacherous French accents. The *Lépé* children went to school, *Maman Lépé* cooked the meals, *Papa Lépé* read the newspapers and by the end of the book, the pupils were supposed to mumble and write French. How could the teacher not be hoarse after hours of yelling? At the end of the class, I was deafened. It was hard for me to envisage forcing the French language into kids that way. But I learnt from Marie-Christine, a French colleague, that this teacher was an exception. Nobody else taught that way.

Discovering Lycabettus

On my way back, I had lingered on the hill of Strefi above Sina street. A breeze coming from the sea was rippling the air. So far I had always gone down, but rising up above Athens, everything was different. The air smelled good from the pinewood on top of Lycabettus. I had wandered in search for a pass between the hills of Strefi and Lycabettus. Steep cement steps went up on the right, to nowhere. On top, after a semblance of street, patches of wild grass took over. From up there the city looked far and remote. As if the last natives on the hill had all gone, leaving their land to the birds and cats. Further on, the tortuous and broken asphalt went down again, opening on a wide esplanade. On that side, stood a kind of Napolitan palace, in beautiful carved stones, surrounded by a small park with old cypresses and pines. And again, the asphalt stopped, giving way to another flight of steps, plunging down a canyon. Hemmed in between Strefi and Lycabettus, Dimokritou Street stunk and roared with an endless caravan of cars stalling in clouds of smoke, fighting their way up to the circular way going all around the Lycabettus.

The asphalt on Dimokritou street was slippery, almost like ice, and I daringly started to ascend along with the cars since there was no sidewalk. From the ring boulevard above, Athens unfurled like a giant octopus reaching as far as the eye could see, starting to climb already the many hills surrounding the basin. On the west side, the sea spread unlimited, spotted with tankers and boats. Above the city, the Parthenon floated, prisoner of cement waves but still proud and free. This was a revelation. Athens was a port, a city by the sea. And there were hills, mountains springing up all around. The wild Lycabettus hill towered above Athens like Mount Monadnock above the plains of New Hampshire. I had found my domain. It was called Kolonaki, and while there was little chance I would be affluent enough to be able to afford living there, the streets could still be mine.

I went down, alert. I was on the hunt now. Somewhere around there, I was sure, I would settle. Quaint little streets had been carved parallel to the slope, like tiers in an open theatre. They were linked by steps which, pieced together, opened a long furrow all the way downtown. I arrived on a street planted with orange trees. I picked an orange and bit into it. It was a bitter wild fruit, a *"nerandzi"* only good once candied. Fokilidou street was wider than the others and totally flat. I had come back reluctantly to the YWCA. I longed for light now, sun, space, and that sea beyond.

I had now abandoned the downtown avenues, drawn irrepressibly by the heights of Kolonaki. I did not drift down anymore. I climbed up the hill now. At the doorstep of the somber YWCA, one only had to look left. Amerikis street went straight up to the wild mountain. Mighty rocks and pines stood there at the summit of the street, flamboyant against the sky. All winter, early nights had hidden them. With daylight lingering longer and longer, they reappeared splendid. I started going up slowly with an even step, like an Alpine hiker. Amerikis street was as steep as a mule track, which it had once been. The streetlights on Akadimias avenue, that I had to cross, provided some respite. Beyond that busy avenue, smells of wood and soil filled the air. Turning my head, I could see Athens now way below. Between Anagnostopoulou and Fokilidou street, I sat on the steps of Pindarou sreet. There, I was level with the Acropolis. The Parthenon was just in focus, right in front of me. Nobody came there, only birds and cats rummaging in the bushes.

The Arab castle

I stayed longer and longer up on the streets of Kolonaki before coming back to the YWCA. It was like leaving a luminous deck for the dark hold of a ship. One night, I had stopped in front of a gate. Made of black wrought iron, it looked as if it had been shut for years. A white house appeared behind, half-hidden by tall Jerusalem cypresses that seemed to stand guard there, hieratical. The style and rhythm of the house was totally out of place. It could have been a small fortress or an island village home. It had nothing to do with the affluent apartment buildings and townhouses around Kolonaki. Built as a kind of pyramid of whitewashed cubes with different levels and small terraces, it seemed to spring up and take off against the sky and above the city. Cats went in and out between the bars of the gate and I watched them regally going up the staircase that spiraled up. In the absence of any visible inhabitant, it was their home. I could not follow them, but I had given a name to that strange house: *"the Arab castle"*. It stood on the slope of the hill like the fancy of an Ottoman Pasha touched by the grace of Greek civilisation. It had become my lighthouse.

When I came back late after dark, the night watchman was already at his post. He had finally deemed me worthy of his conversation. When I had asked him about the Arab castle, he had told me that, years before, the place had been the Consulate of Turkey. As far as he was concerned, he had gone on with a pout, all those *"Levantines"* were not worth much. He knew, he said, because all his life he had commanded boats with Levantine crews. To him, Levantines denoted people from the East: Turks, Arabs, and even Chinese, all inferior compared to the Greeks who, in his view, belonged to the *"race des seigneurs"*.

The Byzantine lady

Like Theodora, the housekeeper, the watchman had had a bright past, which, god knows why, had sunk into nothingness, like an oasis in the sands. His last kingdom was knowledge. He read nonstop but I never knew what. In the morning, he stood up like a captain on the deck, hands in the pockets of his sailor pants, his face ravaged by the long sleepless night, ready to go crash into his bed somewhere as the city awoke.

One evening, I had found him shouting at an old woman who was sitting in the marble atrium. He was telling her to go to hell. I had seen her often before, thinking she was a resident like me. After all, she was not much older than the American lady. She was dressed with long frumpy and colorless clothes, looking with lively eyes at the comings and goings of the YWCA boarders and other people who came to courses and seminars that took place in the building. Her eyes were magnificent, very large, very green and very alert. She seemed to be old and broke, but not unhappy. The watchman could not stand her. To him, he had told me, she embodied all the defects of a degenerate aristocracy.

The old woman had been born in Constantinople, the daughter of a wealthy land and ship owning family, which the watchman envied. Family possessions and positions had long beeen lost and the old lady now lived alone in a basement room nearby. "They never worked those people. Look at that, only good at begging and squatting." "She is not begging", I told him. The old lady was smiling affably with a graceful inclination of her head as he barked at her. "And why do you think she is hanging here all day long? She does not have a cent to eat and warm her room. She goes begging for leftovers at the cafeteria downstairs and then she sits all day enjoying the heat here." To defend the old lady, I told the watchman peremptorily that, contrary to what he thought, the lady was actually quite well off. This was sheer invention. The watchman looked at me puzzled for a second, then he shrugged his shoulders. As a gentleman, as he prided himself on being a gentleman, and in deference to me, he promised he would let the lady alone. But I could hear him still grumbling chosen insults in Greek as the lady nodded politely goodbye from the doorstep.

And what if the *Arab castle* had been hers? I fancied. I had named her *"the Byzantine"* and I plotted a tale of loss and repossession, a tale that would have taken the winds out of the watchman's sails and transfigured the old lady.

A Greek Frondistirio

Waiting for a vacancy in one of the French Institute's establishments, I decided to try my luck with a *"frondistirio"*, a private language school where Greek teen-agers went to learn English. I had spotted a big sign off Akademias Square, just in front of the busy bus terminal. *"Frondistirio Xenon Glosson"* was written in giant letters on a panel covering the whole second floor façade. One evening, as teenagers crowded the sidewalk and poured in and out of the old decrepit Art Nouveau building, I went in. An office with what looked like two secretaries busy typing, had its door open. I asked if I could see the Director. They looked hesitant until one of them asked me what was my query. I was an English teacher, although I was French, I explained and I was looking for a post. She got up and went into the Director's office, and came back, inviting me to come in.

The "Director" didn't know a word of English or any other language, but he glanced at me with half-shut eyes, sizing right away how much he could get out of me. He seemed thrilled at the idea of having a foreigner on his staff. He sent for a teacher to test my fluency. A woman came along and we chitchatted for a while in English. The boss pronounced me pompously as part of his staff from then on. I would be paid five hundred drachmas per fifty minutes course, payable at the end of each month, with the possibility of an advance payment at midmonth. I could begin the next day, a Friday. There was no manual, neither any specific method to follow. I had a free hand.

At six, the following evening, I entered a class of about twenty-five, two-third boys and one-third girls. They were all beginners. The *"frondistirio"*, in fact, had only beginners' classes, and those kids were bound to remain beginners forever. As they stared at me, waiting for the show to begin, I told them "My name is Maria, what's your name?" Until each of them had told their name, asking in turn the kid next to them, "What's your name?" the hour had passed. The following Friday, I entered a classroom of thirty-five pupils, this time with more boys. Before I had even opened my mouth, they had already started enthusiastically, "What's your name?" That day we went on to "How old are you?" The newly registered gang of boys were laughing their hearts out, blinking eyes at each other and staring at my legs. The next week, there were more than forty kids. The Director was jubilating, my class was a huge hit and cash flowed in his coffers. The fourth Friday, the classroom was so full that some of the kids had to stand up. There was no room for more chairs. As I had begun a new series of dumb question-answers, the secretary ushered in two more pupils. Before leaving the classroom that evening, I went to the Director and asked him a cash advance equivalent to the four lessons I had so far given. He readily complied with my request and congratulated me on my success. I left that evening, never to see any of them again. Who knows how many more students had registered for my next lesson? But I did not feel sorry for them. After all, they would not squander their parents' money anymore. As for the Director, I thought he needed to be taught a lesson.

Dithering

The situation in my room was now changing every day. I had grown weary of the constant turnover of roommates. Girls from Australia, the US, New Zealand, Canada, Germany, England came and went every day. Their gigantic rucksacks and bodies hardly fitted in the room. Every evening, they sat in bed with their diaries, writing zealously what had happened to them that day and how much they had spent. They always smiled and cheered, and always asked the same questions. "Where do you come from?" "Where are you going?" I had no answer. Where I came from didn't seem so important anymore, and I had no idea where I was going. I found their inquiries disquieting. Who were those girls to play Sphinx with me? I had nicknamed them the "Janes", they all sounded and looked the same.

At the end of February, the French Institute still had not proposed me any job. I could still go on at the YWCA for a month, but my money dwindled. And I was growing tired of that suspended life. I was now seriously considering going back to France. This time it would be final, I would not go and try to live abroad again. I walked longer every day, reflecting along the way. In Paris, I pondered, what more would I get? No job waited for me and no way I would go back again to my childhood room. March was the wrong season to start all over. Jobs were found earlier or later. If I had three months to kill, it was better to kill them in Athens. Being a bum abroad was of no consequence. No one cared.

Besides, there was something in the air. The capricious Mediterranean weather seemed to foster hope. It seemed that fate could change from one day to the other, like the sea winds. Fatalism was my lifebuoy. "We'll see", said always the Greek, "Be patient and the sky will turn blue" said a popular song. I had lived through the first Halcyon days of my life, smitten by the warm breeze and the insects buzzing in the middle of winter. Cooler weather had come back, but winter was losing ground ineluctably. Night was receding and light was slowly gaining ground.

Iro from Naoussa

Pamela and the other Canadian girls had all left and I missed them. The "Janes" had no companionship to offer, too busy with schedules and routes and all the sights they had to cram into a day. When Iro arrived in my room, I was glad. She was from Naoussa up north. When she announced she was going home for the Carnival recess, she invited me to be her guest. I readily accepted. It was in fact her last trip to Naoussa. Iro had been in Toronto the last three years, studying. There, she had met a Canadian boy she was going to marry soon. Small, with minute childish features, she looked so young that it was hard to believe that she was completing her MA and getting married. The marriage was to take place in Toronto and she hoped to convince her mother to come to Canada with her, and hopefully to settle as well. As for herself, Iro had long ago decided to leave Greece for good.

Like Nasreen when she was going to marry Ahmed, Iro had told me about her doubts. She was glad to get married, although she was only doing it to conform to Naoussa and her parents' mores. She could have asked for Canadian citizenship and lived with her boy friend without getting married. In Canada, she had found freedom and love: freedom to be whom she wished and freedom to marry whom she wanted. She had no regret leaving Naoussa and the gloomy life of her parents. But her heart sank at the idea of leaving her mother behind in Greece. She was an only child. Besides, she hated her father for the cruelty, violence and verbal abuse he had inflicted relentlessly on her mother. For years, he had brutalized and exploited her, making her work like a slave, insulting and beating her up. Her mother had endured everything and stayed with him. Lately, things had changed: the dominating man of the past had become an old man, needy and lonely. Her father behaved like a puppy now, terrified to be abandoned by the wife he had humiliated for so many years. The family owned enormous orchards of apple and peach trees. Still trembling, Iro recounted to me how her father would yell at her mother as she knelt on the ground before him. Day after day, she toiled, picking the fruits, putting them carefully in crates. Her father would come, enraged and frantic, kicking mercilessly the full crates, sending a whole day's work flying in the air. Her mother knelt and crawled, gathering the fruits again while the man yelled like a madman. "My mother has always been sad", Iro said, "At long last, I'd like to see her happy". In Canada, she hoped everything would be different and her mother would start a new life, like her.

Iro thought I would enjoy the Naoussa Carnival, an old Macedonian custom that lasted a full week. While Iro was to come by train from Salonica, I took a bus from Athens. The trip going north was long, reminiscent of my crossing of the American plains going west. Above Lamia, snow patched the whole landscape. Greece looked like Russia now, the Russia I had read about in Tolstoï and Turgenev. When I arrived at night, Naoussa was all white. The air bit sharply. The streetlights were rare. Old minarets from the Ottoman days appeared here and there, pointing to the clear starry sky. From the bus depot, I had followed the directions Iro had given me beforehand, since she would be arriving later in the night. When I got there, her street seemed out of a tale. The wooden houses along the street glowed in the halo of lamps placed against protruding windows, like small conservatories. Naoussa felt medieval and oriental.

I knocked on the door. An old gentleman opened. Dressed elegantly with a suit and tie, he had the same blue eyes as Iro. He made me enter into a huge room, part living room and part kitchen. The mother was stooped over the cooking stove, looking frumpy and grumpy. She nodded faintly to me and went back to her cooking. Iro's father awkwardly started a conversation, asking me about my trip, trying to be social. Iro had not arrived yet from Salonica where she had to fetch papers. The mother banged her pots and pans and seemed to get more and more upset. She finally burst out and asked the father to leave us alone. She still had plenty to prepare for the dinner. The old man looking sorry and helpless quickly disappeared in another room. The mother made me sit on a wooden couch and gave me Greek coffee to drink. The house felt like an isba. There was ice on the windows and a smell of wood burning from the cast iron stove.

When Iro arrived, her father emerged from his room. She kissed them both and seeing her mother frowning, she snarled at her father for bothering her again. The poor man stuttered for a minute and announced that he was going to set the table for dinner. We sat for dinner. While Iro tried to be jolly and her father to be courteous, her mother kept toiling around the kitchen, getting up all the time. When we went to bed, the mother was still picking and cleaning up.

The next day, Iro and I drove to the orchards in the family pick-up. Going through the countryside of her childhood, Iro was happy and nostalgic at the same time. Apple and peach trees were bare and silvery against the shining sky. Miles and miles of them extended as far as the mountains on the horizon. We walked briskly in the crisp air as she looked and beheld, as if she wanted to take stock one last time of the land she was leaving for good.

The Carnival was at its height. The whole of Naoussa stopped to devote all its time to it. Hundreds of men and boys wearing masks and dressed in the Macedonian costume, a white fustanella, white stockings and black slippers with big pompoms, swooped down on the town, shouting and singing accompanied by the monotonous sound of drums and the shrill cries of *"clarinos"*, a kind of trumpet. The masked men were called *"Baoules"*. Late at night and early in the morning, always wearing their masks, they came serenading under the windows of the girl of their dreams. Iro had often heard the serenade on the street under her window when she was a teen-ager, but since there was another girl living in the house next door, she had never been sure whom the serenade was for. The Carnival, breaking the Christian Lent, was like everywhere else an opportunity to eat and drink a lot, and to make merry. Every Carnival evening, all the *"Baoules"* joined in dances on the central square. Iro's father had shown me pictures of her at five, dressed as a little boy in the Macedonian costume, dancing with other children under the proud gaze of her parents. When I left, Iro still had a week to try to convince her mother to come to Toronto. But it was doubtful she would succeed. Her mother was too old and rooted in her past, however painful. It was too late to cut those roots and start anew in a foreign land.

Easter in the deserted city

When Easter arrived, I remained in Athens. The city had turned into a ghost place. Everything was shut during holy week. Athenians went back to the village of their parents or grandparents for the Orthodox rites. The churches and cathedrals of Athens were all lit, doors wide open, the Byzantine chanting hovering plaintive and powerful above the whole city. From the church of Agios Dionysos above the YWCA, I could hear the lamentations and psalmodies of the popes. The tedious sound of the powerful male voices filled streets and squares. On holy Friday, church porches were draped in black. All noise had stopped. Even birds were voiceless. Death had descended on the city and, in spite of myself, my heart felt heavy. At night, the faithful were going up the Lycabettus to the little church of Saint George on top, carrying brown candles to light their way. Again, the YWCA was deserted, and no food was available anywhere. I lay in bed, waiting.

Sunday morning, Panepistimiou Avenue was empty. Even the peripteros were all shut. I was going down dreamily, enjoying the first warm sun since the Halcyon days in January. A man, a Cretan to judge from his breeches and boots, and the thick moustache barring his face, was waiting at a bus stop, with baskets and bags at his feet. He looked puzzled. As I came by, he gestured at me. I came nearer. He wanted to know if he was at the right bus stop to go to Areos Pagos, the Athens *"Champ-de-Mars"*, a huge square, from which left the buses for Central Greece and Attica. I looked on the itinerary on the pole and confirmed to him that he was at the right stop. As I saluted him with the customary *"Ygeia sas"*, the man looked at me embarrassed, as if pondering what he wanted to say. *"Christos anesti"* he whispered quickly, as if those were forbidden words in the city. "Christ is resurrected", it meant in ancient Greek. Those were the words all villagers exchanged on Easter day. *"Nai, Christos anesti"*, "Indeed, Christ is resurrected" I answered, and his face lit up.

Off to Lamia

The week after the Easter recess, the French Institute sent me a brief note offering me a temporary post in Lamia. A teacher there was on maternity leave from April to June. The Director wanted me first to go there and meet Mrs. Varda, the Head of the Lamia French Institute. Two days later, I was off. The bus left from the Kifissou bus terminal, a dump of a place just off a muddy river, more mud than water, surrounded by derelict buildings and smelly industries. Spring had burst everywhere. The landscape looked like French countryside. It was flat and green, with immense fields of cereals. Poplars lined up along the road.

Lamia had no suburbs and no industrial area. The bus stopped on a street opening onto the central square, the only real downtown. The single hotel, one more 1930 building, stood in the middle. It was the tallest building. My room was cold and huge, with a balcony overlooking the empty square. Before meeting Madame Varda, I had a few hours to kill. I went out and wandered at random. The air was fresh and cool. On one side of the square sprawled blocks of new apartment buildings, painted a glaring white with wrought iron balconies curling at every floor and large sliding glass windows. They were not all occupied to judge from the lack of curtains and quiet. This was probably the "new Lamia" sprouting from the shacks that must have been there not long before. Further away, the square tilted down into a large flight of steps. Below them, small alleys wriggled along, bordered by doorless tiny shops. It was the old market. Goods were only hidden by pieces of canvas, if at all. Blood rivulets ran on the hard floor of the butcher shop and a freshly slaughtered sheep hung from a hook, eyes still bewildered. A potent smell of rotting greens and old fish mixed with the acrid scent of burning wood. The market was shut until evening. Only cats ran around. They stopped, staring at me before sauntering away.

At six in the evening, the French Institute was bustling with kids. I went upstairs to Mrs. Varda's office under their straightforward gaze. They whispered as I went by. Mrs. Varda was a very young woman with long hair, holding her neck and torso very straight as village girls do to impress boys when they pace up and down on the main street. She emanated a mix of pride and anxiety to please. I was the first native French teacher to come to Lamia. While we talked, students stretched their necks to glance at me as they passed in front of the open door. I would teach two classes: one with kids sixteen-eighteen years old, one with adults from thirty up. With the kids, I had to follow the regular grammar and fluency program from the prescribed manual. For the adults' special course, I had *carte blanche*. The course was not part of the regular cursus of studies. It had no exams and no degree at the end. Besides those two classes at the Institute, I would teach a private course called "Sorbonne II" for six pupils. Written and oral exams for the "Sorbonne" curriculum took place at the French institute in Athens. The degree gave entry to French Universities. The course was the perk I had been told about. Being privately taught, it carried the impressive stipend of twelve thousands drachmas per month. The ground felt solid under my feet, at long last. I had a job. I was no longer a hobo.

A room "chez l'habitant"

The following day, I went to look for a room to rent. This time I wanted to be able to cook. People renting out were all in the low part of town, next to the old market. I was sent to an old woman who played real estate agent for the rare singles coming to the town. With a scarf on her head, she looked like an old witch, her cunning eyes trying to fathom how much I could pay. She first took me to a small house where an old couple received me in their bedroom. The man sat on top of the conjugal bed, his short legs dangling. "This is a church here", he said with a jovial smile, tapping on his bed. Indeed, crucifix and Virgin Marys hung everywhere on the walls and an iconostasis shone its red little bulb in a corner. The wife stood up silently like a servant while the husband chatted. From what I gathered in the conversation, he was worried about potential boyfriends. The room for rent was a small closet just behind theirs. I said I would think it over.

We went on walking and the old witch took me to another old couple. They were retired butchers who had built a small condominium atop their former shop, just on the brink of the old market. In front of their small building spread a small square paved with large white stones and planted with giant plane trees. Along a high wall, an old washing place was still in use. A succession of fountains with Arabic motifs carved in the marble splurged into thick marble tubs aligned along the wall. The lady, a tall and strong woman with white hair neatly permed, was obviously the chief of the household. Her husband, a small hat on at all times, slightly smaller but very alert, didn't seem to mind. The room had a large window and a tiny balcony. The double bed and the wardrobe took all the room and the door had an opaque glass insert. The perk was the kitchen. I would have my own shelf in the fridge and permission to cook anytime I wished. We sat at the kitchen table to settle the deal. I left a deposit and we drank coffee all together.

Danae, a budding "femme fatale"

As soon as I started my classes, kids came up to me at the end of courses to forward invitations from their parents to come for a meal. I accepted an invitation for Sunday lunch from a notary and his wife whose daughter, Paraskevi, and son, Haris, were both in my class. Their villa was above the town on a small road, with rose bushes blossoming in front. Everything inside was creamy white and fluffy, and all seats big and deep. The notary was round and jovial, as was his wife who was wearing a Chanel-like blue suit and high heels. The lunch cooked by the mother was sumptuous. After coffee in the salon, the kids asked if they could take me out for a drink. We went to sit at the one and only trendy café on the square where all youths met. Haris ordered coca-colas with a rind of lemon, repeating twice to the waiter not to forget that rind that, no doubt, made all the difference between a peasant and a worldly young man. The waiter shrugged his shoulders. As we were sipping the cokes, a girl entered the café with two men.

I knew her. Danae was one of my pupils. She nodded to us as she passed nonchalantly, glancing at us with her peculiar bedroom eyes, half shut because of heavy drooping lids. Harris sat mouth open, his face drawn, almost trembling as Danae planted her eyes on him for a split second. While his sister and I chatted, Haris had forgotten us. Just behind him, Danae was whispering and chuckling lightly with the two men. Now and then, he turned slightly his head as inconspicuously as possible, to spy on her. His eyes were pained and his face pale.

I told Mrs. Varga about the lunch at Haris's parents. She had smiled mockingly. "Haris is a nice kid, but his parents are worried. He has fallen madly in love with Danae." Danae had a bad reputation. She had been seen after hours with dubious men. Parents all over Lamia pointed their finger at her. They all prayed that that precocious man-eater would not enthrall their sons. Mrs. Varda had no illusion. "Haris has no chance with her. She is only playing with him". Danae was sixteen years old. She was not pretty, and not even young looking. Her breasts, arms, calves and even ankles were heavy like in a mature woman. She had a faint black mustache above her lips, and dark hair in her armpits. But her nonchalance and husky voice kept everyone agape.

She always arrived late in class, making involuntarily or not a dramatic entrance. She walked through the class to a free seat as if still sleepy, looking absent-minded, moving her hips and bosom slowly as if she was dancing some voluptuous solo dance. The whole class and I waited for her to sit to resume the course. Girls rolled up their eyes while boys held their breath. All Greek girls tended to purr and swing their hips when males were around, just like kittens. But Danae was another league of animal, a real leopardess. Mrs. Varda's predictions for Danae's future were grim. You could not tantalize and play with males forever. Sooner or later, she foresaw, Danae would arouse mad jealousy and violence. Haris's parents were taking his infatuation very seriously. To nip that love in the bud, they had arranged to send the boy to France the following fall, as soon as he finished high school.

Deportation order

Everything was fine and my life in Lamia had settled to a nice rhythm. All my students were good, working steadily and amazingly considerate. It seemed to be a given in that provincial town that a teacher had to be respected. The teenager class was very crowded and, save for Danae's apparitions, always orderly. The adults' class took place in the evening. There were nine of them, one young guy and eight older women. They were all more or less fluent in French and, based on a text we worked on together, we improvised discussions. Like children, they relished having good marks, even if they were pointless. The *"Sorbonne"* private course took place at dinner time, since the six kids, one boy and five girls, were busy the whole day preparing their entrance exams for the Greek Universities. We met twice a week at the villa of one of the girls. A buffet dinner was prepared and the parents of the hosting girl made a point of being invisible. We sat around the dinner table. We were progressing fast on the rather heavy literature and civilization programme. We had barely eight weeks to go until the final exams in Athens.

Out of the blue, a sealed envelope arrived one day at the French Institute, addressed to me. It bore the stamp of the Greek Home Affairs Ministry. I had violated the Greek labor code, the Ministry informed me. Having entered Greece as a foreign tourist, I was forbidden to work. The authorities gave me twenty-four hours to leave the country. This was a deportation order not to be taken lightly. The same day at noon, I left for Athens on the bus. I was not worried but rather furious and ready to fight. The French Institute had to clean up its own mess. I was ruminating as the green landscape went by along the road. An establishment run by the French Ministry of Foreign Affairs had to be aware of Greek labor laws. They had to solve the crisis.

Lost and redeemed

The Language School Director was not the right guy to meet. I had to see the Cultural Attaché, no less. I went up to his office and asked his secretary for an emergency appointment. I had only twenty-four hours to act I told her. That delay elapsed, I could be taken to the border by Greek police, possibly detained for some time before being driven out. The secretary looked annoyed but I insisted. I had to talk to the Cultural Attaché right away. She called on her phone and entered the office of her boss. A few minutes later, she was holding open the door for me to come in. The Attaché was standing up, bowing to me like Charles Boyer. He made me sit and I repeated my story. I stated haughtily my bafflement at the situation the French Institute had put me in, and that nerve of mine seemed to electrify him. He mumbled apologies and said he could fix the problem in no time. He would send right away a message to the Ministry of Foreign Affairs. The French Institute would argue that they needed a French national for my post. They would have the deportation order annulled. All this sounded easy and painless. But what if the Police was coming searching for me the next day, when the delay had elapsed? The Attaché smiled and told me not to worry. Had he ever had himself to worry about a deportation order? I wondered.

The diplomat kept his word. The Greek authorities had accepted to suspend the deportation until a solution would be found between the two Foreign affairs Ministries. I now had to go to the French Consulate on Amalias avenue. They were in charge of the whole procedure. The Consul was a flirtatious and merry man, a kind of Peter Ustinov with luxuriant white hair and blue eyes. My next stop was a Greek lawyer, a woman representing the French Embassy. Her messy office was off Panepistimiou. She calmly assured me that I would have a working permit and a staying permit by the end of May. I could then come by to fetch them. The deportation order being suspended, I could go back to Lamia, but I had to abstain from working my official classes. This meant that I could teach only the private *"Sorbonne"* class and this, discreetly.

During my absence, the Lamia police had come at the French Institute asking for my whereabouts. Mrs. Varda had told them that I was in Athens to deal with the problem with the competent authorities. I now had only three weeks left in Lamia and that was fine. I had made up my mind. I was going to stay in Greece not only the coming summer, but also the whole next school year and more. But I did not want to live in Lamia or any other provincial town. I wanted to live in Athens. While solving the problem with the French Institute, I had stayed at the YWCA again. My trunk and my big suitcase filled with my gipsy possessions were still in the ground-floor closet. In May, not only was winter gone, it was already summer, reigning supreme in the air and on the streets. Foreign girls roamed everywhere in Athens, legs bare and hair loose as if they were going to the beach. Amazed, Athenian men looked in awe at the cavalcading females heralding summer time.

When I came back to Lamia, I found a new lodger at the butchers'. Marylena had come from Athens to replace a teacher on sick leave. It was her first experience at teaching. It was also the first time she was leaving her parents. Her father had made the arrangement beforehand himself on the phone with the butchers. We cooked our meals together in the kitchen. The butcheress liked having us around. Her only child, a son, was running a supermarket in Canada. They had been visiting there once, but he never came to Lamia. Marylena giggled at everything I said or did and seemed happier by the day. "Someone is writing poems about you", she told me one day and I thought she was kidding. She was not. The boy, a clerk somewhere in town, lived in a small flat in the building. I had heard the butcheress complaining about loud music he was listening to sometimes, which displeased her. I had sometimes met the boy in the hall, but I did not remember even looking at him. He had a crush on me and he had written poems about our doomed love. He had talked to Marylena, begging her to arrange a meeting.

Tsangarada

I had only a week left in Lamia. Before going back to Athens, I wanted to go to Tsangarada. I had read about Tsangarada in Eleni Samiou-Kazantzaki's memoirs. It was the place where she and Nikos Kazantzaki, the Cretan writer, had loved each other for the first time. But I had no clue where Tsangarada was. She gave no directions for finding their mythic village. I had long thought that it must be a village in Crete where she and Kazantzakis were both from, until, unexpectedly, Tsangarada had turned up on a map of Pelion, a peninsula up north of Lamia.

That last week in May, the Orthodox celebrated the Ascension of Christ and I had four idle days in front of me. Lamia was not very far from Volos, the capital of Pelion. There was Tsangarada, down Mount Pelion, by the sea. It faced the eastern Aegean, an open sea going all the way up to Thrace. Like Mount Monadnock, I wanted Tsangarada to be part of my geography. But it was a blind date again. I knew nothing of the actual Tsangarada. If anything, it could be just another brick and cement village by the sea with tourists in the summer. But for the sake of that peculiar music, "Tsangarada" and the long buried bedazzlement of Eleni Samiou-Kazantzaki, I could not resist.

To get there without a car was in fact already a challenge. I had to rely on the capricious bus system. The first and main leg of the trip would be from Lamia to Volos. After that I had to find out when the next bus to Tsangarada, if any, would leave. I started in the morning and arrived in Volos at noon. The town was crowded and merry, with everyone shopping for food and sweets for the religious feast. I grabbed a cheese pita and a tomato and ate while walking around. I still had a third of the way to get to Tsangarada, and it would take another four hours. I had to take three more different buses, with a change at Kala Nera, and another at Miliès. It was a long and segmented trip, but I liked the slow approach. The mountains and valleys above the sea were grandiose and the buses empty. I could cradle nicely, change seat at will, stand up or sit down. I had all the time and all the space in the world inside those buses. At long last, I could spot Tsangarada down by the blue surf, cascading white houses with ochre tile roofs, small and dainty. It would be my first swim of the year, blood-whipping and freezing cold even in the already burning sun.

Back to Athens

The sun pounded on my head as I stood in the courtyard of the French Institute with my pupils and their parents. They all had successfully passed the *Sorbonne* written and oral examinations. I now waited for a new post in Athens. The tall Alsatian Director had been icily polite when I had presented him with my request. The French Institute was starting a new policy, he announced. They now wished to send more French nationals to teach outside Athens in the various regional establishments disseminated all over Greece. Since I had done so well in Lamia, why not go on in another provincial town, he told me. He had a post for me in Larissa. A renowned farming center and the capital of Thessaly, Larissa was a hole and the hottest place in Greece. "This is the only post I can offer you" the Director had said. I thanked him politely, reserving my definite answer, but my decision was taken. I would stay in Athens, job or no job at the French Institute. I had had enough of traveling.

On that examinations day at the French Institute, I had met fellow French teachers. They were all teaching at the Central Athens branch. When I had told them I was just back from Lamia where I had replaced a teacher for three months, they had laughed and jeered. Especially Ariane, who seemed keen on delivering incisive judgments on anything and anyone with her made-up canaille accent. She chuckled when I said my name. She had been at school with my sister in Paris. Michel looked like a personage by Sempé, the French cartoonist. Of medium height, his ways were discreet, his face blank with Christ's hair and a goatee, his blue eyes diluted behind severe round glasses. But once in a while, he dropped ironic remarks on people and things with a hint of a smile. Ariane had left quickly to take care of her busy social life. But Michel had invited me for coffee.

He was a philosophy graduate from Strasbourg University and he had come to Athens because of his Greek girlfriend. They had met on a bridge over the Rhine. She was lost in the city and she had asked Michel for directions. Her law studies finished, she had gone back to Athens and he had followed her. He had now been three years in Athens, perfectly happy. I told him about the proposal for a post in Larissa. "No way. You must stay in Athens" he exclaimed, "Even the Greeks don't want to live anywhere else!" Besides the French Institute, he taught at Moraïtis College, at the American College and at the Royal School of Anavryta, all private schools. He promised that he would inqire about a post for me in one of those schools. Besides, he had plenty of demands for private French lessons which he would gladly refer to me since he could not handle them all. "Private lessons can bring enough to live on. I did it for a year before getting a post", he assured me. "Don't worry", he added, basking in the sun, "In Greece, you live day by day. One day, it's hell and the next is paradise."

In any case, if the Director could deny me a post in Athens, he could not take back my working and staying permits. They were valid until June of the next year, 1978. I could now legally stay in Greece and work for a whole year. I had gone back to tell him I was turning down his offer. "Very well", he had grumbled, getting up and opening the door for me to get out without shaking hands.

The streets of Kolonaki

Objectively, I was on shaky grounds. But Athens had enthralled me. This was the first time in my life I was falling in love with a city. Neither my home city, Paris, neither London, neither New York had aroused so much feeling. There was no explanation. I liked the air, the wind, the breeze, the views, the skies, the marvelous feel of swimming around the city, up and down. Going down to the old town, or going up to the top of the rock of Lycabettus, it felt like music and sea waves. Day after day, night after night of peregrinations in

Athens, I was still in love with the city. Night was maybe my most cherished time.

At night, the streets of Kolonaki smelled like an oriental garden, a *"baxès"* as the Greek called them, using the Turkish word. Jasmine on verandas and orange trees along the curb exhaled all their scents in the cool night air. In the scarce streetlight, buildings, people and cars appeared fleeting and dim like in a dream. I had no fear of the night out in the city. Athens was not Paris. Cars slowed down sometimes. Men whispered through the windows. Passers-by asked for a light. I gently passed my way and they passed theirs.

One night, as I was standing on Solonos Street, waiting for the red light, I heard the frantic tip-tap of high heels on the pavement. Ahead of me, a woman was running down Iraklitou Street, in total panic. Just as she arrived on Solonos, a Jeep veered in at top speed, braking brutally with a deafening shriek. A man jumped out. The woman had already turned back, going up the street again. The man started to chase her. Tall and muscled, he ran faster like a feline. In a few leaps, he reached her, grabbed her shoulder and took her in his arms. Seemingly embracing each other, they went to the Jeep. She kept her head down, motionless. He kissed her, opened the door for her to sit and went on the other side of the car. Just as he was getting inside, the woman jumped out and took off up the street. He got out too and instead of chasing her, watched her disappear. He swore and kicked a tyre, then jumped back in the Jeep and went off with a roar. All was quiet again. I could resume my night walk.

Walking around Kolonaki, I started to read the red and white posters advertising apartments for rent. They were stuck on walls and lampposts. The watchman at the YWCA had told me that Kolonaki was way beyond my means, and filled with those old degenerate he hated so much. He had recommended me Ambelokipous, or Gizi, low-income areas more appropriate to my circumstances. I did not know those areas. I knew Kolonaki, and I liked it precisely for its airs. Greek old-fashioned bourgeoisie lived there. Privilege, I knew, had a lot to do with its charm. Kolonaki was colonial, high and breezy, its buildings flowered and white. Kolonaki ladies, not too young, ambled around Kolonaki square. They gathered with their beaux at the *"Hellinikon"*, an all white leather bar-restaurant that looked terrily chic and cool behind its wide windows. I felt both miraculously carefree and at home on that breezy hill.

Looking for a flat

The little flats for rent in Kolonaki were all in basements and, with their single window opening right on the curb, rather debasing. There were even some that had no windows, only a door opening on the adjacent cellars. The asking price for those kennels was five thousand drachmas and more, which was too much. Michel lived in a huge apartment in Patissia, and I went around the area. Rents were cheaper there. But every evening, I was back in the cool and odorant streets of upper Kolonaki for my walk in the dark. Always back on Fokilidou, the orange tree street. The scent of the orange blossoms had now vanished, but tiny new oranges dotted their green foliage. From the steps of Pindarou, the Acropolis always seemed sovereign and unassailable. On my left, arose the high walls of the "Arab castle", quiet and sovereign too.

Where Fokilidou street ended, in front of the gardens of Dexaméni, there was a house of games. It opened only at night. All its windows were open, the crimson velvet curtains billowing slowly in the breeze. Gamblers in dark suits moved dreamily around green tables in the halo of suspended lights. Further down, Fokilidou opened into Kolonaki Square, the real name of which, but never used, was *"Filiki etairia"*, in memory of an association of bright minds which had concocted *"the Great idea"* as it was referred to, of an independent Greece, freed from the Ottoman rule. The square was busy at all times, like partying forever. Its *"peripteros"* were open around the clock. I stopped at one of them every night, at the corner of Kanari Street, to get the freshly delivered *"Le Monde"*. Newspaper under my arm, I walked back to my dump of a room at the YWCA.

My official papers were now ready. I went down to the lawyer's office on Koraïs street to fetch them. She asked me gently about my life in Athens and how things were going. I told her I was looking for an apartment. A friend of her mother, a Mrs. Papachristou, who owned a whole building, was just looking for a tenant. She had a two-room apartment for rent. Why not go and see her? Of all places, the apartment was in Kolonaki, and right on Fokilidou Street. I could not believe it. The lawyer offered to call Mrs. Papachristou right away. I could hear a flow of words and a rich voice through the receiver as the lady talked. I was to come by the next day around six in the afternoon, to talk things over. But how much did the lady want for a rent? About three thousands drachmas, the lawyer said. Michel was right. One day could be hell, and the next, paradise.

The building was at the end of Fokilidou street, just before the street plunged down into the canyon of Dimokritou street. I stopped in front of a wrought iron and glass door. Three names were listed next to white buttons. I pressed Papachristou and the door opened with a buzz. I went up a narrow staircase, in white marble, past a small kitchen window behind which a hirsute and grumpy female face stared at me. After a small landing in front of a door to another apartment, the stairs went on spiraling around a well of light coming from the sky above. I passed a small terrace on which opened a tall window. On top of the stairs, Mrs. Papachristou was looking at me with her two big eyes behind thick dark-framed glasses. She looked like an owl perched on a branch up there. She welcomed me with her best French. We crossed a messy living room and went to sit on a terrace overlooking Athens, or rather a slice of it, since a higher building on the other side of the street masked a good part of it. From below came up voices and car noises. We sat on old deck chairs and she poured me a glass of homemade lemonade, offering me a slice of homemade cake too. I had noticed silver prints of a ketch on her walls. Her husband had been a sea lover all his life she declared with tears in her eyes. He went sailing around the Thermaïkos gulf, off Salonica where she had lived until her widowhood. She often went along. They tented on beaches and cooked fish on campfires and, judging by her laughing which had succeeded to tears, they must have had a hell of a good time. She had had some people coming to visit the apartment for rent, she told me. But all were men that wanted an office for what she suspected to be extramarital activities. She much preferred a girl like me, a *"Mademoiselle"* as she said in French. She was sure we could get along, she announced candidly.

The flat for rent was just below her apartment. Her kitchen window was overhanging the little terrace I could make use of in front of my living room. The little flat had first been a small penthouse on top of the original roof, before she had elevated the building to build her own apartment. The flat was tiny but complete, with a bedroom, a living-room which opened on the terrace, a miniature bathroom with a small hip-bath and a small dark kitchen with a few cupboards and an old marble sink. There was even a tiny entrance hall. There was no view, but plenty of light from the sky above the terrace. In case I would feel like looking at the city, I just had to go up a flimsy iron spiral staircase to reach the new roof. Up there, I had a sweeping view of Athens all the way down to the sea and the port of Piraeus. I could also hang my laundry to dry on that roof. Mrs. Papachristou asked three thousands five hundred drachmas a month for the flat. There was no telephone line in the apartment, but she proposed to share her phone with me since there was a phone plug in the flat. Every time she would be off, she would bring me her phone to plug in. In exchange I would take messages for her.

Home

Fokilidou Street was my first real home. The Paris garret did not count. I decided to sleep in it the same night. One more night at the YWCA was intolerable. I had missed privacy and freedom too much for too long. I went straight to the left luggage closet to retrieve my steel trunk and big cardboard suitcase. I threw in the few clothes and toiletries I had upstairs in my room and went to the reception to pay my bill. Everything on board, the taxi roared up Dimokritou Street and went boldly in reverse into Fokilidou. He helped me take up the trunk and the suitcase and I finally sat on a broken pot on the terrace, to smoke my first free cigarette. Foyers, pensions, transient rooms were over. I was *chez moi* for good. As I looked up, Mrs. Papachristou's head appeared behind her kitchen window. She seemed to make a point of not looking at me, absorbed in her cooking.

The little flat had its own terrace opening on the sky where I ate my first meal in an earthenware plate, out of my princely service of four plates bought second hand in another life. I had only bread, feta and olives, and red wine for a feast. I had no glass and I sipped from the bottle, sitting on the floor. I put on my Munich radio. The full tragic voice of Vicky Moscholiou sang *"Alytis"*, the story of a Greek tramp, *"xoris agapi, xoris mana kai xoris spiti"*, "without love, without mama and without home", *"Alyti, mes sto voria mikro spourgiti"*, "Tramp, in the eye of the fierce north wind, like a tiny little sparrow".

The next day, I went to fetch a gas bottle and a gas burner. I now had the home we had all been so melancholy about during winter at the YWCA. Sleep swooped down on me all of a sudden. I was exhausted, but I had made it to port. I unrolled my sleeping bag on the bedroom floor, rolled a sweater for a pillow and lay down, listening to faint shrieks of car tyres and voices from balconies somewhere around. I was home.

"The rich", had said Gatsby, "are different from you and me, they just don't care" I had exactly twenty thousands drachmas left. The poor, I could testify, were different. They had to care. Every errand felt like a victory. In the morning, I ran to the "EBGA" shop below on Anagnostopoulou street to buy a yoghurt and two oranges. I ate them sitting on the broken terracotta pot on the terrace. The sun could not reach me, but the air was warm. On Adrianou street, I had gone to buy a *"briki"* to make coffee. It was made of brass and came from Egypt. When the smell of Greek coffee rose and spread around my apartment, I felt truly home for the first time. I turned my cup in the saucer and looked into the coffee grounds. But they were undecipherable to me.

An eccentric landlady

Mrs. Papachristou spent a lot of time in her kitchen. She seemed always absorbed in some intricate cooking experiment and this, at any time of day or night. Her schedules were erratic, as was her life. She was alone, free as the air, with lots of family and friends on whom she lavished her many confections and concoctions. Hence, the cooking non-stop. Her whole apartment was filled with food. Piles of fruits and vegetables filled every horizontal surface in the apartment. The piles collapsed sometimes and everything rolled on the floor. Her giant old fridge was not big enough to keep all the tarts and pies and stews she prepared relentlessly. She stored them on the kitchen windowsill. But food kept rotting wherever she stored it. She looked at all that decay, pondering at the ineluctable. Always in fear of being caught up by that creeping rot, she was obsessed by time and always in a rush, appalled by the merciless passing of time. She cried to God Almighty, the Virgin Mary and all the Saints when the cake or the pie was still not cooked and she was afraid to miss the last bus. Protocol in Greece imposed on one not to come to a house with "dry" hands, i.e. empty-handed. Before setting off to visit someone, she cooked for hours, no matter if it was midnight or siesta time, cold or unbearably hot. Then she took off at dawn or at dusk for Glyfada or Pendeli. Every penny mattered and even if rich, Mrs. Papachristou cared. She ignored cabs and always took the bus. Carrying bags full of her pies and tarts, she had to walk a long way to catch her buses, but she sailed forth like a speedboat on her high heels.

After a month on Fokilidou Street, I had lost twelve pounds just going up and down twice a day. My circumstances intrigued my landlady. I was French, which in itself was the sign of an enviable station in life for her. She gathered I was from a well-to-do family, but she was puzzled by my financial situation. I obviously had no fortune, since I was looking for a job, and my family did not seem to send any money to help me, which shocked her outright. Now and then, she inquired lightly. Once she had asked me if I would have a dowry. I told her that dowries were now a thing of the past in France. Even in Molière's times, they were already ludicrous, I added. She was shocked. Maybe she wanted to find me a husband. I knew that a dowry was not only customary for girls but, in fact, a legal obligation in Greece.

Her love life kept her life busier than mine. The following spring, she seemed to have even more energy and pep. She was off every day after her cooking marathons, running down the staircase, adorned with ever more inspired hats and jewelry. Several times while chatting, she had alluded to sex. She had confided in me about her not having had children because of her very weak health, which for sure didn't show. She had told me too that she could never stand prophylactics when making love with her husband. Her theory was that rubber inflamed tissues and, worse, prevented the sperm to act as a "balsam" on the heated up vagina.

One day, she told me about Polybos. He lived in a villa in Glyfada with his mother, an old lady friend of hers. Mrs. Papachristou visited her regularly, and little by little it had become a good pretext to see Polybos. A retired lawyer in his early sixties, he was still a bachelor. She thought he was afraid of women and sex. Her strategy was to tame him and ingratiate herself. She made no mystery to me of the fact that she wanted to have an affair with him. At some point, the old mother got seriously ill. Mrs. Papachristou was now going every day to Glyfada. Besides the maid, a nurse had been hired to give round the clock medical care to the dying old lady. Polybos spent most of his time in his mother's bedroom with the nurse. One day, my landlady had come back scandalized. She had seen Polybos and the nurse laughing together at the foot of the dying woman's bed. They seemed to be quite well acquainted.

The nurse was in her forties. She would not believe it at first, but gradually truth dawned on her. Polybos liked the nurse and seized any opportunity to grab a piece of her flesh, notwithstanding the old mother lying half conscious on her bed. Or rather, thanks to that half consciousness of the dying, the son was free to do as he wanted, and he wanted the nurse. Mrs. Papachristou was not ready to accept defeat. She went on going steadily to Glyfada, day after day. She even discussed the matter with Polybos, in a sisterly way, trying to make him see reason, to no avail. Younger was sexier, no matter what. She swore she had seen them making out under the nose of the old woman just before her last gasp. The mother died and the nurse moved in.

Mrs. Papachristou did not have an in-house maid as would have befitted her station and means. She only had a cleaning lady who came every fortnight. Frosso was the only being she feared. She needed her badly and the sly cleaning lady knew it very well. Framed by her peasant white scarf, Frosso's face was energetic and beautiful, with solid regular features and wide blue eyes. She worked very hard when she came, bending, kneeling down, climbing on the ladder, stretching to reach dirt wherever she could. She cleaned up with the rural vigor of the YWCA women, brushing, sweeping and throwing buckets of water with bangs of mops and brooms. Mrs. Papachristou was there all the time, attempting once in a while to give her opinion on the way to do things, which infuriated Frosso. When she was doing her job, the cleaning lady considered herself the lady of the place. She did and talked as she pleased. Perched on a chair, she declaimed her insults to Mrs. Papachristou who, bewildered, was rolling her eyes. Being higher on that chair gave Frosso an advantage. Vindictively, she addressed her mistress in the second singular person. Her quick and venomous tongue shot at rifle speed. She tore into her mistress, with zeal and joy, like a Beaumarchais's servant, ready for social revolution. Her cries and shouts resonated in the marble staircase. My landlady was left speechless, unable or unwilling to answer the insults.

"You, you have never done anything in life! You are just plain spoilt, what do you know about work, hard work?" Mrs. Papachristou, mortified, retreated in the depths of her apartment, pleading Frosso in a whisper to talk lower. That seemed to incense the cleaning lady even more. "It's three months you haven't paid me, you *"kleftis"* (robber*)*, yelled Frosso still louder. If I happened to come by on my way in or out, Frosso smiled or winked at me, as to a sister proletarian. But, at the end of the day, Frosso calmed down and sat very civilly in Mrs. Papageorgiou's dining room to share a cup of coffee with her. This was truce time. They talked about shops and family matters. When Frosso left, they kissed each other goodbye until their next fight. Mrs. Papachristou gave her a tart or a pie of her own making and wished her well. She actually admired Frosso a lot, for her energy and for her thriftiness. She could not believe that the cleaning lady had managed to amass enough to buy a big apartment for her daughter's dowry.

My fluency in Greek was improving all the time, and I had thanked Mrs. Papachristou for our conversations. She had looked at me with her big eyes and, with a cunning smile, she had lamented my lack of gratitude. I should have given her free French lessons to reciprocate.

Summer in the city

On my nightly walks, I would find things thrown away with the garbage on the sidewalk. Thus I had got a deckchair with its canvas torn apart, and a folding wooden table. I had sewn the torn canvas until I could buy a brand new one on Pandrossou street. I had sanded the table and put on a varnish. I could now lounge on my terrace, arms up resting on top of the deckchair, relishing my good fortune and the Greek summer, albeit in the city. Summer had reached its peak of heat and Athens, its peak of desertion. Days and nights blended together, wake and sleep overlapped. Heat made the mind forget and the body melt. I had found a couple of cockroaches under the sink and a mosquito on the terrace, but even the cats had gone away. On the roof, the sun beat hard but at least the air moved. From up there, I watched the Parthenon floating immaterial, dangling in the breeze like an all white yacht. We saluted each other like sailors at sea.

My landlady had gone to Glyfada until the end of the heat. The elderly couple renting the second floor had gone too. The ground floor was empty, so was the third floor, which was rented to a mysterious woman, Olga. Mrs. Papachristou admired Olga a lot. She was a single woman and a lawyer from a distinguished family and also a Communist who had done time in the Korydallos jail under the Colonels. That someone could be a wealthy heiress and a Communist at the same time confounded her. Olga still rented the apartment but she didn't live there anymore. I had seen her long silhouette and gaunt face slipping in and out of the apartment, kept dark like a cellar.

When at long last the sun was receding, I opened the shutters and sat on the terrace in my deckchair. I watched the patch of sky above turning to night blue. The temperature did not decrease in the evening, but dark felt cooler. Now and then, the sound of a motorcycle tore apart the silky evening, quickly vanishing like a falling star. The odd car struggling up Dimokritou street sounded like an enraged dog. Telephones rang needlessly from empty buildings around. I drank a coffee and turned over my empty cup on the saucer. The coffee grounds looked like embroideries in the cup. I thought of Nasreen and Faduah. I had a home in Athens, but no friends anymore.

I was away, but away from what? I had no reference point anymore. Living in Athens as on the moon, in a state of weightlessness was thrilling but sometimes alarming. I felt guilty at times as if I had killed my roots. Anchored at random in that city, had I become anonymous? Even immigrants kept together with their ethnic brothers, cultivating their language and customs and dreaming of their fatherland. I was not a female Ulysses either. Ulysses had a wife, Penelope, and a son, Telemaque, waiting for his return in Ithaca. But one didn't come back to Papa and Mama. Was there a slash and burn pattern in my drifting? Was I going to travel from one country to another forever, never to come back? As if leaving carried its curse, destroying any possibility of return. I had left France, America, England, and, someday, was I going to leave Greece? Once gone from the original home, I was beginning to understand that no one, nothing and nowhere could ever be final. I had become the diver of Descartes, like the one in the physics lab at school.

Like during Ramadan, because of the intense heat, life in Athens was going reverse. I was out only in the early hours and the late hours. In between, from noon to night, I stayed indoors in the dark, dappled by sun sneaking through the shutters slits. Like women shut in a seraglio, my entire world was a bit of terrace and a patch of sky. I listened to *Othello* on the record player placed on my steel trunk. The winds in the sails and the bangs of cymbals filled the space. *L'Estro*

Armonico by Vivaldi was my other treasure. I could not tire of its ritornello, spinning and spinning and sheltering me. In the strange void of an abandoned city, a strange gratitude stirred deep inside sometimes, just for being.

Among various possessions, my steel trunk contained also my small *Hermès* typing machine. I had started to throw words on a blank page like pebbles on a beach. I was building a story out of my shaggy feelings and thoughts. Athens was not a city anymore. It had become a vast boat, as big as Noah's ark, with the Parthenon for a mast and sail. Three girls drifted through, one of them Pamela the Canadian, one of them Calliopi the Cypriot, and myself, the narrator. The girls had the fantabulous power to sail the Parthenon as if it were a yacht. They loosened the rigging, unfurled the sail and off went the ancient temple, a magic vessel standing out to sea. Only the deepest of despair or the deepest of joy could work the magic. It could be tough, it could be mad and dangerous, but they would sail off, masters of the magic temple that would bend to their will.

In the middle of the night, I emerged from writing, exhausted. To come back to ground, I cooked, ate some food and drank a glass of wine. Then, I went out. I walked up to the ring boulevard and watched Athens lying below, tame. I went down to Kolonaki square to the *periptero* at the corner of Kanari and bought my newspaper. Night revelers came in an out of *Papaspyrou*, a prominent café, which filled the whole sidewalk, forcing passers-by to meander between tables and chairs. The Greek staccato resounded in the night. Once in a while, trendy four-wheel "Renegade" Jeeps came charging into the square, their tires shrieking on the melting asphalt. Hirsut and tanned savages, albeit wealthy ones, jumped down from their Jeeps and joined friends for a drink before going back to their wild island. I left the square and went on to roam the quiet streets. Lamps dappled through dried up trees whose leaves were starting to fall.

Nobody slept much anymore at night, save the happy few that had air-conditioning. All night, cement and asphalt returned the stifling heat stocked during the day. Old people hung around on the sidewalks in front of their buildings, or on their balconies, in pyjama pants and nightgowns. Looking haggard, they were at a loss to find rest. A stupefied old lady had asked me if it were normal for nights to be warmer than days. The night sleep was now replaced by a siesta, between two and seven p.m. Groggy and drowsy, people emerged in their underwear or nightclothes when the implacable sun was still lingering. The big house of games at the corner of Iraklitou and Fokilidou was still in business. Behind the same wintry crimson velvet curtains, the same players in black suits moved around tables and roulettes like automats. I walked in the asphalt jungle, carefree and fearless like Mowgli. I did not fear Athenian males, no more than Mowgli the wolves. Like them, they knew at a glance if a female was available or not. If not, they went their way. When the first light of dawn appeared on the sea and the thermal breeze started to whistle softly above Athens, I went back to sleep.

Les amours de Marylena

Marylena had not had much of a holiday after coming back from Lamia. She had been to Voula beach a few times with old school friends. Otherwise, she had stuck in Patissia in the apartment of her parents. One day, I called her. She said she was going to the hairdresser. We could meet there. And why not get a haircut? I had never gone to a hairdresser in Athens. A Greek salon de coiffure was a harem-like treat. Women of all ages congregated merrily around hair-dryers, swiveling their chairs, chuckling and babbling about males and cooking, while hairdressers fluttered around them like devoted little bees. Marylena had decided to get a short cut in the style of Vidal Sassoon, which had belatedly made it to Greece. I decided to do the same in the expert hands of Anna, the head of the shop. Anna was a solid woman, dressed in jeans and sweatshirt like an American mom. Her own hair was cut Sassoon-like. We got out of the shop enchanted with ourselves, and our bobbed heads. Marylena looked healthier, her face rosy and smooth. Her small eyes were twinkling and with giggles, she told me she was in love with a guy she had met on the public beach at Voula.

Dimitri was an intellectual, a leftist with many connections. Her whole face vibrated as she was telling me. When Marylena had mentioned me, he had said he would like to meet me. Dimitri's best friend was an old Greek Communist who had lived for years in Paris and spoke fluent French. She wanted to arrange an outing for all of us the following Friday night. Before going out to eat, we would all meet at Dimitri's place for a drink. He lived near Koliatsou square, far down Patission Avenue. As I waited on the sidewalk, his stentorian voice burst out of the speaker down by the entrance door of the building. With a large gesture of his right arm, he opened wide the door of his apartment with a comradely pat of his big paw on my shoulder. Dimitri was barefoot in jeans, his pale torso bare down to his hairy belly. Sitting in a canvas chair, Marylena giggled and blushed. The old Communist sat at the table. His face was half covered with a strawberry mark, his skin flaking off. His rare hair was greasy and speckled with dandruff. He looked at me with shiny mouse eyes. His shirt was open on a thin tuft of grey hair dripping with sweat.

The heat that day was unbearable and even more so in Patissia, a low part of Athens. The window was wide open on a balcony above Patission where noisy and smelly traffic went by at snail's pace. Dimitri was pacing the room, his torso in evidence, his hands up behind his head. He seized a hose on the balcony and started sprinkling the tiles to get some cool. He was standing his back to us, legs apart, carrying on his conversation with the old Communist whom he addressed every second emphatically as *Filé*, "Friend". The old mentor did speak French fluently. He started right away to tell me about his life in Paris on the left bank and how he knew Jean-Paul Sartre very well. Dimitri served drinks, ouzo for Marylena and I and scotch for the guys.

Marylena kept simpering non-stop, wriggling in her chair. Her clothes seemed to bother her. She was readjusting her bra strap continuously. "What is it, *zouzouni*?" asked Dimitri. "A *zouzouni* is a small mosquito" Marylena informed me, "That's my nickname" "It's the sand that bothers you?" asked Dimitri with a soft voice. She wriggled some more. "No, it's the salt from the swim" "Do you want to take a shower?" She and Dimitri had gone to Voula for a swim in the morning. Dimitri asked me about the French Institute. I answered evasively. The old guy was already drinking a second scotch. He declared that he was hungry. "Let's all go to a taverna then" suggested Dimitri. I had a ready answer. I'd be delighted but I was already engaged, maybe another time. The old mentor got up and bowed down very civilly, taking my hand almost to his lips. I kissed Marylena and shook hands with Dimitri. A week later, I met Marylena again. She looked sad. Dimitri had broken up abruptly. He had told her brutally that he was interested in me, not her.

Careless Ariane

Coming back from the open market, I had met Ariane. She was getting out of a trendy Mini-Moke, the funny car of Anouk Aimée in the movie *Un homme et une femme*. She sported high-heeled sandals, swinging her wide hips. She looked at my shopping trolley full of vegetables and laughed at my housewife habits. "Come up for a drink" she offered with her peculiar whining tone. Her apartment was a spacious loft, high enough to be quiet. Ariane wanted to find out what I was after in Athens. My nonchalance left her wanting to know more. "So you don't know a soul here?" Well, I knew Vassilis, and Tito the rooster, and the YMCA watchman and Mrs. Papachristou, but they did not count. She lit a cigarette and poured herself a glass of red wine from a carafe on a small table. She drank it straight and poured another glass again. "Do you want any?" No, I liked wine with a meal, not in the morning. She uttered her judgment, as usual a final one: "Oh, how stuffy you are! It's a very good wine though, the best, from Tyrnavos. I get it in demijohns" She asked me if I was free the next day. "But of course you are, since you don't know a soul!" she answered for me. She had to go to Ramnous to bring back the Mini-Moke to a friend. Her own car, a Beetle, was being repaired.

The next day, we were tearing down Kolonaki, turning at full speed into Vouliagménis avenue. Ariane drove fast and honked nonstop. I held tight to the tube structure of the Mini Moke. She talked nonstop asking questions and answering them. To cover the roar of the engine, she was almost screaming. The guy we were going to meet, she explained to me, had been her lover when her true boyfriend, Alexis, a Greek playwright, was away in Paris. The former was terribly wealthy and terribly boring, but worst of all he had awful hands. She would not hear of sleeping with him anymore, but they had remained good friends. "But those hands!" she kept saying with a grimace of disgust.

I had seen Alexis the playwright around Kolonaki, always a book in hand. A somber and thin guy, with straight hair falling over his dark eyes, he dressed all in black. He sat at *Papaspyrou's* or at *Kosta's* small café on Dexaméni square, reading or arguing with his soul brothers. "I met Alexis because of Tsarouhis" Ariane said, "You know who is Tsarouhis?" I didn't. "He is the greatest Greek painter alive, the only one, all the others are nothing but "petits maîtres". Alexis takes care of his papers. He is the only person Tsarouhis trusts." Tsarouhis was indeed a famous artist, painting sailors and policemen, dressed or naked with round buttocks and thick penises. He painted also dreamy landscapes of ruins in a manner that recalled Le Lorrain.

We were now going along the sea on a straight road. The land was flat, the sky all white. Foggy structures bloomed above the asphalt. Ariane was going at very high speed on the straight road and I was holding my breath. On the right, the flat sea spread motionless as ashen as the flat land. The sun glared in an all silver sky. The air trembled on the horizon. The asphalt had turned white. A black car was stopped on the road. Ariane was driving right into it. I screamed. The black car, hit by us from the back, swerved ahead and the woman who was standing beside it fell backwards, spread out at full length on the side of the road. An old man got out of the car. He looked at us, with his face bewildered and his mouth open. The woman, his wife, was now sitting up, pulling on her black dress, assisted by neighbours who had rushed as she fell. As the man approached us, Ariane's face hardened. She stayed at the wheel while he came to her window. She was well above the frightened face of the man. He opened his mouth but before he could say any word, she barked at him in Greek, accusing him of being parked wrongly on the road. Haggard, the man bowed his head and mumbled apologies. Trembling from head to foot, his wife was now standing up, held by two persons. Pallid, she looked on, appalled by the fierce attack of Ariane, who was still barking and already turning the wheel to go off.

Minutes later, we arrived on the beach at Ramnous, below the ruins of a sanctuary dedicated to Nemesis. She inspected the front bumper. It was bruised and scratched. Her friend, in bathing suit, was coming up towards us, waving with his towel. Ariane fell in his arms and kissed him with a cry. Keeping his arm around her waist, he pulled his thick black beard and frowned. "What happened?" "We had an accident" said Ariane. "But I had told you to be careful, to drive slow." Ariane pouted like a child. "Where did it happen?" Ariane made a vague gesture towards the road. I went swimming while she sat on a towel. As I came out, we left abruptly. The friend needed to go back to Athens fast. He was just back from a trip on his sailboat. He took the wheel, his bathing suit hooked on the car's wing to dry. I sat in the narrow back.

The black car was still on the road. We stopped beside it. More villagers had gathered around. Ariane's friend got out. He towered above the small crowd with his height. His long beard fell on his bare belly. The old man came forward, looking up imploringly, wringing his hands in despair. He seemed on the verge of kneeling down in front of him. The friend asked calmly what had happened. The man was in tears as he explained. He raised his hands in prayer, asking for mercy. His wife was not there anymore, she had been transported to the hospital for head injuries. The man had no insurance for the car and he was terrified that Ariane's friend would call the police. He appeased the old man and told him that there would be no suit. He climbed back in the Mini-Moke and we left. The people remained still petrified around the black car. "Poor chap", said the friend, "His wife is not well. I gave him my phone number." "It's his fault" whined Ariane, "You are not allowed to stop right on the road". Her friend put his hand on her knee and kept silent. The car stopped on Kleomenous Street. He proposed to have dinner later together. Ariane declined for both of us and dragged me into the building. She poured herself a glass of Tyrnavos wine, which she drank in one gulp. "I am going to take a shower", she announced. After she had disappeared, I stood up in the living room a couple of minutes. Ariane had no use for me anymore. I left without a noise.

Marie-Christine

Marie-Christine taught at the Annex of the French Institute on Massalias Street. I had met her when I had gone for training there. As I was sitting in the staff room, waiting for my Greek tutor, she came in explaining to a colleague that she had woken up mistakenly at six am that morning, finding herself at dawn on the street. She had found Athens beautiful at that hour, devoid of noise and fumes. I liked her exhilaration. Seeing me sitting in a corner, she came up and shook hands. She was married to a Greek and had been in Athens for two years. Brought up in Paris, she was born in Dakar, Senegal where her mother's Touareg family came from. Her father was a French diplomat. After work, we had gone to drink coffee at the *Dolce*, a leisurely café off Skoufa Street overlooking the church of Aghios Dionysios and its esplanade planted with tall poplars. The *Dolce* was a sophisticated place, which served Italian *espresso*. Old belles were sipping avidly the winter sun from the sidewalk tables. It was also the rendez-vous of elegant creatures, male and female, who carried on their businesses from the coffee tables.

Dolce the place was indeed, and sitting with Marie-Christine had made me feel at home in Athens, in spite of the rather precarious state of things for me. At that time, I still did not have a flat and proper papers. Marie-Christine was pregnant. She emanated the comforting feeling of someone having rooted in Athens for good. The *Dolce* enjoyed a perfect spot, with sun all morning until noon and a constant breeze coming from the pinewood above. We parted very contented to know each other and promising to meet again. Because she was due to deliver in September, she had not gone to France that summer. She and her husband Kostas were in Athens during the week, but they went on weekends to a house they had built at Porto Rafti, on the coast facing Evia. In June, she invited me to go there for the day. Her husband would meet us in the evening for dinner.

Marie-Christine had come to Greece with a girl friend, three years before. They had made trips to Hydra and Poros and Delphi, but spent most of their time in Athens. She had met Kostas in a café on Syntagma. He had invited the two girls for dinner. The next day Kostas had driven them around. At the end of the week, the girl friend had left. Marie-Christine had stayed behind. Kostas had taken her to Loutraki, a spa resort north of Athens before putting her on the plane to

Paris. At fall, Kostas had come to Paris to meet her parents. They had got married in Athens the following spring. From the beginning, she had agreed to live in Greece. After years living in Africa, where her father had served as a diplomat, she was glad to live in a warm country again.

A Greek success story

Kostas was a self-made man. Born in western Peloponnese in a village near Kalamata, he had left for Athens at twelve. The family owned a shack and the plot around it but there was no land to farm. Kostas was the only son, with three sisters in need of a dowry. The father lent himself as a farm hand, and Kostas was supposed to do the same. But instead he had left for Athens to try his luck. He had arrived penniless and barefoot. Shoes had been his first business. He roamed the streets of Athens looking for and collecting old shoes, which he then sold to a ragman. With the money amassed, he had got his first *periptero* at seventeen, which was a big step forward. A periptero was already a real shop with a roof, a chair and a cashing machine. Finally, he had opened a clothes shop off Omonia square.

A few years later, he had met Bardakas, a seasoned dealer, who was looking for associates to open clothes shops in Athens. Bardakas was from Peloponnese like Kostas, but from Pyrgos. He had understood the new trend in Athens. In the seventies, young Greeks wanted to find in Athens the trendy clothes at decent prices that anybody could get in any western European city. Ermou street, where clothes and footwear shops were concentrated, offered only drab and baggy clothes in cotton or wool and heavy uncomfortable shoes. Bardakas had it all figured out. He first would import direct from Italy, before setting up his own workrooms in the suburbs to copy the Italian models. His plan had worked wonders and he had had to expand fast. Kostas was just the kind of man he was looking for, young and eager to succeed and make money. They had worked out a partnership that left Kostas boss in his own shop off Omonia Square, with a share in two other shops on Stadiou Avenue and in Maroussi. Just as Kostas's business was growing, Marie-Christine had happened. He was now thirty-four and it was time to have children. Kostas did not want to marry a girl like his sisters. He did not want either to marry a Greek girl above his station who would have shunned mercilessly his tramp beginnings. Marie-Christine, wellbred and educated with a law degree, but not prejudiced, was the wife he wanted. She had learned Greek in no time. They lived in an airy penthouse near the Hilton, paved with shiny travertine and surrounded by a big terrace.

While driving through Attica, among olive groves and vineyards, Marie-Christine was telling me about her in-laws. Her mother in law was a stubborn, dedicated woman, working like a slave. Kostas adored her and sooner or later, she was bound to come and live with them, which Marie-Christine feared. She was not keen either on the father in law, a tall man that smoked and drank all day long. Kostas had tried to have him sit at the cash register in the shop, but after two days, he had sent him back home. Of his three sisters, the middle one had married in the village, while the two others had come to Athens where they worked as secretaries. The obligation to provide his unmarried sisters with a dowry had fallen entirely upon Kostas, since the father had drunk all the savings of the family. The younger sister didn't bother much with marriage, she had boy-friends but no intention to tie the knot with any of them. The older one was now thirty-two, getting frantic about finding a man. The first thing any potential fiancé asked about was that dowry.

It was beginning to actually bleed dry Kostas's bank account. One suitor had asked for a six-room apartment in Patissia. Granted the place, he had pondered for a few months before announcing that he didn't want to marry the girl anymore. Tears, gnashing of teeth, the apartment not yet paid for had been resold at a loss. Another suitor had showed up, this time not so demanding, four rooms would do. But, they found out that he was already married to a German woman under German law. Greek men could get away with bigamy since a civil marriage was not recognized in Greece where only the religious Greek Orthodox wedding ceremony was valid. Their foreign wife was then legally a spouse only outside of Greece. The sister was now slowly sinking into despair and spinsterhood, overcome by resentment and shame.

Porto Rafti

The narrow winding road was empty before the weekend rush. We were still going straight on the flat land of the "Mesogeia", the Attica hinterland surrounded by the Aegean south, east and west. Vineyards and olive groves drew lines and dots in all shades of green as far as the eye could see. The plain became hilly all of a sudden and after a few sharp turns, we plunged down towards the coast. Porto Rafti had evolved around the original fishing hamlet, rising up the steep slopes. Levels after levels of white flat-roofed villas piled up to the crests. Real estate developers went on burning whatever woods and scrubs remained around to make way for new building plots. Besides the thousands of villas existing, thousands more were in progress. Steep dirt roads carved out in rock escalated the slopes. Some alleys had been covered with cement to avoid mud in winter and dust in summer. Estates were cut out into small lots, and new batches of villas were delivered year round. Investing his first savings, Kostas had bought his lot many years before. The dirt road going up to Kostas's villa was so steep we stalled several times. The villa was a two-floored building, following the lay of the land, overlooking the pretty cove of Porto Rafti, with pines still preserved on the rocky shore and, beyond, a perfect sea blue. The view extended as far as Evia and the first Cycladic islands.

After a drink, we went down to the pebbly beach for a swim. Kostas arrived at sunset with a couple of friends. In a light beige suit and brown shirt and tie, Kostas looked like Frank Sinatra, thin and dashing. The taverna he took us to eat was in the middle of the reeds behind the beach. Tables were out in the open under the moon. The owner had prepared a *"psarosoupa"*, a soup made with a giant grouper that lay in state on a huge plate, his juice in a big bowl, rice and vegetables in separate dishes. Kostas and his friends were regulars, hence the special service. A sauce made of olive oil and lemon juice mixed together was spread on the fish meat and they could not believe I had never sampled *ladolemono* before. Thanassis and Maria, their friends, were both chubby and short like a pair of children. Thanassis looked like a double of Danny de Vito of whom he emulated the humor. After we had eaten everything on the table and had had coffee, we started back for Athens. Since the friends had a much bigger car, I went in theirs while Kostas and Marie-Christine went in her little Peugeot. As sprightly after the meal as he had been all along, Thanassis proposed to have a nightcap at the new apartment he had just bought in Maroussi.

In the wan halo of streetlights, we stopped on a dusty street not yet asphalted and fringed with a string of working sites at different stages. We walked up marble stairs yet without balustrade. Plaster dust flew off at every step. We got into their apartment, an enormous expanse of rooms smelling fresh paint. Thanassis made us touch the travertine on the floor, which had been shipped direct from Italy. The furniture was already in place. Chest of drawers, coffee tables, night tables, cabinets, side-boards were all made of a yellow wood, spotted like a leopard's skin and lavishly lacquered. We sat on a giant couch spreading along two walls and Thanassis got behind an enormous bar counter to prepare drinks. He and his wife pottered around the giant living room, touching and smelling everything, as if they still could not believe the place was theirs. We drank to their luck, their place and their happy future and left them, standing at their door, looking slightly annoyed at having to stay there all by themselves.

The French Institute nomenklatura

The grouper meal in the moonlight had been the last warm night of the summer. It was still August, but the sun was losing ground, slowly and inexorably. Athenians were coming back. My trip in fiction had ended, the story I had invented about three girls in a boat at the Acropolis of Athens was finished. I was now back on earth, still feeling the wings of dream in my wake. I was at the end of my money too. I had gone back to the French Institute to inquire for work again. The tall Alsatian had left, replaced by a short man with a crushed face and a childish smile, a Mr. Risette whose name meant just that, a child smile. He had told me that the Larissa post was still vacant and I was still welcome to fill it. The French Institute could not offer me anything else.

At any rate, I could enjoy free of charge lectures, movies and spectacles organized by the Institute. Informed by Michel, I had gone to the get-together of all teaching personnel in the great auditorium on September 15th. The whole French nomenklatura was there: the Consul, the Cultural Counselor, the Cultural Attaché and his brand new wife saluting everyone with large smiles and emphatic exclamations. The teachers of the *Lycée Français* and the French Institute, the ones enjoying an advantageous expatriate status, were also there. Michel belonged to the migrant worker category, teachers that were hired locally and paid about a sixth of what the others got.

There was also a diva at the meeting. A fat woman, her tight skirt crumpling up her flabby knees, Constance Alladase was a gawky sight. She was not terribly tall, nor young, nor pretty, but she obviously was an important personage considering the impressive crowd queueing up to pay homage to her. Her official role was to set up the overall programme of cultural activities. She contributed herself personally with lectures on contemporary art, which made Michel laugh hilariously. Once upon a time, Constance had been a primary school teacher, "like the Alsatian Director by the way" had remarked Michel. She had been sent abroad in various countries the last twenty years. Before coming to Athens, she had been posted in Buenos Aires, Argentina. There, two major things had happened to her. She had fallen in love with a man, and she had ingratiated herself with contemporary artists. The result was the constant presence at her side of a sinister guy, dressed like a retired army officer, whom she referred to as *"my uncle"*. "For very good reasons" had said Michel enigmatically. The other outcome was her self-promotion as a twentieth century art specialist. In short, Constance was a fraud. People tolerated or admired her, but no one seemed to dare question her noisy incompetence. Even Michel whispered calumnies behind her back but bowed and smiled when he was next to her.

 I had been to one of Constance's lectures. She paced the floor with her solid step and hard Minnie heels, her skirt going dangerously up on her thighs, emitting her endless logorrhea with a bass tone that could suddenly rise to an unexpected shrieking soprano in crescendos accented with wide arm gestures in the air. The uncle was there in the first row, next to the "crème de la crème". His face and hands were covered with age spots and tobacco stains. He chain-smoked nonstop. His dark eyes looked tired but ever alert. Strapped up tight in a green army greatcoat with belt, which accented his wide shoulders, he looked like a man in his sixties. His past was as dark as his allure. Once upon a not so far away time in France, the uncle had been a zealous collaborator during the German Occupation. After the war, he had been condemned in absentia to death by a French court. He had already left France long before, seeking refuge in Argentina where he had lived quietly until the beginning of the seventies. When he had met Constance, the man was at bay. The new Argentinian president had no sympathy for war criminal refugees and was ready to extradite him to France. Greece had come as a blessing. Since 1967, Greece was a dictatorship with exactly the kind of chaps the uncle felt comfortable with. Constance had managed to get a post in Athens and the couple could now enjoy a peaceful existence, albeit as "uncle" and "niece". I never knew the name of the "uncle". Everybody referred to him as Constance's uncle only. But Michel was positive that the guy was responsible for many arrests and deportations of Jews and Resistance fighters. In 1977, the Greek colonels had already been long in jail, but nobody had yet bothered the uncle. Constance, I would learn later, had been the instigator of my nomination to Larissa, and my ensuing disgrace for refusing to accept it.

I remained stubborn. I would not leave Athens. The French Institute was not to decide where I should live. I would do without them. As promised, Michel sent me one of his pupils for French lessons. A fat and spoilt boy, he was the grandson of the President of the Republic. My folding table found on the street would do for a desk to begin with. I ran to Monastiraki to find seats. Two old Viennese café chairs with arms turned perfect once I painted them a coffee and milk color. The boy, tall and enormous, had the gait of Jean Renoir. An only child brought up by a single mother, his whole aging family spoilt him. The one thousand drachmas per lesson already covered my monthly rent of three thousands and five hundreds drachmas. Once the rent was paid, I was left with only five hundred drachmas for food and other essentials. I was back to tomatoes and olive oil like at Crosby Hall in London, but that applied now to all my meals. Feta and eggs were my luxury. My teeth hurt a lot lately, my gums bled and I could hardly chew meat anyway.

Hitchiking in Evia

I had met Claire, a French girl, at one of the French Institute evenings,. Two years before, she had completed her degree in political sciences in Paris. She had worked for a while, until one day she had been smitten by an uncontrollable panic. She had collapsed on the street and quit her job. Her family had been making apparel and underwear in Bar-le-Duc, Lorraine for six generations. All her sisters and brothers were married with children. Still single, Claire was the odd duck in the household. After a trip to Greece, she had decided to stay in Athens. She was independent, the monthly rent of her Paris flat securing her living. She had rented two rooms on Dafnomili Street, on the hill of Strefi. Jobless and free, Claire was always off somewhere.

As winter came, the sea became unpredictable. Claire now limited her outings to the continent. She had suggested we go together to Evia, an island linked to Attica by a bridge. She hiked with a skirt and moccasins, and she was tireless. The bus had taken us to Halkida from where we had started walking towards the north. Our goal was the northwest coast, which her guidebook praised as pristine and beautiful. Out of town, we raised our thumbs to hitchike. At noon, we had already got to Limni, a small town by the sea. We had only ten kilometers to walk to the pristine beach. We sat outside a pastry shop for coffee and sweets. I had one baklava while Claire ate two. But she was still hungry. She went in the shop again to buy a creamy pastry called *"galaktoboureko"*. When we went to pay the lady inside, the door to the kitchen was wide open. Big baking trays with honey dripping leftovers were spread on a long table, waiting to be cleaned. Claire glanced through the door, her face flushed. As I was paying the lady, she darted through the door, running to one of the trays. Grabbing a spoon, she started to gulp down all the honey syrup she could while the lady was busy giving me change. Before the lady could notice, Claire was back still licking her fingers in delight. I learnt on that trip that she was obsessed with food, obsessed with diets and addicted to amphetamines.

Out of Limni, there were woods and lots of green on both sides. We stopped every now and then, hopeful, putting thumbs up. As far as the eye could see, the road was empty. It was early spring and days were still short. There were no rooms for rent in the area we wanted to go. We had to be back to Limni for the night. As we had abandoned any hope of a lift, an engine started to roar in the far distance. We looked back. A red sporty car was approaching, with swarms of lights blinking from all sides. Wondering what that could be, we did not raise our thumbs. It stopped anyway. The inspired driver was an employee at the Greek national electricity company. He had transformed his car into a magic coach. Every time he braked, plastic flowers on the dashboard and the back shelf, whose hearts were actually red lights, turned on. On the back and front of the car, he had four sets of car lights and added lamps were sprinkled here and there, in and out. We got a full demonstration. He asked us our names. Claire had said her name was Solange for the fun of giving the guy a hard time pronouncing it. He repeated "Solaanz" several times while she laughed up her sleeve. We asked him to drop us ahead of the beach and he offered to wait to take us anywhere we wanted. We declined politely. He said "Good bye Solanz" and we burst out laughing as he disappeared blinking and roaring. In front of us lay the pristine beach. It was a dump with high chimneys and decrepit factories at one end. It smelled like putrefied eggs. Dead fishes floated their belly up and we wondered where on earth guidebooks got their information from. We left and went back to Limni with a bus sent from heaven just as we wondered what to do in the dwindling sun.

Trizinia, the land of Phaedra

I was not put off by Claire's neurotic ways. Her personality seemed totally split in two. Sometimes, she was fierce and daring, ready to walk and climb for miles, even all alone. Sometimes, she suddenly broke down in tears, depressed, despairing of ever getting thin, or ever having an orgasm, or ever finding a man, or ever having children. Trips seemed to be the best medicine for her depressive moods.

She suggested another trip to Trizinia in Argolida, the land of Phaedra. The tragic heroine of Racine had lulled our ears in secondary school, *"Fille de Minos et de Pasiphaé"*. My teacher had a passion for Phaedra, torn between Theseus, her old and unfaithful husband and her beautiful stepson Hippolyte, who was the same age as her. At the eastern tip of Peloponnese, Trizinia was the place where she had consumed herself in cravings and remorses, finally hanging herself from an olive tree on her own land. I still remembered the scene of Phaedra confessing her forbidden love to Oenone, her confidante. *"J'aime"* roared our teacher, a passionate unmarried woman, "Hear now the crowning horror. Yes, I love. My lips tremble to say his name". I could still hear the bass voice of Mademoiselle M., a short ungainly woman but illuminated as she impersonated Phaedra.

The bus had dropped us at Ligourio by the sea. We had another forty kilometers to go. Any vehicle would do for us. Sometimes in the back of pick-up trucks, sometimes on tricycles, we finally arrived in a dull and flat countryside with sparse olive trees and small fields. The palace of Theseus and Phaedra was nothing but stones whitened by the millenniums. So, this was the land where Phaedra had erred, mad with love. The bareness of the place somehow gave credence to the story. Boring and lonely, it was the right terrain for passion to grow.

From Trizinia, we had gone to Galatas, a town across a small channel separating the continent from the island of Poros. There, we were far from the tragedies of ancient times. Galatas was a thriving port town, named after the Galatas of Istanbul. But instead of a bridge to link it with Poros, only a few hundred meters away, Galatas used small boats, roaring their two stroke engines day and night. The small channel between the island and the peninsula was busy at all hours like a miniature Bosphorus. We got into a boat so low one could dip one's hand in the cold seawater. The one-minute trip seemed to condense all the bliss of a sea crossing. On the other bank, the Poros promenade meandered along the old houses. Before Easter, there were no cruise crowds from Piraeus. Poros was its plain self. We started up towards the peak of the village where the bell tower of a church stood out. We looked back from time to time. The view over the island, the channel and Galatas on the continent grew larger and larger. When we arrived at the church, it was dark.

Steps from it, a house had a sign "rooms for rent". We knocked on the door. It opened and a young girl saluted us. We asked her for a two-bed room, and as she nodded, two very small children appeared behind her, clutching her skirt. She seemed annoyed. The door was still open. The little kids seemed very hectic, whining incomprehensible words. She tried to keep them inside, but, as we were going out with her to see the room, which was in a neighboring house, the little creatures darted straight outside. They stopped, jumping up and down, in front of the place. In the glare of a streetlight, they looked like little Chinese creatures with black hair, frumpy little faces and curved little legs, the size of two-year old children. They went into the house with us, letting out shrieks of excitement and, instead of walking, they started rolling their strange little bodies. The next day, they were on the lap of a boat captain as we motored back to Galatas. The two small creatures were actually two midgets known all over the island and looked after by all inhabitants. The captain told us that they were both sixteen years old. The girl who had shown us the room was their younger sister.

The Royal School of Anavryta

Back to Athens, luck struck: I had an offer to teach four hours a week at the *Scholi Anavryton*. Michel had kept his word and found me a job. *"Anavryta"*, as it was called in short, had been founded by King Paul of Greece. His son Constantine had attended the school. The Royal school was a Greek version of a British public school: same green lawns, luxuriously watered all year round, a huge park with beautiful trees, and plenty of time for all possible ball sports like football, baseball, handball, tennis, badminton. The school, initially only for boys, had just begun to accept a few girls. All pupils wore a uniform, navy blazers, grey pants or skirts, striped ties, long-sleeved shirts and caps, whatever the season. Ceremonies with hymns and choirs were held at the beginning of the school year and at commencement. Michel had no time left to do the job. If I wanted it, I could have it. I would be paid five thousand drachmas a month, including a month off, but no social security was included. The course was optional and the class would not be more than fifteen boys at a time.

Anavryta was in Maroussi north of Athens. I went down to Omonia to take the subway, old and wooden, rattling and shuffling like a train in the ole' far west. After a few stops, the train was out in the air, above the roofs of sprawling suburbs. From the station in Maroussi, I could either take a bus or walk twenty minutes to the school. The beautiful park *"à l'anglaise"* which surrounded the college was an oddity in Greece. Cedars, araucarias, oaks and pines with bushes and plants arranged in slack borders composed a fancy British landscape just miles from Athens.

Before starting to teach, I had met with the Director, a thick-lipped and obsequious man who had taken my hand in both his for a long time. He had introduced me to a fleshy younger guy, looking like Tom Hanks, with a big head and tiny little blue eyes. He was the personal assistant to the Director. He would supervise the course and attend whenever he had the time. I was to refer any matter to him. The Director had kissed my hand to say goodbye.

I now had a monthly stipend and a status, however minuscule it was. That was an enormous relief. To get to Anavryta and back took more time than the one actually spent in the classroom, but time I had plenty of since this was my only regular job. My pupils were between twelve and sixteen years old, officially semi-beginners but well above average. Anavryta was a very selective school, and a genuine center of excellence. The curriculum was extraordinarily heavy, comprising more than twelve subjects. History, geography, mathematics, chemistry, physics, ancient Greek, literary Greek, colloquial Greek, grammar and syntax, two foreign languages, religious matters et al. At Anavryta, the kids were studying Latin also and a third, optional, foreign language. It was an elitist school, filled with privileged upper class children, but open also to deserving bright children, referred to Anavryta by local headmasters. My pupils were hardworking and progressing fast, save for a fatty boy, the son of a lawyer from Agrinio, always laughing up his sleeve. After a month, he was sent back to his hometown.

The supervisor that looked like Tom Hanks attended my class virtually every time until the end of the schoolyear. He sat in the back and he distracted the kids, making them nervous. I couldn't stand his ever-smiling little blue eyes. He was a slimy guy, with fat fingers and a soft caressing handshake that I had found unpleasant from the beginning. He spoke English with a strong American accent and he had told me that he had many "very wealthy" American friends, both in Greece and in the US. He kept asking me when I would be free to go out for dinner with him and some of those friends. He would go on telling me about their cars, their Porsches or BMW, or their yachts. It sounded like a catalogue of socialites on a magazine front cover. What annoyed me most was that, when the guy chatted with me, my pupils looked at us out of the tail of their eyes, probably thinking something was cooking between the slimy supervisor and me. They didn't seem to like him very much either, leaving fast before he could talk to them at the end of the class. Repeatedly, he insisted on driving me back to the subway station in his big Chrysler, telling me of his programme for the week-end, on so and so's yacht or at the Astir Vouliagméni, the palace hotel on the coast. He had tried to come and fetch me at the subway repeatedly and I had deliberately dashed away before he could spot me.

Gentrifying my home

Besides the course at Anavryta, Michel had given me more private lessons that I could want. My first savings had been to buy an electric radiator for the winter. My apartment had no heating, and no sun entered through the windows because of the extension built above to accommodate Mrs. Papachristou. At fall and in spring it was colder indoors than outdoors. I had pondered a whole day about buying that radiator. It cost one thousand eight hundred drachmas. That was also the price of a wooden trunk I had spotted at Vassilis's shop on Abyssinias. I had told Vassilis of my dilemma, but he had urged me to go get the radiator, which was more important for going through the winter. On his part, he promised to keep the trunk until I would have the money for it.

A month later, I came back down to buy it. It was a small painted trunk with two iron handles and a damaged lid. Vassilis had taken two old pieces of wood to repair the lid. After a cup of coffee, I had climbed in a tricycle next to the driver, with whom Vassilis had bargained a price for the ride up Lycabettus to Fokilidou street. The tricycle was going at snail's pace with a deafening din. When we started to ascend Dimokritou street, I shivered with fear. We stalled and stopped a few times, but finally managed the turn into Fokilidou Street, no matter the oneway sign, The man carried the trunk upstairs for me and put it in my little living room. I sat down and looked at it. A brownish layer blurred its motifs in black and green, with hints of red and yellow. A sudden genteel feel had irrupted in my tiny home. I first sanded the lid, which was not painted and made it shine with wax. Then, I tried with some soap to wash the brownish dirt off the motifs. Some did go. Emboldened, I tried with a more radical cleaning product. The dirt was dissolving fast and a garland of white, yellow and red flowers appeared, vivid and merry. Numbers emerged also: 1866. The trunk dated back one hundred and eleven years. I went down to tell Vassilis. "Good" he said happily, "That means it has quite a bit of value". Judging from the motif I described, he thought the trunk had been made for a young bride's trousseau.

My living room called for more improvements. I bought an old desk with drawers on one side, opening back and front so my pupils and I could sit facing one another. For my few books and record player, I considered putting in bookshelves: one on each side of the window opening on the terrace. Claire had made some herself, Michel too. It was only a matter of piling up bricks, interspersed with wooden planks. Bricks could be pinched discreetly from working sites. I needed about eighty of them, which meant a lot of pilfering. Luckily, I had spotted a building in progress on Sina Street and I started to take one or two at a time in late afternoon when the workers had gone and everybody was having a siesta. After a month I had my quota. I didn't know at the time that Marcel Duchamp and his wife Teenie had used the same trick in New York City, stealing a few bricks here and there every time they were walking to a friend's house for dinner. They hid them in paper bags. But the bricks stolen by the Duchamp had a higher purpose than a bookshelf. They were intended for a mysterious piece of art kept at the Barnes foundation, *"Étant donnés: le gaz d'éclairage"*, which shows a wooden door embedded in bricks with two peepholes through which appears a naked woman, legs apart. If the bricks could be pinched however, the wood planks had to be bought. I had found down in Monastiraki, on Adrianou Street, a young guy sporting a baseball cap and opaque sunglasses, who, with a multiple sawing machine as high as the wall, could cut planks to any dimension I wanted. It was fascinating to watch him manipulate his pet tool, delivering in seconds a pile of joinery bits, planks or legs. I got ten planks that a cab driver consented to carry with his trunk open. In minutes, I had built up my shelves like a Lego game.

One last item was still missing to really make me part of the normal world: a refrigerator. When it finally arrived in my kitchen, carried by two sweating guys, I felt as happy as I had been when my mother had got her first one in 1960 in Paris. Then, my sisters and I were so moved that we had arrived late at school, telling our teachers "it was not our fault, it was the fridge that had arrived at home!" The teachers had looked incredulously at us, trying to figure out why a fridge could be such an event, since everybody but we had already had one for ages. I now woke up in the middle of the night, listening with awe to the purr of the cooling engine, emitting its mysterious message in the dark. From one day to the next, my life had changed. I could now shop once a week at the open market and have fresh fruit and vegetables at will. I could buy meat and fish too. I could start to cook in earnest.

Private lessons

At first, private lessons seemed to require very little work. I mostly talked with my pupils on the basis of texts or books they had to read at home. But after a few hours, I felt inexplicably exhausted, all my energy drained. Those pupils, two boys and four girls, came from wealthy families. All of them were spoilt and unhappy children. Although they were very good at it, learning French was not their main preoccupation, it was first a way to get out of their home, and also to get the attention of someone neutral. Instead of a French teacher, I was being turned into a kind of shrink. In that language foreign to them, they sometimes talked gibberish, but they felt free to talk and express whatever they felt like. French constricted them to a difficult and different syntax, but it freed them of the conventions and taboos of their mother tongue.

In awe, I was watching French, my mother tongue, making wonders, the same English and Greek had made for me. Foreign languages freed energies, liberated the mind, traced new paths and opened new worlds. Language learning was as magic as a trip in Wonderland, my pupils confirmed. One girl had told me of her anorexia, another was in full confrontation with her control-freak mother and another was thirsty for love and terrified of getting trapped. The boys were quieter. Mothers seemed to demand much more from their daughters, never satisfied with them. Those girls arrived at my place, their faces usually strained and tired. When they left, the strain and fatigue was on me. Although all my pupils came to my place, I had accepted to go to the home of one of them, Athina, in Halandri. Athina would have probably loved to escape her parents' overwhelming control and come to my place, as did all my other pupils, taking advantage of the opportunity to meet their boyfriends on the way. But her parents had insisted on my coming to their place. The French lessons were Athina's idea, not her parents'. The mother, a very elegant woman who spoke perfect English, had told me that Athina would in any case go to America after completing secondary studies at the American College in Athens. She thought that French was becoming *passé* and provincial. English, on the other hand, was the language of the new elite that led to prominent public and industrial positions.

When her mother was around, I could see Athina getting taciturn and frowning, bending to pressure but champing at the bit, like a nervous horse. Mute and tense, she waited stoically for her mother to stop talking and disappear. Once alone in her little study with me, she started reading and talking in French, carefree and voluble, suddenly pacified by a language she was the only one to master at home.

The comfort of a legal status

In February 1978, I was finally called back by the French Institute to replace another pregnant teacher going on leave. They needed me, which was flattering. But I needed them too. My work permit as well as my staying permit were only valid until May 1978. The Royal School at Anavryta was not willing to be my official employer, therefore I would not have been able to renew my papers through them. They had hired me as a private teacher, undeclared, but they paid me a decent sum every month, which they acknowledged one way or the other in their books. The French Institute, on the other hand, paid a miserly sum to its locally recruited teachers, but the official contract they signed with us allowed us to apply for the papers that were crucial to legally stay in Greece. I did not want to risk a deportation again. Besides, working at the French institute gave me a right to social security, a sickness insurance scheme and a pension scheme.

Back in France, my family had had to put up with my decision to live in Greece, but my parents kept arguing that it was sheer madness to work without proper insurance. At twenty-seven, I was far from obsessed with sickness, even less with retirement. But my parents had got on my nerves with their reproaches. Like my pupils, I wanted to make them happy to keep them quiet. The post at the Patissia annex of the Institute was a blessing.

Ariane and Michel taught at the Institute's headquarters on Sina Street, which was the flag establishment. Whining Ariane had made no bones to me about the disgrace of teaching in a suburb. I couldn't care less. At any rate, the pupils in Patissia would be less stuffy than the ones going to the headquarters. Like in Lamia, I would be in an all-Greek environment, save the Director who was French. I had met him first as he was giving a recital of French songs, together with a young Greek teacher who impersonated Juliette Greco, but in a blond version. With a severe face, austere suit and combed back white hair, that little man cultivated a vague resemblance with Paul Claudel, the writer and diplomat. Like Claudel, he had made almost all his career abroad, and he obviously considered his French Institute Director's position as prestigious as a diplomatic function. His ambition was actually to become the next Cultural Attaché, which was unlikely, due to their recruiting strictly among high-ranking academics or civil servants. The little man had become a star in the small world of the French colony in Athens, multiplying his appearances on the stage, tirelessly putting on spectacles, poetry readings and songs recitals. He recited Apollinaire, Rimbaud and Verlaine, and sang the poems of Aragon put to music and love duets together with the Greek blonde teacher. But he had a problem. By the end of the coming academic year, after twelve years abroad, he was due back to France as a primary school teacher in the state system as he had started. His prestige and expatriate financial comfort would evaporate from one day to the other, unless he found a solution. Which he would, by joining the Alliance Française, a private undertaking, becoming Director at their Mexico branch.

I had twelve hours to teach per week at intermediate and superior levels with kids from twelve to eighteen years old. After my stint in Lamia, I now knew the ropes well enough to feel comfortable, although my classes were much bigger with next to forty kids in each. The job gave me another ten thousand drachmas a month and on this, I had to pay a heart-wrenching three thousand drachmas for my social security every month.

Now reasonably paid and insurance-covered, I was beginning to dream of getting my driving license, and a car. The only way to go to Bassae was by car. I had not forgotten that dim lit room at the British Museum and its exquisite phantasmagoria of Amazons, Centaurs and Greek warriors. I had finally identified its location. The temple of Bassae was perched on a mountain in a lost valley of Arcadia, near Phygalia, the surviving village. The map indicated a dirt road, not much more than a mule track. No bus went there. The best way to get to the temple would have been to walk, but it was a long way and getting lost in a lost valley was a frightening possibility. Nobody around me seemed terribly interested by the temple. I would have to go alone and for that I needed a car.

At the Kaningos Police station

In March, I went to the Police station. The first year, I had got my papers through the French Consulate lawyer. This time, I had to go myself to get them. I had decided to go with Michel. If we were to spend the whole day there, at least we could keep each other company. The Police station was on Kaningos Square, the dreariest square in Athens, decrepit and shabby, a place for lost dogs. We went up the marble staircase, littered with discarded forms and newspapers, as if the building had gone to the dogs too. The work and staying permit section was on the second floor, an immense room, immerged in neon light from tubes going across the ceiling from wall to wall. All around, police officers were sitting behind metallic desks. At one end, the big boss was sitting behind a desk as big as a bar counter. His green lizard eyes seemed on permanent alert, sweeping non-stop across the entire room. His face was square and solid with big jaws contracting rhythmically. His enormous hands were busy all the time, grabbing the papers brought by his subordinates, seizing various seals which he banged down at amazing speed on the pile of documents in front of him, handing back stamped copies to the applicant sitting in front of him, piling up the rest on his desk. He looked and acted like a machine, but the green eyes kept moving and a big holster hung down from his side. When he moved into his chair, the grip of his black pistol appeared in the leather sheath.

Many foreign girls hung around the room, accompanied by their Greek boyfriends. Some of them, being denied a staying permit, cried in front of police officers, as impassible as movie villains. We had arrived at eight in the morning. There was already a long queue to get the forms, another queue to file them with a police officer in charge of screening applicants. The longest queue was in front of the last and third hurdle, the major one: the big green-eyed boss. The boss could interview applicants as long as he wanted. In fact, it was more lile a police interrogation, as if we were all guilty of something. He could delay stamping the documents, he could ask for more proofs of this or that, he could just deny a permit, he was God. After four years, Michel knew well the guy's moods and tricks. He had briefed me before about the procedure. We had to wait and wait and shut up at all times. Questions did not have to be answered by words. Greek way, a nod with the head to say yes, face and chin up to say no, was enough. Never explain, never complain, Michel had adopted the British motto. Don't smile too much either, nor frown, nor avoid their eyes. I barely dared breathe and I felt naked. What was a migrant worker worth? That was my status, migrant worker. Five hours later, I had forgotten the long wait. I was still an alien, but I had papers for one more year.

The lake of Stimfalia

To celebrate victory, our courses not resuming for two weeks, we decided to go hiking to the lake of Stimfalia. Jean-Jacques and Lise, both Swiss from Valais, had joined Michel and I. Ariane had announced that she would join us there. The only bus going there left at eight in the morning. The road ended at Lafka, the highest village in the valley. We would sleep there. Michel had planned everything ahead. A robust lady was waiting for us at the communal guesthouse, which she had opened especially for us. Normally, it was shut at the end of August. The rooms were impeccable, but, even in daylight, freezing cold. By early afternoon, it was already dark. The sun had sunk behind the mountains. The air was crisp and translucent as in the Alps. On Michel's orders, the lady had prepared a stew for dinner.

We decided to walk around before the cold and dark prohibited it. The mountain slopes were densely forested. A small torrent ran at the bottom of the valley. The village smelled of dung and wood smoke. It was quiet, with everyone already indoors. Here and there, animals' heads popped behind stonewalls. A somber billy goat was locked into a rocky pen, looking forlorn. Stray chickens and cats raced by. We came back tottering in the dark on the stony path. Twinkling stars and the wide milkyway tore the night. Meanwhile, Ariane had arrived with her car. Her back hurt from the ride and she lamented the stupidity of having come to Lafka, that hole of a place. Michel promised her a great meal. "With wine?" Ariane whined "All you want!" he said. The stew was a goat stew. Its juices were served as soup in a bowl. After a kilo of wine from the barrel all to herself, Ariane had become more lenient to her surroundings. She scoffed at our plans to get up with the roosters the next day. We went early to bed. There was no hot water and no heating and temperature went down well below zero Celsius at night. Pushing away the top sheet, I rolled myself in a blanket with two more on top, head under, to keep warm.

As the rising sun fast inundated the valley, we were up. Breakfast was served by the infallible lady, moving at high speed since she had to run back to her cattle and poultry in between tasks at the guesthouse. Ariane was still in bed. Michel had knocked on her door and she had screamed, telling him to go to hell. We all started happily down the path. The day was glorious, with the colors coming out at their richest under the lush sunlight. I remembered Mount

Monadnock. It was the kind of weather that made you feel strong and contented. We were going down the valley towards the lake of Stimfalia. From there we would go up towards a medieval monastery and the village of Kastania. We all had rucksacks with flasks of water and fruits. We would get solid food at the village across the plain.

I remembered the story of the birds of Stimfalia, which scratched lost travelers' eyes out and then cut to shreds their entrails. The lake looked sinister and dead. There seemed to be no life in its stagnant waters, neither in the herbs and bushes sprouting around. We went by without stopping. We stopped at the monastery of Saint George. As we were standing in the courtyard, looking up the white washed façade, a white-bearded monk clad in black appeared on the balcony, flushed and agitated. He didn't seem at all happy at our intrusion. Michel greeted him in Greek, saying we were from France. He called a friar, in a blue robe, to take care of the infamous papists, and disappeared. The friar opened the chapel for us. Its ancient icons were badly molded. We were given the customary coffee with a glass of water and a dried up loukoum before going.

When we arrived in Kastania, the town streets and cafés were overflowing with men. Local elections were taking place to choose a mayor and the town councillors. Raucous villagers discussed and debated everywhere. We sat at a taverna outside in the sun on a high terrace that looked over the valley. Around us, conversations buzzed like swarms of bumblebees. If men poured everywhere, women were nowhere to be seen, save a few in the scullery behind, cleaning vegetables and cooking. We came back lazily to Lafka in the afternoon, cheeks flushed and in a good mood. Bored stiff, Ariane had already left. We got on the last bus to Athens.

Mets, a bohemian haven

Claire had introduced me to Caroline. She lived in *Mets*, a quiet area nestled between the old Olympic stadium, the Arditos pinewood and the Athens cemetery. *Mets* had the lure of a provincial town just minutes from downtown Athens. Most houses dated from the previous century. They were stonebuilt, often at street-level, with terracotta-tiled roofs adorned with ceramic neo-classical motifs. An iron gate opened on their side into a passage leading to a courtyard in the back, usually centered round a lemon tree with flowers and plants in pots. The air was fresher, the cars rarer, the hard-pack sidewalks sprouting weeds after the rains. A trip there still felt like countryside. But lately, *Mets* was changing. With the irruption of heavy blocks of flats, the old pretty stone houses were beginning to look like forlorn dissidents.

I went there walking, first down Kolonaki and then across Vassilissis Sofias Avenue. Beyond started Irodou Atticou, a cool and green avenue shaded by the National Garden on the right and lined with white marble buildings on the left. The slope of the street felt pleasant. It was gentle and relaxing. Along the fence of the National Garden, which everyone still called the Royal Garden, the National Guard was on duty round the clock, like in front of the National Assembly. On the sunny side of the street, the left one, there was always action. Midway stood the *"Megaro Maximo"*, the ex-Kings' Palace, which had become the Prime Minister's office and residence. Heavy police squatted around the clock in front of the palace, with talkie-walkies and pistols. Limousines crammed the roadway, the policemen jumped around, hysterical and red-faced. The *evzones* guards kept their cool in their thick wool garments, even during heat waves. My preferred time on Irodou Atticou Avenue was after the rain in spring, when all the trees in the park shone and shook in the sun, like dolphins jumping in the sea.

Further down on Konstantinou Avenue, the world changed. The air was loaded with fumes from the heavy traffic heading towards Syngrou, Vouliagméni and the airport. After the delights of a royal avenue, the walk up to Mets was steep and stifling. But I liked to walk under the cement arches and stop there for *rizogallo*, a milk and rice sweet, in a small dairy shop. On top, Plastira square was a small roundabout with trolleys colliding and people swarming, like a mini-Omonia square. Archimidous, the street of Caroline, opened wide at one end. She lived at the end of it. While traffic flooded Plastira square and any street going downtown, Archimedes was always empty like a dried summer riverbed. Post-war buildings with whitewashed façades and round art-déco lines gave way to little houses and tortuous streets still unpaved where winter rains made pools and muddy rivulets. Caroline lived on a rooftop in a faded apartment with a view as magnificent as it was unexpected. Her windows were exactly at the height of the Parthenon which, from there, appeared as if it were a neighbour. One could even count the columns of the temple.

Gladys from Scotland

Caroline was Anglo-French, married to a Greek who was away in Rhodes for his military service. She was going there every two months by boat to see him. The sea trip lasted fourteen hours. In between, she relied on her girl–friends that were all English and living in *Mets* too. Like many foreigners, they all did some translation work and gave private lessons. Gladys was the only real professional of their group. She was a draughtsman and she had been working for more than a year putting together illustrations for an English language manual. We had gone to her house one day for coffee. Her street was ensconced between two walls of rock and red soil that had been carved out brutally by a bulldozer. Before that, her doorstep had been level with the dirt alley it opened on. The bulldozing had suddenly put the house on top of a man-made cliff where it perched now, tiny and fragile, like a doll's house rescued from an earthquake. She had painted it pink with light grey shutters. It looked exactly like the little cottages she sketched on her drawing board.

In sync with her little house, Gladys was a very minute woman, with a delicate complexion and a small squirrel face. Behind her round Mary Poppins glasses, her eyes stared. But her fragile appearance was deceptive. That day, she had a scarf on her head and a blue overall stained all over with paint. She was painting her kitchen, which doubled as a living-room. She moved about like an elf, putting on the kettle to make us filtered coffee, going back to her painting job and chatting to us while we sat. Her son appeared in the corridor with his guitar and she sent him back to his room to work his music some more. A cat sauntered about gleefully and she put down her paintbrush to fill the cat's dish with canned food. The kettle burst into whistling and she poured the boiling water in the coffee pot. She shook her brush and dipped it in a tin, which she put outside, grimacing at the potent smell of turpentine. "You live in Kolonaki?" she said, looking at me wide-eyed, "It is nice there. I wish I could afford it." "When is Alexander coming back?" she asked Caroline. "In a year!" sighed Caroline. We reflected on the lengthy Greek military service. Her husband had been lucky. He had only eighteen months to serve since his mother was a widow and he was an only son. "Greece is still at war" remarked Gladys, "Since 1974, they have not put an end to the war with Turkey."

From the boy's room came the laborious sound of a guitar, stopping, starting again. Gladys sighed suddenly and bent her head on the kitchen table, stretching her arms. "It's spring" she said, "but I feel so tired" "When is the baby due?" asked Caroline. I had not remarked that she was pregnant. "Around Christmas. But it's not the baby that tires me, it's just that bloody Greek bureaucracy".

Gladys had no papers at all. She was in Greece on a tourist visa, which she had to renew every six months. That obliged her to get out of Greece to obtain a new visa on re-entering the country. She would drive her Volkswagen van to the Bulgarian border, going out through one border post and coming back through another one the same day. Going there and back took less than three days if everything went well. To get a new visa however, she had to prove that she had an income. Like many other foreigners in Athens, Gladys used an easy trick. She went to the main branch of the National Bank of Greece on Syntagma Square. There, many affluent tourists came to change foreign currencies into drachmas. Each transaction was recorded on a slip of which a pink paper copy was remitted to the tourist. Most foreigners dropped those pink slips carelessly on the floor as they went out of the bank. Barely legible, they were easy to forge and Gladys could pretend having changed enough money to live on for months. "I'd like to go back to Edinburgh" she said, as a sudden shower battered at the roof. A year later, after giving birth to her baby whose father was the handyman who had fixed the roof, Gladys had had to go back to Scotland in a hurry. It was an emergency. Terminally ill with cancer, stretcher-borne, she was evacuated on a medical flight.

Exarchia the anarchistic

Caroline had a night job with the Greek Information Agency where she worked late into the night, sometimes until dawn, translating non-stop Greek dispatches into French and English. Her office was in the basement of a drab public building at the foot of Kolonaki, on Kriezotou, a small street off Akadimias avenue. At two or three in the morning, she didn't feel like going to sleep, she needed to unwind. Every now and then, I went to meet her and we would go and have a bite in Exarchia where there were plenty of unexpensive tavernas. Exarchia was reputed to be the nest and cradle of the anarchists, which in Athens meant all kinds of drifters, free souls, and also real extremists. Their dissidence was a powerful mixture of anti-capitalism, anti-americanism and nationalism. The rebels from the dictatorship days had found a new cause in their fight again the rich and the Americans. Once in a while, masked bands burst on Exarchia square, making headlines the next day with the helmeted policemen facing them. The protests could be ferocious, but were usually over at dawn. Athenians did not fear them much. For them, the anarchists were part of the picture.

There were also many freewheeling whores around the narrow, sunk in streets. Asklipiou, Ippokratous and Mavromixali Street darted in parallel, straight along the north side of Lycabettus hill, never touched by the sun, darkish and foggy from fumes trapped between their high buildings. No wind or breeze ever blew in those streets that felt like tunnels at all times. Little red bulbs dotted here and there the grim façades, lit day and night. At the touch of a bell, the usually fat and mature women popped on their doorstep, like quaint housewives.

Exarchia square had only cafés. Like the brothels, tavernas nestled along the treets in the few shacks or holes that had survived the profitable condominium building, much denser on that side of Lycabettus. Caroline had taken me on Mavromihali street to the taverna *"Lefkes"* named after one small rachitic poplar tree in its yard. In the hard pack courtyard, Kolonaki liberals mingled with Mets and Exarchia libertarians all year long. Wooden tables were rickety, wine barrels were aligned all around and the owners looked rural enough to make it endearing to nostalgic Athenians. The food was more peasant and cheap than elsewhere with black-eye beans and wild greens. The wine, sold by the kilo direct from the barrel, tasted good but left you stunned for the night and the morning after. Coming back on foot was wiser. The narrow sidewalks of Mavromihali street reeled gently and the façades billowed like sails in the wind. Caroline took a cab home, while I walked in a daze back to my side of Lycabettus hill.

Fernand, ex-1968 firebrand

I had made a friend in Exarchia. He lived at the beginning of Mavromihali Street, not far from the University. Fernand was Swiss, from a village in Valais. He was a member of the *"Parti du Travail"*, the discreet Communist party that the Swiss Confederation would not have tolerated under that name. Born on a farm, he had been dazzled by art in his early teens from the first time he had seen a book on Claude Monet's nympheas. One schoolteacher had taken an interest in him and had taught him the basics of the painting craft.

At the beginning of the sixties, Fernand had gone to Paris, bumming around, squatting at wealthier friends' homes. He had followed courses at the Ecole des Beaux Arts and had participated heartily to the May 1968 fantasia, from the barricades to the free republic of the Sorbonne, frantically painting all over the walls and sidewalks, drunk with joy and spring, and booze too. By the end of the summer, the happy revolution had stopped all of sudden, as a merry-go-round that abruptly falls off its axis. Fernand and his friends had pondered where to go to pursue a life dedicated to art, while living on a shoestring. Plenty of Greeks having fled their country roamed the Paris left bank since the 1967 Colonels' coup. When they had come back to Athens in 1974 after the fall of the dictatorship, they had dragged their Paris friends in their wake. Fernand talked now about the battle of Paris like a veteran, which gained him handy access to people that knew the ropes for a cheap life on the edge. In his first year in Athens, he had married an Exarchia budding pasionaria who had quickly left him to live with a woman psychoanalyst in Filopappou, a sophisticated and affluent bohemian district next to the Acropolis.

I had met Fernand at Nathalie's, a French teacher at the Lycée Français and a neighbour of Claire. He looked pretty worn out then, his hair greasy and his face swollen from too much drink. He didn't paint anymore, he worked freelance as a graphic designer, doing book covers and advertising material. But I had found his rare talent for telling stories quite endearing. In spite of his unattractive face, his bad smell and incessant, rather feminine, chuckling, I found him fascinating. He had invited me for a drink one evening at his apartment on Mavromihali. Fernand's place was roomy and empty, save a drawing table, a mattress on the floor, a few carpets made of handwoven rags and an easel. The walls were covered with old posters of Che Guevara and Godard's movies. A subdued light oozing from low lamps gave the place a grotto feel, with pieces of Indian cotton hanging as virtual partitions to make the two rooms look like twice as much. Fernand had poured ouzo which we had drunk sitting on the mattress. In my honor, he had put on a red cotton sweater and brushed his hair and beard, looking now like Savvopoulos, a hot star of Greek pop, with the same round glasses and persistent smile. I felt dizzy from the ouzo as we went out to eat. "We are going to the tavern of the Communists" laughed Fernand, "rather half-baked ones", he added, chuckling.

The tavern of the Communists

When we arrived at the place, there was no sign outside. Fernand rang the bell. A young guy opened the door and saluted him with a slap on the shoulder and a brotherly *"Yassou, Mastora"*, "Salutations, Mason". The place was big, with a very low ceiling, plunged in medieval chiaroscuro with candles in bottles set on low tables. We crouched down to sit on small stools. The place was empty. As we waited to order, two guys and two girls came in. One of the guy raised his left arm as he saw Fernand. He had a thick tuft of hair falling on his right eye like a bad boy played by Jean Gabin. "I can't stand him" hissed Fernand between his teeth. "That guy is the typical little macho." His girlfriend, a frail and very young brunette, looked at her bad boy in awe. Fernand had ordered "a kilo" of red wine to begin with, still foaming from the barrel in an old recycled bottle. Before any food had arrived on the table, we had already sipped the whole kilo. The chef of the day, since the taverna was a collectivist venture where everyone took turns being either chef or waiter, had made a *"kokkinisto"*, a red colored goulash with beef and tomato, french fries and sausages. We ate heartily, Japanese way, bending towards our bowls on the low table lower than our raised knees. Another kilo of wine had come on the table. I felt warm and floating. The dessert was a semolina pudding. Fernand seemed nervous as more people were coming in, all puffing frantically on cigarettes. The taverna was full and a haze of cigarette smoke blurred the picture. He snapped his fingers several times at the overworked guy who ran now non-stop in and out of the kitchen. I managed to get a glass of water with the bill. We paid and got up, leaning on the low table.

Out, the cool night air was slightly reviving. Fernand walked slow but straight. I was not very sure of the ground under my feet. We stopped at a minuscule café right on the curb and sat at one of its two tables for coffee. Guys argued about money inside the café and cars flitted by very fast on the street. I left Fernand in front of his building and went on with small steps, taking the first left street going up. That was the overall direction if I remembered correctly. Climbing the steep oblique street, I panted. But the effort was getting all the smoke and wine out of my system. Fortunately, the street landed right on the ring boulevard around Lycabettus. From there on, it was thankfully going down.

That evening, Fernand had told me about some of the underground stars of Exarchia. Gina the red was one of them. She was jeered at and mocked by her comrades who considered her as a " *petite bourgeoise"*, *"mikroastiki"*, a air head and a nuisance. Gina was in her early twenties. After a few years studying in Paris, or pretending to, she had come back to Athens. She lived on Emmanuel Benaki, a street perched high along a rare piece of unspoilt green. Walking with Fernand, sometime later, we had spotted Gina on the curb. A pretty girl with black hair foaming around her chubby face, she wore a red pullover and, pointing her to me, Fernand had chuckled, "Here comes Gina the red". That name was a mock one given by her brothers in arms. Railing at the cowardice of the leftist males, Gina argued that it was time for girls to shake things and organize their own movement. She could have preached in the desert.

Bassae

The new academic year 1978-1979 was starting. Boldly, I had decided to drop my classes at Anavryta. It was not worth the hassle of a three hours trip. I had more private lessons now, and ten hours with the French Institute at Patissia. That was ample enough to live on and it left me with much time free. Assessing my savings, I had gone to France that summer to buy a car duty-free as my expatriate status allowed me. Taking it back to Athens had been adventurous. In Ancona, the ferry was overbooked. My car had to be put on the next one. Going down to Piraeus two days after my arrival in Athens, I saw my little white car standing alone on the vast deserted quay. At noon, all ferries had already left. I took the wheel, nervous but thrilled, up Piraios avenue, across Omonia, up Stadiou, across Syntagma, across Kolonaki square and at long last, I arrived on Fokilidou street. My nerves and my brakes had survived. Having a car was like having wings suddenly. I could now go anywhere, like for a start Bassae.

Since my wanderings in the British Museum and my discovery of the miraculously intact friezes taken away from the temple, I had wanted to go to Bassae. I had had a hard time finding it on the map. Common maps of Greece did not mention Bassae, the location of the temple, but only Phygalia, the ancient village nearest to it. The Phygalia inhabitants, in a fit of splendor, had called on Ictinos, the same architect who had erected the Parthenon of Athens, to build a temple to *Phoebus/Apollo* for them. An old French *guide bleu* at the French Institute library had finally given me some clues. The temple was in the heart of the mountains of Arcadia, fourteen kilometers from Andritsaina, the nearest agglomeration. It would be a long drive across Peloponnese through Corinth, Argos, Tripoli, Megalopoli and at last Andritsaina. My plan was to sleep there and go to the temple the morning after. I had not forgotten the hair-raising account by Leonard Woolf of his trip there in the twenties with Virginia, with a taxi. They had driven up and down the mountainsides, he swore, as if a taxi could hike. Nobody I knew had ever been to Bassae, neither did they seem interested in going. I was hoping that, fifty years on from the Woolfs' visit, the road would have improved.

In March, I decided to go. I knew I should have waited. The spring rains could dangerously furrow the already bad roads. When I arrived in late afternoon in Andritsaina, the sun had long disappeared. It was very cold in the mountain village. Smoke festooned the air above the roofs. The high stone houses had graceful wood-carved verandas. In the morning, all traces of winter had gone. It was sunny and mild. I took the road happily. Locals had told me optimistically that no one could miss the temple, it was at the end of the one and only road.

The austere mountains of Arcadia stood up all around, shutting the whole valley. I was now trapped until I would reach Bassae. It was impossible to turn around. The track was not wide enough. Going up, I had the mountain on my right and an unfathomable precipice on my left. The landscape recalled the desert of Gobi, a stony infinity pictured in geography schoolbooks. But instead of being flat, it was a mountainous Gobi, a dead terrain where only stones and rocks could grow, arising in rounded or needle-shaped peaks. Birds of prey circled in the sky above. Driving was slow and required unfailing attention. The dirt road was pitted with holes and littered with broken rocks. A big rock suddenly appeared ahead of me. It took center stage on the road, and I had to go around it, inches from the drop. The winter rains had left a muddy border all along the route. My only advantage on Leonard and Virginia Woolf was that I was at the wheel of my own car while they had been at the mercy of a mercenary driver. But was it such an advantage? I got out of the car to get an idea of the situation. I looked behind, I looked ahead, but I did not look down. As a comfort of sorts, I thought about *"Le salaire de la peur"*, Henri Clouzot's nightmarish movie.

    The magic temple could not be that far, I was telling myself. I had now been an eternity on that infernal road. Either I had to go back driving backwards, or I had to chance it. I finally decided to go, skidding around the obtrusive rock. The road ahead was steeper and narrower. If anyone came down, I had no clue what to do. The old law of the mountain gave priority to the one ascending, but I could not prejudge a stranger's ethics. But there was nobody, no car and no animals, not even goats. Only birds of prey seemed to live on that planet. A little green plateau appeared at last. Sheep were grazing placidly and a guard with a kepi stood up ahead, looking at me incredulous. It was well past noon already. The sky had grown foggy. On the grayish background stood the grey temple of *Apollo-Phoebus*, like a dark knight loitering in the forgotten mountains. Stiff and numb, I got out in awe. All columns were standing up, as was part of the roof and the central naos, a closed cell where the friezes had been until Lord Elgin had carved them away. I climbed into the nave, treading carefully. *Bassae* seemed to have come onto the land of men, like fallen from heaven. Its grace remained but the temple seemed to cry for its past and the savage wounds inflicted by the brutal Lord.

Naxos

It was again the end of another schoolyear. For the first time, I would go off to sea in June, without waiting for the cheaper September. Time in Athens seemed to speed up as years went by. Three years had passed since I had landed in Greece on a cold night. On the quay at Piraeus, boats were wide open like whales ready to swallow. I decided for one going to Naxos.

The gently curved port was quiet and soft-colored like those faded pastels of Italian towns by the sea. It faced a spit of land on which stood, waiting, abandoned and absurd, a lonely marble door. The school year was not finished yet. Boys and girls in blue aprons dotted the quays. The old fortified city, a Venetian Kastro, stood up above the modern town. I walked left onto a cobbled street that ran parallel to the seashore. I was looking for a lady who had rented Michel a room in the past. That room was already occupied. She asked her husband to bring me to another lady that could rent me one. The husband was part mason, part roofer and plumber as the need arose. Besides, he sold almonds, melon seeds and peanuts, which he grilled and salted himself. He biked his self-made vending cart along the quay in the evening. At his favorite spot midway along the promenade, he opened the glass lid above his portable shop and lit a fishing lamp hanging from above. With his lanky body and gentle smile, he recalled irresistibly Jacques Tati's *Mr. Hulot*.

Mr. Hulot and I walked back towards the sea again and went away from the port on the long street that ran parallel to the shore. Houses on both sides were all built alike, with double staircases going from the street up to a walled in doorstep. We stopped at a house with magenta red shutters.

Before going up the steps, Mr. Hulot yelled the name of the lady, *"Kyria Katerina!"* She appeared right away on top of the stairs looking like a stunned bird. Under a hairnet, her face looked strange. On her very white face, her eyes were very dark and deep, with underlining dark shadows. She wore a silk robe. She had just arrived from Athens to spend the summer in Naxos. Although exhausted from the trip, she quickly recovered her civility and smiled, politely welcoming us.

The house was in shambles. Dust and bits of plaster had fallen from the ceiling, the beams of which were made of cypress wood still bearing dried fruits. Almonds, apples and tomatoes were spread on the ground and a light sour smell pervaded the house. On one side, the corridor opened on a kitchen with a long hood above the cooking stove and, on the other, on a salon with carpets thrown on the wooden floor, two run down wing chairs and a long wooden settee. A high fireplace occupied the bottom wall. The shutters were still shut all over the house, which had two bedrooms. The lady opened the door of the small one for me. She rejoiced aloud about my being French and, as if to make me feel comfortable, she mentioned that the Ursulines, a French nun order, had run a girls' school until very recently up in the Kastro. The little room opened on a patch of abandoned walled in garden. A stone throw away, the sea broke on piled rocks. While lying in my small bed, I could hear the surf, breaking and receding with changing tempos as the wind blew from varying directions all over the Cycladic archipelago. Further down the street, the bells of the Orthodox Church rang the hours and, leaning out of the window, I could see its blue dome.

Katerina, a woman with a past

Katerina was from Salonica. She had been born and married there. But her mother was from Naxos and had left her the patriarchal house, the *"patriko"*. She came from June to September and then went back to Athens where she now lived with her only son. She was full of humor, evolving in her disorganized house, graceful and carefree. Her door was open at all times and I moved in and out like a free cat. I was just careful not to make noise in the evening since she went to bed early. I did not know her exact age, but she must have been well past eighty years old since she had mentioned her son was in his sixties. Once in a while, she prepared tea or coffee for both of us. Her voice was particularly endearing, melodious and youthful as she let out now and then snatches from her past. They sounded like tales, where any lingering sadness or regret had been woven in so skillfully that they could barely be recognized.

The first tale was the story of a cat she had had as a young girl. At night, that cat disappeared, sometimes for days on end, but she always came back. Once, the cat had reappeared with a beautiful silky bow around her neck. A little message was hanging from it. *"Despinis"* or *"Kyria"*, it said, "Miss or Mrs", "Whoever you are, your cat came to visit me last night." She gathered the message was from a boy but it was not signed. Counting on the cat to go off again, she had attached her answer around the cat's neck. The go-between had gone on traveling to and fro, from her house to that mysterious neighbor for a year. Obviously the boy knew who she was, but she did not who he was. Many years later, when she was already married, and ill married, she had been able to identify her admirer.

Her life had been rocky thereafter. Her husband was a wealthy trader from Thrace who, first, had covered her with jewels, Russian jewels brought back from his travels. Her happiness had lasted a year, until their son was born. Afterwards, her husband had gone back to his two passions, gambling and philandering. He had gone to live apart with his changing mistresses. She saw him sporadically, usually when he needed money. Gambling had taken its toll on his wealth, and philandering, a toll on his health. But he went on, and every new conquest seemed to require more presents to be kept happy. One day, he had asked Katerina to lend him the Russian jewels so he could pawn them. She had complied, under no illusion. The jewels would go to some usurer. The house in Naxos was the only possession she had rescued. Only there she felt at peace, free from her painful past and free to do as she pleased. In Athens, she had to make do with her daughter in law, but besides her son, her saving grace was her two granddaughters. One of them was going to leave Greece to go study in the US. To allay her grief, she had asked not to be told of the date of the girl's departure. It was quite likely she would not see her again.

The Kastro ladies

Every morning I went up to the Kastro. Under the inaugural arched passage, there was a door, a thick studded wood door, which had remained open for centuries, since the day the last sea lords had left with their booty, never to come back. Beyond, the fort city opened like an old trunk, filled with strange shivers and quavers coming out of thick walls, cobbled stones and abandoned houses. A flow of sunlight occasionally leaked between walls, building new lines of stone and sky, of white and dark. It was like walking in time lost but regained. The stubborn little fort seemed to imprint little by little its secret map on my feet. I was being made to follow a pattern, leading to minuscule squares, bringing me to an edge. There was no dead end, the alley went on and on like a tale, repeating itself or trying variations, but ceaseless. I only could decide to put an end to the convolutions and jump aside, getting out of the enthralling mesh.

Only one Catholic vicar and some old women lived in the Kastro. The old ladies were descended from Venetian families who had come a thousand years before with Marco Sanoudo. They lived demurely in their ancestral homes. Like their houses, they didn't look like much at first sight. They were dressed like spinsters, in skirts and heavy shoes, with poor little chignons on top of their heads. But the Kastro belonged to them. They did not mingle with the handful of foreigners that had come of late from the West, Europe and Americas, renting and restoring abandoned houses.

Mary, a retired British schoolmistress acted as leading light for the foreign community. A kind of self-styled Bloomsbury mimicry, she had the right hint of shabby chic and Albion's gift for condescension towards natives. Naxos had become her main residence. She fled to England in July and August when the island was as its hottest and most crowded. Any foreign would-be resident in the Kastro had to go through Mary. Mary acted as a kind of honorary Consul for all non-Greek newcomers and as a go-between with the Venetian ladies and with the Catholic vicar. She happened to be a Catholic herself and going to church had become a must for any foreigner wishing to ingratiate himself with the reigning caste. Sunday mass, thanks to her, had also become a very social occasion where the aristocratic and the plebeian communities could sit together in the church, if not on the same benches. The Venetian noble ladies had their pews in front, the rest of the faithful, either foreign or Greek sat behind them.

The only rebels to that custom were a couple of German who had been the first people to buy and restore an old house in the Kastro. The man, Werner, was a painter, who had not left the island for more than a decade. His wife, Gertrud, was entirely devoted to her husband's career. She took care of the sales, the shipping, the exhibitions' catalogues and she alone did all the traveling to and from Germany. They had come upon the Kastro by chance in the sixties when like many other counterculture or "alternative" freaks, they were looking for a cheap and freewheeling place to live. Long summers and sunlight were an added attraction. Werner and Gertrud had bought for a song a small house with a tiny enclosed garden. It had views out to sea from its top and a tiny studio no bigger than a little workshop in an oriental souk, its window level with the outside cobblestone alley. The place was in pitiful state, and they had repaired little by little everything by themselves. Their achievement had woken up, and probably worried, some of the Venetian families who had come back to their Kastro houses, at least in the summer.

Werner and Gertrud didn't give a damn about the old ladies and their Catholic Church, which impressed the old hags very much. Like any upper class, they invested themselves with the exclusive knowledge of who was worthy of their attention, and they couldn't stand social climbers. Hence, the reverence of the Kastro ladies for Werner and Gertrud who did not give a damn about them. As for the rest of the population of Naxos, Greek or non-Greek, to them they were undistinguished "plebs". At best, they could become servants or suppliers of goods.

Wandering in the Kastro, I had seen coats of arms above the doors and, sometimes, when a window was open, very high ceilings in decorated wood. I had noticed also the old faces of the inhabitants taking a peek at me from behind their curtains. While walking through the alleys, I had seen a swift church mouse of a lady coming back from the Catholic church. I had seen also a very fat lady panting and sweating as she ascended the alley. She was the wife of the only apothecary on the island, a proud Duke. The Duke was small and mousey like his sister who had married an Athens judge. That Duke and Duchess had produced a son, blond and blue-eyed. His round rosy cherub face always smiling beatifically. He was known and looked after by all inhabitants of the port. They treated him like the child he would remain forever, although he was already in his thirties. He wandered down to the port at all hours, barefoot, a flannel vest on his chubby torso.

The Archbishop's house

Adjoining the Catholic church, was a large house with a pepper tree balancing its branches in front of its doorstep. I had elected it as my favorite. The house was surrounded by a garden, which was unique in the Kastro. All other houses had only balconies looking towards the sea, vast terraces on the multi-leveled roofs and, at best, tiny enclosed gardens like the small patches kept by church vicars aside their presbyteries. This magnificent house was planted in the middle of its own garden. Behind an old rusty gate kept shut with a cheap bicycle lock, the house offered its beautiful balanced façades to the passers-by. Hanging in the middle of the pepper tree was a mobile made of corks, pebbles and bits of painted wood, which dangled and moved in the air with a faint musical sound. An old deck chair lay abandoned in the parched and wild vegetation, its canvas ready to give. A few geraniums had mushroomed here and there, uninhibited and standing the summer drought as if aware they were alone to defend the honor of the lonely garden. The shutters were closed. Nobody was there. The house was standing on the very top of the Kastro, precisely where the original Venetian castle had crowned the hill, enclosing in its embrace the whole city of Naxos. The Catholic Church was on one side, the city Museum on the other. In front, a kind of esplanade extended which would have offered a breathtaking view of the sea and the other islands beyond, except for a monstrous and hideous building standing right opposite the house, erected by the Ursulines nuns to house the girl convent school Katerina had told me about. Its mass blocked off any light, sky or sea.

Katérina knew the house quite well. She had told me it had belonged to an eccentric old lady, unmarried and blue-blooded like her Venetian cousins. The lady dressed and behaved as a kind of ethereal princess of dreams, with light umbrellas to filter the sun and extravagant hats. Her dresses were made of silk and lace, long and fluffy. She put on heavy make-up and sat on the small terrace on top of the steps leading to the door. Just after she had died, a terrible storm had set fire to the house. Under the violence of the lightnings, the paved floor had collapsed, opening a gaping hole into the dark cellars. The lady had bequeathed her house to the Catholic archbishop of Greece who resided in Syros, the capital of the Cycladic archipelago. The house was no longer abandoned. A few months before, it had been rented to friends of Werner, the German painter.

Back in Athens, I had seen Claire again. She knew the lucky tenants of the Archbishop's house: Natalie and Manfred. Nathalie was French. She taught handicrafts to primary school pupils at the Lycée Français. Manfred was German and made mobiles. The mobile in the pepper tree was his making.

Stranded in Amorgos

The next year at Easter, I decided to go to Amorgos. Easter came early that year, in mid-March, a time when the sea could turn abruptly into a raging maelstrom. The huge ferry was near empty. All day we had advanced in the sea at the pace of a camel in Arabian sands. Beyond the Cycladic islands, there was no land anymore in sight. Time had stopped and so had thinking. I felt vacant through and through. We didn't meet any other boat. The rustle of the prow cutting through the water and the cry of seabirds breathed life and sound in that strange planet of a boat, suspended in time and space. Land appeared at dusk. A long line of land, like the end of the earth when people believed it was square, like a wall shutting the horizon. I had no clue what I was going to find there. But Amorgos had tempted me for its sibylline syllables. "Amorgo" in Spanish meant bitter. It sounded fierce, forbidden and forgotten. It had tempted me too because of a lady playing the piano on a small islet out of Amorgos, Antikairi.

She was a distant relative of my family, whose husband had built there, with his own hands, a tiny stone shack. His plan was to live on Antikairi all year long. She compared him to a limpet stuck to its rock. As for her, six months a year in Antikairi were ample enough. When an aunt had mentioned to me a woman "who played the piano in the middle of the sea", I had pricked up my ears. She had taken her piano there to fend off boredom. Life on top of an islet only peopled with goats that were disembarked every spring was for hermits. When the piano had arrived in Amorgos, it had been easy to find men to give a hand to help transport it to Antikairi. Nobody on the island had ever seen a piano. Four men had quickly volunteered to lug it onto the couple's boat and to travel with it to Antikairi. Once on shore, they had carried it, carefully as if it were a coffin, on their shoulders up to the couples' stone shack. The lady had sat and played music for them while they crowded the minuscule rooms.

Before getting to Katapola, the main port, we had first anchored off Aigiali, its port was too shallow for ferries. During the anchoring maneuver, a procession of fishing boats started to come from the shore. As they approached, I could see piles and piles of pink matter on every one of them. Hundreds of carcasses of freshly slaughtered lambs crammed every boat. They were the most important harvest for Amorgos farmers who reaped from their sale every Easter their main income for the rest of the year. The carcasses were to be loaded one by one on the boat through a door opening just above the waterline on the port side. Two hours had passed and more *kaïkia* were coming alongside to pour more lambs into the belly of the ferry. The men shouted and grabbed the flesh, holding it high with excitement and pride before throwing it to a sailor inside. There must have been one hundred boats. On the horizon, Aigiali looked like a green Irish land dotted with little white houses. Night had fallen when we left with three siren blows, making the last fishing boats jostle on the mighty wave the ferry made, as we turned round.

The port of Katapola was deserted and the ferry towered above it. A fierce north wind was rising. A fat man with an Arabic wool bonnet and large pants ran out of a shop, rushing to catch the rope thrown from the boat and pull in the thick cord, swiftly attaching it to its mooring post. More men arrived to help. The one single taxi of Amorgos, alerted by my Antikairi relatives, knew I was coming. A room had been prepared for me up in *Hora*, the capital, for the night. We went up an abrupt and meandering rocky path, akin to the Bassae road, on which we keeled dangerously. The village looked like an old Christmas tree lit with candles. Halos of light came out of asymmetric small windows dotting the houses piled up at random like little white mounds. The constellations up in the sky echoed the village lights in the night. The air was freezing cold, loaded with so much oxygen that it burnt the throat. A young woman with blond hair under her thick black cotton scarf called her shy husband to take me to the room in an adjacent little house. All night long, the wind cried and growled like a wounded animal wandering in the mountains. In the morning, cold and wind had not subsided but everything shone in the sun, from the stones to the green grass and the faces of people. The shy husband was in charge of a small café and prepared me bread slices and coffee. A handful of old men jingled their prayer beads with their fingers, grinding time with a non-stop logorrhea. A foreign girl with long hair was sitting in the background, reading a book. For the three days I stayed, her eyes remained unflinchingly lowered down, on the page or on the floor. She had anchored at the café for an unending meditation. The shy man brought water or coffee to her table and she nodded politely while he smiled with embarrassment.

I had had to go back down to Katapola, the port, to make a phone call to Antikairi. There was no phones up in Hora. The line went off and on but I had been able to talk to the husband. He was there alone. His wife had gone to France. He was ready to come over with his fishing boat to take me but the north wind had gathered strength during the night and it was risky to get the boat off its mooring. We had to wait and see. Around Amorgos, they all knew him and they had respect for the French man who, at seventy years old, having retired from his career as a radiologist, had decided to have his childhood dream come true. From his early teens, he had been dreaming about Amorgos. He had gone there in the sixties. His dream was to build a house for himself just like the *Amorgiani*, with curved walls and low ceiling that made human habitat feel like a garment around the body. But he was French, a foreigner, hence forbidden to buy land and to own a house on Amorgos, a so-called "border land" classified as of vital security interest for Greece, off limits to non-Greeks. In the seventies, a shepherd who owned land on the islet of Antikairi had offered to let him build his abode there. For all its desolation, Antikairi was famous for the statue of a 1500 BC *kouros*, which had been found there, together with Cycladic figurines dating back to even earlier times. All artifacts were in the National Museum of Athens.

The demureness and extreme gentleness of that old French man impressed the Amorgiani. The fact that he had been wounded in the right arm and hand, during World War II and was now maimed for life added to their consideration. In spite of his age and handicap, he manned himself his *"kaïki"*. He fished and cultivated a tiny garden patch to subsist. Even when the fierce summer north winds started to hoot and sweep over the islet day after day, he stuck to his rock and routine. Over the bad phone connection, his voice was quiet and gentle like plainchant. I was not to meet him ever though. The wind was gathering strength by the hour and we had reached ten on the Beaufort scale. No way he could come and fetch me during the week I would be around. It was easy to sail towards Amorgos, but near impossible to berth because of the formidable backwash created by the huge waves.

I had gone down the dirt road and then up the endless stone steps to the Monastery of the Hozoviotissa. The wind was not purring anymore, it was growling and slapping nastily my back as I was going up the endless steps. Looking at the vertiginous rocks falling straight in the foaming sea, I held my breath under a scarf I had rolled around my neck and head to fence off the assaults of the wind that menaced to choke me. At the monastery, an old monk opened the gate. He wore a cotton black bonnet that made him look like Rasputin. He smiled sardonically at me, pointing his finger to a small gold medallion of the Virgin Mary I was wearing around my neck. *"Katholiki!"* "Catholic!" he exclaimed, as if I were damned. The rooms behind the façade that stretched along the falling rock were as narrow as cupboards. In the small chapel, the icons were disappearing under a green mold. More than a holy place, the monastery felt like the devil's lair. Leaving in haste, I had gone down the vertiginous steps, dangerously fluttering above the precipice like a feather.

The next day, the phone was off, the electricity too. The island like tens of others in the Aegean was cut off from the world. A tempest could last three, six or nine days, so went the saying. We were at the start of the fourth day. I would not go to Antikairi. I was stuck. With gale winds, all ferries had been stopped. I could not hike. I could only sit in the café, drink, eat and sleep. I was stuck and shut in. When I asked about the weather, or the next boat scheduled to come, I got the same chin-up mimic from everyone, which meant: "I don't know, neither do I care, that's the way it is". I knew that the other side of fatalism was inalterable faith in change, but I felt pretty hopeless. I decided to leave Hora and to go down to the port to try and find a way out. I took a room in the street parallel to the quay. There I could hear any boat coming.

After two nights and two days, I suddenly heard a siren. At dawn, it resounded louder than the gale. A boat had come in. I got up and dressed and ran to the quay. A huge white boat filled the whole port. Not an old ferry, powerless against the tempest, but a splendid liner. The boat was cruising the Mediterranean, going from Nice to Istambul via Sicily and Greece and back with neat elderly passengers, crowding the decks to look down . An hour later, they were all going down the gangway, with sun hats and rubber shoes, looking fresh and happy like new-born babies, leaving their cocoon to explore the wilderness of Amorgos. The few little shops had rushed to put out their postcards and knick-knacks for them. An assemblage of trucks and old bangers was gathered on top of the pier to take them up to the village and to the monastery.

I paced the quay waiting for some quiet to resume. Two men from the boat were smoking a cigarette on the gangway. I saluted them and asked where the boat was bound to. "To Piraeus" they told me, "with a stop in Naxos". The name Naxos fell on my mind like a revelation. On such a boat, I could be there in a few hours. I asked to see the Captain. The older guy ordered the young one to bring me to the Captain's quarters. The stocky and short Captain was jolly and gallant. I asked him to take me aboard to Naxos. There, hopefully, the tempest would abate and I could take a regular ferry back to Piraeus. But before going back, I hoped to be able to sleep in the Venetian Kastro at the pepper tree house. The captain readily granted me permission to come aboard and invited me to share a coffee with him.

When the passengers got back, their noses red and their faces hilarious from the excursion inland, hoarded like precious cattle by the frantic Greek drivers, I was leaning on the rail, safe and happy to escape. As I was daydreaming, a blonde woman came up to me. "Who are you?" she asked abruptly. I said my name. "You are not on the cruise" she objected, frowning. "You can't stay on this boat" she added peremptorily, her arms crossed and her tone furious. "The Captain gave me permission to travel to Naxos". "What?" she yelled, all flushed, and she went rushing down the deck on her high heeled sandals, her swishing large skirt rustling like a sail. Minutes later, she came back. "Listen" she barked, "The Captain has decided to take you aboard and I cannot go against his decision. But, you will sit in this corner" she pointed at it imperatively, "on this chair. And you won't move, you won't talk to anybody and when we get to Naxos, you'll get off the boat immediately." I sat and didn't move, didn't go to the bathroom, didn't talk to anybody. Some passengers came by, saying hello and smiling, eager to start a conversation. I remained speechless and impassive like an idiot. In a matter of hours, the heights of the Kastro were pointing above the waves. The sun was getting warmer. The tempest was abating. I walked down the gangway, my eyes blinking as I started up the tortuous alleys.

Naxos, the grand way

The gate of the pepper tree house was open. I went up the steps veiled by the tree foliage and knocked on the door. Nathalie opened. I stepped inside, amazed. The huge room was so vast and high that it felt like being in the middle of a cathedral. Ceilings culminated at sky level with windows so high up the wind could come into the room without disturbing the space below. The floor was paved in huge slabs of white stone, polished by time. Like on a theater stage, a tiny door opened on the side. Behind it spread a long wing. On the north side, bathed in a subdued light, the wing had an ancient view of green fields and hills dotted with sheep and cows, with a small white monastery visible far up. Nathalie was alone. Manfred, her husband, was traveling. His art was all around the main room. Huge pieces made of wrecked wood, reeds and stones, like musical mobiles, which, touched by the air or by a hand, delivered surprising melodies. Nathalie had almost immediately invited me to stay at the house.

Behind those walls, it felt like a very different world from the one most everybody knew. It was a world unto itself. One could live shut up that house, there was enough air to breathe and space to pace, as on a large boat. From the main part of the house, there was no view. The massive abandoned Ursulines convent on the other side of the alley blacked it out completely. To see the sea, one had to escalate a ladder in the kitchen, step on a small roof and, from there, climb again on the higher roof above the main room. There, the eye engulfed the whole of Naxos and the sea beyond where faraway islands seemed to ooze from the haze.

That house exerted a strange power, at once soft and formidable. Once in, it was difficult to go out. Nathalie didn't venture much beyond the market just below the Kastro, a small web of alleys called the "Borgho" where, like in Venice in the past, Jewish families following the Venetian rulers of Naxos, had first settled with their shops and crafts. Everyday, it took determination to break free from the thrall of the place. But once out, walking down was all the more rewarding. The sea, the sun appeared intermittently, on and off. The walls along the alleys could be cold and damp or warm like sand on a beach. Just coming out from winter and tempest, my eyes blinked, my head swam, dizzy with too much light. The air carried smells from the fields and from the sea. At the bottom of the Kastro, the quay unfurled like an old lateen sail, gently billowing. At the south end, nude rocks with a church marked the end of the port town. Beyond, dunes, swamps and potato fields surrounded by reeds stretched in the distance, with beaches and coves and more rocks along the water. On the way back, at all times, the Kastro was up ahead, showing the route home.

Katérina was not in Naxos yet, neither were most of the Venetian ladies who wintered in Athens or Rome. On Sunday, Nathalie had gone to church with the required zeal. It seemed to be part of her deal with the Catholic Archbishop of Syros to whom the house belonged. Manfred could not care less, but Nathalie abided by customs and good manners. Eyes, ears and tongues in Naxos, and all the more in the Kastro, were alert to any sign of discrepancy. They could even smell the faintest misdemeanour. It was therefore no surprise to Nathalie when rumours of her affair with a local fisherman started to go around. She played her part very well though, smiling caressingly to the Greek Catholic Vicar who lived just next door. Although, he could not totally ignore Nathalie's private life, trouble was not to come from him. If anything, he was happy to have a neighbor in that vast house that had remained empty for years after the death of the owner. His only demand was for Nathalie sometimes to listen to him recounting his dream days in Rome where he had attended the seminary.

A cabal against la "Française"

Real trouble started when her tryst with the fisherman came up to the Venetian ladies through Naxian women, exasperated by *"la Française"* who had taken for a lover a married man, father of two. At first, Nathalie laughed. Who cared about the old hags even if their titles were one millennium old? She took precautions though. She had shown me the secret passage into the cellars of the house that led outside into a quiet alley. The fisherman came up on moonless nights and left at dawn, or sent a car to fetch Nathalie and bring her to his boat at a remote mooring. But the old shrews had a good nose, formidable ears and eyes. But, as the years passed, Nathalie cared less and less about the gossip. "Everyone tries to manage as he or she can", she had told me, shrugging her shoulders.

But the politics of the Kastro were as intricate as its mingled population. Besides the old Venetian families, Werner the painter and his wife Gertrud and Mary who lived year round in the Kastro, there were many more Germans who lived more or less permanently in rented rooms in the port. While the Kastro foreigners played it gentry-like and kept polite if superficial relationships with the Kastro ladies, the foreigners who lived in the port paid no attention to such protocol. Nevertheless, on a small planet like Naxos, everyone knew each other and carried on at least some neigborly relationships. The only one totally out of all that was Nathalie. She did not speak English, she did not speak German, and she considered that whatever aristocratic credentials the Venetian ladies had, they were not worth much more than the titles and the long history of her own family. Her only notable contacts were with a few locals down at the port, with whom she gabbled broken Greek, and with the Catholic priest, her immediate neighbor. None of the very Catholic ladies had judged very orthodox the intrusion of Nathalie and Manfred, too bohemian a couple for their Kastro. Manfred, the husband had immediately been seen in the company of German girls drinking loads of wine and ouzo to go through the damp island winter. When German girls slept with men, it was of no consequence for the secluded world of the Kastro, but the dalliances of Nathalie with a Naxos man brought the devil to the heart of their territory. It was like discovering that your apple is being undermined from within by a nasty little worm. Some good souls had warned Nathalie gently to beware. "I won't be dictated to by a bunch of silly old trouts!" She had exclaimed one day as she was telling me about it.

Nathalie, as a native Provençale, understood perfectly the situation, but not only didn't she fear at all the old trouts, she was also ready to give them a piece of her mind. In her fight against prejudices, she had found an ally in her lover. Like all Naxians from birth, the fisherman resented the haughtiness of the Kastro ladies, Greek themselves but sneering at their fellow Greek citizens by virtue of their noble non-Greek origin. Symbol of that haughtiness and enduring privilege, the Kastro palaces high up above the port loomed like an inconquerable domain where they, the people of Naxos, were outlawed. "One day, I'll piss right down into the sea from their palaces", the fisherman had declared defiantly, punching his fist on the table, as he was sitting at the little pier café. He was drunk and so were all his pals making chorus.

Nathalie too was drunk that afternoon when I arrived. March was cold, damp and melancholic. A house and an island, however beautiful they could be, were but a house and an island. But that house was terribly important to her. She thought of it as her own and people in Naxos complimented her just as if she had been the very landlady of the house. It was also the only spot where she managed to meet every now and then her flitting husband. Manfred had installed his studio in the northern wing. The house was also a magnet for many a man whom she had taken a fancy to. When I left Naxos to go back to Athens, the sky was dark and heavy and the sea turbulent again, heaving under a powerful swell that banged brutally into the hull. Nathalie waved and smiled from the pier, looking like Ingrid Bergman in *Stromboli*, alone and poetic. But trouble was brewing in her paradise. Her affair with the fisherman was not the cup of tea of the Kastro ladies.

Of the Naxians, whom could Nathalie really trust? If war erupted, would they remain faithful? There had been no proof over the milleniums that a woman at the source of a scandal was ever protected or spared: neither Helen, neither Phaedra nor Medea had escaped their fate. Naxos had indeed been a haven to Ariane, the Cretan princess abandoned by Theseus, her ruthless spouse, but then no Venetian ladies had been there to object to Ariane's dallying with Dionysos. So far, the foreign community seemed out of the cold war between Nathalie and the Kastro ladies but how long could they remain neutral? Although nobody knew under what conditions the house had been rented to Nathalie, there was a lot of envy. The penniless foreigners in the lower town hoped for a bargain rent. Some entrepreneurial British, friends of Mary, were beginning to sketch a great financial investment. The Kastro ladies were getting ready to oust away *"la Française"* no matter what, even if it meant jumping out of the frying pan into the fire by getting a whole gang of anglo-saxon sybarites on their side.

Fire redemption

I came back to Naxos the following summer. Up in the Kastro, full-out war was now raging behind the walls. Nathalie's house had been put up for rent. The Catholic archbishop had made known his intention to terminate the lease in a blunt registered letter. The night I had been traveling on the ferry, a fire had broken out at the presbytery. Coming at the door to greet me, Nathalie looked like a ghost. All night, she had passed on buckets to the Vicar and a handful of volunteers. Meanwhile, the Kastro duchesses had slept the sleep of the just. So had Mary, the British schoolteacher, Werner the German painter and his wife, Gertrud, and all the Sunday mass faithful. A Parisian girlfriend of Nathalie who was visiting had helped too. Nathalie was fed up, and ready to throw in the towel. The friend, a minute brunette woman with the raucous voice of a Paris street urchin, was pacing the main room, exhorting her not to give up the fight. She too had a stake in the house. She was spending all her summer vacations at Nathalie's. Fatigue had quelled Nathalie's rage and made her a rag doll. The friend made her dress in Sunday clothes, made her gulp down coffee and forced her to smile. They were going to confront the enemy straight eye to eye. Born in a rural town, the friend had not forgotten the lesson of the French provinces. A stranger always had to go and visit the local notables in a spirit of allegiance. Only thus could one hope for a degree of positive recognition in the local community. The friend considered as unbearably *bourgeoises* all those dreadful conventions but *"quand il faut, il faut!"* she proclaimed, pacing and smoking. And the house was well worth a few hours of humility.

The night fire had pumped all energy and hope from Nathalie, but her friend was galvanized, alert to the momentum to seize. After all, she reasoned, they both had saved the presbytery, the church and the Vicar itself by carrying all those buckets of water all through the night. If there was a God for the believers, and a mercy for the sinners, that night of fire was to be their redemption too. Fearless and courageous, they had braved the flames and the dark for the sake of the priest. For a moment, I wondered if the friend had not set the fire herself, throwing a *"Gauloises"* butt into the right spot at the right time...

Nathalie looked like a little girl going to a birthday party, her hair braided, a modest scarf covering her shoulders and her dress coming down to her ankles. But she had not resisted sporting a pair of very conspicuous topaz earrings. The afternoon was sizzling on the cobblestones, at least wherever the sun could hit since the Kastro was like a hogan in the Prairie. At the height of summer, the house was at its best. The house did not feel like a cathedral anymore, it felt like an oasis. Like an odalisque, one could live indoors for days on end. There was enough space to promenade and breathe.

The whole afternoon had elapsed and the shivering heat was beginning to lift in the evening breeze when Nathalie and her friend, at long last, came back, exhausted. The panel of Duchesses had sat placidly, tea cup in hand, telling Nathalie about family values, family spirit and family ties, while Nathalie smiled as politely as possible to the point of feeling pain in her zygomatics. She had perfectly got the message. She was enraged as she came back. She banged shut the thick door with so much might that the monumental walls trembled. "Family values!" shouted Nathalie, throwing her neat little handbag on the table and rushing to her bedroom to take off her *comme-il-faut* clothes as if they burnt. Back in her usual shorts and unbuttoned shirt, she kept on cavalcading around the house to vent out her anger. "Family values! The old bitches!" Her friend had opened a bottle of port and poured generous glasses. "I think we won" she said calmly. Nathalie was sipping her port, slowly recomposing herself. "I wonder what the English woman's role has been in all this" said Nathalie, thoughtful. "And Werner and Gertrud?". Her friend shrugged her shoulders. *"On s'en fout!"* she said *"C'est fini maintenant."*

The old violinist of Apeiranthos

The lease was renewed that year and no one talked about the sex life of Nathalie anymore. In any case, she had now a new lover: a very old man, the most famous violinist on the island. She had heard him many times at villages' celebrations of their Saint's day. He came from Apeiranthos, a remote mountain village in the north of Naxos where people had come originally from Crete. They worked in the marble quarries and raised cattle and, according to Katérina who could not stand them, stole cattle as well as women, following an age-old Cretan tradition. The sexagenarian violinist had carried his courtship swiftly and efficiently, yet with the manners of his age. He had had *"billets doux"* remitted to Nathalie celebrating her beauty and asking her to come to his concerts. Cars were sent to wait for her at the southern entrance to the Kastro. She had gone several times, with her precious topaz earrings and a silk shawl, shivering with excitement. Every time, dishes and sweets and wine were already on her table in front of the orchestra. After the concerts, a car took her and the violinist to a remote taverna where the old man played again his violin but for her only. She was thrilled and flattered by the exuberant attentions of the musician. He too had been granted the honor of coming to the house through the secret passage. "It's like meeting again Papa, a shrink would say" Nathalie had told me. In September, shortly before she would leave to go back to Paris, Nathalie had asked me to go with her to visit the violinist and his wife in their village of Apeiranthos. The man himself had asked her to come and meet his wife whom, he had insisted, he had never betrayed up to his encounter with Nathalie.

The mountain village of Apeiranthos looked liked dead ashes under the afternoon sun. It was the end of the road.

The bus stopped there until early evening. We climbed the deserted alleys, sweating and panting. All shutters were closed, no cats appeared in the dull, colorless village, white under a white melting hot sky. One sensed abandonment and malediction behind the blinding whitewashed walls, of a life bleak and black. We arrived at the door of the violinist and knocked with the hand-shaped knocker. The man himself opened the door and made us sit in the salon while he went to fetch his wife. The salon of the violinist was crammed with tapestry armchairs, the *grand siècle* motif of which was repeated on the carpet and the sofa. A heavy dark wood pedestal table was in the middle of the room, with an embroidered napkin under glass in the center. Against the wall, a cupboard of the same dark wood with relief decorations displayed china cups and more embroidered napkins. As the formal salon of the house, it was not used often and a smell of soap and dust pervaded its rarefied air. Black and white pictures in silvery frames of the violinist as a young man and of his wife adorned the buffet. Bigger blown up foggy pictures of his parents and grandparents hung on the wall. The old man came back, smiling, asking us to excuse his wife for a few minutes. His hands were surprisingly small and his complexion very pale. With his small blue eyes and rosy flesh bulging around his neck, his very silvery hair, he almost looked English. His wife appeared in black at the door of the salon. Under the rare white hair, her face was sallow and pale and her eyes dreamy. She seemed melancholic. After bowing in front of us as if she were a servant, she didn't sit and quickly retired again to prepare coffee.

The violinist knew Manfred. In fact Manfred himself had first brought him to the house. Nathalie and Manfred were then throwing their one and only party to celebrate their first Kastro year. The violinist had come to play the whole night. At dawn, the revellers had all gone out, down the alleys, following the violinist to the port. The violin had kept playing the whole way, under the windows of the Kastro duchesses, all through the Borgho and down to the sea. He could not stop playing, nor could they stop following him. The violinist had jumped in the sea, still playing, with water up to his waist, walking towards the tiny church of the Virgin Mary, "Saviour of the sailors", standing on a small platform off the quay. Everybody had jumped after him and the procession proceeded with shouts and laughs. Suddenly, a policeman had arrived shrieking and running on the pier, his vest unbuttoned and his eyes incredulous. Reluctantly, everybody had had to get out. It was getting cold in the water anyway. The café up the pier was just opening and the first customers already sitting on the outside chairs looked at the party noncommittally, eyes half shut. All the revellers had sat at the café. After three last strokes of the bow, the violinist had broken the strings of his instrument. The concert was over. Everybody had clapped. They had ordered coffee and knocked their cups for a last toast, wishing each other many years to live ever after.

After visiting the violinist, Nathalie and I descended again from Apeiranthos to the port of Naxos. Our bus got blocked for a long time at the entrance of Filoti, a town surrounded by terraced mountains like in China. A funeral was being held. All the villagers stood clad in black along the main street while the coffin went across the town for a last promenade. Carried by four men, a woman was laying in her open coffin. This was the first time I was seeing a dead person. The sun fell on her tranquil face, eyes shut, framed by a black scarf tied under her chin. The bus driver and all the passengers crossed themselves as the coffin went by. I did to.

Patmos

That same summer, I went off to sea again, sensing urgency. Slowly inflation was gathering pace in Greece. And time, like money, was shrinking too. I was going to Patmos, where Saint Joan had lived in a cave, writing the *Apocalypse*. The sea was very rough with giant waves shaking and beating the ferry. But in spite of the tempest, the sky above was at its bluest and the sun at its shiniest. Sitting up on one of the wooden boxes containing the lifejackets I had got wet from the seaspray that splashed against the hull and reached up to the second deck. It was the middle of August. The boat was very full with Athenians as well as foreigners. While we were still at high sea, miles away from the continent, a thin white line appeared, slightly more steady than the white line of the foam above the swell. Winds blew and whirled ferociously like in a witch's pot. But that white line remained in place, cresting the raging sea. The tempest was beginning to get the better of my stomach. I kept my eyes riveted on that white line. In the blinding fog of spray and sun, a fortress was emerging looking like strange cloudy formations rising above waters when wet air meets dry air in the atmosphere. The white line had now become crenellated, crowning stonewalls, real walls. It was a citadel. The giant waves rushing towards it would have made me terribly dizzy, had I not been able to focus on those strong walls sitting straight and stubborn in the middle of the indomitable waters. This was Patmos, heroic and fearless like a corsairs' haunt.

While tourists submerged the port, Skala, I walked up to the town on a mule path with wide cobbled steps. Up there, the Monastery reigned unchallenged. The whole island was actually under the absolute authority of the monks. After twelve hours at sea on the boat deck, the walk wiped away the fatigue and the dizziness. The town high on the hill was empty and quiet. Granitic houses faintly rosy or green lined the cool alleys, with arched porches in the roman style at street level and small balconies supported by sculpted stones, sometimes with fine spiralling columns and Venetian lions keeping watch on balustrades. I asked an old lady drowsing on her doorstep if there were any rooms for rent. She indicated a house further on where I knocked. Getting no answer, I pushed the garden gate. Not a sound emanated from the enclosed garden and the balconied floors surrounding it. I put down my rucksack and waited. The landlady emerged from her siesta. For a room, she offered me her attic with a mattress on the floor. There was a minuscule window perched like a nest high under the beams. A ladder was resting on the wall below it. It was the way out to a terraced roof. I could wash at a faucet on the floor below.

An old man, always in a dark suit and hat, lived on the main floor below. He was a retired civil servant, a bachelor, who went three times a day out to the sole taverna in the village for breakfast, lunch and dinner, always before the tourists crowded the place. The rest of the day he walked the length of the town which was not much more than the length of a liner and came back to his room, coming out on the balcony sometimes, his shirt sleeves rolled up on his arms, to exchange salutations and a few jolly words with the landlady. Everyday I heard his chitchat about God's bounty and his own undeserving soul. "God will have a little corner for me, I hope, up there in the sky when I die." The landlady was unmarried too, but she had inherited from her deceased parents the house, which gave her independence. Although dressed in black, because of the death of her parents, she was still elegant and winsome. Her house was a self-contained little fort on three levels. Accessible from the street, the ground floor was a suite of cool vaulted cellars with a well and the naked rock showing in places. The first floor was level with the enclosed garden all walled in and had a vast kitchen and pantry. All around the garden ran a balustrade on which opened all the rooms of the main floor: bedrooms, salons, dining room. To get to my garret, I had to climb a ladder from the corridor. The north wind raged everyday from morning to dusk whistling like a steam engine in the walled alleys.

From the first day, I adopted more or less the habits of my landlady. I was first getting breakfast at the only place that served as café and eatery on the rectangular square, which, like in Venice, just appeared at the last minute after a curve of the street. Smells signaled everything needed: bread and pastry, groceries and spices, fish, meat. With a day's worth of sustenance, I went on. Walls along gardens and houses were no higher than human eyes, allowing one to see faraway on the sea. From up there, only water was visible, the walls hiding the slopes of land and the port below. Patmos seemed totally stranded, like a *Mont Saint Michel*, secluded and solitary.

It had long been perilous to get to Patmos and to leave it, which was appropriate for the Monastery of Saint Joan. The Monastery was immense, a city in itself with turreted walls and dungeons. Its treasure was a library with books carried all the way from Constantinople by the monks, after the invasion of the city by the troops of Mehmet II. The enormous books, some dating back to the fifth century, looked fit for giants, bound with heavy wood and written on thick parchment made of goatskin. After the sacred fort, the descent to the port was an abrupt change. Down by the sea, Skala, with all its nigh-clubs and tavernas, felt like Las Vegas in the middle of the desert. That Las Vegas belonged in fact to the very wealthy and omnipotent Monastery, which drew a substantial income from all its pagan activities.

The island still had many inhabitants who tilled their land under the implacable sun. Their harried, dried and knotty bodies and their silent gaze made them look alien on their very own land, which was, slowly but steadily, changing hands. Answering my customary Greek salutations, they often stopped their work for a while, leaning on their shovel while mules and donkeys where all ears to our conversation, moving them rhythmically with great interest. The farmers mentioned God casually as if he was one of their kin. The ochre soil and the tormented bushes in the Mediterranean sun looked like a piece of the Biblical Palestine. The farmers still lived with the memory of the Christ's apostle, Saint Joan, who had sought refuge in a grotto no bigger than an animal lair just below the town. Freely and effortleslly, they often quoted the *New Testament* and the *Apocalypse* of Saint Joan.

Their main worry was the rising price of land, not that they needed to buy land - they all owned enough - but because of the tremendous temptation to sell it. Patmos had now become a magnet for speculators from all over the world. It had long been loved by very rich people, but luckily not by investors. Those people wanted residences for themselves and also properties that would grow in value. They often wanted to build new rather than restore the old. A man I had been talking to had shown me a small islet off Patmos, which he owned. He sent his goats there by canoe in spring when the rocky soil was covered with a green downy grass. A Swedish promoter had offered him tens of millions of drachmas for it and the figure haunted him. He was torn apart. He needed cash money to send his children to secondary school and maybe university. But once sold, land was lost forever. Besides he had read about Swedish tourists bathing in the nude and making whoopee like antique satyrs, and that bothered him too. He was trying hard to hear what God had to say about it all.

An Irishman from Brussels

After much sweating and swimming, and with only corned beef, bread and tomatoes swallowed along the way, every evening I was eager to eat a real meal. I walked in the silent alleys in the glare of the moon, falling always as if by accident on that little square where the taverna stood in a halo of light. By seven pm, the taverna was already overcrowded with Northerners, mostly British, Dutch or German, who ate very early. After ten though, it started to ease a little. The owner and his two aides kept running until dawn, unfailingly. But even late one was not always able to find a chair, let alone a free table. One night I had only found a chair next to two languid girls, looking bored and yawning. I had asked in English if I could sit. They had looked at me with a stern look, not saying anything. I had sat. I had no other choice. As we waited stoically for the waiter to take the orders, a bearded guy with smiling blue eyes arrived prancing about in his shorts and, before I could say anything, held out his hand to take mine with a friendly "Hello! Where are you from?" The "hello" sounded more like "hullo". The guy was Irish. The chair I was sitting on was his chair, and the girls his friends. As I was getting up hurriedly, he made me sit down and went to get an empty chair from outside, carrying it high above the diners at arms' length. Erwan quickly introduced himself and his friends, and we all ordered piles of food.

Both girls were from London. The petite blonde one was recently divorced from a defrocked priest. The tall brunette looked like a horse with long eyes and a long flat nose. She was living with a painter thrice her age. She was terribly thin with all her bones protruding, her ribs, her cheekbones and her shoulder blades. I was not sure the girls were terribly happy at my intrusion. Like myself, their acquaintance with Erwan had been fortuitous. They had met at the same taverna and went hiking together. Erwan suggested that I join them the next day. I went to meet them on a stony beach. On the way down, negotiating the stones that kept rolling on the rough path, I had been stung by a big brown and yellow insect in the neck, a *sphinga*. Erwan was sitting on a rock above the water reading his book, sun hat on and legs crossed like a yogi. The petite blonde was turning crimson in her bikini, braless and without any sun hat, reading a magazine. The tall brunette was sitting in the water, her legs apart, letting the sea come up her thighs. I put out my picnic and offered them a bite, which they all declined. They only ate grapes and figs during the day. Erwan had a big flask of water and drank from it every now and then. When the sun started to drop, we started back uphill.

A wild dancer

After two days, the girls had got a little tamer and I had become part of their landscape. Erwan was Irish but French too, son of a Britton gone to Ireland during WWII troubled times. He lived in Brussels, a civil servant at the European Commission in Brussels. We were well organized now and the first of the group to arrive at the taverna tried to grab a table outside. Inside, the heat was hell, with the kitchen stoves burning hot. Out on the little square, the breeze was at pains to blow through because of the tricky pattern of streets, but at least we could breathe. It was more fun too with the village veterans sitting at the café opposite the taverna, watching us as eagerly as a TV screen. Most of the diners didn't stay in the village, which offered only a few rooms. They slept down at Skala, the port, where all the pensions and hotels were gathered. There were also yachting people who had moored for the night in Patmos.

One evening, a whole Italian family had come up, very elegant, very stiff and probably very rich. Besides the parents and a young boy, the daughter sat with her fiancé. She was beautiful but her face was sad. When they had arrived on the square, everyone had looked up. The parents and the fiancé surrounded the girl and her sad eyes seemed to ask for help. As if she were hostage to a demanding family, all her beauty concurring only to her doom. I was not the only one mesmerized by the Italians. The old men at the café stared at them. The family ordered food and started to eat, speechless. Around them, all diners laughed and talked and ate and drank with a lot of noise. The beautiful girl did not even eat, gazing disenchanted with her wide turquoise eyes. Suddenly, another group arrived on the square: two boys and a girl, arm in arm, dancing together and reeling, drunk and merry.

A man in the café started to play the violin. The trio broke and the boy in the middle leapt forward by himself. The violin had the upper hand while the boy danced, obedient to the cords yet free to improvise. He rose and crouched and leapt and turned. The violin rose and fell and cried and cringed. Boy and violin were now married for better or worse. His friends had remained standing up, clapping their hands and moving their hips, unable to follow that will-o'-the wisp. The dance was now getting fierce and the violin angry. The graceful and ample circles of the beginning had stopped. The boy had become possessed and the violin could not command him anymore, it could only follow him. His arms and feet kicked madly, his eyes wild. The girl put a glass on the ground. The boy knelt and smashed it with his hand, pieces of glass flying around.

Agape and in awe, everyone watched. The Italian family was in the first row. Riveted on the jingling legs of the dancer, the melancholy daughter' eyes glowed in the dim light coming from the few bulbs hanging above the tables,. The violin pushed and pushed, the boy seemed beyond exhaustion, he could not lead anymore. The musician now did, with merciless skill. The boy grinned in ecstatic pain, his eyes shut. He knelt down again and broke again a glass, his right hand now bleeding, and down again, and broke another glass, this time with his left hand. Behind the old men, younger men from the village had gathered to watch him. Muscles twitched on their maxillaries and their eye apples got sharper and larger. A light smile floated now on the Italian girl's lips. Completely engrossed in the boy's dance, she had now forgotten her family. He danced for her and the men frowned. They did not like that. His friends approached the dancer, the girl taking his left arm and the boy his right arm. They danced with him a moment until he let his head fall backwards as if to rest, sustained by his pals on each side. They gently pulled him away. The violin wept now. The trio jumped one last time, moved out of the light, out of the square and disappeared in the dark. A pout came back on the lips of the Italian girl. The waiter swept away the broken glass while cats sniffed the fresh blood.

A Patmian Gatsby

Patmos nights were loud and loaded. So far the monks tolerated the Babylonians making merry, as long as the sins took place in Skala by the sea. Foreign girls liked to drink and local boys readily supplied them, easily adding their sperm to the nightly summer orgy, the girls wanting it or not. The police reacted mildly to complaints from girls who had woken up on the sand, disheveled and frightened, their clothes in disarray. Rapes happened every night on beaches and one local boy was suspected. He was the son of the port grocer, and helped his father during the day. The trendy tourist crowd affected a casual friendship with him and invited him around as the island mascotte. The boy was going to lush parties in the pretty houses of wealthy Athenians and international trendsetters. He was good looking, thin and elegantly athletic. He seemed to be everywhere on his little motorbike. His summer friends gave him drinks and drugs. But when summer ended, the boy was left with a raw island, emptied of its revelers, cold, bare and lonesome. For the rest of the year, he had to make do with his Patmian fellows and the family grocery store. The pleasant camaraderie and pre-dawn fits of sympathy, the champagne shared in the rising sun, it all disappeared in a wink with the last flurry of ferries filled to the brim with his once friends leaving Patmos.

The boy was rumored to be sick. The sudden and sharp decrescendo with the coming of fall precipitated him into depressions and frightening fits of violence. A conversation could turn into a fight for whatever reason, his fists quick and hard. If he ran amok, no one could contain him. Even local men got away fast when he fell into that dangerous mood. Besides hurting himself, the boy could hurt others badly with a chair, with a bottle, with whatever was near at hand.

A young couple who owned a house in Hora, opposite the shop where I had met them, had invited me for dinner. He was a Greek from Alexandria, come back to Athens with his parents after Nasser had pushed them out. His wife was Swiss and they had got married in Patmos the spring before. Their house's main floor, above the street, opened on an impressive tableau of water and rocks, the sea towards Turkey and the islets of Lipsi and Arki. They prized so much their view that they had had their bed raised on a platform so as to have that living art piece just level with their eyes when lying down. The medical doctor in residence for the summer had come to dinner too with an American girl. After dinner, we had all gone for a drink in Skala. The bars were full of brass and teak, bright lights and bright women. Puffy fifties dresses were the vogue in Patmos that summer, with ballooned skirts and narrow waistlines. The whole quay looked like a resurrected Saint Tropez of young Brigitte Bardots. The pretty grocery boy was there, perched on the hood of a small yellow Autobianchi. He was smoking a joint. My new friends had stopped to say hello to him. "I just had two of them, ten minutes ago, right here on the wing of the car" he was boasting. "Them" were two foreign girls camping on one of the famous beaches of Patmos, Psili Ammos. The boy's expression was disturbing, both pretentious and spineless. He seemed lost and, at the same time, eager to show he was not, with violence most likely.

The battle of Patmos

On August 30, my Irish friend was leaving the same day as I was for Athens. Our ferry, coming from Rhodes, was scheduled for ten p.m. We had gone down to Skala together to have dinner before boarding. At ten past, we had long finished dinner and still no boat had appeared in the clear night. The quays were full to the brim. It seemed that everybody was leaving the island. No one was surprised that the boat would be late. Most everything and everybody in Greece was late. At midnight, some people started to fret, getting up from their café chair and pacing around the quay. The trip lasted ten to twelve hours and lot of them had a plane to make. Time was running out. The grocery boy was sitting on the lap of a pretty young Greek woman, drinking from her glass. All of a sudden, he threw the brandy he was drinking in the face of the husband. The woman screamed and we all reflexively got up to get away. The boy had started punching the husband in the stomach and on the head. The guy fell down on the ground while his wife started running barefoot towards the port authority building, screaming for help and yelling, "He is going to kill him! He is going to kill him!". The boy was now brandishing a broken bottle, defying anyone to dare approach him. Local Patmians ambling on the quay pretended not to have seen anything. The guy on the ground was bleeding. Two policemen arrived, but the boy had disappeared as swift as a monkey. In the moonlit night by the warm sea, it all looked like a film set. Yet, the smell of death lingered. The boy had wanted to kill, passionately. The bleeding husband was now on a chair. His wife and friends comforted him, dabbing his face with a napkin soaked in the glass of *raki* he had been given to drink.

It was now two a.m. Nobody was joyous anymore. We were all tired and anxious. The last revelers had gone to bed. All would-be passengers dragged their luggage on the pier towards the empty mooring. Some locals were standing around. I asked them if they knew what was going on. "The boat is already full" they said, "They already filled in Rhodos. They will stop in Patmos only to take passengers with cars." Around me, no one spoke Greek. A beautiful BMW had just arrived on the pier. My Irish friend was looking at the couple, flabbergasted. "This is Commissioner H., in charge of European external relations at the Commission" he said. Next to the couple stood a little blond man, Axel Springer, the Berlin media magnate. The European Commissioner and his girlfriend had been his guests at his house on the heights of Patmos. A daily reminder of Springer's presence on the island was the repetitive gun sound of his private helicopter, which went to and from Athens any time of day or night.

In a flash, I understood what was going to happen. The hundreds of people gathered on the pier had no clue about the trick that was to be played on them. The Commissioner and the Athenians, all with cars and first class cabins, would get on the boat while all the others, with boat deck tickets, would be left out in the cold, their tickets lost, having to wait for an improbable boat to take them and sure to miss their charter flights. I told my Irish friend we would not be able to get on the boat. We found an old wood box. I climbed on it and clapped my hands. "Listen everybody", I yelled in English, "The boat we are waiting for is already full. We won't be able to get aboard. Only people with cars will be allowed on. We have to do something. Come with me to the Port Authority so they find a boat for us that will bring you back in Athens in time to catch your flights home." People looked at me, at first incredulous. I repeated my plea. "Let's all go to the Port Authority. I shall do the talking in Greek, but I need you to support me. Alone, I won't be able to achieve anything." I repeated my little speech in French and in Greek.

When I jumped down from the wood box, everybody had awakened. We all went up in big strides to the Port Authority building. Two officers sat in a drab room, filled with massive desks covered with worn out files and piles of papers. The one sitting behind the biggest desk looked up at us, half drowsy, half flippant. I stood in front of the group and told him we knew the boat coming was already full and would not take any passenger. All those people had to catch a plane, the Port Authority had to find a boat to take everyone back to Piraeus before noon at the latest. The guy put on his officer's cap and pouted. He fidgeted with a short wave radio. We all waited silent and determined. "I'll try" he said reluctantly "But you have to go out. We cannot work with all those people in the office." I translated the message to all. "No" they all yelled, "No, no way, we won't get out until we are assured you have found us an appropriate boat". "The boat is coming" shouted someone, "Let's all go back to the pier!" By then, we functioned like a well-trained pack.

We all ran back to the pier, ready for action. We all stood on the edge of the quay, a human shield ready to block the roaring cars from getting on the boat. The ferry lights appeared in the night and we all screamed. It approached slowly with the scraping sound of the anchor raking the sea bottom. Positioned in front of the mooring, the ferry started to let down its heavy door. We yelled more. From the back deck, the crewmen looked at us, dumbfound as if we were a mob of cannibals on a wild island. The captain yelled back, telling us to go backwards. The roaring BMW, its motor on, was parked slightly aside but just by the water, the European Commissioner and his mistress seated in and waiting. The ferry door was going down when it stopped halfway. We stood speechless now. The door resumed its descent. It was about one meter from the pier ground. The most daring, rucksacks on their backs, grabbed the edge of the metal door with their hands, trying to get aboard. The door went up again, instantly, lifting a boy that refused to let go. He hanged now, two meters high, his hands tight on the rusty metal, his legs dangling. The door went down a little and the guy jumped off. Terrorized, the ferry was turning back. In no time, it had disappeared in the dark.

"Let's go back to the Port Authority!" I said, up again on my soapbox. This time, the officer was calling all the boats in the area. One was now coming, making a detour just for us. It would be in Patmos in two hours time, around five am. We all cheered and clapped. The battle of Patmos had been won. But Axel Springer had not abandoned the fight. The little blond man suddenly erupted right in front of me, his face crimson. "Who are you?" He yelled, his fist right under my nose. "Are you a Communist or something?" My Irish friend and others immediately had got between him and me. "She is just one of us, leave her alone!" Axel Springer retreated at once, fuming and trembling. This was the man owning "Bild Zeitung", the famous gossip magazine.

The sun was rising as we were leaving Patmos at long last, shivering in the dawn dew. It was burning hot when we arrived in sight of Cape Sounion, at the tip of Attica. The radio operator on the boat had gently given me his chair to drowse on while he was going to his cabin. I fell asleep, carefree. The prow ploughed its way through the Aegean blue, purring and lulling. In Piraeus, in a rush, Erwan and I hopped on a taxi. I had got off in Syntagma, while my Irish friend was going on to the airport and had no Greek cash left. I gave him enough drachmas for the fare. "Let's hope I see you in Brussels. If I can help…" he said, waving good bye.

Times changing again

Back in Athens, everything was going awry. Greece had become the tenth member of the European Union. Behind the wagging flags and the triumphant photographs of Prime Minister Karamanlis, the country was being kneaded like a piece of dough to fit into its new European persona. This entailed a drastic readjustment of prices for all basic products. Sugar, dairy, fruits, olive oil, feta, tomatoes, cucumbers, rice, meat, fish, even bread, the price of everything was doubling overnight. Caviar and champagne were not affected. Frantic Greeks emptied the shelves of shops in a desperate attempt to beat the inflation. There was no time left, and it would never be the same anymore. 1980 was Greece, year zero. My twenty thousands drachmas a month which had been ample enough so far, suddenly were no more than pocket money. Drachma value melted like snow in the sun. Whoever had had just enough to live on, now could not subsist anymore. In a matter of weeks, I had gone below the poverty line. I could not afford any longer the basic requirements of food, lodging and utilities. The economic tempest meant I had to sail off, but where? My chances were nil in Athens. I would never get a job other than teaching at the French Institute and this, on migrant terms.

All over again, I felt quicksand under my feet. Once upon a time, I had found escapes: to America, to London, to Greece. This time, there would be no haven anymore. Greece was catching up with all the countries of the western world. Suddenly, frugality was no longer enough to survive. I had no solution but to go. This meant going back to France, for good this time. Since I had left for the US in 1970, my first attempt at escape, ten years had elapsed. I was not twenty anymore, I was thirty. I now belonged to a segment of population supposedly stabilized in work and marriage. My student days were over, so were small jobs days. But, comparative literature and linguistics were not exactly the knowledge company managers were looking for.

I had resumed my walks around Athens like in the days I had had no home. Athenians were getting frantic, their cars stalling in heavy traffic jams, their carts collapsing under mountains of products in supermarkets. Breathing deep, eyes half shut, I tried to swim again in Athens, my beloved city, that whale of bounty where I had landed, alone, one cold November night with a steel trunk and a knapsack. From Syntagma square to Amerikis street, from the YWCA to Kolonaki, to Fokilidou street and its *Arab Castle*, to the Church of Saint George on Lycabettus, and down to the kingdom of rags and fleas in Abyssinias Square, down to the ancient agora, at the foot of the Acropolis, and up to the Acropolis, under the frail shelter of the dismantled Parthenon, I was walking again the city that I loved. Like a spider fallen in a storm, I tried to weave the web again, from one place to the other. The city was still here, all the spots were still in place, but I was pushed out, irreparably. Before I had even left, Athens had left me.

I suddenly remembered a stifling hot day, back in May, four months before. Our trolleybus going down to

Omonia square was stuck. Our trolley had got off the wires. Police cars roared by, their sirens screaming, and a motorcade forced the passage of a procession of black limousines. The driver stood in the middle of the avenue in a loud concert of cries and honking. Sweating and focused, he was trying to hook the trolley back on the wires high above him, his hands manipulating the two poles as a child would a kite. Standing up, crushed on all sides by the crowd of passengers, I sweated like everyone else while old women cried at the mercilessness of the sun, *"Ilio! Ilio."* Now and again, the poles of the trolley touched the wires with a rain of sparks without getting properly hooked on. Stalled traffic filled the whole of Panepistimiou up to Syntagma and beyond, including the off streets. Cars were now interwoven in such a way, that it was hard to see how any vehicle would manage to break free. All of a sudden, the shriek of police sirens set off in a triumphant solo on top of the honking background. *"O Ziscar d'Estaingue!"* had said one guy all of a sudden, *"Inai o Ziscar"* The French President was in Athens for the signing of the Greece's Accession Treaty to the European Union. That was the first day of a revolution, and nobody knew.

Claire was leaving. She was going to Brussels to do an internship with the European Commission and live with a Belgian boyfriend she had met in Donousa, a small Cycladic island. "Why don't you apply like me for an internship?" She had told me joyfully before leaving, as if internships were given away like gifts in supermarkets. I had shrugged my shoulders "Why should the European Commission want to hire a literature specialist?" Claire at least had a very serious degree in political sciences, and handy political family connections. "But you speak and write Greek so well" she had added encouragingly, "You have been living in Greece for three years. I am sure they would be interested in that." I was flattered but the truth was that I did not think Belgium, Brussels and the European institutions were for me.

I had often walked past the European Commission Delegation on Queen Sofia Avenue. This time I went in and asked for an internship form. The secretary asked me to wait. Only the Head of the Delegation, that was their bizarre rule, could decide about giving them out. I was ready to leave, but the girl urged me to wait a moment. An elderly Greek woman, with a dark ravaged face, her braided black hair arranged as a crown around her head nodded sternly as I went into her office. I told her in my best Greek of my intention to apply for an internship at the European Commission. She raised slightly her brows as I went on, lauding myself impudently, my knowledge of Greece, my many degrees, my fluent knowledge of Greek and English. The bitch quietly listened to me, gazing at me with her snakelike eyes, trying to assess how much clout and string-pulling power I might have. I dropped casually my Irish friend's name. That seemed to trigger the right reaction. She pulled open a drawer and took out an application form, which she gave me, albeit reservedly. "Could I have two forms just in case?" I asked sheepishly. She smiled indulgently and produced the second form as one gives a lollipop to a child. As I got up, she whispered casually that there were thousands of applications for only two hundred internships. I took back my hand she had clasped in hers and left. The answer arrived in November. My application had been accepted and I would receive a scholarship.

On the tenth of December, I was off. The road to Patras was flat and bare, as if leading to nowhere. When I arrived, night had fallen, the port was deserted. The ferry had not yet come from Italy. Dense rain soaked everything. I still had hours to wait. A small shack of a café was lit on the quay. I went in. Tired and bored dockers stood around, sucking their cigarettes, grumbling between whiffs and sighs. Outside, it was damp and cold. Inside, it was damp and warm, and foggy with smoke and steam. The small windows were opaque with condensation, letting through glares from the quay. The café owner pottered slowly around, sparing his steps and his words. He and the whole place seemed sunk in time like wrecks at the bottom of the sea, contented and undemanding. Sounds of trucks and shouts of men woke me up. The *Karageorgis* ferry had arrived. I got up and said a dry and manly goodbye to the café owner and customers, my right hand up. *"Kala, kala na paté"* they all growled like benevolent monsters in a Japanese tale, screwing up their eyes in a blessing smile. I opened the door and plunged in the dark cold night.

EPILOGUE

"*Pyrame ti zoï mas, lathos, k'allaxame zoï*" I hummed the poet Séféris's words on the deck. "We took our life, no, we were mistaken, we changed life". I had taken aboard everything I had. My painted trunk, my books, my typewriter, my carpets and covers, even my gas cooker and my broom, I had taken my life with me.

It was but an illusion. Life would never be the same anymore. It would change and the old one would melt away. Georges Séféris had leant on a ship's rail the day he had left Alexandria, his life all tucked in his soul and luggage. He knew about parting. He knew all the exiled always believed their life would go on, more or less the same. But, once gone, life in a new country always changed forever.

Where had it all begun? Where would it all end? Would it be one life after another? Or was it one life only running like one continuous thread? I looked for the vital lead of all those bits and scraps, people and cities. None. One had to be content with that. America had opened me the world. The Greek had taught me the way and the method: take your life wherever it goes and whatever it becomes.

At thirty, many more lives awaited me along the road.

Printed in the United Kingdom by
Lightning Source UK Ltd., Milton Keynes
140813UK00001B/145/P